THE STONE AND THE WIRELESS

Mediating China, 1861–1906

SHAOLING MA

Duke University Press Durham and London 2021

Printed in the United States of America on acid-free paper ∞
Designed by Aimee C. Harrison
Typeset in Minion Pro and Trade Gothic by Westchester

Library of Congress Cataloging-in-Publication Data
Names: Ma, Shaoling, [date] author.
Title: The stone and the wireless: mediating China, 1861–1906 /
    Shaoling Ma.
Other titles: Sign, storage, transmission.
Description: Durham: Duke University Press, 2021. |
    Series: Sign, storage, transmission | Includes bibliographical
    references and index.
Identifiers: LCCN 2020036881 (print) | LCCN 2020036882 (ebook)
ISBN 9781478010463 (hardcover)
ISBN 9781478011477 (paperback)
ISBN 9781478013051 (ebook)
Subjects: LCSH: Mass media and culture—China. | Mass media—
    Semiotics—China. | Mass media—Political aspects—China. |
    Mass media—China—History—20th century. | Popular culture—
    China—History—20th century. | Technological innovations—Social
    aspects—China.
Classification: LCC P94.65. C6 M35 2021 (print) | LCC P94.65. C6 (ebook)
    | DDC 302.23095—dc23
LC record available at https://lccn.loc.gov/2020036881
LC ebook record available at https://lccn.loc.gov/2020036882

Cover art: Wang Sishun, *Apocalypse*, 2015–19. Stone, iron, copper,
polystyrene, aluminum. Dimensions variable. Courtesy of the
artist.

The Stone and the Wireless

**SIGN, STORAGE,
TRANSMISSION**

A series edited by
Jonathan Sterne
& Lisa Gitelman

For S. B.

CONTENTS

ACKNOWLEDGMENTS

If it is a truism that one never finishes writing a book, certainly it has to be because every page is a record of gratitude. While acknowledgements incline toward retrospection, writing them during the global COVID-19 pandemic—a testament, if there is one, to how we must *not* return to "how things were"—demands that gratitude also be a work for futurity. Sam Solomon has unfailingly shaped and inspired my thinking of the many figures of the stone; this book thus exists as our echo. I am indebted to my PhD advisor, Peggy Kamuf, for all her guidance throughout my time at the University of Southern California, and for encouraging me to "return," without guarantees, to the unfamiliar site of "China." Akira Lippit, Karen Pinkus, John Carlos Rowe, Panivong Norindr, Dominic Cheung, Anne McKnight, Roberto Ignacio Diaz, Brian B. Bernards, Michael du Plessis, David Lloyd, Jack Halberstam, Viet Nguyen, and David Rollo have variously expanded my intellectual horizon in ways I could not imagine. Many friends have paved the way: Lindsay Rebecca Nelson, Caterina Crisci, Emilie Garrigou-Kempton, Seth Michelson, Vicki Conti, Colin Dickey, Nicole Antebi, Manny Shah, Carlos Yu-kai Lin, Géraldine A. Fiss, Jessica Stites, Nisha Kunte, Chris Farrish, and Adrienne Walser. I remain warm in the light from Sandy Sohee Chi Kim and Nada Ayad.

I am deeply grateful to my colleagues at Yale–NUS College: Risa J. Toha, Gretchen Head, Mira Seo, Scott Cook, Matthew Schneider-Mayerson, Brian McAdoo, Rajeev Patke, Nienke Boer, Andrew Hui, Geoff Baker, Nozomi Naoi, Claudine Ang, Chen Yanyun, Lawrence Ypil, Laurel Flores Fantauzzo, Joanne Roberts, Jeannette Ickovics, Tan Taiyong, and countless others. The Yale–NUS college librarians, Priyanka Sharma, Sarah Ruslan, and Jadely Seetoh were indispensable in helping me with source materials and image rights. My students, who are too many to name, have not stopped teaching me. The college's start-up grant and the Tan Chin Tuan China research project pocket grant have generously supported research related to this book. Special thanks are due too to Petrus Liu, Andrea Bachner, Jing Tsu, and N. Katherine Hayles for reading and commenting on previous drafts, and to Eric Schluessel for his thoughtful edits. At this time of tremendous precarity in the humanities and academic publishing, I cannot express more gratitude to my editor, Courtney Berger, her editorial assistant, Sandra Korn, and others on the editorial team at Duke University Press for the most galvanizing publishing process that any first-time author could possibly ask for. Without, moreover, Lisa Gitelman's early interest in the project, I would not have had found such an ideal home for the project. The book's weaknesses are entirely my own.

John William Phillips and Ryan Bishop taught me everything I needed and still need to know about critical theory and cultural studies when I was an undergraduate at the National University of Singapore. I am beholden to Kyaw Yin Hlaing and Benjamin Wong for supporting my intellectual migration from political science to the humanities. During my years at NUS, I had the fortune of being in the company of Sim Joo Jin, Jing Hsu, Jeanne Hong, Raiman Abdullayev, Ching Lim Lee Ching, Ingrid Hoofd, Sandra Manickam, Serene Lim, and Ong Shengpei. Mayee Wong's kindness and strength have consistently inspired these pages and their author.

I wish to thank my former colleagues at Pennsylvania State University: Hoda El Shakry, Sarah Townsend, Judith Sierra Rivera, Marco Martínez, Carey Eckhardt, Eric Hayot, Erica Fox Brindley, Shuang Shen, Jonathan Eburne, Hester Blum, Jonathan Abel, Jessamyn Abel, On-Cho Ng, Jade Atwill, Charlotte Eubanks, Reiko Tachibana, Kate Baldanza, Bo An, Octavian Darwin Tsen, Victoria Lupascu, and Max Larsen. The days of late would have been dull without the cheers of Louis Ho, Juria Torame, and Kevin Riordan. Immense thanks go out to colleagues in my extended Sinophone and Singapore-Malaysian studies family: E. K. Tan, Brian Bernards, Cheow-thia Chan, Weihsin Gui, Elizabeth Wijaya, Nadine Chan, Cheryl Naruse, Joanne Leow, and Fiona Lee.

Early versions of parts of chapters 2 and 5 were published in *Science Fiction Studies*, special issue on China, 40, no. 2 (2013): 55–72, and *Configurations* 26, no. 1 (2018): 1–26, respectively. These chapters have been substantially revised and expanded for this book. All translations of Chinese-language materials are mine, unless otherwise stated. The inclusion of Chinese characters alternates between the traditional and simplified script depending on the sources from which they are cited.

I have not been the most pleasant person to be around at some of the most challenging moments of research and writing. Despite this, my parents,

x

Lishun Ma and Yunlan Ma Liu, sister, Shaowei Ma, and in-laws, Ed and Susan Clark, have offered me unconditional support and love. My son, Elliott Ren Clark-Ma brightened the end of each long, exhausting day by asking me if the book was ever going to be done. My daughter, Sula Lei Clark-Ma's first words and steps continue to leave indelible marks on the different stages of research. To Emelyn Cabaccan, who has left her own family to help take care of mine: thank you. I dedicate this study to my enduring partner, interlocutor, and friend, Justin Tyler Clark, with whom there has never been any need for mediation.

The Forms of Media

What do media do? Over the last few decades of the Manchu Qing dynasty (1644–1912), writers, intellectuals, reformers, and revolutionaries grappled with this question without knowing they were doing so. They could not know because, just as in the case of the etymology of English "media," the Chinese term *meiti*, referring to "technical media," did not exist until after the popularization of communicative devices in the early twentieth century. Before that time, individual devices were simply referred to as this or that "machine" (*ji*, *qi*, or *jiqi*).[1]

Indeed, the ubiquitous and undifferentiated machines that characterized the experience of this period were on the minds of many Chinese, among them the customs clerk Li Gui (1842–1903), a member of the court's delegation to the historic 1876 Centennial Exhibition of the World's Fair in Philadelphia, USA. If the entire "cosmos" had turned out to be "one vast machine" (*ji*),[2] as Li, dazzled by the displays in the Machinery Hall, exclaimed, there was no place especially carved out for media. Because the steely progress of the Second Industrial Revolution impressed this visitor with its potential to transform production, all machines were to fulfill the same basic purpose to "benefit the [Chinese] people." Even though observers such as Li knew little about technical media as such, their writings generated discursive and dynamic processes of mediation between emerging conceptions of the old and the new, China and the West, and between culture, tradition, and technology. The late nineteenth century thus witnessed a gradual convergence between more intangible mediations and their perceptibly heftier, machine counterparts, whence the media question was beginning to emerge. The passage below, excerpted from Li's travel diary, *Huanyou diqiu xin lu*, translated and published as *A Journey to the East*, offers such an opening.

As I wandered about gazing at these machines, I wanted very much to single out and write about those with real utility. In this, however, I was hindered by the complexity of their workings, which proved impossible to completely recount. In addition, the group of visitors was very large and the movements of the machines were deafening, so when meeting with others, I quite often could not hear them speak. The interpreter, too, could not help but distort some things in conveying the finer points of the different devices to me. For all of these reasons, I am able to report only on those things that I could see and inquire about with comparative ease.[3]

No media device, barring anachronism, appears in this excerpt. Even in subsequent paragraphs, when the author mentions the typewriter and glass-etching machine, he barely distinguishes them from manufacturing and production technologies for digging coal, pumping water, or forging and smelting. To Li, they are all wondrous innovations worthy of documentation in terms of their cost, speed of production, the amount of space they occupied, and the number of people needed to operate them. Certainly, his account of the typewriter makes for an impressive historical anecdote of early Chinese contact with the "novel inscription technology."[4] But even the communicative functions of the printing press, typewriter, and glass-etching machine appear garbled. As far as the customs clerk is concerned, both kinds of machine produce noise: while the industrial machines' "deafening" sounds thwart his attempts to find out more about them, the typewriter and the glass-etching machine do not inscribe Chinese characters, and Li does not read English.[5]

No media device, not even one recognized as such, mediates on its own. Mediation happens where communicative processes (the bodily functions of hearing and speech, writing, translation, and print) overlap and interact with historical contexts and social relations. On the most immediate level, Li's diary records the conversations between the interpreter and himself, and those among other international visitors, as well as any miscommunications amplified by the "deafening" movements of the machines. Beneath the diarist's conscious awareness that he is able to "see and inquire about [things] with comparative ease"[6] lies a configuration of cognitive functions, sensory synapses, and muscular relays, which distinguishes between the numerous useful and useless devices, and later recalls and records them. The physical, legible marks of Chinese characters give Li's diary its physical form, but not without the larger forces of history that help shape how and what the diarist writes, including deliberations over the precise form of the technological, of what counts or does not count as a machine with "real utility." The Centennial Exhibition in Philadelphia took place slightly more than a decade after the conclusion of the Taiping War (1850–64), which was partly quelled with the help of Western weapons. It was the Imperial Maritime Customs Service, founded to recover custom duties from foreigners after the Second Opium War (1856–60), that sent Li to document the world's fair and represent the Qing Empire's industrializing efforts at international events.[7]

There are *media forms*—that is, physical properties of communicative devices and their mechanical processes—and there are linguistic or visual *forms of media*—tone, metaphors, tropes, composition, visual imagery, lines, narrative voice, and so on. The first converges upon the technical or instrumental; the second encompasses aesthetics and the theoretical. These seemingly conflicting varieties of media meet in the politically charged circumstances of late nineteenth-century China on the international stage. Their encounter was by no means accidental, and even less so is this book's restaging of their rendezvous. At a time when observers like Li knew nothing about the specificity of media forms, their writings nonetheless registered curious forms of media. To the question "what do media do?," *A Journey to the East* thus responds with handwriting made reproducible through the technical imprints of mechanical printing, and with the historical and cultural specificities that imbue such inscriptions with form and meaning. Of all the things, peoples, and circumstances that media mediate, mediation attends first and foremost to the relations between a technology's material forms (its physical format, function, reproduction, and circulation, and so on) and elements of such materiality signified in linguistic and visual texts. To grasp just how intertwined and yet at odds these two formal registers are, we need only to return to the above quote from Li, where technological forms—clanking devices producing "deafening" movements—on the one hand prevent the diarist from detailing the exhibition accurately, but inform the style, structure, tone, and imagery of his diary on the other. When the diary, an inscriptive medium meant to document machines with "real utility" records instead the by-products of mechanical friction—that is, their noises, materiality coheres formally as irony.

If the current state of media studies, according to one diagnosis, suffers from a surplus of media devices and a deficit of mediation,[8] the solution is therefore not to do away with devices and instruments but to acknowledge their material specificities while scrutinizing their representability in texts and images. As it turns out, the vacillating relations between technical or material and aesthetic-theoretical forms are exactly what proponents of mediation need. This proposal is not meant to fold media theory into a sub-set of literary criticism or visual and cultural studies, but to reveal that the distinction between media as "technology" and media as "cultural forms," to evoke Raymond Williams's terms, to which I will return, remains a media question through and through.

THE "CASE" OF LATE QING CHINA

Yet, how does the road to such an immanently mediating inquiry—whereby "media" announces both the object and method of study—lead to China? The historical, compared with the second, more conceptual rationale, appears justifiable on its own grounds. The years 1896 to 1906 span a period in China when old technologies such as the phonograph, telephone, telegraph, early cinematic devices, and photography were indubitably both new and foreign,[9] and enthusiastically documented by print, frequently with some controversy. Photography can be said to begin either with Jules Alphonse Eugène Itier's (1802–1877) employment with the Imperial Maritime Customs Service between 1843 and 1846, only a few years after the invention of the daguerreotype in France in 1839, or, as the Canton mathematician Zou Boqi (1819–1869) claimed in *Sheying zhi qi ji* (*An Account of the Camera*) in 1844, with his attempt at building his own camera.[10] Scholars point to the August 1896 screening at Xu Gardens as the origin of Chinese cinema, although disagreements over nomenclature could easily have this history begin with newspaper reports of lantern-slide screenings from as early as 1875 instead.[11] Guo Songtao (1818–1891), the first Chinese ambassador to Great Britain, provided the first account of the phonograph in April 1878, if, that is, there is no confusion as to whether he might have been describing the telephone. In 1880, the Chinese Telegraphy Bureau was established in Tianjin as a lu-crative "government-supervised and merchant-managed" (*guandu shang-ban*) enterprise. The bureau took over the Danish Great Northern Telegraph Company and British Eastern Extension A&C Telegraph Company's control of Chinese telegraphic communication. Official court documents (*gon-gwen*) made good use of this vast, growing network, thanks to an 1898 law conferring court-issued telegrams the same official status as edicts delivered by courier.[12] At the same time, most literate Chinese read republished tele-grams in newspapers sooner than they would get to send one themselves.

4   The history of media, perhaps even more so than other histories, directly concerns who reported what, when, and *through which specific medium*. Yet, the historical objects of this book name media in the plural and not individual

mediums in the singular. I could very well also name China in the plural. This choice speaks not lightly of the admirable reconstruction of any individual communicative innovation, but is one consciously undertaken in order to enact a method or practice of mediation as the dynamic interactions between the material and technical process or device, and its discursive significations in texts and images. Mediation, defined throughout this book as media's cleaving and bridging of technics and signification, applies just as vigorously to the rifts and unions of history and concept. The history/concept problem, as Rebecca Karl observes, is in turn welded to the "cycle of nativist/foreign (Chinese/Western) claims."[13] A work like *The Stone and the Wireless*, which has elected to take mediation as its object as well as method of study, thus moves between the historicizing of then new media and the conceptualization of mediation for rethinking the communicative milieu of the *fin de siècle* that helped shaped China. Mediation, in other words, entails what Xiao Liu identifies as a "'worlding' process" of "temporal and spatial reorganization" that "generates new relations, conflicts, and negotiations."[14]

Hence, this study eschews a typical periodization of the late Qing that begins with the First Opium War (1839–42) or the First Sino-Japanese War (1894–95) and ends with the Xinhai Revolution of 1911–12.[15] Instead, the establishment of the Ministry of Foreign Affairs (*Zongli yamen*) in 1861 and the centralization of transportation and communication under the Ministry of Posts and Communications (*Youchuan bu*) in 1906 bookend my study. The Ministry of Foreign Affairs was responsible for an emerging bureaucratic culture: its new documentation procedures, such as the diplomatic diary (*shixi ji*), the focus of chapter 1, did not just contain invaluable observations of new media technologies, but more importantly recorded and shaped China's changing worldview. The establishment of the Ministry of Posts and Communications signaled an end to the state-private cooperative structure that oversaw the development of telegraphy, which is a central topic of the book's last two chapters. My focus on early media, instead of romanticizing past technological innovations, looks to a longer history of entangled social relations and identities.[16]

Beyond challenging conventional characterizations of Chinese semicolonialism and victimhood, as New Qing History since its rise in the late 1990s has effectively achieved,[17] or simply sharpening such revisionism with a technical edge, this book addresses some of the more elementary and yet intransigent concerns in area studies, critical and media theory, and comparative studies. Mediation itself names neither a Chinese or Western concept but really a comparative method, since it refers to the "specific conditions through and in which concept and history are mediated, that is, the structured historical conditions demanding mediation" without which we risk promoting the "reifications of imputed native authenticity or of some external conceptual unity."[18]

Little doubt that the space available for a mutually reinforcing media history and theory remains a tight one to maneuver; how a concept of mediation would illuminate media history, not to mention a specifically Chinese media history, warrants further explanation. For if uncovering media cultures outside Europe and North America valiantly expands disciplinary horizons, to avowedly dust off such cultures with a theoretical brush invites allegations of parochialism of a specific kind. Harnessing media theory for China, after all, risks reviving the taboo of encumbering "Chinese reality" with "Western theory," to evoke the title of Zhang Longxi's 1992 essay, worth revisiting for its minor but significant remarks, on telecommunications. In this polemical piece first published in *Critical Inquiry*, Zhang lambasts Rey Chow's reduction of the 1989 Tiananmen Incident—that is, Chinese reality—to its derogatory representation on American television *sans* a critique of the brutality of the Chinese state or a discussion of the protesters' demands. Such elision of historical reality exemplifies, for Zhang, the cost of Western theoretical sophistication.[19] While the means of transmission is not the focus of Zhang's objection, the essay's plea to regard "television texts" not just as "mere fictional representation" but also for their "worldliness and circumstantiality" inadvertently wedges technical media between "Western theory" and its competing "Chinese reality."[20] Television's "worldliness and circumstantiality" ought to amplify "Chinese reality." Yet, in being deployed for a critic's "fictional representation," television ends up buttressing "Western theory" instead. If, in other words, we can accept the mediatedness of Chinese (or any other) reality while simultaneously considering media's concrete historicity and materiality, could the "West" and "China" not then be unhinged from their tortured gridlock with "theory" and "reality" respectively? If such an unmooring is possible, surely even the relatively straightforward task of *historicizing* the development of communicative media in late nineteenth-century China becomes an immanent *theorizing* of what media do.

As long as the West continues to have a monopoly over theory or method, leaving China or other parts of the non-West irrevocably wedded to reality, history, context and so on—assuming that we can even agree on the meaning of these terms—animosities between these conceptual pairs will only persist regardless of the number of times we put them in scare quotes. Many critics have from their specific disciplinary perspectives attempted to loosen the deadlock. Haun Saussy, for one, suggests that since deconstruction's fantasies of

6

China are so foundational for its historical formation as a theory or method, it was "'Chinese' theory [that] modifies Western 'reality.'"[21] But these were not the first attempts. Nearly two centuries before such contemporary debates in literary and cultural studies, Qing reformers unwittingly performed their own "chiasmus on the predicates" of what would only later be reified in North American academia as text versus context, and Western theory versus Chinese reality.[22]

In the aftermath of the Qing state's devastating defeat during the Second Opium War (1856–60), military and scientific advances preoccupied many members of the court. Li Gui's visit to the 1876 Centennial Exhibition was made possible by the outcomes of the war, and his enthusiastic report of the machines displayed there a mere morsel of a sizable cultural archive documenting similar wonders. One of the ways that reformist officials who formed the Self-Strengthening Movement (*yangwu yundong*) (1861–1895) made sense of this reality was to justify the adoption of Western technology on the basis of their Chinese origins. Verdicts on this thesis, which could be traced to the Jesuits missions of the early sixteenth century, have been quick to pass: the notion that China had originated the scientific and technological know-how that Europe later came to develop could be derided as proof of China's failed modernity on the one hand, or examined seriously as a sign of careful political maneuvering on the other.[23] Less emphasized in existing scholarship on this period of Chinese reform, however, is the logic undergirding one of its most famous slogans, whose cleaving of "Chinese learning as essence" (*zhongxue weiti*) from "Western learning as practical use" (*xixue weiyong*) remarkably previews the discourse of "Western theory" versus "Chinese reality" mentioned above.

It was the scholar-official Feng Guifen who first advocated for Western learning as practical use in his "Jiaobinlu kangyi" ("Protest from the Jiaobin Studio") in 1861, and Zhang Zhidong, in his 1898 "Quanxue pian" ("Exhortation to Study"), who subsequently popularized the distinction of Western from Chinese learning based on Feng's proposal. According to Chen Depeng, proponents of the Self-Strengthening Movement were not opposed to including within the category of Western learning both its politics (*xizheng*) and techniques (*xiyi*), and yet doing so risked making redundant the structural distinction between fundamental principle and practical use.[24] In order to maintain this structural integrity, the category of Western learning came to be limited to the practical domains of Western science and technology,[25] and the result was a definitive epistemology produced out of a realpolitik that was neither strictly foreign nor indigenous but a historical, 7 semicolonial enmeshment of both. To historicize these distinctions between Western practice and Chinese principle far from renders them "nugatory and useless," or in deconstruction parlance, simply "unstable." Instead, to historicize distinctions is to make their "usage more precise."[26] That imperfect equivalences exist—as if this were an exception rather than the rule of all translations—between the essence (*ti*) of Confucian precepts and the academic high-speak of theory, between and the use or applicability (*yong*) of Western techniques and historical contextuality, rather proves instead of invalidates the point that I am here making. What is considered foundational, abstract knowledge rubs against practical functionality; the two, moreover, are sharpened on the backs of political rivalry, and linguistic and cultural difference. Such was the Chinese reality or historical context, which, to borrow again from Karl, spell the "specific conditions through and in which concept and history are mediated" in the first place.[27]

Latter-day observers of the gap between Western theory and Chinese reality (and I count myself as one) can thus learn a lesson or two from the above episode of Qing intellectual history: the distance separating any theory from any reality is indeed real—that is, it is historical through and through. When the historical context in question orders the very terms in opposition, the question that confronts us becomes: Whose theory? Whose reality?

The road to an immanently mediating inquiry—whereby mediation announces both the object and method of study—does not have to lead to China, but it might well start there. The turn of the twentieth century more than denotes a period in China when old communicative technologies were new and foreign, but also a time when writers and intellectuals were struggling to demarcate machines and technical know-how from what were perceived to be the fundamental and yet more nebulous roots of their very identities. Qing reformers having to distinguish Chinese from Western learning in order to justify their adoption of foreign technologies thus helped shake the very grounds on which twentieth-century Chinese studies scholars struggle to steady themselves. Therein lies the historical reality driving my theory: mediation refers to the tireless contestations between science, technology, and their national and cultural implications staged in an absurd hall of mirrors where the real and the material appear embellished with signification, and discourses on machines confront concrete media as their self-image.

8   After the Self-Strengthening Movement failed to secure China's victory in the First Sino-Japanese War (1894–95), more progressive reformers sought to renew the Qing state by turning to the West not just for technology but

also for cultural and institutional change.[28] Hence Yan Fu (1854–1921) attributed Western supremacy to educational reforms and commitment to social and political justice rather than industrial and technological strength.[29] Zhou Shuren (1881–1936), better known as Lu Xun, mocked his countrymen of little talent for clamoring over Western material (*wuzhi*) achievements such as modern weaponry, steel, and railways instead of valuing its spiritual (*jingshen*) emphasis on the individual.[30] Both would have scorned Li Gui's overenthusiasm at the Machinery Hall of the 1876 Centennial Exhibition.

It is unclear, however, who might have had the last laugh. Yan Fu and Lu Xun's criticisms of their intellectual predecessors, after all, play on an incipient division between the as-yet-uncodified disciplines of science and the humanities.[31] With much help from actual media devices and communicative processes, mediation therefore also takes issue with both periodization and the nation-state as the *sin qua non* of historical contextualization. Beyond their immediate political and social concerns, late Qing intellectuals prefigure C. P. Snow's 1959 critique of a division between "two cultures,"[32] recently reframed in Bruno Latour's works.[33] Challenging the dichotomy between science and technology and culture, Latour, not insignificantly, calls those who walk the narrow path between the West and other cultures "mediators" (*des médiateurs*), and the uncharted territory beyond the strictly modern and postmodern perspectives "the Middle Kingdom."[34] Such wordplay, to which I will return, demands careful consideration. There were indeed both human and nonhuman "mediators" in the "Middle Kingdom," and they star as this book's protagonists. The diplomats Guo Songtao and Liu Xihong, and the technical contraptions they imperfectly record in their diaries (chapter 1); Jia Baoyu's time-travels inscribed on stone (chapter 2); photographs extoling selfless, patriotic femininity (chapter 3); the Boxers (*Yihe tuan*) in chapter 4 with their incantations and uprooted telegraph poles; and an aspiring entrepreneur of biomedia technology (chapter 5) were all mediators in the strongest sense of the word because their active negotiations of technology and culture, reform and rebellion, China and the world were made possible by developments in transportation networks as well as inscriptive, print, and early audiovisual, electronic-wireless media. Insofar as these mediators also evoke yet-to-be-invented communicative processes and networks, this book thinks the ancient stele alongside the wireless so as to enact "temporal interdependency without telos, movement without suppression."[35]

9

Should resistance against associating Western theory *a là* Latour with Chinese reality present itself, it does so once again by ignoring that Western technological transfers coupled with indigenous adaptations were part and parcel of that very reality. The field of Chinese histories of science and technology has debunked the "Needham paradigm" postulating the supposed absence of modern science in China, and repositioned late Qing and Republican Chinese technoscience as active rather than receptive.[36] Such works also join scholars elsewhere in questioning the "easy separation of scientific practice from social and political agendas."[37] And yet, it is both puzzling and remiss to exclude media technologies from a rethinking of the convergence between science, society, and politics. Mediatory processes did not just "happen" frequently during the late Qing; its men and women also avidly grafted mediation onto their encounters with innovations in recording and communication. As John Guillory demonstrates, theories of mediation as variously expounded by German idealism, linguistics, semiotics, cultural materialism, social theory—and, to add, Latour's contribution to science and technology studies—have always been insufficiently assimilated into the study of actually existing media.[38] If this estrangement is attributable to the "disciplinary division between media and communication studies, on the one hand, and the cultural disciplines, on the other,"[39] no doubt the rift is even more pronounced when, beyond disciplinary divides, national, racial, cultural, and linguistic differences enter into play.

The Stone and the Wireless is a study of late nineteenth- and early twentieth-century Chinese media culture as well as a theoretical inquiry into mediation. Instead of proposing indigenous, philosophical notions of social and cultural mediation that have little to do with communicative media and then extraneously applying them to the latter,[40] I begin from their middle ground. I explore scenes of recording, transmitting, and interconnectivity set up around existing and imagined media—books, phonographs, human-stele hybrids, telephones, photography, brain electricity, letters, shamanistic rituals, early cinema, feminine sentimentality, telegraphs, and newspapers—and ask what it is exactly that they *do*. Surely, all communicative techniques from primitive scribblings on stones to wireless technologies perform mediation, at least in some minimal, loose sense. But they do not mediate between this and that thing, entity, or process—nature and artifice, the mythical and the social, the human and the technical, and the individual and the collective, to just give a few examples—without first mediating mediation itself. That is to say, a medium always mediates between some version of its already mediated form— following Carolyn Marvin, technology's larger social and cultural "drama"— and the unmediated "instrument" or device.[41] Any tension between discursive representations of the technological real and the intensities of an embodied,

10

technical experience lies *within* and *not* outside the primary realm of mediation. Rather than distinguish a "philosophy of mediation" centering on the proliferation of "multiplicity" from a "philosophy of media" that reifies "objects,"[42] this book integrates mediation into what media do. That there are no two separate philosophies or theories tending to media in one instance and mediation on the other is not to suggest the eradication of difference *as* philosophy, but that we do not need to create another field of study altogether when what needs to be challenged are the disciplinary histories legitimizing the distinct methods of our study and its objects.

Arvind Rajagopal argues that Cold War politics effectively contained communicative studies within Western academia since media technologies were deemed to be unfree in party-controlled communist countries. The emergence of the discipline of communications, which influenced "successor terms such as media" occurred simultaneously with the exclusion of the study of technology from area studies, as the latter focused more on the linguistic and cultural aspects of undeveloped countries.[43] This book is an attempt to redress such prejudiced separation of technical media from languages and cultures, together with their respective "areas" of development. To "mediate China," as my subtitle suggests, means enacting its argument through its topic, area, and historical period.[44] More than simply acknowledge the history of communicative technology in late nineteenth-century China as inextricable from the realities of global technological transfers and semicolonialism, I examine recordings, transmissions, and connections in terms of such inextricability, as the complex web of relations at once tying and differentiating machines and the sciences to *and* from their cultural significations.

The development of audiovisual technologies, as any overview of their history is quick to demonstrate, has always been global in nature. Yet to underscore cultural differences in media's transnational origins is not to allow "machines [to] slip unremarked into the domain of an implicitly racialized sense of culture," but merely to historicize the ways in which late Qing writers embedded machines in questions of national, racial, and cultural identities.[45] So closely intertwined were technological innovations with the fate of the Chinese state that a writer like Wu Jianren (1866–1910) estimated its progress by the extent to which Chinese inventions could be models for foreign imitation and learning. Hence in Wu's utopian novel *Xin shitouji* (*New Story of the Stone*, 1905–6), which I analyze in chapter 2, no device goes unmentioned without an emphasis on its indigenous Chinese origin and superiority to its Euro-American counterpart. The more fantastical techno-ethnocentrism gets, the more unfeasible it is to separate the technical medium from its mediation by questions of identity. If media, as one of its most representative think-ers frames it, are extensions of men,[46] they have to navigate the distances between shores of perceived cultural difference. The scholarly consensus ad-vanced in part by media scholars Jay Bolter and Richard Grusin's influential study that all newer media remediate older ones neglects another equally necessary process of remediation: between what are too simplistically per-ceived as "Western" technical mediums and their "non-Western" appro-priations and imitations, between the technologies "themselves," and their scripted dramas and ramifications.

The main impetus for this book, therefore, lies less in expanding the hitherto largely Euro-American focus of the so-called Edison era,[47] how-ever heartily it embraces the call for "an adequately materialist history of the emergence of media cultures in the colonial world."[48] Just as late Qing "reality" or "context" conceived from an early historical vantage point frus-trates the distinctions between China and the West, and reality and theory, China at the turn of the twentieth century is more than simply an "example," "episode," or "case study" in non-Western media history. Equally important it is, then, to resist framing the subjects of this book as cultural or aesthetic responses to Western science and technology, since part of what rethinking media and mediation entails is to contest prejudices and habits of oppos-ing culture or aesthetics to science and technology.[49] China at the turn of the twentieth century subsists beyond a case study of non-Western media history because it conceptually renegotiates mediation's role vis-à-vis media studies' posthermeneutic, anti-interpretational turn, while extending me-diation beyond the vantage point of the technological to incorporate ques-tions of the social collective, nationalism, gender, and political economy as generated by semicolonialism and the unevenness of capitalist development. Specifically, this book reinserts mediation into media forms while reading media as possessing other forms—that is, as having been mediated through textual and discursive practices. The first is a move toward the material condi-tions of communication, the second a continuous regard for social practices and cultural forms.

English-language scholarship on the Qing *fin de siècle* has largely em-ployed the term *mediation* in terms of an *intervention* or *intercession* in processes or relationships involving different or at times opposing enti-ties. Mediation has been useful in emphasizing the historically exceptional transitions between linguistic differences,[50] tradition and modernity,[51] failure and success,[52] essence and function, and China and the West.[53] For Lydia Liu, the phrase *linguistic mediation*, more so than translation, more strongly illustrates overlaps between the linguistic and the sociopolitical, while for Michael Gibbs Hill it is precisely the lines separating translation from "other modes of mediation" that need to be more sharply drawn lest all mediations collapse indistinctly into "cultural translations."[54] Technical media fall outside the focus of these works; yet it is not difficult to see how communicative devices and processes could help reinforce the importance of social and cultural mediations. Studies of pre-Republican Chinese visual and material cultures, on the other hand, congregate at the other end of the analytical spectrum by downplaying nontechnical aspects of mediation in communicative scenarios.[55] Thus when scholars of mid to late twentieth-century China such as Bao Weihong and Xiao Liu more ambitiously develop expansive understandings of mediation that attend more to the socioeconomic, political, and cultural implications of communicative technologies,[56] they inevitably foreground the propensity of technocultural theorizations to follow conventional periodizations of modernity. It does appear that knowledge production around China ought to, following Haun Saussy's proposal, welcome the manifest mediations of conceptual categories such as "Western, religious, metaphysical, Communist, imperial, didactic, modernist" rather than see them as "danger[s] to be guarded against."[57]

Nonetheless, to prevent the proclamation that "mediation is our authenticity—whoever 'we' may be"[58] from sliding into aporia, this book refrains from employing cultural, linguistic, and textual processes of mediation as metaphors for what media do. The historical processes that mediate China do not "figure" as external factors or even effects, intended or otherwise, of inscriptive machines, wires, and other communicative devices when they are an essential component of how these devices function. At stake is thus less what media "are," an ontological claim or an axiological inquiry into what "good" or "bad" technologies do, but more of a modest call for a praxeology, which, in contrast to existing applications of the term in modern social philosophy and the social sciences, points to the study of nonhuman and nonpurposeful media operations in the theoretical humanities.[59]

READING FOR MEDIA

Precisely because the indelibly technical operations of a medium cannot be reduced to their textual and cultural significations, such irreducibility must be read, accounted for, interpreted, and wrangled with. In other words, this challenge to read for media presupposes the truism long entombed by

13

Marshall McLuhan's legacy. Yet it also recognizes that technological media engender formal dimensions such as tone, metaphors, tropes, composition, visual imagery, lines, narrative voice, and so on, which through interpretation illuminate the social dimensions of communicative practices. Rather than simply declare that physical devices, their networked infrastructures, and the ways in which they have been imagined and written about matter equally, and leave it at that, this book takes the forceful tensions and relations between materiality and its formal signification as its primary inquiry.

The question of form has been a major, though obscured, fault line in new media studies. Lev Manovich's foundational *The Language of New Media*, according to Alex Galloway's assessment ten years after the book first appeared, considers "media as pure formal devices." That is to say, both digital media and its cinematic predecessor employ specific techniques—their own "languages," as it were—that are worthy of study independently of their social and institutional practices. Together with Friedrich Kittler and McLuhan, Manovich's media formalism thus lies opposite to Fredric Jameson's "poetics of social forms" as well as Raymond Williams's cultural materialism.[60] Writing in 1974, before media theory exercised considerable influence across various disciplines, Williams sharply diagnoses McLuhan's work as "a development and elaboration of formalism which can be seen in many fields, from literary criticism and linguistics to psychology and anthropology, but which acquired its most significant popular influence in an isolating theory of 'the media.'"[61] Formalism, then, surpasses McLuhan's media analysis and is instead recast as an interdisciplinary ground even as discipline-specific practitioners do not recognize it as such. We can even go as far as saying that fields in their individual capacities erroneously assume that their subjects of study are the sole cause to which all other causes are then "reduced to effects," when in fact something like "the media" can extend across literature, the psyche, human behavior, and other determinants. In assessing McLuhan's media analysis, Williams thus practices what he preaches—namely, extends a "parallel" or "homological analysis" between McLuhan's "technological determinism and his avant-garde aesthetic formalism."[62] The question of form becomes that on which "technology" and "cultural form," to evoke the book's subtitle, converge.

Interestingly, cultural materialism is ensnared in its own methodological version of the problem of form. In Paul Jones's evaluation, Williams's critique of McLuhan is made possible, paradoxically, by his attention to form. He has to maintain television's distinct roles as "technology" and "cultural form," while also exploring the "*form of relation* between the two."[63] The same conundrum preoccupies Williams's discussion of determination as a "real social practice." While rejecting technological determinism, the Marxist critic is equally skeptical of its opposite—namely, the notion of a determined technology that views technology as sheer effect instead of as cause.[64] Hence we learn that television determines certain aspects of society without doing so with a "wholly controlling, wholly predicting set of courses." In his later work *Marxism and Literature*, Williams develops the concepts "typification" and "homology" to further emphasize different social practices as a "complex of specific but related activities." To be sure, homologies are distinct from "formal" relations insofar as they are "examples of real social relationships."[65] Yet, to be a useful analytical tool—as an example surely must be—for understanding media, homologies name the forms of relations between media forms and their significations in texts and images.[66] What Williams develops through the homological as a general concept for thinking through the relations between different social practices—"general" insofar as it serves the ambitious project of cultural materialism *writ large*—I more modestly term *mediation*.

Williams's disagreements with McLuhan remain quietly monumental, not just for media studies but also for the larger stakes of humanistic, theoretical inquiries. I draw upon what Williams sees as McLuhan's main weakness, and intentionally redistribute the weight of media formalism onto the turn—or rather, the return—to form in the humanities over the last few decades. After what can be perceived as exhaustion from an exclusive focus on ideological critique and historicist perspectives on aesthetic production, calls for a renewed attention to close reading and to the nuances of individual texts have resounded from the fields of literary, cinema, and affect studies.[67] As so many advocates of this revived formalism drawing from Frederic Jameson and other Marxist scholars of the twentieth century demonstrate, reading for form can intensify rather than dilute "other theoretical, political, and ethical commitments."[68] The focus on media as formal devices by Manovich, Kittler, and McLuhan, then, appears to swim against this intellectual current insofar as it favors the flows of information over the work of interpretation, the scaling of infrastructure over the representation of media. Attempts to wrest media from meaning under the pull of posthermeneutics,[69] the infrastructural turn,[70] or the technolinguistic,[71] however, often backfire. In emphasizing the precedence of devices, technologies, and material networks over their more symbolic counterparts, such scholarship has to presume the processes of mediation between devices and their historical contexts, technology and culture, material networks, and their representations. But the work of

15

such conceptual mediations, once again, does not happen independently of the media technologies in question. Without physical devices and technical processes of communication, there would be no need to mediate between them and their textual representations. Conversely, *sans* the reading and writing of media, how do we gauge their worth? In this respect, the works of Kittler, the German media theorist and literary scholar, remain exemplary.

"Media determine our situation." So begins the masterful dictum that sent media scholars into a frenzy when it first appeared in English publication in 1999. To this day, loyal and begrudging citations alike stop short before the second half of the opening line in *Gramophone, Film, Typewriter*: "which—in spite or because of it—deserves a description."[72] Kittler deftly accomplishes this description—or dare I say, close reading. Seldom do we find such a tender paean to the written text as in the sentiment, "how that which is written in no book came to pass may still be for books to record."[73] No doubt Kittler shakes the pedestal on which books were placed in traditional literary studies, pushing mediality to the fore instead as "the general condition within which something like 'poetry' or 'literature' can take shape."[74] His "cavalier" preference for the "sudden ruptures" of historical change at the expense of "genetic causalities" overstates new media's supplanting of print.[75] Nonetheless, it is through textual analysis of writings about technology, and not some abstract appeal to the "technological real," that he assesses writing's ability to punctuate the new aural, visual, and inscriptive functions of the titular trio. In Jean-Marie Guyau's 1880 piece "Memory and Phonograph," Kittler finds the retreat of the psychological sciences and the advent of the phonograph as the embodiment of the brain and memory, so much so that the "trace preceding all writing . . . is simply the gramophone needle."[76] And yet, none of this can be read off the needle. With similar perspicuity, Kittler locates in Maurice Renard's "Death and the Shell" of 1907 the first of a "long series of literary phantasms that rewrite eroticism itself under the conditions of gramophony and telephony."[77] The book's examination of Thomas Pynchon's *Gravity's Rainbow* is classic literary analysis at work; the prognosis that the novel reflexively depicts the overtaking of "sound film and video cameras as mass entertainment" only underscores the fact that it is Pynchon's language that engulfs, in Kittler's words, the "total use of media."[78]

Contrary to the statement that "books (since Moses and Mohammed) have been writing writing; films are filming filming,"[79] the constellation of poets, novelists, philosophers, and inventors that dots *Gramophone, Film, and Typewriter* testifies to the contrary—namely, that books do not just write about themselves but also about other media. Kittler himself acknowledges writing's versatility, its willingness to attempt what he calls "the impossible."[80] Hence, "Schnitzler's novellas simulate processes of association in phonographic real time, Meyrink's novels in filmic real time."[81] In the chapter "Typewriter," Kittler distinguishes between Nietzsche, who typed out the statement "Our writing tools are also working on our thoughts," and Heidegger, who proclaimed in "old German hand" that "Technology is entrenched in our history."[82] It is little surprise then that Kittler declares Nietzsche "the first mechanized philosopher" to launch "the transvaluation of all values."[83] At the same time, credit should be given to the first German professor of literature to teach computer programming for writing a cautionary tale of technological determinism. A review of *Discourse Networks* as "a narrative history surprisingly unreflected with regard to its methodological procedure,"[84] entirely overlooks the care with which Kittler grants literary texts the position of "a methodological center . . . in contexts that explode the two-cultures schema of our academic departments."[85]

I began this introduction with no less of an outburst, but in an entirely different context: Li Gui, writing in 1876 as an educated Chinese male in what was then the United States' second largest city and the site of the nation's founding, and under pressure to represent China's interests in industrial progress, draws attention to the inscriptive form of his diary through the communicative failures that it nonetheless registers. The boisterous clamor of industrial machines transforms into an irony that effuses Li's diary, and mechanical sounds double as narrative tones mediating between the hefty machines and their discursive significations. Nonhuman entities direct some measure of *The Stone and the Wireless*. Yet accompanying devices were late Qing men and women like Li, who, as anachronistic media theorists, anticipated, mobilized, and transformed many of the inquiries in media studies today, often without full knowledge of the machines they encountered, let alone any conception of media as such. To the extent that they nonetheless grasped mediation from beyond a solely technological vantage point, these historical figures—not all of whom, as my study of the Boxers in chapter 4 shows, were intellectuals, or, as chapter 3 elucidates, male—remained committed to questions of the social collective, nationalism, gender, and political economy generated by China's semicolonial status and global modernity. Despite, or rather because of, the dominance of posthermeneutic criticism in media research, the culture of interpretation remains central.

Joining the recent momentum toward the postcritical in literary and cultural studies, this study's oxymoronic mandate to read for media remains

17

indebted to the established practices of close reading while wary of the fetishizing of textual exegesis and suspicious hermeneutics.[86] Equally respect-
ful to the technology itself and its myriad cultural forms, the project undertaken here approaches texts and images less with the aim to demystify
and unearth hidden meanings, but to amplify their communicative roles. I
thus embrace Ellen Rooney's definition of reading as a more "inclusive" process than critique, one which is heavily imbricated with the question of
form beyond the main purviews of the literary.[87] Indeed, like Louis Al-
thusser's determination to read Marx's *Capital* "to the letter," with an effect of
producing in his prose "critical puns, paradoxes, ironies, and oxymorons,"[88]
my own interests in textual and visual forms of media, and, following Williams, in the forms of relation between them, must, rather disconcertingly,
resemble wordplays. There is something too literal about such repetitive use
of "media," "mediation," and varieties of "forms"; something ploddingly obvious about emphasizing the commonality shared by media forms and forms
of media, not to mention defining what media do in terms of mediation and
not another term. But such play on words arises from a commitment to, and
not as an accident of, reading: it "makes a formal demand" on readers to
open themselves to a materialist experience of language, whereby "form
is produced as an opacity not to be pierced, penetrated, or described but
displaced."[89]

Accordingly, readers may find my dogged pursuit of communicative devices and process from the literal—the transportation of books, the phonograph, the stone, and lithographic presses—to the more figurative—
light, lines of telegraph poles, feminine sentimentality—reminiscent and
yet strangely at odds with surface reading. Against symptomatic reading's
penchant for hidden meanings and ideologies, surface reading advocates
re-appreciating texts at "face value."[90] Yet, what evinces in "plain sight," as
Cannon Schmitt teasingly emphasizes, simultaneously "escapes notice."[91]
Otherwise, there would simply be no job for surface readers to do. If "surface is the new depth," then, correspondingly, postcritique cannot but be
mired in critique. Eschewing the binary of surface/depth, this book, following Schmitt, favors the slippages between the literal and the figurative for the
simple reason that a literal or denotative reading, rather than jettison symptomatic reading, would "force interpretation to account for what is hidden
in texts in conjunction with what is plain to see."[92]

Whereas, for Schmitt, the "figurative, repressed, or ideological resonances
of texts" find their fruition in "the sheer facticity of fictional worlds,"[93] *The
Stone and the Wireless* often mobilizes literal readings of media to ring in the

materiality of media forms. Hence chapter 1 considers Guo Songtao's dizzyingly monotonous detailing of foreign objects and technologies in his diary as a traditional, textual substitute for newer communicative networks made up of the telegraph, postal networks, the telephone, and the phonograph. Chapter 2 suggestively traces an otherwise nondescript, not to mention mundane, contraption such as a book cart in *New Story of the Stone* to the philosophy of *wen yi zai dao*, commonly translated as "writing as a vehicle to convey the *dao*." While the literal association of a physical vehicle with the more complex meanings behind the word *to convey* (*zai*) may frustrate those who seek more consistent philology, such play on words highlights mediation as that which is both obscured and in plain sight. Hence chapter 3 places the notion of a poetic medium in an actual vessel—that is, the steamship—and returns lyricism to early twentieth-century women's writing, interpreted as conduits for older and newer means of self-expression. Chapter 4 examines photographic, lithographic, and textual depictions of damaged telegraph poles and half-burned ships in war-stricken China precisely because they image literal, and not allegorical, states of communicative breakdown during the 1900 Boxer crisis. When such representations evince disruptions plain and simple, they also allow us to delve deeper into the relations between the different mediums to excavate their latent significations.

MEDIATIONS ALL THE WAY DOWN

To say that media mediate risks saying nothing at all. Yet, as a number of recent works devoted to the explanation of key concepts in media studies attests, "media," "medium," and "mediation" are nonsynonymous terms whose heterogeneous, if not obfuscated, meanings can be traced to diverse etymological origins.[94] Throughout this book, I use the noun "mediation" and the verb "to mediate" to refer to the production of tensions between technical media's physical forms on the one hand, and their political, social, and cultural meanings as they are generated and made legible through textual and visual representations on the other. Mediation, as the arrangement of technology and its Other, names what a communicative medium does. Every medium is specific, as inscriptions can be made on paper, stone, or photographic paper, and their contents transmitted variously through light, electrical wires, radio waves, or as concurrently purported by nineteenth-century believers of telepathy, mesmerism, and animal magnetism, through ether or thought itself. Just as the latest technical medium claims its specificity from its continuity or divergence from an earlier model, the term's

19

linguistic and cultural signification resonates through historical trajectories. Therefore, reading for media aims not to strip a technical medium of its materiality or historical importance, but to revitalize it. This book grounds the indissociable links between historical developments in communications technology and the social processes of mediation in a study of turn-of-the-century Chinese depictions of media forms. From this perspective, debates between positions that are deeply invested in technology's social meanings—such as nationalism or semicolonial modernity—and a posthermeneutic stance aimed at liberating technology's robust materiality are not secondary to the media question. Rather, they are intrinsic to it.

At stake is how we approach media history when our very sources documenting technical innovations in communicative technologies—newspapers, journals, letters, telegrams, edicts, diaries, artistic renderings in poetry, prose, and illustrations, photographs, and other representative systems—are undeniably part of the consideration of media forms. For this reason, any media history, if done right, is at its heart a theorization of the formal exigency in reading for media. Hence even the most prosaic appearances of communicative devices in late Qing texts and images alert us to the fact that media and mediation are irreducible "to the elucidation, essentially of the paraphrase of themes."[95] This is the precaution with which I approach Li Gui's *A Journey to the East*, eschewing the thematically more relevant, not to mention more widely discussed, passages in his diary regarding the printing press, typewriter, and glass-etching machine to highlight instead the writer's hesitant reflections on what he could and could not communicate. If limited to places where communicative devices appear, mediation would simply name a theme. It would miss a complex operation modulating Chinese writers' vacillating obsessions with the new, the scientific, and the technological on the one hand, and what these technologies signify on the other in their historical milieu.

This move to re-center language and representation in media theory in the face of an ever-extending reach of information technologies in the humanities can only appear jarringly outmoded, given new media studies' attempts to amplify the "new" in discourses around new materialism. To the claim that renewed interest in materialism is "already present in the way technical media transmits and processes 'culture,'" such that we can jettison "philosophical traditions" in order to "read modern physics, engineering, and communications technology as mapping the terrain of new materialism," an insistence on the materiality of language screams nothing short of futility.[96] What if, however, the changing of the guard for such disciplinary gatekeeping even has its historical precedence in the very philology of the word: media?

When the media concept finally emerged in response to the development of new technical media in the later nineteenth century, it also, in Guillory's formulation, "perplexed the relation between the traditional arts [from poetry, to music, rhetoric, logic, and dialectic] and media of any kind."[97] The rather late appearance of the media concept in the Western tradition thus results, paradoxically, from *a lack of mediation* between older and newer fields of study. That is, to return to the "two cultures" debate presciently staged by reformers of the Self-Strengthening Movement, there exists a gap between theoretical knowledge or ethical precepts grounded in language and culture, and ostensibly more technical devices that are no less inscriptive and yet relatively less determined by signification. This rift between literature and media is all the more surprising, given their philological proximity in both the Greek and Chinese origins of the terms.

One of the earliest English translations of Aristotle's original word for mimesis was "media" or "medium," where the latter has no equivalent in classical Greek. The Chinese character *mei* gives us the compound words for "medium" (*meijie*) and, later on, "media" (*meiti*), but it has no similar basis in "mimesis." The Chinese term for "mediation" (*woxuan*), however, carries mimetic implications since the character *wo* refers to the mechanics of turning made a handle (*wo*) as well as a literary device. The Song poet Luo Dajing (1196–1252) uses the interdependence between the axle and the wheel's rotations (*woxuan ru che zhi youzhou*) in order to emphasize the equal importance of finessing substantive (*jianzi*) and function words (*huozi* or *xuci*) in poetic compositions.[98]

Europeans and Americans at the turn of the twentieth century did not describe the telephone or phonograph as "media," and yet this did not stop subsequent media scholars from canonizing this period of media history as the Edison era. Correspondingly, my engagement with terms like *media, medium*, and *mediation* hinges upon their being translations for likewise absent original lexicons (*meiti, meiji, woxun*) in Chinese. An alternative to switching between different forms of the word—media, medium, mediation, media forms, forms of media, and so forth—would be to come up with an entirely different set of vocabulary and define it. This practice, however, would betray the very premise of the book—namely, that mediation as concept and as material processes are irrevocably enmeshed. To employ terms outside of the *medias* root would be to admit that cultural or social mediation—including, of course, language—has nothing to do with technological change.

So far, this philological digression highlights the ambling trajectory of the media concept as it has been, in China, historically wedged between tradition and modernity, indigeneity and foreignness, and culture and technology. All such epistemological figures, Williams reminds us, are misconstrued as stable, opposing poles around which values could then be constructed *post festum*.[99] Mediation trumps the passive term *reflection* as an analytical concept to dismantle these oppositions since reflection presumes a distance between the "real world" and the material processes of artistic activity.[100] Yet mediation remains insufficient, according to Williams, when it is used as a "metaphor" maintaining "separate and preexistent areas or orders of reality, between which the mediating process occurs."[101] Certainly, as long as "technology" and "writings about technologies" are kept distinct, it is easy to exploit the figurative potentials of mediation. Yet, so long as the term specifies what media do, including what a written medium like Li's diary fails to do, limited as it is by what the author "could see and inquire about with comparative ease,"[102] the concept remains committed to, and yet irreducible to the technical facts of, media. Mediation, in this case, more than figuratively or tenuously evokes technologies. The "mediators" I examine in this book, to draw again on Latour's name for those who work between science and culture,[103] integrate the discursive processes of mediations between China and the West, essence and function, culture and machines, and other oppositional terms into what it is that a technical medium *does* quite literally: mediate.

Resistance against the collapsing of the technological real into discourse, which the interdisciplinary cultural critic Mark B. N. Hansen in *Embodying Technesis: Technology Beyond Writing* critiques as *technesis*, ought to translate into more efforts at reinforcing the relationship between media and mediation. Instead, discarding mediation risks also throwing out media altogether. *Embodying Technesis* deems "cultural materiality" to be an interdisciplinary trend responsible for an "impoverished concept of technological materiality"—without, it must be noted, engaging in cultural materialism as a specific disciplinary subfield within cultural studies or in Williams's works.[104] From this perspective, mediation has no place in the book's critique of major thinkers of technological modernity from Freud, Derrida, Lacan, and Foucault, to Deleuze and Guattari. The problem, once again, is that all technologies are referred to broadly as the "robust materiality of technology" or the "technological real." Without letting specifically communicative machines perform their role of making connections and distinctions between technology and its perceived other, mediation cannot even be mustered as metaphor.

The underlying significance of not defining the "technological real" is obvious. In more moderate instances, Hansen acknowledges that technology does not exist outside social systems and cultural meanings, even playing "an essential role as part of what allows for the very existence of the social as such."[105] Technology, in other words, helps construct its opposite. On more forceful occasions, however, the book holds poststructuralist criticism responsible for reducing technology to "mere supplements or material supports for the production of knowledge/thought/desire."[106] To remedy the becoming-instrument of technology, Hansen extracts the latter from its embeddedness in social and cultural realms. It is one thing to attack the "wholesale assimilation of technology's materiality into the domain of thought."[107] It is, however, quite another to refuse technology some kind of role or agency in the still-unknown relation between thought's encounter with the real. To have "robust ontological status as 'agent' of material complexification," Hansen argues, technology must be rid of its "role within thought."[108] In its preference for a functionalist over a representationalist model, *Embodying Technesis* could have articulated what it is a technology *does*. Precisely because it is unfair to expect a single work to provide an answer to what is undeniably a vast philosophical question, it would be more prudent to focus more narrowly on specific kinds of devices and process rather than analyze technology in the general. Hansen, however, would object to such a "simplification" or "reduction," which he accuses the "master-thinkers" of technology of doing when they "thematize" and "treat technology descriptively, through the category or figure of the machine."[109]

It goes without saying that technologies are more than textual figures or metaphors. But textual or inscriptive machines are not all metaphors, and likewise, not all descriptions of inscriptive technologies are reductive. I share some of Hansen's skepticism about Latour's definition of science as translations, which risks including everything as an inscription device for transforming a "material substance into a figure or diagram."[110] I sympathize with his criticism of Paul Valéry and William Carlos Williams for equating a poem with a machine.[111] Nonetheless, I remain unconvinced as to why Hansen overlooks Derrida's account of the movement of *différance* in "electronic card-indexes and reading machines" as concrete, material examples of technology.[112] If the reason is that such instantiations only further subordinate technology to the larger philosophical principle of *différance* and the *gramme* or mark of writing, the question then becomes whether any definition of technology could indeed lie outside means or instrumentality, as an unadulterated principle in and of itself without utility or function. As I demonstrate in chapter 3 and the conclusion, a technical recasting of femininity's relationship to media technologies can either disrupt or enhance the more figurative, and not coincidentally, instrumental employment of femininity as a medium or conduit for reimagining a new China.

The drive to liberate technology from its philosophical constraints as "a mere machine—a technics in the service of language" ends up reifying it as a transcendental signified.[113] A pursuit of the technological real and its robust materiality ends up appealing to reality and materiality only in their negative senses as *not* culture, *not* text, *not* interpretation, *not* description, and therefore *not* specificity. This posthermeneutic stronghold, which reintroduces the poststructuralist, and specifically deconstructionist angles of critique it so admonishes, appears in other fields, notably affect studies. Eugenie Brinkema, in a sharp diagnosis of what she calls the "fantasy of something that predates the linguistic turn and that evades the slow, hard tussle of reading texts closely," suggests that the escape from signification maintains the very problems it is intended to challenge.[114] Indeed, Hansen's telling injunction to "bypass the mediation performed by the 'semiotic element' of a word or an image in order to engage physically with it"[115] ironically points to the necessary endeavor of the present book: to return mediation to words, meaning, *and* media so as to engage with them in all their specificities.

TECHNOTEXTS, LOOPS, AND NEW CHINESE WRITING

If a medium is form, then the media of language—that is, words and their significations—are materiality formalized. To claim that the urgent methodological task facing media studies today is to track the divergence and convergence between a particular technical form and its content requires us to return a sense of wonder to McLuhan's overused dictum in *Understanding Media*. Rather than take the copula "is" in "the medium is the message" for granted, we should interrogate how the equivalence comes about in the first place.

I have repeatedly risked stating the obvious: not all technologies are media in the strict sense, and not all media actively represent—that is, mechanically inscribe through writing or imaging. This distinction prompts media historian Lisa Gitelman to remark that "machines get some of their meaning from what is written about them in different ways and at specific junctures, in research plans, patent applications, promotional puff, and so on. Writing machines, in particular, get some of their meaning from the way they are used, including the writings they produce."[116] Such devices, in other words, are especially fecund for analysis, and it is no surprise that they form the backbone of much interdisciplinary scholarship that straddles both media and literary studies such as my own. Writing machines, appropriately, make for the title of Katherine Hayles's book, which examines the media in which literary texts appear—print, computers, and other devices—and also the activity or process through which these "technotexts" illuminate "the machinery that gives their verbal constructions physical reality."[117] What defines a literary work as a "technotext" is that it effects a "reflexive loop" between the "imaginative world it creates and the material apparatus embodying that creation as a physical presence."[118]

But a technotext does not have to be a literary work. A telegram or photograph equally qualifies as one by foregrounding the connections between its material artifactuality (form) and its verbal or visual signification (content or message). A technotext, moreover, transforms its "material apparatus" into elements of textual or visual form, while also representing other media, peoples, and communicative processes that are not usually regarded as technical media proper. An American traveling photographer and war correspondent's photograph depicting the Boxers' destruction of telegraph and railway lines, the topic of chapter 4, does not so much reveal the material conditions of photographic production as it indexes other telecommunication and infrastructural networks, including the cultural and commercial systems in which visual media traffic. In her "Ziti xiaozhao" ("Self-Inscription on a Photograph," 1906), the revolutionary martyr Qiu Jin (1875–1907) incorporates poetic and photographic forms of address and indexicality, respectively, to channel what I foreground in chapter 3 as the figure of the female medium. The loop in Hayles's study should thus be seen as more of a plural, self-generating structure: "media constantly engage in a recursive dynamic of imitating each other, incorporating aspects of competing media into themselves while simultaneously flaunting the advantages their own forms of mediation offer."[119] In late nineteenth- and early twentieth-century China, it would be difficult to pinpoint who or what does the flaunting, since the recursive dynamic of the technotext applies to both the medium and its signification.

In this regard, Hayles's concept of a technotext extends Derrida's notion of "*arche*-writing," the antecedence and iterability of the mark, to other technologies of storage and transmission. The French philosopher Bernard Stiegler, similarly building on Derrida's concept and the related notion of the supplement, emphasizes mnemonic technologies in terms of this essential exteriorization of memory.[120] An *arche*-writing does not have to be a "machine reduction of technology," "a static and mechanical figure [of the machine] that is by nature secondary and posterior to the primary and constitutive movement of thought and to whose sway, consequently it can pose no threat."[121] Outside thought, an *arche*-writing takes on material forms as print, the grooves scratched by the phonograph needle, the ink ejected by the pressing of a typewriter key, and so on. Indisputably, these material marks serve their intended inscriptive functions, beyond which they also take on symbolic meaning. Such dual identities do not reduce media's impact on our experience to cultural constructivism, but they do mean that language and form constitute part of this experience.

Hayles's notion of the technotext and Derridean *arche*-writing thus excavate the material richness of textuality and writing. By claiming that a focus on literary and aesthetic forms, theory, and close reading far from contravenes the study of communicative media, *The Stone and the Wireless* encourages further conversations between scholars of Chinese literature and culture, those working in *Medienphilosophie* or media philosophy, cultural techniques, and what Thomas Bartscherer, in his review of Alex Galloway, Eugene Thacker, and McKenzie Wark's *Excommunication*, calls "the New York school of media theory."[122] For this reason, this is a study largely driven by questions of disciplinary and epistemological formations. If *Television*, with its critique of McLuhan's media analysis, marks Williams's full elucidation of "material cultural production," *Marxism and Literature* extends the theoretical implications of all of the cultural materialist's previously more "detailed practical work."[123] There, literature serves as one example among others, but also a consistently theoretical concept with which to tie in other examples of cultural production. Specifically, literature is "a particular kind of work in the medium of language."[124] More generally, its forms testify to Williams's long commitment to the importance of literacy for communicative compositions as social material processes.[125]

> The hearing of certain traditional arrangement of words: the recognition and activation of certain rhythms; the perception, often through already shared themes, of certain basic flows and relations and in this deep sense real compositions, real performances: all these are parts of some of our most profound cultural experiences.[126]

This constitution of cultural experience is evidently more complex in the creation of a new form, and with it, novel arrangements of linguistic elements, subjects, and compositions, which require "newly shared perception, recognition, and consciousness [that] are offered, tested, and in many but not in all cases accepted."[127] Innovative forms characterize social systems undergoing transitions in certain value systems from which a new form must necessarily distinguish itself, but this distinction does not therefore amount to an individualistic endeavor. On the contrary, the "historically variable" distance between collective modes and individual projects, but also between material linguistic elements and consciousness, emblematizes the "function of real social relationships." Every occasion to promote a new form, moreover, must underscore the components of its material elements and the means with which its materiality could be perceived and, hopefully, widely disseminated. In the case of speech and writing, the "materials" of forms pertain to "words, sounds, and notations." "The ultimately formative moment," Williams argues, is "the material articulation, the activation and generation of shared sounds and words."[128]

For a society around the turn of the twentieth century, obsessed with the sense of humiliation as well as the dynamism that accompanied its semicolonial experience, the introduction of new ways of writing hinged upon the very success of "the activation and generation of shared sounds and words."[129] "Given that writing was so clearly marked as indigenous," Theodore Huters argues, "the contradiction between preservation of the national tradition and the need for thoroughgoing reform were to prove particularly vexing in this period."[130] This dilemma was acutely felt in the rise of the Chinese novel (*xiaoshuo*) as a dominant genre toward the end of the nineteenth century, and one modeled on Western and Japanese works, which were seen to be more politically instructive than traditional Chinese novels.[131] Yet it was precisely its foreign import that tempered enthusiasm for the genre, and many theories of the novel from the period tackled this issue head on.

In 1902, the author and political reformist Liang Qichao (1873–1929) wrote an essay entitled "On the Relationship between Fiction and the Government of the People," originally published in his journal *Xin xiaoshuo* (*New Novel*). It remains to this date a classic text in the history of Chinese literary criticism. Some scholars have traced its intellectual basis to the Meiji tradition of political novels in Japan; others to Liang's interest in Buddhist philosophy around the same time.[132] Yet what has escaped scrutiny is how fiction's visceral, bodily effect on readers jars uncomfortably with larger forces of literary form such as the marketplace and language. However, the more stress is placed on novels' immediate hold over their readers—that is, on the transparency of the form—the more the essay helps expose what Williams calls "the materializing of recognition."[133]

Already in 1899, Liang evoked the power of novels to directly immerse and nourish (*jinrun*) citizen's brains.[134] In the better-known 1902 essay, Liang elaborates on fiction's power of influence, employing the Buddhist terminologies of thurification (*xun*), immersion (*jin*), stimulation (*ci*), and lifting (*ti*) for illustration. To highlight the extent to which readers are unconscious of these four powers' effect on their minds, Liang depicts their fondness for fiction over and above other kinds of writing as a "spontaneous psychological phenomenon beyond human control."[135] Even those who do not read fiction cannot help but "inherit" the lessons it imparts to society. The essay concludes with the hyperbolic comparison of fiction's indispensable role with air (*kongqi*) and subsistence (*shusu*). In addition to being indispensable needs without which one cannot live, air and subsistence also function as mediums. The new novel, according to Liang, should allow his fellow countrymen to absorb reformist and nationalist ideas, such as the ones espoused in his essay, as easily as breathing or eating.

If a "revolution in the realm of fiction" can "renovate the people of a nation," their "morality," "religion," "politics," and so on,[136] the essay intends its battle cry to sound less through the materiality of "words, sounds, and notations" and more through spontaneous, immediate transmissions. Liang's reliance on the Buddhist principles of thurification, immersion, stimulation, and lifting, along with his proclamation of the novel as the "Great Conveyance for literature"—"Great Conveyance" referring to the most powerful means of realizing Buddhist truths—can be seen as a way to downplay the sheer utility of the novel as an instrument of reform.[137] It would be challenging to find another view of fiction more at odds with Williams's materialist conception of form. Yet, in the face of such spirituality, or, rather, the conceptual framework that religion offered, it would be difficult to slough off all traces of materiality, the appeals to air and food being just one such slippage. Even the most idealistic understanding of literature's functions, of which Liang's essay is exemplary, cannot be entirely vague when it comes to the means through which fiction is transmitted. Hence, in admitting that the "power of stimulation" varies according to the kind of content in question, Liang addresses writing's effectiveness over speech's "spatial and "temporal" limitations.[138] Within writing, the vernacular is preferred over classical language, and the parable over grand, serious discourses. It is easy to blame a traditional literary form for causing undesirable behaviors such as superstition and lustfulness; such simplistic, one-to-one causality becomes more complex when the essay concludes by wedging booksellers' markets between individual consciousness and material linguistic elements.

"On the relationship between Fiction and the Government of the People" thus does not simply demonstrate the competing allures of traditional and foreign literary models. By revealing a related, though less detectable, contradiction between literature's immediate transmissibility and the irrefutable substantiality of air and food, not to mention the physical, written form and the marketplace of print, Liang's essay admits to the materiality of communication in the promotion of a new literary form. Similar contradictions confound other fiction writers of Liang's time as they, too, attempt to innovate Chinese fiction by insisting on the immediacy of literature, only to underscore what Williams calls the "work" undertaken by "the medium of language."[139] The stone and the wireless exemplify this conundrum in *New Story of the Stone* and "New Tales of Mr. Braggadocio" respectively: the two vastly differing technologies, which also title this book, emblematize the complex communicative processes through which oft-didactic messages of national and individual enlightenment can manifest in the first place.

I have chosen to reinterpret the likes of Liang, Wu Jianren, Guo Songtao, and Qiu Jin, all of whose works have long received critical attention for their visions of the Chinese nation and its literary modernity. I recast them here as witnesses to the new media technologies of their time with the hope that such reevaluations of their recordings (*ji*), transmissions (*chuan*), and self-writings (*zhuan*)—in short, their attempts to connect (*tong*)—may complicate or even contradict some of their by-now exhausted views on Westernization, semicolonialism, racial and ethnic classifications, as well as class and gender. If the result is that media and the concept of mediation uproot late Qing men and women to a field of study seen as removed from their historical contexts, such removal evinces once again the hitherto lack of mediation between literature, culture, politics, and science and technology; concept and history; and between amateurish Chinese tinkerers and celebrated European and American inventors. And if the present project succeeds in extending media theory to questions of sociality and governance outside Europe and America, the credit falls once again on the historical mediators shuttling back and forth between technical devices and the discursive processes of their signification.

CHAPTER OVERVIEW

The book's five chapters are organized around three inquiries into the medi-
ated effects of "recordings" (*ji* 記), "transmissions" (*chuan* or *zhuan* 傳), and "interconnectivity" (*tong* 通). Each of these three headings captures a techni-

cal function or mode of inscription as well as a set of mediating principles or theories. These progress through the book through gradually increasing levels of intensity in the mediations between media forms and their formal significations in literary and visual texts. I alternate between nonfictional genres and works of science fiction and poetry in order to foreground the mutual interactions between forms, historical meanings, and technical media both real and imagined. Lest we expect imaginary media to be found only in fictional works, this book claims that diplomatic diaries, official telegrams, newspaper articles, letters, biographies, and photographs are equally capable of looking beyond the historical and material constraints of their times into possible futures. Both nonfiction and fiction, moreover, exhibit an extraordinary sense of self-reflexivity.

Despite the significance that early Chinese science fiction played in documenting media technologies,[140] this book distances itself from a genre study. Nathaniel Isaacson, in *Celestial Empire: The Emergence of Chinese Science Fiction*, attributes the rise of the genre to China's semicolonial status, which forced science fiction writers to engage not just with "foreign powers or alien invaders" but "the country's own indigenous traditions."[141] Needless to say, imperialism drove late Qing intellectuals in an oscillating frenzy between foreign and indigenous ideas. I am, however, primarily concerned with the extent to which media technology helped guide that frenzy's momentum. For this reason, I examine *New Story of the Stone* and "New Tales of Mr. Braggadocio," and conclude my study with the recently published *Waste Tide* for their defamiliarization of what it means to record and connect, and not because they fulfill any generic criteria.[142] *New Story of the Stone* enters the science fiction realm proper only in the second half of the novel, but even then, the author labeled it as "social fiction" (*shehui xiaoshuo*), and stylistically it shares similarities with travel narratives and utopian fiction. Such inconsistencies are unsurprising, given how confusion accompanies taxonomic proliferation during this period of literary production and translation. Liang himself listed ten genres of fiction, and at one point grouped Plato's *Republic* and Verne's *Twenty Thousand Leagues Under the Sea* together under the heading of "political fiction."[143] As an emergent form in Williams's sense, the science fiction examined in chapters 2, 4, and the conclusion foreground form not as the "passive disposition of material elements," but the activation of "social semiotic and communicative processes."[144]

Recording (*ji*), which branches into the first two chapters, is one of the four categories of imprint in the traditional Chinese classificatory scheme,

30

along with classics (*jing*), histories (*shi*), and philosophy (*zi*).[145] Its rich etymology in the classical tradition of record-keeping also extends to the functions of storage, production, and reproduction germane to new media processes.[146] Chapter 1 compares the plotting of old and new media experiences in three contemporaneous Western diplomatic reports or diaries (*shixi ji*) authored by Guo Songtao, his deputy Liu Xihong (?–1891), and one of his translators, Zhang Deyi (1847–1919). Despite their political differences, all three diplomats envision alternative communicative mediums and mediating processes unavailable or at least not yet known to them by name. Such imaginations, however, are belied by writing's anxieties about faithfully depicting new audio and visual recording mediums, an anxiety which spills over into chapter 2.

Like the diplomats I analyze in the previous chapter, Jia Baoyu, the protagonist of *New Story of the Stone*, ruminates on his Chinese identity vis-à-vis new technologies—albeit not in nineteenth-century England but in semicolonial Shanghai circa 1905 and, in the second part of the novel, in utopian China. Like the original character from the classic *Dream of the Red Chamber* on whom he is based, Baoyu, by the end of the novel, transforms into a piece of stone on which his entire adventure is inscribed. The story is then patiently copied and edited into vernacular Chinese by a minor character, Lao Shaonian, a bureaucrat of the utopian kingdom. Focusing on the use of the stone in the historical context of lithography's ascendance in Shanghai, where much of *New Story* is set, and the novel's obsessive detailing of documents, this chapter claims that the intertwining of the human observer, writer, copyist, and stone inscription reflects larger anxieties toward state bureaucracy, commercialization, and the status of work.

Chapter 3 mines the polyphonic meanings of 傳 as both transmission (*chuan*) and historical biography (*zhuan*) in poetry, photography, and the new hybrid form of photographed biographies and autobiographies of exemplary women. These mediums dramatize the transformations brought about by new media technologies through various constructions of female sentimentality specific to their formal structures: poetry, through lyricism; photography, through the tension between the photographic index and the deixis; and the text-image relation in photographed biographies and autobiographies. The question, then, is not whether women can represent their gendered consciousness "in" these new mediums but to radically posit gendered consciousness *as* a lyrical medium, one that no longer serves as instrument or tool for the project of nation-building. I begin by analyzing Huang Zunxian's poem "Jin bieli" ("Modern Parting," 1899), which employs

31

conventional notions of feminine sentimentality to foreground the relation between the poetic medium and new communicative technologies. In contradiction to this more instrumentalized deployment of feminine sentimentality, Qiu Jin's "Self-Inscription on a Photograph," written on the back of her own photographic portrait, challenges normative prescriptions of women's feelings and the erasure of femininity's "lyrical traces" by early Chinese feminists, both male and female.

The final section, "Interconnectivity" (*tong*), analyzes the ultimate dream of connectivity borne from the period's preoccupation with electricity. *Tong* indicates a constellation of principle meanings related to openness and thoroughness, penetrability, and exchangeability.[147] These inform the compound "to join" (*goutong*), the Chinese term also indicating the physical intersection of waterways dating to the *Zuozhuan* of late fourth century BCE.[148] We find it again in "communications" or "infrastructure" (*jiaotong*), which is also the intersection of roads in *Taohuan yuan ji* (*Peach Blossom Spring*, 421 CE) by Tao Yuanming (365?–427). *Tong*, as both noun and verb, appears at times better suited than the common translation for "communication" (*chuanbo*) for embodying general states of communicative accessibility. Wang Tao (1828–1897) praised newspapers for "connecting external affairs to the interior" (*tong waiqing yu nei*).[149] The reformist Tang Caicheng (1867–1900) lauded the popular press for its ability to connect literate people in different social strata, who could, by "grasping the changes and patterns in one phenomenon, infer those in others" (*chulei pangtong*).[150] Liang Qichao, ever so visceral in his appeals, invoked *tong* when he compared the nation without newspapers with the physical ailment of "having one's throat and tongue blocked" (*houshe butong*).[151] *Tong* also comprises the first half of "general history" (*tongshi*), which, in contrast to "dynastic history" (*duandai shi*), speaks to a total view of human activities. With the advent of the telegram, "circular telegrams" (*tongdian*, sometimes "public telegrams" *gongdian*) relied on an increasingly connected official infrastructure.

Chapter 4 continues the heuristics of disruption from the previous chapter, this time examining conflicting representations of interconnectivity in telegrams, letters, eyewitness reports, newspaper articles, and visual media leading up to and during the tumultuous events of the Boxer Rebellion and the Siege of the Legations of 1900. The telegraphic imagination's straddling of ineffable spirit and bodily matter, and its distortion of time and space when crossing over to print as public or circular telegrams, I argue, was a complementary medium, not an opposing one, to the Boxers' use of magic and public communication. By engaging with the recent turn from mediums to infrastructure in media studies, this chapter demonstrates that the breakdown of transport and telegraphic communication during the Boxer Rebellion, instead of constraining the production of texts and images depicting the crisis, in fact helped fuel their global circulation.

The last chapter of the book settles appropriately on the fantasy of all communications: a medium that connects everything including the very distinction separating itself from other media. Toward the end of the story, the protagonist of "New Tales of Mr. Braggadocio" by Xu Nianci (1875–1908) invents brain electricity, the power of which replaces existing energy sources, transportation, and communications media, and eventually causes worldwide unemployment. I trace the genesis of this invention to earlier moments in the short story where a multiplication of the first-person narrative perspective stands in for the problem of representing the masses or the collective. At the same time, the problem of narratology intersects with the late nineteenth and early twentieth centuries' fascinations with neurology, electricity, and the powers of mental healing in New Thought and Spiritualist circles. More than a motif, brain electricity thus disconnects theoretical and discipline-specific interests in connectivity from more abstract concerns, bringing the notion of interconnectivity (*tong*) to resonate with developments in advertising, technical education, and economic productivity in this period of Chinese history.

The Stone and the Wireless concludes by extending early Chinese science fiction's imagination of boundless interconnectedness to Chen Qiufan's (Stanley Chan, 1981–) novel, *Huang chao* (*Waste Tide*, 2013). The latter's depiction of class warfare aided by augmented-reality technologies and cloud computing continues my analysis of the enigmatic ending of "New Tales of Mr. Braggadocio," whereby narrative form and subjectivity coalesce with the historical problem of an individual's relationship to their larger collective in the political economy. At the same time, Chen's novel, by martyring women's bodies and sentimentalities for the abstract, greater good of humanity at large, reintroduces the problematic figure of the female medium that both divides and connects this book. While I argue in chapter 3 for a technical instead of moral valorization of the feminine example, my concluding assessment shows that women's relationship to media technology remains easy prey for contemporary science fiction's digital exploits. If media mediate the tensions between the technical and the political-ethical undergirding early twentieth-century gender and class relations in the nascent nation-state, the work of mediation, to state it plainly, runs on overdrive in order to make sense of global China today.

33

The effort this book directs at unraveling the conceptual implications of mediation rather than at giving a history of any individual media technology means that the tumultuous events and works as treated here would find themselves awkwardly placed in existing media histories of the turn of the twentieth century, or even in political or literary studies focusing on the last decades of the late Qing, lurking rather as footnotes to more ostentatious parades of the new. If so, such a result would be fitting. With my study ending in the year 1906, I stop before the Xinhai Revolution of 1911–12, before the 1914 May Fourth Movement, when the Chinese language is often said to have been renewed, before the serious beginnings of Chinese film and gramophone industries in the 1930s, before the centralization of telecommunications, postal, and transportation networks during the Republican era, and before the fervent transnational imaginations of the Chinese typewriter during the interwar and postwar years. *The Stone and the Wireless* closes before these moments so as to capture the manifold, unpredictable potentials of media and mediation before they were eviscerated once they, as we say now, "went live."

PART I
記 // | RECORDINGS

GUO SONGTAO'S PHONOGRAPH | THE POLITICS
AND AESTHETICS OF REAL AND IMAGINED MEDIA

In a speech delivered before the Teachers' Association of California in December 1896, and published in the following year in the *Chinese Recorder*, John Fryer (1839–1928) criticizes the traditional literary examination essay for "impart[ing] a uniform stamp upon every educated Chinese," very much like "the use of one of their engraved wooden blocks from which their books are printed."[1] We would be quick to judge Fryer for speaking as if later printing techniques such as moveable type, the printing press, or lithography do not strive precisely to reproduce exact copies of the original with more efficiency. After all, Chinese inventions are not the only ones Fryer, a British missionary turned promoter of Western science and technology extraordinaire, singles out for his media metaphor. Because of the literary examination essay, the speaker alleges, the Chinese student becomes a "mere literary machine, with a prodigious memory, but with about as much original thought as a phonograph or a typewriter."[2] Like a good Kittlerian before Kittler, Fryer equates Chinese literary writing to a storage device, which records and reproduces but fails to create and inspire.

A racial stereotype underlays Fryer's image of engraved wooden blocks from which literal stereotype plates are molded to cast high-quality facsimiles. Exemplifying Katherine Hayles's definition of a "material metaphor" that traverses "between words and physical artifacts," Chinese woodblock printing lends the mechanics of its printing process for less than neutral ends.[3] It is tempting to dismiss Fryer's Chinese stereotype not simply for the speaker's condescension but, ironically, his sheer unoriginality: is there no end to the Euro-American fascination with how the Other mimics using mimetic technologies? Yet, as Michael Taussig reminds us, the mimetic faculty has its complicated histories, and every witnessing of mimesis "invokes just that history and registers its profound influence on everyday practices of representation."[4] The nuts and bolts of mimetic technologies—movable type or wooden blocks—help anchor essentializing notions of mimetic behaviors that contribute to racialist discourses.

Certainly, Fryer chooses woodblock printing, the phonograph, and the typewriter for their mimetic capabilities even as these techniques, far from producing perfect copies, in fact create new media content.[5] Yet a quick glance at their foreign origins and Chinese adaptations reveals a deeper politics, one tying technical functionality to questions of national identity. Woodblock printing or xylography, as is well known, developed in the early Tang dynasty (618–907), almost eight centuries before Gutenberg's birth. In North America, Thomas Edison (1847–1931) invented the first sound recording device in 1877. Remington and Sons successfully commercialized and produced in 1874 the Scholes and Glidden typewriter; but it was the American company's famous Remington rifle, which the Tianjin and Jiangnan arsenals were reproducing in large numbers by 1872.[6] During the Self-Strengthening Movement (1861–1895), state-owned industries situated along the Yangtze delta and elsewhere manufactured firearms and warships, and not phonographs and typewriters; even then, Chinese-made Remingtons continued to be more expensive and lower in quality compared with imported ones.[7] The point, however, is not to determine who made what first and made them better,[8] when the reformers themselves learned firsthand the inexorable dialectics of originality and imitation. Since a strong part of the critical discourse of the movement, as I discussed at greater length in the introduction, involved the view that China had earlier invented most of the sciences and technologies, which it now had to imitate, outcomes of the First Sino-Japanese War (1894–95) proved on the one hand that claims to originality did not exactly benefit or speed up China's nation-building process, and on the other hand, that not all supposedly inferior copies are made equal.

Nineteenth-century Chinese arsenals did not manufacture phonographs or typewriters. Yet mediation occurred where industrial machines, which built firearms and warships, operated alongside cultural practices tasked with the translation and dissemination of information. In 1868, the School for the Diffusion of Languages (*Guang fangyan guan*), previously the Shanghai School of Foreign Languages (*Tongwen guan*), moved into the Jiangnan Arsenal. There, Fryer headed the translation section of the school and worked with brilliant scholars like Li Shanlan (1811–1882), Xu Shou (1818–1884) and Xu Jianyin (1845–1901) to translate Western books on the sciences and applied sciences into Chinese.[9] Classical learning continued to be taught at the arsenal, separate from the translation department. It was in this hybridized environment where Fryer witnessed firsthand, for twenty-eight years, Chinese students being "drilled in the eight-legged essay" alongside subjects like modern mathematics.[10] On the one hand, the Englishman's subsequent derisory comparison of Chinese literary writing with woodblock printing, the phonograph, and the typewriter levels the differences between each inscriptive medium's recording, copying, and communicative capacities. On the other hand, his remark, seen in light of his experience, accentuates the dissonances effected by the coexistence of technological transfers, linguistic translations, and the dissemination of both indigenous and foreign learning.[11] That the educated Chinese resembles "mere literary machine[s]" thus lays bare all the physical grooves and indents that distinguish the literary-cultural and industrial processes of reproduction and inscription from another in astoundingly inchoate and uneven ways.

This chapter sidesteps Fryer to follow instead the figure of the overly exact Chinese inscriber in three contemporaneous diplomatic reports or diaries detailing Qing embassies to the West. These are authored by Guo Songtao (1818–1891), the Qing court's first ambassador; his deputy Liu Xihong (?–1891); and one of Guo's translators, Zhang Deyi (1847–1919). Each text registers various communicative devices and processes and exposes writing's abilities as well as limitations vis-à-vis newer audio and visual recording technologies. Not unlike the trio of woodblock printing, phonograph, and typewriter in Fryer's description, Guo, Liu, and Zhang's writings pit Chinese inscriptive techniques against American and European inventions, and help highlight the dynamic interactions between Chinese classical learning, Western science, and the nitty-gritty workings of physical machines. There, the ties between politics and technics converge and diverge, couple and decouple. Whereas conventional historicism of the late Qing would presume that an author's political-ideological position determines their views of Western science and technology, my analysis of the three diplomatic reports shows that even a conservative or more chauvinistic disregard for Euro-American scientific practices shores up mediation as the intertwining of technical objects and processes with their textual and cultural legibility. A politics of representation, in other words, sways but cannot fully explain how media are represented.

For this reason, the myriad shapes and hues in which mediations appear in the three diplomatic reports render the usual labels of "progressive"

39

or "modern," "conservative" or "anti-modern" only marginally useful. Certainly, Guo's pragmatic, statecraft-school thinking shaped his *Lundun yu bali rij* (*London and Paris Diaries*).[12] Compared with his subordinates, the Chinese ambassador promoted political reform and exalted the benefits of Western science and technology very enthusiastically; yet it is his diary that most anxiously registers the new temporal economy effected by the new sound recording technology of phonography. Wary of how Western-style practical learning (*shixue*) will contaminate the Chinese classics, Liu's *Yinyao siji* (*Private Diary in an English Carriage*) may turn a blind eye to newfangled inventions. And yet, upon closer inspection, Liu no less traverses the distances between the political and the technological.[13] Zhang's *Suishi Ying-E ji* (*An Account of My Journey with the British and Russian Emissary*), as the most ethnographically detailed of the three, bridges Guo and Liu's respective positions.[14] In harnessing the ideographism of Chinese characters to visualize otherwise unfamiliar objects and customs, Zhang liberates the written script from its elevated status as civilization or learned discourse (*wen*), foregrounding instead its materiality as a visual medium.

The origin of the diplomatic report or record of the West (*shixi ji*), moreover, epitomizes the indissociability of genre, history, and media-specific materiality. It emerged in the second half of the nineteenth century as a hybrid primarily between the diary (*riji*) and travel journal (*youji*), related also to genres such as "jottings" (*biji*) and external records (*waiji*).[15] As early as the Northern and Southern Song dynasties, officials traveling to foreign states used the diary form to document their experiences. The late Qing diplomatic record shares its genealogy with the travel journal (*youji*), which dates back from as early as the Eastern Han dynasty (25–220 CE). In this chapter, I switch between the terms *diplomatic report*, *record*, and *diary* in reflection of this flexibility. As a hybrid genre, the diplomatic report is an official document often written with a personal voice. However, unlike Western travel narratives, where the first-person point of view often accompanies psychological reflections and narrative techniques that would be incorporated into the modern novel, Chinese travel tales focus on "telling" (or describing) rather than characterization and story,[16] a quality essential for compiling a media sensorium, a point on which I will elaborate later.

The Welsh Baptist missionary Timothy Richard (1845–1919) thought little of these diplomatic records, dismissing them as superficial, amateurish, and disorganized works by officials who did not understand foreign languages. Contemporary scholars studying the late Qing genre as diplomatic history, biography, or comparative intellectual history added little to Richard's assessment as they continue to evaluate the diplomatic records according to the binaries of tradition versus modernity, and view this new composite subgenre of the record or account (*ji* 記) as evidence of the empire's admission, albeit belated, into the international family of nations.[17] All of these positions overlook the diplomatic report as a media-specific document, which helps a dynamic bureaucratic culture in managing and controlling information flows over a rapidly expanding geographical space. The institution responsible for this emerging bureaucratic culture was the Ministry of Foreign Affairs (*Zongli yamen*), established in 1861, which, according to Jennifer Rudolph, developed a "managerial style" that centralized the government's management of foreign affairs.[18] While Rudolph's study focuses on the ministry's active involvement in requiring, receiving, and processing documentation from provincial and local sources within the empire, I attend to the new diplomatic reports' significant extension of the ministry's paperwork traffic to a global scale. Thus in 1866, when the ministry ordered local and provincial officials to send, on a quarterly basis, reports on "all incidents of negotiations with Westerners,"[19] it also demanded that the informal delegation to Great Britain led by Bin Chun (1805–?) "record (*jizai*) the country's geography, customs and cultures for documentation and verification back home."[20] Whereas the Board of Rites, the Court of Dependencies (*Lifan yuan*), and at the apex, the Grand Council had traditionally controlled all memorials regarding foreign affairs to the throne in a hierarchy,[21] the direct delivery of local, provincial, as well as overseas diplomatic reports to the ministry beginning in 1866 created a new horizontal chain of communication. Indeed, a month after Bin Chun's return, the ministry copied his *Chengcha biji* (*Notes on an Embassy*), and without consulting the Grand Council, presented it to the throne.[22]

With each subsequent diplomatic mission, the ministry gradually took on the Grand Council's status as the Qing's repository of information on foreign affairs.[23] In 1876, upon the formation of the first official embassy to Great Britain headed by Guo Songtao,[24] the ministry issued the following decree:

> the delivery of speedy reports being more accurate than one's eyes and ears, all envoys must record (*jizai*) in detail and inform at all times matters having to do with lands and customs, so that in years to come, Chinese officials can refer confidently to these documents for the handling of foreign affairs. When inspecting foreign strengths and weaknesses, officials need to write what they have experienced themselves (*qingli qidi, shineng bizhi yu shu*). . . . Should information be hidden and undisclosed, the fear is that foreign situations will forever be obscured, and the emissaries' tasks,

41

as good as falsely constructed (*xushe*). Hence it is ordered that diplomat-officials record (*dengji*) on a daily basis all events big and small, and send back to the ministry a monthly compilation for filing and assessment. Translated foreign books, newspaper publications, etc., related to the events are also to be sent back as evidence.[25]

James Hevia, in his study of writings of the British diplomatic corps, scrutinizes the routines of "collection, processing and storage" that constituted the British imperial archive of China.[26] Likewise, the Ministry of Foreign Affairs' institutionalization of the diplomatic report of the West (*shixi ji*) inculcated in its emissaries the daily habit of diary-keeping followed by the monthly practice of compiling and remitting. This discipline was meant to help the Qing Empire construct "truthful" accounts of the outside world. If China and the West each deployed their bureaucratic writing machines, their confrontation staged not Deleuze and Guattari's model of deterritorialization and reterritorialization, where only one side determined the decoding and recoding of material flows. Instead, the scene of writing in the paradoxical status of the Chinese empire-cum-semicolony executed what Robert Young, revising Deleuze and Guattari's model, calls the palimpsestual inscription and reinscription of cultural contact, where "cultures were not simply destroyed but rather layered on top of each other, giving rise to struggles that themselves only increased the imbrication of each with the other and their translation into increasingly uncertain patchwork identities."[27]

The palimpsest, of course, is a verbal figuration derived from its technical functions, much like Fryer's Chinese stereotype.[28] Since overlaying Guo, Liu, and Zhang's handwritten diaries are also the diarists' impressions of the Chinese and British presses, heliography or sun-writing (one of the earliest photographic processes), daguerreotype, Morse code, paint, and sound recordings, each palimpsest, if we were to employ the metaphor materially and accurately, thus consists of more than one kind of inscriptive technology superimposing itself onto another. The Ministry of Foreign Affairs, by its request that its ministers deliver their diaries together with physical copies of "foreign translated books and newspapers," thus received more than it asked for. While newer media often overwhelm and obscure older inscriptive forms, we can also see how *ji*, a traditional storage medium as well as the conceptual keyword of the present and the subsequent chapter, superimposes marks left by more advanced inventions.

Insofar as multiple layers of the palimpsest can outstrip each other, whether they are British or Chinese, old or new, it is not just the layers that must be interpreted but the outstripping itself.[29] It would be unsatisfactory to treat the emissary's writings simply as "windows" or "doors" to older and newer media, and then simply trade our linear accounts of media history for a more complex "*remediation* or *layer model* of media."[30] More rewarding, and also more challenging, would be to analyze Guo, Liu, and Zhang's diaries *as* layers, opting for an immanently mediated form of presentation that switches back and forth between the three writers, and in so doing mimics the very sedimentation of the foreign events, technologies, and practices that the diaries uncover. Encapsulating the stories that the diplomatic reports tell of past and present media formats is the uneasy mediation between the politics of technological adaptation brewing in the Qing court—the pressures of Westernization and modernization and the conservative or traditionalist backlashes against them—and the actual confrontations with physical machines and technical processes.

If the turning from a particular theme in one diplomatic diary to another in order to enact the palimpsestual inscription and reinscription of cultural contact appears somewhat unruly, this chapter would have succeeded in embodying Alex Galloway's notion of the unworkable interface, which obstructs any conjoining of a "thing and its opposite" in a "neat and tidy manner." Rather than a "door" or "window" understanding of mediation, an additional "intraface" complicates the interface, leading the latter into incoherent rather than coherent regimes of the political and the aesthetic in absolutely "nonnormative terms."[31] What the media theorist means by an unworkable interface thus translates into "a medium that does not mediate," in other words, an understanding of mediation that does *not* lead to transparent immediacy. Likewise, as this book argues, mediation crosses the threshold that separates media objects and devices on one side from their textual forms on the other in order to facilitate their mutuality. Just as there exist workable and unworkable interfaces promoting both coherence and incoherence,[32] it cannot be denied that some media mediate more than others.

Beyond a palimpsest of the old and the new, and the indigenous and foreign, the ministry's decree also primed the diplomatic diaries to record the not yet recordable. Officials' reports from their tenure abroad were to serve not only as reliable information for future reference, but also as the very means of verifying their diplomatic mission, without which the emissaries' tasks would be "as good as falsely constructed (*xushe*)."[33] Yet what if the reports themselves evince false constructs? According to the Chinese narrative tradition, *ji* is a genre in both history and fiction, as with others in the bibliographical taxonomy of the *sibu* system.[34] In Plaks's evaluation, what is called truth is "always something more subjective, more relative, more directly limited to specific human context," therefore on a gradient with the "obvious untruths of hyperbole, supernatural detail, or ideological distortion."[35] For this reason, Zhang Deyi, who kept diaries for all the eight different embassies that he served between 1866 and 1906, originally titled each of them "a narration of the strange and the marvelous" (*shuqi*).[36] Just as the true or the historical and the illusory or the fictional overlap rather than diametrically oppose each other, the term *strange and marvelous* (*qi*) can also be interpreted as that which is "particularized (*qite*), and hence concrete."[37] Within the bounds of the narration of the *qi*, these diaries project a realm of imaginary media and unlikely mediations, and so break with the confines of the political present.

I will unravel how Guo, Liu, and Zhang's accounts of their experiences abroad span this gradient of the real and the concrete, and the fictional and the strange. All three envoys, through their varying commitments to science and technology, come to envision alternative communicative mediums and mediatic processes unavailable or at least not yet known to them by name: Guo's unintentional evocation of the telephonograph; Zhang's peek at early cinematic technology; and Liu's hints at the techniques of political representation. Therefore, the best way to contest Fryer's indictment of Chinese unoriginality is to follow his comparison of the traditionally educated Chinese with a "mere literary machine" to the letter—that is, to scrutinize instances in the diplomatic reports where writing *about* machines challenges inscriptive fidelity, leaving in its wake uncanny and hybrid media experiences that traverse temporal as well as spatial borders. Precisely because the diplomatic reports fail to provide exacting accounts of physical devices and their specific functions, they forecast, through apparent inaccuracies, unfamiliar modes of seeing and hearing. By discovering "potential or possible media; dreamed media, fantasized media," these three late nineteenth-century Chinese, not unlike scholars drawn to imaginary media in the subfield of media archaeology, envision "how human communication can be reshaped by means of machines."[38] But more provocatively, Guo, Liu, and Zhang's reports also test the possibility that human-machinic communications can *take shape* at all—that is, manifest through literary styles, the arrangement of sources, and other formal devices "that travel beyond the boundaries of their home texts to attract allies, generate attachments, trigger translations, and inspire copies, spin-offs, and clones."[39]

It would be fair to ask whether the presence of imaginary media affects the three diplomatic reports' status as historical records (*ji*). If media innovations are often born from the frustrations that result from the inherent limits of human communications, the Chinese diplomats' perceptions of cultural difference mixed with national inferiority and superiority show that such frustrations neither "transcend . . . their specific historical context" nor escape "technological construction and determination."[40] For what does it mean to find in these late nineteenth-century diplomatic reports implicit, yet to be realized, and perhaps frustrated desires for alternative ways of communicating, when both existing and future technologies were and will be conceived outside the Middle Kingdom? Do we read into these desires a doubly compensatory gesture, or does the thin veil of perceived technical inferiority muster some minimal resistance on the level of signification? Through the formal interplay of textuality and visuality crisscrossing time and space, the diplomatic reports from China's first embassy to Europe overwrite the unidirectional model of technological transfer undergirding modern media history, and in so doing reposition mediation at the unruly crossroads of materiality and signification.

THE MOVEMENTS OF *WEN*

While Guo was not the first Chinese official to document his official stay overseas, the original *Shixi jicheng* (*An Account of My Embassy to the West*) was the first diplomatic record compiled for the Ministry of Foreign Affairs in accordance with its 1876 regulation, and also the first to be banned. This is how the eminent reformer Liang Qichao summarizes the controversy around *Shixi jicheng*, whose print blocks the Manchu court ordered to be destroyed:

> In the second year of the reign of Guangxu, the ambassador to Great Britain Guo Songtao wrote a travel diary. In it is a paragraph that roughly says, "foreign nations are different now, they also have 2,000 years of civilization." Goodness! This was incredible; the book traveled to Beijing and enraged the entire court. Everyone despises it and writes motions to oppose it until the decree to destroy the diary was passed.[41]

Hyperbole notwithstanding, Liang's observation captures Guo's politics and its reception at court. A year before his posting to Great Britain, specifically in a 1875 memorial titled "Tiaoyi haifang shiyi" ("Debating the Benefits of Naval Defense"), Guo recommends going beyond the adoption of Western technological know-how to incorporate the "whole system" or "core values" (*benmo*, literally "the root and the branches") of parliamentary politics and trade.[42] While the more conventional approach of the period advocated by the Self-Strengthening Movement entails Chinese imitation of Western "techniques and crafts" (*jiyi*) as "means or instruments to an end"

45

(*mozhong zhi yijie*),[43] his suggestion that Western nations possessed fundamental principles beyond the sphere of pure instrumentality proved to be a bitter pill to swallow. Even more radical was his claim that China in fact lacked *dao* 道, the "Way," hence its continuing defeat by foreign countries.[44]

Guo's dismantling of the then popular dichotomy between essence and application or principle and technique in an effort to connect Chinese and Western learning dovetails with his recognition of the need for a communicative network once he was appointed the empire's first ambassador. The recoupling of such reified conceptual distinctions calls for both the construction of physical infrastructures and their subsequent representation in writing—such being the necessary collusion of concept and infrastructure, materiality and signification. Before his departure for England, Guo established the Shanghai post office (*wenbao ju*) responsible for receiving and sending foreign mail and official documents through commercial ships that sailed between Tianjin, Beijing, and foreign countries.[45] The postal office greatly aided emissaries' task of corresponding with the Ministry of Foreign Affairs until the end of the 1870s, when the telegraph took over as the main line of communication. Through this new infrastructure, Guo was able to have Chinese-language papers such as *Shenbao, Xinbao, Wanguo gongbao*, and the English-language *Zilin xibao* delivered to London.[46] There, he subscribed to the *Times* and other English newspapers and visited numerous press agencies. To illustrate how the ambassador relied on the missives of print media networks for his own report, his *London and Paris Diaries* mentions at least thirty-three titles of foreign presses, most frequently the *Times* (twenty-seven times) followed by the *Shenbao* (twenty-one times).[47] When Guo received letters from other state officials and family members back home and abroad, his notes often prioritized the method of their delivery—the name of the ship and shipping company, day on which it was sent and received—over and above their actual contents, which in many instances go unmentioned.

So laboriously detailed are events, customs, people, places, items, letters, and demonstrations of inventions, all ordered by chronological dating, that no reader could easily overlook the diary's listing or indexical effect. From a narrative perspective, Guo's account can be said to "be" narratives without necessarily "possess[ing] narrativity"—that is, without eliciting narrative responses.[48] Its sparse, literary style means that readers would have to put up with, in Yi Dexiang's assessment, the author's "flat and overly broad account."[49] Unlike the development of modern travel narratives in the West, Chinese travel writings, as predecessors to the diplomatic report, share little affinity with the modern novel. Whether it is in the depiction of external reality or psychological interiority, both travel writings and the diary form remain in the narrative mode of "telling" rather than "showing."

From the viewpoint of media, then, the indexical effect in Guo's *London and Paris Diaries* accumulates to form, following Matthew G. Fuller, "a system of objects arranging itself in composition with as yet unknown combinatorial principles."[50] Unexpected combinations enclose readers in a "sensorium," where there exists a "simultaneous reeling off of information and reeling at the implications of each element making it up."[51] Guo's extensive use of lists provides just this maximal intensity or, in more metaphoric sense to highlight the diary's storage function, a "compositional drive" invaluable for "developing an account of medial interconnection."[52]

In this sensorium, diplomatic writing, unexpectedly, traffics in an extra-diegetic account of the state of worldwide communications, and of the particular infrastructure that controls its flows. Hence, days when nothing of interest happened but for the letters or newspapers the ambassador received and read are followed by personal visits to the telegraph post office, and digressions into the histories of British railroads, telegraph system, and shipping.[53] In the same entry where the ambassador reports the loss of a letter he has been expecting from China, he also praises the invention of heliography, which in his words "uses sunlight to send letters."[54] Light as a pure medium signifies speed and efficiency: on April 12, 1877, right after his observation of heliography, the ambassador waxes lyrical about his tour of the Crystal Palace with its innovative use of plate glass to build a structure of transparency and luminosity.

In commending the English national postal system for its leading role in developing international shipping routes, Guo, after all the efforts in sending his diary back home, must have been hard hit by the Qing court's censorship.[55] Interestingly enough, it is in a peculiar entry on the telephone where we can best make sense of the ambassador's attention to the interlayering of different inscriptive media. The telephone, in Guo's words, adapts Western studies of "light, electricity, and sound" to execute the principle of "whatever moves becomes *wen*" (*qi dongchu bi cheng wen* 文).[56] While "movement" (*dong*) refers reasonably to the telephone's conversion of speech into electronic signals and their subsequent transmission along wires, Guo's inclusion of the study of light in early telephone technology, in contrast, appears confounding. Even less explainable is his employment of *wen* instead of *yan* 言 (speech), *sheng* 聲 (voice or sound), or *yin* 音 (sound) to account for telephony. Initially used to denote patterns or markings in nature and the cosmic order, *wen* was only later associated with written compositions (*wenzhang*) and the modern term *literature* (*wenxue*),[57] and includes within its wide semantic range today writing, speech, belles lettres, civilization, and moral refinement. Even though classical exegesis on *wen* does not exclude eloquent speech and musicality—Liu Xie (465–521) consistently borrows from oral-aural elements in his magnum opus on the topic[58]—Guo's equating of *wen* to sound vibrations and electronic signals reads as strikingly novel. But what is all the more memorable in this nineteenth-century description of the telephone in terms of the "movement" of *wen* is its simple and unencumbered functionalism, which assigns to *wen* neither a pure immediacy with nature nor the illuminating status of poetry. Guo is also less interested in elevating *wen* to a science as he is in defining it as a physical effect, since telephony already adapts studies of light, electricity, and sound to create movement, which in turn produces *wen*. Given the diary's emphasis on the circulation of print media and the infrastructures of transport and communication—that is, on the movement of information rather than the mind or body—its author's particular explanation of the telephonic function designates *wen* as simply one aspect of a larger media ecology.[59]

By focusing less on individual technical mediums or overarching philosophical paradigms and more on their dynamic, combinatory potentials, the *London and Paris Diaries* anticipates Richard Menke's understanding of media in his analysis of nineteenth-century American fictional representations of technologies. Media as a "concept" did not yet exist but would become ubiquitous a generation later to refer to the network of "nonprint technologies as well as print forms created for a mass audience."[60] Already, Guo observes in a visit to an English printing factory that its lithographically printed products range from letters to envelopes, railroad tickets, schedules, bills, telegrams, and invoices for wire transfers. The diverse nonprint and print usages accounted for in this entry rise in significance especially when the ambassador immediately contrasts them with Chinese printers who employ the same number of workers to manufacture half the number of products, limited to letters and accounting ledgers.[61] It would be too easy to attribute the dominance of print in the Chinese example to the country's technological lag behind England. At the time of Guo's writing in the 1870s, after all, the railway and the telegraph were seen as cumbersome foreign innovations. Even toward the end of the nineteenth century, a moment fortuitously captured by the onset of the Boxer Rebellion (1900)—the topic of chapter 4—villagers, often supported by local officials, resisted the spread of both technologies. Print, far from unaffected by the communicative crisis of 1900, played an active role in dramatizing events before and after the rebellion. Guo's admiration for English printers' diverse profits from advancements in rail, the telegraph, and the international banking system thus reflects more of the increasing intersections of print and nonprint communications, in which nexus China would soon be caught, than of the isolated functions of any individual technology.

Like the ambassador's animated descriptions of heliography and the telephone, which through movement creates *wen*, newer media such as telegraphy thrive off older technologies of inscription. Yet more lies at stake than simply the encounter of older and newer media, but the pace with which they are combined in order to effect what Fuller calls "an account of medial interconnection."[62] Certainly the quick and elliptical nature of Guo's impressions has much to do with the limits of the writer's technical knowledge; to praise this overall listing or indexical effect for its brilliance would paradoxically rob the *London and Paris Diaries* of its very media form. Instead of depth and concentration, the diaries opt for flatness and breadth, almost impatient to move from one sight or sound to another. If we can read into Guo's daily entries the formal quality of movement, it is because the latter as a tone and overall mood captures the writer's way of adapting to multiple devices. Stasis, in contrast, would signify physical immobility as well as the inertia of knowledge systems and thought itself. This concept plays a vital role in Liu Xihong's diary, to which I now turn.

NAMING THE *DAO*

The comparison of Guo's record with that of his deputy ambassador cannot pivot on the superficial observation that the former provides a more detailed account of new inventions and technical media than the latter. Insofar as this book defines mediation in terms of the discursive interactions with physical devices and material processes of communication, that Liu Xihong pays much less attention to the strictly technological side of the equation does not mean that his account fails to contemplate mediation *tout court*. Besides, Liu's *Private Diary* is a much shorter book based on the author's brief nine-month stint in London. Its thirty-six entries take up only 192 pages, in contrast to Guo's thousand-odd pages, which are subdivided into thirty chapters, each containing at least ten days' worth of entries. To evaluate *Private Diary* on the same grounds as Guo's media sensorium would be to commit the kind of crude technical or material determinism that this book rejects from the outset. At the same time, to ignore how each writer's attitude toward the technical or the material shapes the ways in which he observes his external surroundings would be equally absurd.

49

As always, what was not recorded did not matter, though in this case, the victor also lost. Liu's sojourn in London began with an episode of bureaucratic oversight, one that would tarnish the deputy ambassador's relationship with his superior even after both had left their posts. After arriving in London in January 1877, Liu discovered that the letter of credence issued by the Manchu court only stated Guo's and not his own official designation. As a result, Liu was unable to present himself to the British in any official capacity.[63] Despite eventually being granted an audience with Queen Victoria, Liu nevertheless resigned out of resentment of Guo's failure to check for Liu's accreditation in the court letter. Liu was reassigned to represent the court in Germany, while Guo was sent to France. In 1878, the court ordered them both back to China on account of the pair's continued animosity.[64]

The deputy ambassador's decision to keep his own report of the emissary's affairs in Great Britain exacerbated the conflict. From Guo's perspective, Liu's diary consisted of fraudulent entries intended only to further smear the former's troubled reputation at court.[65] Implicit in Guo's accusation was that only the ambassador, and not his deputy, had the authority to report to the Ministry of Foreign Affairs about their official duties overseas. The two officials' interactions before they left for Great Britain did little to cultivate amicable working relations. In contrast to Guo's embrace of Western technological know-how, Liu opined that it was "sufficient to purchase [useful machines] from Westerners" and avoid manufacturing them in "Chinese arsenals."[66] Given this lukewarm attitude toward "techniques and crafts" (*jiyi*) or "technical craft" (*jiqiao*), Liu would undoubtedly share none of Guo's enthusiasm for British parliamentary politics or for more thorough reform from the ground up. As a clear illustration, Liu, in a letter to Li Hongzhang (1823–1901), assigns Western languages and writings to the category of techniques and crafts secondary to the "Way of governance" (*erwang zhidao zhiben*); as such, they should not be taken too seriously."[67]

Undergirding Liu's Luddite-like aversion to the phenomenal world of industry, craft, and technology is his commitment to upholding fundamentally opposing epistemes, which distinguishes true learning from mere tools. In a visit to the Shanghai Polytechnic Institute (*Gezhi shuyuan*) prior to his departure for England, Liu criticizes supporters of Western learning for naming the college after a concept meaning the "investigation of things and extension of knowledge" simply because the institution "stores machines."[68] According to Liu, *gezhi* in the tradition of the "Great Learning" (*Daxue*), the central text of Neo-Confucian teaching, intimates the Way (*dao*) and not "objective things" (*qi* 器). In keeping *gezhi* on the side of the noumenal principle (*li*) or Way (*dao*), Liu excludes from it the study of science and natural philosophy that the organizers of the institute had intended the term to mean.[69] The problem was not that Western nations' wealth and progress had no source or foundations (*gendi*), but that one cannot call them a "Way" (*dao*).

There are two ways to interpret the writer's position on science and technology from this quibble over nomenclature. On the most immediate level, a strict adherence to the "study of principle" (*lixue*) tradition of Neo-Confucianism forecloses Liu to its practical applications. Yet he may also have perceived, a century before the contemporary Chinese scholar Wang Hui, that *gezhi*, in its trend toward objectification after Zhu Xi (1130–1200), was still limited by its own tradition and therefore not a particularly appropriate term to indicate scientific knowledge and Western technology.[70] To be fair, Liu admits that Western nations derive their wealth from "fundamental principles" over and above the realm of manufacturing.[71] Rather than crudely oppose Liu's conservatism to Guo's pro-foreign progressivism, a point necessitating a revisit, I am more sympathetic to an alternative interpretation that views both as merely inheriting different aspects of Confucian learning. Whereas the ambassador humbly and enthusiastically opened himself to learning Western science and technology, his deputy stressed the steadfastness of moral ideals. While the former followed the practically minded statecraft school (*jingshi*) of Confucian thought, and the latter adhered to the importance of universal principles (*li*), both were Confucians through and through.[72]

The two diplomats nonetheless diverge when it comes to their opinions on mediation. While Liu's *Private Diary* unmistakably elevates the Way above the sheer instrumentality of objective things, Guo's media sensorium, with its listing or indexing of other informational processes, performs a similarly connective function as the global communications network it depicts. Liu, in other words, would likely strive to distinguish his own writing from functional communication, whereas the author of the *London and Paris Diaries* inadvertently finds himself on the opposite end with the form of his report mirroring its content. When Guo redeploys *wen*, with its elevated connotations of writing, speech, belles lettres, civilization, and moral refinement as a conveyer of information in the manner of the telephone, what is he doing but showing that the Way belongs to the world of objective things? By relying on the Chinese *wen* to explain the working of a ringing contraption without fetishizing the cultural edifice buttressing the term's etymology, Gu would be well placed alongside commentators from Fryer to Kittler and Fuller, who variously grasp writing as fulfilling a storage function and a "compositional drive" connecting to other media.[73] Liu, on the other hand, would not quite fit in with this lineup; and the task falls rather appropriately on Zhang Deyi, the emissary's translator, to moderate Guo and Liu's respective reports of the communicative functions of language.

WENZI AS VISUAL MEDIUM

Zhang's long diplomatic career began when he was, at eighteen years old, one of three students from the School of Combined Learning (*Tongwen guan*), the Qing college of translators, who accompanied Bin Chun on the 1866 delegation to Britain.[74] Subordinate to Guo and Liu, Zhang nonetheless surpassed his superiors in experience. The eight volumes of his travels abroad, which roughly bookend the end of the Tongzhi period (1861–75) and the beginning of Guangxu's reign (1875–1908), also signal Zhang's adeptness to the then new genre of the diplomatic report or record of the West (*shixi ji*).[75] A comparison of how all three officials describe the foreign press in their diaries reveals their respective attitudes not just toward the society in which they were stationed, but also toward public discourse in general. Whereas Guo subscribes to the *Times* for its "balanced, objective accounts,"[76] Liu erroneously assumes that all London newspapers practice the Chinese culture of "pure talk" (*qingyi*),[77] which refers to a style of public debate controlled by conservative scholar-officials and literati of the purist faction (*qinqliu dang*), who opposed the introduction of foreign methods and ideas by more liberal-minded officials such as Li Hongzhang.[78] In contrast to Guo and Liu, Zhang neither extols the press's objectivity nor forces it to conform to the standards of the Chinese secret memorial system that Liu upholds—in other words, to pure subjectivity. "All the listed newspapers," Zhang expounds using striking wording, "are equally communication (*chuanbo*), the grand lives of brush and ink (*cheng bimo zhi yida shengya ye*)."[79] And communications, as the translator vouches firsthand, are no straightforward affairs: when his English fails him, Zhang informs his readers that he has to transliterate the titles of foreign newspapers the best he can. Yet there remains five or six other newspapers whose names he simply does not know how to put in writing. Indeed, many of the thirty-odd English newspaper titles Zhang lists do not make much sense to a native speaker.

The author of *An Account of My Journey* may have overlooked the advances of mechanical printing when he equates the printing press to the labor-intensive process of "brush and ink"; in this regard, Zhang does not share Guo's penchant for documenting the sheer multitude of technical objects, infrastructure, and processes. And yet to the extent that Zhang's diary directly employs the linguistic medium for imagistic rather than semantic purposes,[80] it surpasses Guo's diplomatic report in foregrounding the materiality of the communication. Hence in one entry, the character 页 depicts the shape of a microscope.[81] Meanwhile, 串 conjures the shape of an acrobatic configuration that the translator saw at a circus performance.[82] And 皿 resembles the ceremonial crown used at an inauguration ceremony.[83] Chinese characters, not uncontroversially, as I will soon elaborate, become pure imagery. Very often, Zhang isolates a radical in order to exploit its shape. A uniquely shaped table thus takes the form of 匚.[84] Similarly, 凵 stands in for a swing hanging in the main hall of the Shanghai Polytechnic Institute on which a mechanized doll sits.[85] On other occasions, the translator abandons any semblance to written characters altogether and draws lines and shapes in accordance with what he sees. Take for instance his depiction of English public restrooms shaped like [ ].[86] When depicting Russian snow hats, Zhang uses the symbol ▽ for the front view, and ⌂ for the side view.[87] Whether they are actual characters, isolated radicals, or geometric shapes, Zhang refers to them broadly as characters (*zi*). It is as if, when in new lands and recording new sights, the diarist cannot stress enough the flexibility of the Chinese character as a visual medium, while undermining, in these instances, its phonetic element, which in fact constitutes a major principle of the language.

Going even further than Guo, who describes the telephone as that which in movement becomes *wen*, Zhang manipulates the shapes and sinews of the linguistic medium to represent less familiar events, objects, and cultural practices. The experience of seeing Chinese characters used this way in *An Account of My Journey* becomes more arresting when yoked to the long tradition of Western discourse around the Chinese written character—that is, its unique link with material reality by virtue of a supposedly pictographic nature, as opposed to the alphabet's phonetic quality. Philosophers, writers, and artists from Gottfried Wilhelm Leibniz, Georg Wilhelm Friedrich Hegel, and Ezra Pound, to Julia Kristeva, Jacques Derrida, and Jacques Lacan have treated Chinese writing as either a positive or negative example of an order of signification more riveted to the material world. So much ink has been spilled on this topic that the critique of the Western imagination of the Chinese pictograph has generated a cultural industry for comparative literary and cultural studies in the English language. Yet as Andrea Bachner's contribution to this subject illustrates, the analytical richness of the Chinese script or sinograph transcends the Western/non-Western binary when cultural and national identities are themselves "scripted" in the alterities inherent in the sinograph. More must be done than simply expose the hallucinatory nature of the Western imagination, or reclaim native authenticity for Chinese writers like Zhang, who exploit the pictographic force of Chinese writing. What the Qing translator's diplomatic diary highlights instead is "the heterogeneity of scriptural effects . . . a difference of media at the heart of the sinograph, or, indeed, any single script."[88]

We can say with some confidence that Zhang did not have the history of Western ideographic myth of the Chinese writing script in mind when he made use of graphic characters and symbols to depict England, Russia, and Western-influenced objects. *An Account of My Journey* is no work of art; yet its direct reporting style ends up commenting on aesthetics and the sensorial experience of reading and writing. By employing characters, radicals, and geometric shapes non-discriminatingly as characters (*zi*), his entries interject accounts of foreign architecture and cultural practices ranging from political institutions to food with a script-like visuality no longer completely recognizable as "Chinese," and yet whose resonance with certain features of the Chinese script writing remain visible. Unlike Liu, for whom linguistic signifiers must not lose their original context and meaning lest *wen* or *dao* be contaminated by technical craft, Zhang allows for writing to abandon semantics for physical form.

In so doing, *An Account of My Journey*'s pictographic insertions underscore the visual and linguistic tension within Chinese written characters: the former seemingly flushed with the immediacy of the signified, and the latter having to shoulder the immense tradition of culture and meaning. The question this tension raises is whether visuality itself, more so than inscriptive significations, efficiently portrays the unfamiliar and the foreign. Before answering this question, we need to return to Guo's diary to unravel the complications and heterogeneities *within* verbal communication.

THE MEETING OF SOUNDS

The association of *wen* with cultural refinement and thus a certain gravitas was not unique to China; as new inscriptive technologies made their mark on Europe and North America, textuality was designed for serious use rather than frivolity. This is indeed how Thomas Edison marketed the phonograph, derived from the Greek words for sound and writing, as a textual device "with dictation in mind rather than entertainment."[89] And such intent did not falter in the machine's global itinerary. An 1890 article introducing Chinese readers to the phonograph (*jisheng qi*) published in *Gezhi huibian* (*Chinese Scientific Magazine*) characterizes Edison's machine as a "wondrous craft" (*qiqiao*) often misunderstood for being of purely frivolous and entertainment value (*qule kaixin zhi yong*).[90] The phonograph's ability to reproduce stored sound, the article continues, means that it can actually bypass "the inconvenience of book writing" (*shuxie zhifan*) and preserve "good speeches of famous men" (*minren shanyan haoyu*). From its inception in North America, the phonograph foregrounded linguistic distinction as its storage and transmissive function. The cultural significance of phonography, as Gitelman maintains, thus lies in its liaisons with other textual practices such as shorthand reporting, typescripts, printing telegraphs, and silent motion pictures.[91] And yet mediations varied in their significance and ease: when Guo's written record pits itself against early sound recording, it jolts the media sensorium that the ambassador has carefully constructed.

On April 19, 1878, after returning to England from Paris where he was attending the World's Fair, Guo meets a certain Aidisheng. The latter demonstrates to Guo and others present a *chuansheng ji* invented by a Scottish émigré to the US named Geliyin Beier.[92] This is how Guo describes the machine in his entry:

> It holds a 3 inch disc, made from thin metal as thin as a membrane (*lian bo tiepian ru zhumeng*). Below is placed a metal needle (*tiezhen*); two inches above lies a large-mouthed cylinder (*jukou tong*) that receives sounds (*shouna sheng*). Attached is a shaft holding a tin cylinder (*tongyuan tong*) punctured with tiny holes (*huanzao zhenkong*) held by an axle (*yongzhou xianzhi*). Said cylinder rotates with the operation of a motor . . . [W]hen the machine (*chuansheng ji*) moves close to the motorized wheel (*zhuanji lun*), the needle comes into contact with the cylinder's holes, and sound is naturally produced.[93]

The demonstrator Aidisheng then proceeds to explain how the apparatus adheres to the basic principles of sound vibration produced by the eardrum. In sum, Guo provides an accurate description of the mechanics of the phonograph. Guo's subsequent account of the live demonstration of the device, however, sounds a little more curious:

> After speaking into the mouthpiece covered by a brass cap, the sound travels through some organ (*jiguan*) and the transmitted sound (*ji chuanyan*) is

55

stored in the cylinder (*nazhi tongzhong*) enclosed by the brass cap. When the needle closes in on the wheel and its holes (*qizhen jinbi lunkou*), and as the latter turns, the transmitted (*chuan* 傳) sound is sent out (*chuan* 傳) from the enclosure. . . . When two people converse continuously (*chuan-yan* 傳言), their voices are sent out (*chuanchu* 傳出) [until] every sound meets another, in the middle of the room (*zhongjian shaojian, yiyifuhe* 中間稍間, 一一附合).[94]

What device did Guo see presented by this mysterious Aidisheng? While Guo fails to note the significant innovation of the double electromagnet and its coiled current transmission, and observes "holes" on the "cylinder" instead of grooves, it is not difficult to identify *chuansheng ji* as the phonograph and the transliterated Aidisheng as its inventor, Thomas Edison, making the *London and Paris Diaries* the first Chinese account of the device.[95]

How Guo records the device he had seen shapes both the meaning and technicality of the medium. The Chinese neologisms foreground an inherent ambiguity in technical functions, and it is this inherent technical ambiguity, which demands that we read and reread the mediated form of the inscriptive device in question. This is also what makes the *London and Paris Diaries*—along with other texts studied in this book—a historical document of media as well as a theoretical inquiry into mediation. While Guo's description of the tin cylinder "punctured with tiny holes" fits the grooved engravings of the phonograph cylinder, and that of the thin metal "membrane" the diaphragm, his choice of name—*chuansheng ji*, with the character *chuan* 傳—emphasizes the transmission of sound over distance, contrary to the phonograph's technical breakthrough in storing (*liu, cun,* or *ji*) sound. The image of two people conversing and their voices meeting each other most likely refers to a version of the phonograph that directly connects listeners through earphones, and yet the emphasis on the relaying and simultaneous emission of their conversations (*chuanyan*) evokes the telephone. The machines are quite different in their construction, appearance, and function, and indeed newspapers and magazines from the same period used distinct Chinese terms to differentiate the telephone from the phonograph.[96] The November 1890 issue of *Feiying ge huabao* (*Feiyingge Pictorial*) includes an illustration of the phonograph, which it calls a "recording-sound device" (*jisheng qi*). The accompanying text lauds Edison's newest invention for being more marvelous than the existing telephone, referred to as the "transmitting-sound device" (*chuansheng qi*), since the phonograph not only plays sound (*chuansheng*) but also "stores" (*cun yu qi zhong*) and "moves" the sounds elsewhere (*yi song ta chu*). After

56

playing the phonograph, we are told that its recorded sound both stays (*liu*) and is passed down (*liuchuan*) for "tens of hundreds of years" (*shu shibai nian*) without dissipating.[97] Another article in *Zhixin bao* (1898) praises the phonograph (or "sound-retaining device," *liusheng ji*) for surpassing telephony by not just transmitting but storing sounds over "a longer period of time."[98] At stake in the Chinese words for a phonographic recording is the dual functions of broadcast or dissemination (*chuan*) and temporal permanence (*liu*).

Guo's account of the new audio-recording technology is, it goes without saying, one guided (or misguided) by the contingencies of any live demonstration, which, carried out in English, must moreover be instantaneously or subsequently translated by someone else in the audience with the ambassador. This circumstance is compounded by the fact that the "Wizard of Menlo Park," as Edison was affectionately called after his invention of the machine, was not in England at all in 1878. It was a William H. Preece, an electrical engineer, who gave the first public demonstration of the phonograph in England at the Royal Institution in February 1878, and it is possible that it was he and not Edison whom Guo saw showcasing the device. Without an exact match with the date of Guo's entry (April 19, 1878), evidence of a May 8, 1878 lecture delivered by Preece on the phonograph nonetheless suggests that a series of demonstrations could have taken place around the same time.[99]

Between hearing the phonograph recording, understanding the working of its mechanical components in his native Chinese, and later documenting the device in writing, there exist several temporal lags without which Guo's recording (of a recording) would have been impossible. Technically speaking—and what is the phonograph but a technology that speaks?—such lapses in time (not to mention distance) are especially significant for the form of the Western diplomatic report or diary as well as the bureaucratic practice behind its dissemination. The speedy delivery of Guo's diary, while far from being telecommunicative, helped the Ministry of Foreign Affairs to control the Chinese empire's information flows over an expanding geographical space. As a storage device, the same document preserved for "years to come" the court's future management of foreign affairs.[100]

That the *London and Paris Diaries* performs functions analogous to both the telephone and the phonograph also points to the formal similarity between the two machines themselves. By formal similarities, I mean that both the telephone and phonograph share structural commonalities that allow them to function *analogously*—a word that the North American magazine the *Scientific Monthly* employs to highlight the two inventions' mechanics. Hence the "elasticity of the phonograph needle point" corresponds to the "condenser" in the telephone, the "pivoted needle arm" a substitute for the telephone's "transformer or repeating coil," and the "elasticity of the diaphragm" in the early acoustic phonograph is comparable with the condenser in the earlier device, and so on.[101] Edison developed the idea for the phonograph, after all, while he was an employee at Western Union competing with Bell's patents and improving on the telephone.[102] While recorded sound appeared superior to telephony for both North American and Chinese communities in terms of its social functions and cultural significance, the mechanical advancement of the phonograph over the telephone was perhaps overrated.

Technical or structural similarities between the telephone and the phonograph therefore accentuate the duality of form that this book has been tracking: both inscriptive media's physical forms (formats, capacities such as memory space, and shelf life) and the reworking of such forms in literary, cultural, and social texts. Both kinds of forms can be "read" for—that is, interpreted and given new contexts—but they emerge as "product[s]" of different kinds of "reading," which cannot be "known in advance."[103] It is one thing to analyze the phonograph—needle, cylinder, axle, and all—and another to examine Guo's description of these components in his diary. The latter, as a storage medium as well as a narrative form or genre, multiplies this tension at the same time as it helps produce it.

In pointing out Guo's ambiguous use of the word *chuan* (to transmit or relay) when *ji* or *cun* (to record, inscribe, or save) would have more sharply specified the phonograph, it is not my goal to revise existing consensus and propose that the machine witnessed by the ambassador in 1878 was really Alexander Bell's telephone instead.[104] Uncertainty over the identity of the demonstrator notwithstanding, Guo's technical description, however wanting, fitted that of the phonograph. The problem of lexicon, then, serves more as symptom of the encounter between an older inscriptive medium and a newer one, and their respective temporal economies. Whether or not the ambassador was referring to the transmission of speech over distance or both the relaying *and* conservation of speech speaks of a larger anxiety over the "economy and durability" of inscriptive media and their cultural significance.[105] Unlike the telephone, which "reproduce[s] speech at a distance," an inscriptive communication device such as the phonograph is able to "reproduce again and again 'at any future time' because of the delicate spirals inscribed on the surface of records."[106] Because of this, Edison's invention stimulated larger contemporary phenomena such as "the tensile bureaucracy of managerial capital, the ideal of objectivity in the professions and media, and the success of new popular culture forms."[107]

Whether or not such phenomena impacted China at or around the same time in the wake of the phonograph's inscriptive revolution, and if not, whether their belatedness reaffirms certain truisms of semicolonial modernity, are worthy questions that nonetheless belong to another project. Here, I return instead to Fryer's material metaphors to make an impression, or in this case an indent or groove, in the aesthetics of Guo's inscriptive—and inscribed—representations. The possibility that Guo's phonograph may only telephone *without* simultaneously storing and reproducing sound reflects first and foremost an anxiety over writing's ability to account for and keep up with newer inscriptive media technologies in the ambassador's immediate historical context. The question to ask then is this: Does the *London and Paris Diaries* record anything of value, worthy of reproduction at any future time, or does the Qing court's banning of the publication spell its truncated lifespan? Relatedly, is Guo's writing phonographic—that is, is the diarist able to, in Gitelman's phrasing, "have [his] copy and send one too"?[108] Or is it merely tele-phonic, transmitting information without recording and preserving? Does the ambassador's diplomatic report, because of its advocacy for adopting Western politics and practices not restricted to science and technology, sound more like a distant voice at the other end of a telephone line to which somebody is only half listening?

This vacillation between a recording and a transmission punctuates what Wolfgang Ernst calls the "sonic time" of technological media, which in turn impacts how we conceive of temporal relations in general. "With phonographic recording sound immediately becomes inscribed into a nonhistorical, nonhuman, signal-based archive of a new kind. This archive requires a temporal motion itself (like the turning disc) in order to become re-presenced, de-coupling the past from history."[109] To properly capture "the sonic—sound as sound and sound as time," Ernst's methodology prefers an "archaeology" over a "history" of sound insofar as the former prioritizes nonlinear temporalities. A linear temporality of history governs the rules of telephony, and Guo's description of two people "conversing continuously" until "their voices are sent out [and] every sound meets another" even forms a visual image of a line connecting between two points.[110] An "ecstatic" temporality bouncing off and away from "historical time," on the other hand, characterizes phonographic time: the replay(ing) of what Ernst calls an "acoustic event" is enabled by the motor, rotating axle, and the needle-and-groove contact in Guo's account.[111] Since the *London and Paris Diaries* undulates between telephonic, linear time and phonographic, ahistorical time, the impression it makes is less to do with an archaeology of sound and more with the politics and aesthetics of inscription.

After all, Ernst's critique of the dominance of linear temporality wholly attributed to the development of "an emphatic philosophy of history in the age of Enlightenment"[112] borders on cultural generalization. As Prasenjit Duara claims in *Sovereignty and Authenticity*, anxieties brought about by the modern perception of linear time resulted in "a circular return to mythical origins."[113] Paola Iovene particularly questions such a "return," especially when the idea of linear time is widely perceived to be imported from the West. Scholars of Chinese classical thought, for instance, debunk the narrative of a "monolithic Chinese 'cyclical' time that was allegedly replaced by a new model of linear temporality."[114] While a linear perspective dominated the diary format and the genre's descent from traditionally dated historiography (*jishi ti shishu*), Guo's phonograph has us spinning around with no promise of a steady landing.

What if, no longer choosing between the ephemerality and linearity of telephone time, and the phonograph's splitting of historical time in its replaying of an acoustic event, Guo's entry affirms both continuation *and* rupture by ushering in a medium not yet in existence? Toward the end of his May 18, 1878, article "The Phonograph and Its Future," Edison announced that the phonograph will perfect the telephone, which at its current stage was limited by its inability to leave any "record of its transactions, thus restricting its use to simple conversational chit-chat, and such unimportant details of business as are not considered of sufficient importance to report."[115] With these words, Edison thus put into print and by 1878 prototyped what would only manifest in 1924 as "a very simple device"—namely, the telephonograph or carbon telephone (later called the "telescribe")—that allows the "speaker to simultaneously transmit and record his message." By asking "can economy of time or money go further than to annihilate time and space, and bottle up for posterity the mere utterance of man, without other effort on his part than to speak the words?" the inventor banks confidently on the temporal economy about which Guo Songtao's phonographic imagination is only able to speculate.

As Jentery Sayers observes, the telephone-and-phonograph amalgam was less about a perfect recording than the disciplining of conversations and verbal agreements serious enough for purposeful communications.[116] Paradoxically, however, the invention's promise of acoustic permanence also "afforded its construction, malleability, and artificiality." In the telescribe, sound, once rid of its "liveness" or immediacy, was no longer ephemeral; the hybrid device simply reproduced the selective process in the making of a phonograph record with a pneumatic switch allowing users to go "off the record and to save only what they desired for wax." The machine, despite advertisements to the contrary, could not actually "eavesdrop" on telephone conversations. A telephone operator, in this regard, had more control in a telephone conversation than a telescript's account, since the latter was more "subject to the discretion of participating parties."[117] Moreover, the telescribe was not automated. One party's recording differed from another's because of their respective "acoustic settings, frequencies of pneumatic switch usage, [and] specifications of wax cylinders."[118] By Edison's own account, there was only the weak promise of a machine that simultaneously transmits and records "the mere utterance of man without other effort on his part than to speak the words."[119] The year of the tinfoil phonograph, 1878, heralds then the historical making of "fabricated fidelity . . . a technocultural moment when synchronous verbal communications were—if they were not already—transforming into asynchronous messages to be referenced and played back later."[120]

Linguistic ambivalences in the Chinese ambassador's account of the phonograph are no mere instances of wordplay insofar as they also correspond to technical slippages, which unwittingly summon an alternate communicative medium before its time. For reasons Sayers outlines above, it would be overly hasty to call the telephonograph a more advanced technology; equally foolish would be to dismiss the importance of its cultural imaginary just so as to maintain a false binary between the materiality of a medium and its discursive significations. This is why Guo's diary, in presenting a *tertium quid* between telephonic, linear time and phonographic, ahistorical time, helps rethink what it means to read and write under, not to mention *over*, the impressions of new media.

THE SPECTACULARITY OF ACTIVITY

Addressing his audience toward the end of the nineteenth century, Fryer found it necessary to denigrate the lack of originality in Chinese cultural production not only through the metaphor of woodblock printing, but by comparison with the phonograph. The *pas de trois* of xylography, phonograph, and typewriter, however, highlights how textuality could be at odds with sight and sound. In her study of visual modernity in China, Pang Laikwan uses the flexible notion of the distorting mirror to examine the ways in which "Chinese urban subjects viewed the West and modernity as objects of inquiry, desire, and consumption," which in turn actively shaped the construction of new Chinese subjectivity.[121] Such "realist desire" to understand a changing world characterizes the "pictorial turn" in nineteenth-century China, when the visual, for the first time, "directly competed with the written

61

as a communication tool."[122] In the realm of print culture, the tension between image and narrative, like that between Chinese viewing subjects and Western objects, reigns supreme. Yet Pang's study, and understandably so, grants writing lesser intricacy or significance. Hence the visual emerges as "more multiple, elusive, and unexpected" than its textual counterpart, which comparatively appears as a mere tool to "explain and tame" the former.[123] The double functions of explaining and taming occur elsewhere in Pang's book, even though textual explanations do not only tame but equally provoke. In her analysis of an 1889 lithograph of a cross-dressing courtesan in a restaurant, for example, Pang argues that whereas the visual image emphasizes her recognizable femininity (bound feet, raised pinkie finger, and accompaniment by a male patron) through "spectacularity," the narrative text, written from the first-person perspective of the courtesan, raises the significance of her agency through "activity" in its emphasis on temporal duration.[124] Narrative thus serves more than to reflect or explain the visual image as such but, to use the book's ruling metaphor for vision, *distorts* it through its temporal economy of duration and sequence.

Thus it is with both the potentials and limits of the visual that we return to Zhang Deyi's *An Account of My Journey*, whose imagistic manipulation of Chinese characters already complicates the "pictorial turn" in nineteenth-century Chinese print culture. His diary further engages with the question of temporal duration earlier raised by Guo's representation of the phonograph, this time in a controversy involving another pair of older and newer media— namely, portraiture and photography. On August 20, 1877, Zhang details Guo's engagement of the British painter, Walter Goodman (1838–1912), for a commissioned portrait. The ambassador fears that he will be too impatient to sit for the portrait, and so Goodman suggests that a photographic "blueprint" (*lanben*) can be taken instead.[125] During the photographic session, Guo requests that the pearls on his official hat finial be shown and his profile be kept straight, while declining to wear his official dress. The ambassador's British secretary, Halliday Macartney (1883–1906), checks on the painting as Goodman works on its final stages. Upon its completion, the ambassador's portrait is displayed to much public acclaim at the Royal Academy, and later at a Liverpool gallery for forty days. In adhering to the European tradition, which was uncommon in China, of circulating images of high-ranking officials,[126] this episode puts the finishing touches on Guo's already popular image in England as a Westernized, enlightened Qing envoy.

Yet it falls on the press, and not art institutions, to become the final arbiter of the ambassador's reputation. Zhang's diary proceeds to relate an article in the well-known Chinese newspaper *Shenbao* that presents quite another version of the portraiture process, supposedly informed by Goodman himself:

> Guo was extremely reluctant to sit for the portrait, and only agreed to do so after much persuasion. He had his hands firmly hidden in his sleeves, and insisted on having both, and not just one of his ears depicted lest viewers think that the other had been cut off. In addition, the ambassador insisted on drawing the feathers adorning the back of his official hat; I advised him that this request was impossible given where they are positioned. Guo then leaned forward till his head was almost on his knees, and asked, "what about now?" "But now," I replied, "how do we even see your face?" to which the ambassador laughed, and agreed to place his hat beside him instead. When I asked him to don his official dress, the ambassador declined out of fear of being embarrassed in front of the British public.[127]

What appears to be reasonable requests on Guo's part in Zhang's original account are here blown to comical proportions by the Shanghai newspaper. The *Shenbao* article concludes by identifying Goodman and an unnamed British newspaper as its sources. The ambassador was so taken by the portrait's "wonderful likeness" (*weimiao weixiao*) that he commissioned the painter to draw his wife next.

The portrait's resemblance to its subject is thus never in question. What the newspaper article mocks is the period of action *before* Goodman commenced his portrait. On the one hand, it matters little which version is correct—whether, according to Zhang, Guo's portrait was based on his photographic image, or in *Shenbao*'s case, that Goodman painted the ambassador in front of him since the photograph, its claims to indexicality notwithstanding, could not verify the temporal sequence of events leading up to the painting. Yet it is not insignificant that the introduction of photography prioritized the subject's sitting, previously sidelined in the Chinese portraiture tradition, and in so doing scaffolded a new technical regime of visual truth premised upon objectivity, itself dependent upon historical contingencies, varying understandings of realism, and discourses of national characteristics. While the European portraiture tradition has called for the sitter, commemorative portraits accessible to the larger Chinese society since the Ming dynasty did not demand similar physical presence. "The realistic representation in Chinese portrait painting," the art historian Yi Gu contends, aims less to provide a "onetime observation" but more to "transcribe the features that were most fundamental and least subject to change."[128] Hence many commemorative portraits were done posthumously, and even those painted during the subject's lifetime emphasized physiognomy rather than direct observation.

Part of the Chinese aversion toward sitting for a painting is the worry that the sitter may "stiffen up" in front of the painter, thereby preventing the painter from being able to "transmit" or "transcribe" (*chuan*) his or her subject's "spirit" (*shen*). To transcribe (*chuan*)—last seen in my discussion of Guo's diary to denote the movement of sound from one place to another, as in the Chinese term for telephone, *chuansheng ji*—now signals the transfer of a person's innermost, imperceptible essence to another medium.[129] Photography's ability to capture the sitter "alive in [even] her spiritual likeness" (*huode shensi*), as a 1909 illustration in *Tuhua ribao* (*Pictorial Daily*) that contrasted photography and portrait painting in two side by side panels claims,[130] meant that any difficulties when sitting for one's photograph hint more at the sitter's personal idiosyncrasies. And yet, photography, paradoxically, cannot fully evidence such idiosyncrasies; only a medium capable of narrativizing a sequence of events could. What the *Shenbao* article scandalizes is neither Guo's image itself nor Goodman's craft but rather textual narrative's contestation of visual "truth" or "objectivity."

During the 1860s and 1870s, nearly two decades before Arthur H. Smith published his controversial *Chinese Characteristics* (1895), how the Chinese posed in front of a camera generated much speculations about racial and cultural differences. *Shenbao*'s comical portrayal of Guo requesting that both of his ears and the back of his official hat be shown appears as part of a larger historical trend rather than an anomaly. John Thompson, a well-known British photographer working in China during the period, published a parody of Chinese photographic portraits that highlighted the sitter's insistence on a full frontal view with both ears showing, which suggested an overall unnaturalness, and a propensity to arrange setting and props in the most artificial manner.[131] If photography made irrelevant differences in visual perspectives and conceptions of optics, which guided stylistic distinctions between Chinese and Western-styled paintings, written accounts of Chinese responses to the new technology nonetheless revived and augmented putatively irresolvable national and cultural differences. Studies of both Chinese and Western photographic portraits of the same period have revealed, unsurprisingly, the exaggeratedness of such constructions: Chinese photographers arranged their clients according to Western ways of sitting and posing, while the sitter's awkwardness in front of a camera as described by Thompson was also found in Western studios.[132] What set accounts such as those by Thompson and the *Shenbao* writer apart from visual examples—say, the cartoon carica-tures of Oriental physical traits in nineteenth-century European and North American popular presses—has overwhelmingly to do with narrative: the *sequence* of events including the sitter's conversations with the photogra-pher, how the former arranges his or her attire, backdrop, and overall com-posure in front of the recording device and so on.[133]

As in the rare possibility hinted at by Guo that a stored recording—be it the phonograph or, allegorically, his banned diary—may only be played or read once, Zhang's diary entry detailing two versions of the story behind Guo Songtao's portrait suggests that neither painterly nor photographic veracity can fully capture the "essence" of a Chinese sitter with as much political and cultural significance as Guo. Earlier, I showed how the telephone and pho-nograph's sonic temporalities impinge on the anxieties induced by the court's censoring of Guo's diplomatic report. Here, the *Shenbao* controversy accen-tuates the difference between narrative as a primarily temporal medium, and the spatial order largely governing painting and photography.[134] What the paintbrush either on its own or with the advent of the camera could *not* reveal—namely, the Qing ambassador's provinciality—writing helped filled in. Such was the so-called Chinese photographic style that someone like the photographer Thompson, putting down his camera for the pen, and readers of the prestigious *British Journal of Photography* wanted to "see." Guo's por-trait, however, provides the occasion to challenge the Western tradition of ordering time and space according to ideological and aesthetic hierarchies.[135] Media mediate, and rivaling media mediate absolutely: in the last instance, Zhang's account of Goodman's painting privileges neither text nor picture but conjures instead the time-space synthesis made possible by early cine-matic technologies.

I emphasize the capacious function of time-space synthesis over and above any specific technical origin of cinema, following the works of Thomas El-saesser, Laurent Mannoni, and Jonathan Crary, which variously stress the birth of the motion picture in conjunction with other visual forms.[136] The early history of cinema in China is similarly embedded within existing print, visual, and theatrical media. Of particular significance are recent disputes over whether China's earliest motion picture screening, according to the authorita-tive *Zhongguo dianying fazheng shi* (*A History of Chinese Film*), indeed took place on August 11, 1896, in Shanghai's Xu Gardens.[137] Not unlike my study of Guo's attribution of telephonic transmission to the phonograph, revisions to this prevailing interpretation center on nomenclature, arguing that *xiyang yingxiang*, the term taken to denote cinematographic film, could have been referring to lantern slides all along. According to Chinese film scholar Tang Hongfeng, it was in fact a lantern slide show, not a motion picture screening, that occurred in Shanghai in 1896.[138] Not only does this refutation move the beginning of cinema in the country to earlier accounts of lantern slide shows—for instance, a May 1, 1875, article in *Shenbao*—it also shifts the conceptual terrain of cinema scholarship by highlighting the *function* of visual imaging when the actual *apparatus* itself escapes concise naming and identification.

Mediation occurs where the medium as a recognizably defined device remains absent; such is media's paradoxical modus operandi that this chapter has been defining. Zhang's detailed reportage of the events surrounding Goodman's portrait of Guo sourced from the press may serve no greater purpose than to offer another episode of court gossip. Yet from a media perspective, the diary's description of a controversy that essentially belies the visual arts' imaging of reality shows that photography and portraiture can step outside their technical perimeters to envision the possibility of creating and recording motion *in time*. Here, writing, far from "explain[ing] and tam[ing] the visual," becomes the latter's distorting potential.[139] In the face of *Shenbao*'s smear, the Chinese ambassador might have hoped for a device that recorded the period of time during which he sat for his portrait (or photograph). By simultaneously corroborating *and* invalidating photography's claim to visual truth, and in so doing dramatizing its complex role in contemporary mockeries of Chinese characteristics, the 1877 Guo-Goodman controversy distances writing from its usual characterization as a nonvisual medium, imbuing it instead with a visual perspicuity not unlike the moving image.

In this light, Guo's recollection of the phonograph demonstration he witnessed on April 19, 1878, as one person's voice "meeting" another "in the middle of the room," appears prescient in its emphasis on movement.[140] In 1891, an article in *Geizhi huiban* (*Chinese Scientific Magazine*) titled "Aidisen xinchuang jisheng jixing qi shuo" ("Edison Invents the Sound-and-Image-Recording Machine") announces a new machine that combines the phonograph (*jisheng qi*) and camera (*zhaoxiang ji*) in order to record (*ji*) a song as well as its singer's appearance and movement.[141] Most likely a reference to the kinetoscope, the peephole version of Lumière's cinematic projection, the article emphasizes the breakthrough in being able to create continuous movement through visual illusion: the singer "moves as if she is alive (*huodong rusheng*)!" While literature, painting, and photography endeavor to "transcribe the person's spirit" (*chuanshen*), Chinese accounts of early cinematic technologies, from magic lantern slide shows to the kinetoscope, highlight "movement" (*dong*). The same article, moreover, explains how the illusion of movement is created: Edison's kinetoscope is able to capture "forty-six images in one second using perforated film wrapped around an electric motor, as compared with slower precursors [possibly Eadweard Muybridge's zoopraxiscope], which take one image per second and project sequential images drawn around a glass disc."[142] Despite the writer's optimism, the kinetoscope's simultaneous projection of image and sound remained wanting in the 1890s, and even the improved version that Edison introduced in 1913 would have trouble synchronizing the music accompanying the film.[143] The technical infidelity between sound and image, such as that between the simultaneous transmission and recording of sound in the telephonograph, persisted alongside perceived cultural discrepancies. Zhang's 1877 account of Guo's portrait, in tracking writing and photography's distinctive temporal economies, also advances the kinetic potential of the phonograph as it appears somewhat *tele*phonetically in the ambassador's diary entry one year later.

OF LOCOMOTIVE AND LOCAL GOVERNANCE

If both Guo's *London and Paris Diaries* and Zhang's *An Account of My Journey* bring together disparate technical functions in imaginative textual forms, so far Liu's *Private Diary* alone corroborates Fryer's belittling equation of traditional Chinese learning to a storage device that merely regurgitates from memory without producing anything original and interesting. If this reading is deemed a foregone conclusion because of Liu's conservatism, magnified through his animosity with Guo, it would do little more than reduce communication and mediation to the direct reflections of some "concrete reality" rather than, Raymond Williams proposes, conceive of them as active processes of meaning-making.[144] At its worst, such a reduction resembles what has in literary studies gained pariah status—namely, the intentional fallacy. Even a more generous reading of *Private Diary* that brackets the author's background would find the comparative absence of real and imagined media in his report, at least compared with his peers, striking. Paradoxically, the member of the embassy most apathetic about science and technology in his time abroad writes most like a storage device.

Per Edward Said's method of "contrapunctal reading," which he defines in *Culture and Imperialism* as the evaluation of a text based on an external perspective "with an effort to draw out, extend, give emphasis and voice to what is silent or marginally present or ideologically represented" therein,[145] the lack of media devices in Liu speaks volumes about the kind of recording that *Private Diary* performs. But as George M. Wilson shows, the problem of Said's contrapunctal reading, despite its advances, is that it abstains from "full involvement in the imaginative enterprise encouraged by the text."[146] Sidestepping the seduction that such a contrapunctal reading offers then, I ask if it is possible to find anything imaginative about media and mediation in the most technologically averse of the three diplomats.

In an entry dated April 15, 1877, Liu recollects his conversation with the king of Prussia a few days prior, when the latter attempted to commiserate with the deputy ambassador about their countries' weakness compared with nations like Russia and Great Britain. There exists, however, an advantage to not progressing, Liu contends, in privileging benevolence and justice (*renyi*) over wealth and power (*fuqiang*).[147] Why envy the West, the Chinese diplomat retorts, when "the one who walks slowly has lesser risk of falling, and military conquests take so many lives?"[148] When further queried by the king as to why China fails to produce its own trains, Liu replies that the Qing court already has at its disposal "hundreds of officials for hundreds of thousands of citizens, such 'method or procedure' (*xing* 行) being the fastest, [covering] hundreds of miles in one day, that there is no need to wait for coal-driven trains."[149] Having earlier credited the railway for "alas, almost shrinking the earth" (*yuhu suodi yi*),[150] and now praising local government for being more efficient than trains, Liu implies that the language of the obliteration of time and space commonly used in accounts of the railway and the telegraph is also applicable for non-technological "methods or procedures."

I am far from suggesting that the deputy ambassador is advocating for democratic reform,[151] but merely that Liu's patently feeble justification inadvertently closes the distance between political representation and technological advancement, which otherwise runs wide in his larger account. To be fair, Liu is not afraid of complimenting Western-style parliamentary politics, in particular British politicians' elocutionary skills and their ability to reach compromises in parliament, and he even openly admits the superiority of Western-style debates.[152] At the same time, he criticizes the corruption and elitism of the House of Lords for exploiting the state's wealth in the name of the people's welfare (*minli*).[153] Consistent with his overall resistance to economic, political, and technological progress, he pinpoints the influence that merchants and traders assert over members of the upper house as the major drawback of the system.[154] Elsewhere, Liu singles out the dangers of commercialization and trade (*shangjia*) on rural agricultural communities (*qiongxiang pirang*), linking railway expansion to such economic risks.[155] No doubt misconceptions about national and international economy might have colored the Qing official's overall reservations toward Western science and technology. As historians have noted, more conservative politicians often exploited concerns over the people's livelihood (*minsheng*) to resist the development of the railway, telegraph, and postal infrastructure. A fine line, to say the least, separates a reasonable level of economic protectionism from self-interest.[156]

Once again, it is easy to attribute Liu's anti-reformist views to his sense of cultural superiority. Paradoxically, such a popular diagnosis ends up reifying the binary of an immutable traditional Chinese essence versus an equally problematic generalization of Western beliefs about endless progress—in short, the anti-modern as opposed to the modern, to which I will return later in the chapter. It would be more useful to detect in his conservatism—and conservative he was indeed, especially compared with fellow Mandarins Guo and Zhang—an awareness of the complex mediations between political initiative and economic base, both of which are necessary for the most minimal enthusiasm for technological adaptation and infrastructural overhauls. Certainly Liu's writing offers little room for either existing or future technologies such as the telephonograph or early cinema gleaned from between the lines of Guo and Zhang. The deputy ambassador's cavalier dismissal of modern railway networks in front of the Prussian statesman affirms the proud insularity that is a hallmark of the Qing dynasty's failed reforms during this period. As the next chapter shows, however, insularity also fed the period's fecund utopian imagination. Liu's admittedly absurd rationale that the "method or procedure" of local prefectural politics forms a faster and more efficient network than trains begs the question of the relation of technological development to representative politics in feudal, dynastic China. For someone who staunchly maintains the purity of linguistic forms, cultural traditions, and fundamental principles distinct from the world of "objective things,"[157] this is undoubtedly where contamination occurs. In this regard, *Private Diary* brings mediation to bear not upon the interstices of technics and textuality, but leverages its discourse to negotiate the relation between a fantasy of direct communicability and bureaucratic governance.

NON-MODERN PAPER SHUFFLERS

Facing further attacks from court officials, who were not content with destroying his diary's printing plates, Guo, after more than a year in his position, asked to be repatriated on account of illness. His supporters delayed his resignation, but Guo returned home from England in January 1879 and subsequently withdrew from politics.[158] Upon his death in the seventeenth

69

year of Guangxu (1891), the Qing court still decreed Guo's overseas writings to be too contentious to be circulated. With historical hindsight, the first Chinese minister overseas would likely have wished for his intended readers to behave more like Fryer's description of the Chinese student with which this chapter opened, with mimetic powers and storage capacities like those of the phonograph and typewriter.

Nonetheless, the original diary's failure to circulate also attests to the success of its mediation between other inscriptive media and their political and cultural legibility in the context of China's first official diplomatic mission. Alexander Galloway, Eugene Thacker, and McKenzie Wark, sharing an ethos that similarly propels this book, advocate for "no more talk about" media either old or new, and more about "media and mediation as conceptual objects in their own right."[159] If we were to think less about "senders and receivers," and more about "questions of channels and protocols," less about "writing and reading, and more about structures of interactions,"[160] we would attain an understanding of media beyond that which always serves to communicate and perfectly translate. Their work thus explores mediative situations whereby messages announce their own limits and ineffability, such that "every communication evokes a possible excommunication that would instantly annul it. Every communication harbors the dim awareness of an excommunication that is prior to it."[161] While the theological implications of "excommunication" do not apply to Guo, his writings are nonetheless excommunicated in the sense that they served as the reason for his expulsion from the community of purist (*qingliu*) scholars opposed to Westernization, whom Ku Hung Ming compares with a "Confucian High Church Tory revival."[162] Moreover, the court's indictment of Guo's *Diaries* also spells what the three media scholars call the "paradoxical anti-message" at the heart of excommunication.[163] By continuing to write from abroad, and, more importantly, by continuing to evolve writing alongside other inscriptive media, Guo registers the resilience of his response, or, rather, his retort to the community that refused his communication.

Around the time when the court banned Guo's diaries, deputy ambassador Liu accused his superior of being a traitor for wearing a Western coat even when he was nearly "freezing to death" in the cold. On another occasion, Liu berated Guo for standing to salute the king of Brazil, merely an "insignificant sovereign."[164] History's judgment on Guo Songtao's and Liu Xihong's contributions to this period of Qing politics and scientific development would not fail to center on the former's modern, Westernized outlook on the one hand, and the latter's stalwart traditionalism on the other. Yet does Guo stand so indisputably as a figure of late Qing modernity, and his deputy of its undoing? Should more complex examinations of mediation, which go beyond the lens of perfect communications and stand-alone devices, not complicate a modern stance that predetermines what it is examining?

In *We Have Never Been Modern*, Bruno Latour argues that the word *modern* designates the practice of "purification" that separates "a natural world that has always been there" from "a society with predictable and stable interests and stakes," and this practice relies on "a discourse that is independent of both reference and society."[165] This presumption of distinct "ontological zones" dividing nature, society, and discourse during the historical period known as modernity, however, has relied on the complementary practice of "translation," which commingles, for example, "the chemistry of the upper atmosphere" with "scientific and industrial strategies," "the preoccupations of heads of states," and "the anxieties of ecologists."[166] The paradox of modernity is that the more purification forbids hybridization, the more the latter proliferates, and the more impossible modernity becomes. Yet modernity's self-sabotage does not announce the triumph of the premodern or any nostalgic primitivism since the premodern suffers from the opposite ailment of overcommitting to hybrids, and thus to their purification.[167]

The possibilities that Latour's analysis holds for the recasting of late nineteenth-and early twentieth-century Chinese literary and cultural production as versions of an "incipient modernity" are far-reaching and deserve separate treatment.[168] Suffice it to say, rethinking the late Qing as that which has curtailed its own modernity means viewing Guo's embrace of foreign politics, culture, and technics as a simultaneous delinking *from* modernity. That is, the combinatory effect of his diary's "media sensorium" linking the railway system with heliography, the telephone with *wen*, and Chinese with Western learning manifests in Liu's anxiety over the encroachment of ancillary "techniques and crafts" (*jiyi*) into the whole system of "roots and branches" (*benmo*). Guo's hybridization, *together with* Liu's conviction in the purity of linguistic form uncontaminated by historical and cultural differences, would, in light of Latour, embody the modern critical stance.

> So long as we consider these two practices of translation and purification separately, we are truly modern—that is, we willingly subscribe to the critical project, even though that project is developed only through the proliferation of hybrids down below. As soon as we direct our attention simultaneously to the work of purification and the work of hybridization,

71

we immediately stop being wholly modern, because we become retrospectively aware that the two sets of practices have always already been at work in the historical period that is ending. Our past begins to change. Finally, if we have never been modern—at least in the way criticism tells the story—the tortuous relations that we have maintained with the other nature-cultures would also be transformed.[169]

We have therefore never been modern because any record (*ji*) of modernity, to foreground the key concept of this chapter, embodies the inseparability of translation and purification. As inscriptive documents, the diplomatic reports I study testify to the incessant mediations between media materiality and signification. Guo's *London and Paris Diaries*, to put it perversely, needs Liu's *Private Diary*: the deputy's suspicion toward linguistic translatability, as his quarrels over the use of *gezhi* demonstrate, could have taught the ambassador a lesson or two about the imprecise use of the telephonic *chuan* to express the phonographic function. And yet the ambassador's projection of another alternative beyond the dichotomy of telephonic, linear time and phonographic, ahistorical time would not have been possible without first risking the instability of writing as an inscriptive medium. Reading *for* media, for the obfuscating neologisms, ideographs, and the temporality of media forms in writers with such different political and ideological positions, generates surprising results that exceed the search for intermediaries and seek instead "mediators—that is, actors endowed with the capacity to translate what they transport, to redefine it, redeploy it, and also to betray it."[170]

In *The Interface Effect*, Galloway advocates for a comparable betrayal, one no less satisfying than the making incoherent or unworkable of both politics and aesthetics. Whereas a coherent aesthetics "centers" the artwork, "coalescing" it around a specific being, an incoherent aesthetics "unravel[s] neat masses into their unkempt, incontinent elements."[171] If a coherent politics aims for "stable institutions," "centers of operation, known fields and capacities for regulating the flow of bodies and languages" as best executed by nation-states, an incoherent politics "tends to dissolve existing institutional bonds" with no interest in upholding a center, in galvanizing existing coalitions, or to continue an undisrupted historical trajectory.[172] Hence Guo's account of the phonograph jeopardizes his record, while aesthetically, such a dispersive effect explodes the articulation of his political view as "modern." Liu's politics determines what and how he writes, and while *Private Diary* appears as the most ideologically consistent of the three, it nonetheless disturbs the non-modern or premodern prescription that Latour encourages us to reconsider. Through the Guo-Goodman controversy, Zhang Deyi shows that writing helps visualize what painting and photography both fail to depict. The incoherence of Zhang's aesthetics—distanced from any negative connotations of quality or normativity—paradoxically reveals comparatively little of his political position.

Going beyond the Ministry of Foreign Affairs' order to "record (*jizai*) in detail and inform at all times matters having to do with lands and customs,"[173] these diplomats' evocation of unrealized or partially invented communicative scenarios cracks John Fryer's mold of the learned Chinese as a "mere literary machine." The emerging genre of the diplomatic report of the West (*shixi ji*) that grants media objects and processes their textual afterlives foregrounds the complicated symbiosis between politics, discourse, technology, and aesthetics. This is where Young's metaphor of the palimpsest, signifying the interlayering of cultural contact, needs to be inscribed and reinscribed on the rotating phonograph cylinder, which Edison later adapts for his kinetoscope. But this also signals how Galloway's appeal to an unworkable interface with incoherent rather than coherent politics and aesthetics helps return the mechanics of wheel-and-axle to meaning-making and not a little hermeneutics.[174] Because writing, as a traditional storage medium, registers the reverberations of both physical media and their textual forms, we continue to read *for* media. Evidences of their delegation to Europe between 1876 and 1878, these emissaries' accounts of media both real and imagined have never been modern.[175]

73

STONE, COPY, MEDIUM | "TIDBITS OF WRITING" AND "OFFICIAL DOCUMENTS" IN *NEW STORY OF THE STONE* (1905–1906)

The 1876–1878 diplomatic diaries written by China's first emissaries to Great Britain were never "modern" in the Latourian sense because they spectacularly recorded media both real and imagined, and reflexively conveyed their own recordings as the mediation between materiality and signification. Around two decades later in the early twentieth century, the novel *Xin shitouji* (*New Story of the Stone*, 1905–6) by Wu Jianren (1866–1910) conjures a hybrid medium in the very body of its protagonist, who doubles as both the observer of media's social and cultural significations and the physical medium of the record, chronicle, or notes variously represented by the titular literary genre, *ji* 記. This human-machine coupling, in updating contemporary discourses of posthumanism around the development of intelligent machines with a distinctly ancient, Chinese mythology, thus continues to blur the boundaries between the premodern, modern, and postmodern examined in chapter 1.[1]

The story of the Goddess Nüwa has been read as a creation narrative and cultural archetype, but it also exemplifies Bernard Stiegler's thinking on the co-originarity of humans and technics.[2] Nüwa famously created humankind out of clay. However, when this method proved to be too labor intensive and time consuming, she decided instead to weave together a thick rope, dip it in clay, and so create multiple clods at the same time. The clods came alive upon landing on the ground.[3] According to the *Huainanzi* (second century BCE), a great flood and earthquake occurred shortly after her creation. In response, Nüwa smelted five colored stones to mend Heaven, cut off a turtle's feet to prop it up, and collected reed ashes to slow the wild waters. Of all the tools that the Nüwa mythology depicts, it is the stone whose literary adaptation installs it among the mortal world of the rich and the famous. *Shitou ji* (*The Story of the Stone*) by Cao Xueqin (1715–1863)—more popularly known as *Hongloumeng* (*Dream of the Red Chamber*)—opens with the one large stone block leftover from the 36,501 used by the Goddess Nüwa to repair Heaven.[4] Endowed with both sentience and magical powers of transformation, the remaining stone incarnates into a piece of precious jade. The novel's protagonist Jia Baoyu is born along with this piece of stone and is so named "Precious Jade." The stone, as Baoyu, enjoys a lifetime of sensual opulence only to experience eventual disillusionment before returning to its mythical form with an account of its life in both the spiritual and mortal worlds inscribed on its back.

The stone of the Goddess Nüwa and its illustrious afterlife in Chinese vernacular fiction do not end with Cao's eighteenth-century classic, but endure to sharpen the intersections of technics, signification, and the nation-state in China at the turn of the twentieth century.[5] Wu's *New Story* revives *Dream of the Red Chamber*'s original protagonist from its previous dalliance in "romantic passion" (*ernü siqing*) to fulfill the more "serious enterprise" (*zhengjing shiye*) of "nation-building" (*dingguo anbang*) (151).[6] The first twenty-one chapters chronicle Baoyu's experience as he witnesses his fellow countrymen's corrupt ways in the Barbaric Realm (*yeman jingjie*) of turn-of-the-century Shanghai and Beijing. The second half of the novel transports Baoyu to the Civilized Realm (*wenming jingjie*) ruled by a family of inventors as erudite in modern science and technology as they are in Confucian ethics. Following its predecessor's narrative structure, Wu's late Qing novel inscribes Baoyu's adventures as text on his nonhuman form. Before departing the Civilized Realm, Baoyu gifts his utopian guide, Old Youth (Lao Shaonian), his birthstone. The new owner accidentally drops the souvenir, and tracking it to a deep mountain ravine, discovers that it has transformed into a large rock on which is inscribed a marvelous text. Not wanting the text to go unread, and worried at the same time that readers may not comprehend its density, Old Youth copies it by hand in his spare time and edits it into the vernacular Chinese text of *New Story* (407).[7]

Since the second or third century BCE, texts have been carved on stones for monumental and commemorative purposes and to preserve canonical Confucian, Buddhist, and Daoist writings.[8] Because of the quantity of well-preserved and readily accessible stone inscriptions, their study profoundly informed scholarship on the history of the Chinese writing system, more so than the study of bronze inscriptions, which were more valuable than stones because they were dated to earlier periods, but more inaccessible because they belonged to "private or imperial collections."[9] As Jing Wang suggests, the stone's earliest divine association with Nüwa's creation gradually evolves into a symbol of human artifice as a "medium of written words" whose "verbal potential" may have been latent in another strand of folkloric beliefs in the stone's power of fertility.[10] Appropriately, the stone (with or without inscriptions) serves as a ritual object in altars worshipping the deity Gaomei, the divine matchmaker and the mother goddess of birth, one of whose many personae is Nüwa herself.[11] The character *mei* 媒 in Gaomei, with its etymological origin as the sacred source of matrimonial union and procreation, later forms the compounds *meijie*, "medium, intermediary, or mediator" and *meiti*, "mass media." Insofar as the inscribed stone as the "mediator between Heaven and Earth" has always been a communicative medium, it is not difficult to see how it has consistently bridged the human and non-human, navigating between different forms of signification ranging from the supernatural to the worldly, the official to the private.[12]

From these folkloric origins, *New Story* reintroduced the stone of the Goddess Nüwa to the Chinese popular imagination at a time when the relationship between human communications and machines grew in traffic and complexity. The enigmatic stone, when recast in the turn of the twentieth century, records (*ji*) the false binary between physical media infrastructures and their discursive significations. Between 1881 and 1908, nearly 45,450 kilometers of new telegraph lines joined the corners of the Chinese empire.[13] While telegraphy began as a commercial enterprise controlled by Danish and British companies, the importation of foreign machinery and engineering talent enabled its transformation into a joint public-private (*guandu shangban*) enterprise at the end of the nineteenth century. Concerned with China's overdependence on foreign expertise, the viceroy and trade minister Li Hongzhang (1823–1901) requested in 1880 that a number of Chinese students studying in the United States devote themselves to telegraphy, and he established a telegraph school in Tianjin in the same year.[14] Western missionary and commercial interests, which introduced lithography to China in the late 1870s and movable lead type by the 1890s, transformed indigenous technologies of printing and laid the foundations for modern political journals.[15] In international concessions in the treaty port of Shanghai, a burgeoning print and visual culture benefited from access to imported paper, printing machinery, and, thanks to extraterritorial protection, a degree of freedom from the threat of imperial censorship. In 1885, almost a decade before he blamed the Chinese literary examination for turning the Chinese mind into lifeless woodblock printing, which can only duplicate and not originate, John Fryer helped open the Shanghai Polytechnic Institution and Reading Room (*Gezhi shuyuan*), which published and sold scientific journals and textbooks.[16] It would be an understatement to say that Shanghai made itself legible as a city of new inscriptions.

New technologies certainly aided the transmission and reproduction of information, but whether they were themselves capable of human cognition and verbal skills posed a question of considerable interest to urban, newspaper-reading Chinese. *Huanqiu zhongguo xuesheng bao* (*Global Chinese Students' Paper*) reported on a new German-made robot named Enigma who walked and ate but could not talk.[17] *Dongfang zazhi* (*Eastern Miscellany*) boasted of a more advanced model, Occultus, who could not only speak, laugh, shout, and sing, but was capable of following instructions and responding to questions.[18] Indeed, if there could be machines for "transmitting sounds" (*chuan sheng*) and "storing sounds" (*liu sheng*), an article in *Zhixin bao* (*Chinese Reformer*) predicted that there would soon be a device made specifically for telling jokes.[19] Not all reports assumed such lightheartedness, however: since a worker who operated a steam engine looked as if his "vitality" (*shengji*) might well "leap into" (*yaoru*) the machine's metal casing, a commentator warned that the human spirit (*jingsheng*) could never reside in the mechanical.[20]

New Story's tale of the sentient stone and its metamorphosis into human form made a timely reappearance amid these turn-of-the-century considerations about automation and mechanical life. As an emblem of this chapter bookending my larger study, moreover, Nüwa's stone records the ever-reflexive dynamics between media's historical contexts and their more theoretical implications. First, the stone's inscriptive functions in the novel must be seen against the backdrop of lithography's ascendance in Shanghai, where much of *New Story* is set. The technique of lithography (meaning "stone writing") based on the immiscibility of oil and water on limestone plates was most suited for the reproduction of fine lines in illustrations and for reprinting instructional works and Classical texts necessary for taking the imperial examinations.[21] In 1876, the Jesuit owners of the Tushanwan printing house were the first in Shanghai to use lithography to create religious illustrations.[22] Two years later, Ernest Major, after a series of successful business ventures including running one of the most important Shanghai newspapers, *Shenbao* (founded in 1872), and other industrial plants and trading companies, purchased hand-cranked lithograph presses and launched the Dianshizhai lithography studio, the first privately owned, commercial printing enterprise.[23]

In an 1884 illustration of the Shanghai illustrated newspaper *Dianshizhai huabao*, the man-machine relationship plays out alongside, or rather on the surface of, the stone as the ancient site of inscriptions. The text accompanying the illustration of Major's new studio, not unlike the unnamed narrator at the beginning of *New Story*, boasts of reviving the material while transforming its very function. In the novel, the stone reincarnates to fulfill its original goal of "mending Heaven" (*butian*), a popular late Qing reinterpretation of the traditional mandate of Heaven. In the following description, the new reproductive technique using limestone plates does not just remove the tedious labor associated with the older procedure of engraving and rubbing, the stone itself almost undergoes a charmed transformation.

> In olden times, the classical writings were all engraved in stone [for people to get rubbings]; the state of Shu [Sichuan] under the Meng [in the tenth century CE] was the first to change this by means of woodblock printing. Here now [in the Dianshizhai] comes another stunning innovation, even more extraordinary; again based on stone, it creates a new procedure. No need [anymore] for cutting and polishing [the stone slabs and woodblocks]; and none for engraving and carving them. . . .
>
> The craftsmen with the Heavenly gift and the carvers with the uncanny skill [needed for carving the stone slabs and woodblocks] are gone without a trace.
>
> The machine rolls over it, the stone shimmers wet, and collected tidbits [of writing] or official documents are transferred to the smooth stone.[24]

The same stony surface of "olden times," after being overshadowed by wooden blocks, returns to the limelight in present-day Shanghai with a different technique of ink application and reproduction. What the first line refers to as rubbings (or squeezings) taken from an engraving even shares with lithographic printing the basic principle of "obtain[ing] duplication on a piece of paper," which may have inspired printing.[25] As Christopher A. Reed amply demonstrates, late nineteenth-century publishers chose lithography over the older woodblock and the emergent letterpress printing for its ability to meet market demand for reprints, as well as its aesthetic appeal in retaining the elegance of the Chinese script.[26] The stone, according to this enthusiastic pitch for Dianshizhai, transmits texts independently

2.1 Dianshizhai print shop, from *Shenjiang shenjing tu* (Shanghai: Shenbaoguan, 1884). Source: MIT Visualizing Cultures.

of the authors who composed them, and the carvers and craftsmen who helped publicize, duplicate, and memorialize them. As indicated in the last paragraph, the machine, not people, is the subject of action, along with an indiscriminate mix of written genres from "collected tidbits" of writing to "official documents." The illustration by Wu Youru (1840?–1896?), however, with its depiction of workers outnumbering machines—at least four working on each press and paper stack—glaringly undercuts the text's hyperbolic praise for automation, showing, to the contrary, that lithographic stone does not ink, impress, and print by itself.

The famous illustrator's work featuring two hand presses, five hand-cranked flatbeds, and photolithographic presses was "itself printed litho-graphically" for *Shenjiang shengjing tu* (*Scenic Spots of Shanghai*), a Shanghai miscellany (figure 2.1).[27] Hardly a scenic spot by conventional standards, the

79

printing room is organized into grids: each hand-rotated flatbed press and its hunched-over male workers form a unit of production identical to another. The combination of men and machine thereby visually mimics print's conformity with the industrial logic of reproduction. Or, perhaps the text's erasure of labor conforms slyly to the pictorial representation after all: low-skilled print workers deemed to possess little individuality are less visible than traditionally trained engravers. In any case, there is little denying the labor-intensive nature of the lithographic process. Even though the print and paper industries hired fewer workers than other light industries, the 1,300 or so employees in Shanghai's Chinese lithographic shops alone were, by 1894, significantly greater in number than those working at both Western- and Chinese-owned letterpress printers all across China.[28] An observer recollecting the process from the period remarks that "each press [required] eight men, divided into two groups taking turns rotating [the press]. One person fed in the paper, two received it. The process was troublesome and full of surprises. Its output was barely several hundred pages per hour."[29] If the author of the statement were to consider too the difficulty of handling the limestone tablets, they likely would have accounted for more manpower. To return to the Dianshizhai image, we see large, rectangular stones piled on the floor in the center of the illustration, their blank surfaces and uniform size resembling the stacks of paper placed on tables throughout the printing room. While the artist clearly spent more time detailing the machines and raw materials than the actual building, the tilted roof with its awkward attempt at depth perspective draws viewers' attention to the two-dimensional surfaces of paper and stone tablets alike. With square-rimmed windows and a ceiling divided by crossbeams resembling the square blocks of the Chinese script, the illustration references the material shapes of printing media as well as those of writing, the generic medium of language.

In *The Language of New Media*, Lev Manovich defines old media by its need for a "human creator who manually assembled textual, visual, and/or audio elements into a particular composition or sequence," from which "numerous," "identical," copies could be duplicated.[30] In contrast, a new media object processed automatically by computers is capable of producing variations. Variability, however, is not always a programmed operation assembling and customizing "sequences" and "discrete samples."[31] It can also refer to how all copies of digital images, not unlike and even more so than their analog counterparts, experience degradation and loss of information upon pixelation.[32] In other words, no copies of either old or new media objects are perfect duplicates. The same exaggeration of duplicability—and its opposite, variability—could be said of the distinction between stone rubbings or tappings and lithography. A rubbing, Wu Hung finds, bears the original stele inscription as well as different kinds of blemishes: those on the stele through the weathering of time, the rubbing itself from paper's wear and tear, and, last but not least, damages to the stele made by the practice of rubbing.[33] By the same stroke, lithography is hardly immune from variability. According to renowned Chinese lithograph artist and arts educator Quan Xianguang, the distinctive characteristic of lithography lies in its creative, and not simply reproductive, ability: the drawing of a master copy and the particular chemical reactions between oil, water, and ink on the stone's surface are all elements that give rise to slightly different effects each time.[34]

What truly ties older engravings to contemporary lithography, Wu Youru's 1884 illustration and its accompanying text claim, is the enduring, even mystical inscribability of the stone's flat surface. The indispensability of the printing technique's material form, however, continues to beg the question of other kinds of embodiments, specifically those of human beings and other artifacts. Wu, who later left Dianshizhai to start his own lithographed magazine, *Feiyingge huabao* (*Feiyingge Pictorial*), brags elsewhere in a poem that lithography, with no need for "polishing" or "cutting," now assumes "a supernatural workmanship that is completely effortless."[35] Therein lies another aspect of such a glorification of the ancient stone: its evidence of an indigenous tradition modifying a foreign imported technology. Wu implies, according to Reed, that the "lithographer's stone was not really something new in China."[36] Assertions of cultural identity thus help close the gap between older and newer media, showing once again that the social processes of mediation are inseparable from technological innovations in communications.

New Story was first published serially in 1906 in the Shanghai newspaper *Nanfang bao* (*Southern News*). Two years later, the Shanghai Reform Fiction Press (*Shanghai gailiang xiaoshuo she*) reprinted the novel, which because of its inserted illustrations was retitled *Huitu xin shitouji* (*The Illustrated New Story of the Stone*).[37] In all likelihood, the illustrations were lithographic prints. The point in this digression into the self-representations of the lithographic process, however, is not to exploit the stone's fictive inscribability in *New Story* in order to shed light on an existing printing technique *à la* new historicism. Since this book historicizes media *through* late Qing media theory, I am committed to showing how the third-person center of consciousness turned inscriptive medium, and the questions of media and mediation this metafictional narrative structure raises, cut across text, historical context, *and* medium simultaneously. In her study of the stone motif in *Water Margin* (*Shuihu zhuan*), *Journey to the West* (*Xiyou ji*), and *Dream of the Red Chamber*, Wang Jing links the poststructuralist concept of intertextuality, "the intertwining patterns of communication" between texts and contexts, to the "Chinese tradition of textuality" or *wen*, which has been figured as "sexual intercourse" and the intermingling of objects and phenomena.[38] Modifying the Chinese interpretative tradition's privileging of historical allusions in contextual studies, Wang wrests intertextuality from the dominance of "source" or "influence," moving the "burden of proof of historicity from the conscious speaking subject/author" to the reader and the text itself, as well as to the spontaneous connections between individual texts.

Material media, however, acts as the missing link in this grid of text, context, and intertext. The stone's intertextuality in both *Dream of the Red Chamber* and *New Story* materializes as an engraved textual surface and recording medium: in the two novels, a fictional reader (Vanitas in *Dream of the Red Chamber*, Old Youth in *New Story*) receives the stone text and copies its inscribed text by hand. If both novels similarly showcase stone engravings and manuscript culture, the late Qing adaptation distinctively aligns these inscriptive processes alongside early twentieth-century lithographic techniques. Borrowing Wang's terms for my analysis, it would be fair to say that the eminent stone traversing both Cao's original and Wu's adaptation manifests as intermediality. Within the late Qing novel itself, the stone also plays intramedial witness to the story's various representations of inscribability *across* different media, thus assuming a *trans*media identity.[39] Intermedial, intramedial, and transmedial qualities of the stone of *New Story* converge to form what can be called "metamedial." While metafiction defines a literary work's self-commentary on fictionality and its relation to truth, metamediality, less preoccupied with ontology, characterizes instead the stone's ultimate inscriptive role in recording other media and their messages, which relay the very intimacies between physical structures and their social meanings. Readers averse to neologisms may be more comfortable with knowing that "metamediality" simply spells a loftier name for "mediation" central to this book, defined as the cleaving and bridging of the distances between technical media, their historical contexts, as well as their formal representations in texts and images.

This then marks the "newness" of *New Story*, what sets it apart from its predecessor despite retaining its narrative structure: the late Qing text documents Baoyu's recursive transformation from an observer of technologies, media, and their social and cultural significations to also the medium of the narrative itself, which is then read, copied, and rewritten by Old Youth, a modern bureaucrat. Wu Jianren first labeled the first eleven chapters published in *Nanfang bao* (1905) as "social fiction" (*shehui xiaoshuo*), after which the entire forty-chapter text appeared in printed volumes three years later as "idealistic fiction" (*lixiang xiaoshuo*).[40] But rather than recapitulate the division of the novel into two parts based on an ideological distinction between barbarism and civility, or genre, my focus on the story's form vis-à-vis its content—namely, its representation of inscriptions—situates it in the interstices of modern Chinese media history that are not completely filled by book histories and scholarship on the modern press and book publishing. Despite the rich variety that makes up Shanghai's burgeoning media culture, scholarly interests tend to converge upon specific genres in the official world of print.[41] *New Story*, on the other hand, supplies a hodgepodge of less easily classifiable records.

BEYOND CIVILIZATION AND BARBARISM

In the first half of *New Story*, newspapers, ship tickets, company brands printed on merchandise, books, luggage tags, bank passbooks, and scraps of paper with English words on them reflect the commercial and Westernized influences of Shanghai. In the utopian realm, however, imperial edicts, government telegrams, business cards, inscriptions on medals awarded by the emperor, and instruction manuals for state-owned machinery—in short, official and unofficial paperwork associated with bureaucracy—greet Baoyu. And yet "paperwork" is here—as it is increasingly in our world today—a misnomer since paper is only one of the materials central to the novel's inscriptions, entangled with other mediums, some older and newer than itself, of which the stone is but one example. While literate characters read and write in the Barbaric Realm of early twentieth-century Shanghai—Baoyu, Xuepan, and Bohui being active participants of this inscriptive economy—the recording and transmission of information for any use or in any format within the Civilized Realm belongs to the stock and trade of higher-ranking technocrats on the one hand, and unnamed clerks on the other. As Theodore Huters argues, the best way to classify the new Baoyu, who emerges from his earlier incarnation in *Dream of the Red Chamber* as the classical "*wenren*, or literatus" with a "private sensibility" untainted by pursuits of wealth and fame, is as a "critical intellectual" (*wenhua ren*, literally "cultural person").[42]   83
The Baoyu we see after he enters the Civilized Realm, however, hardly fits this description. There, he recedes into the background of a flurry of routine

communications whereby information and its association with knowledge of the new or the foreign appear redundant to an authoritarian state perfected on the principles of Confucian morals and minimal bureaucracy.

It would be inaccurate to characterize the two halves of *New Story* simply in terms of "barbarism" and "civility." Instead, inscriptions in the two realms consciously address turn-of-the-century tensions between reformist and commercially oriented outlooks on the one hand and a state-centered perspective on the other. The interstices between them help link up what would still ultimately be an incomplete picture of the erratic presence of media in this period of Chinese history—erratic because media belongs neither strictly to technology nor culture, and are irreducible neither to the teleology of print and modernity nor to the wastebasket of disposable scraps.[43] Reflecting nonetheless the communicative environments in which documents circulate, *New Story*'s textual artifacts emerge as "patterns of expression and reception discernible amid a jumble of discourse."[44] Because Baoyu is, at least in the first half of the novel, curious about the phonograph, company brands printed on merchandise, and names of ships, his immersion in this inscriptive world further expands the "media" and "formats" of documents beyond "more elevated uses of texts, as in 'the literary,' and from more elevated forms of text, like 'the book,'" to include a wider array of "things" or material objects not just "bearing" but also *producing* "semiotic traces."[45] He can be best seen to pursue what Gitelman, following Latour, calls a "deflationary" interest in the mundane and the everyday, preferring "an embarrassment of material forms" over and above "grand catchall categories like 'manuscript' and 'print.'"[46]

Utopian China in the second half of the novel has its equal share of inscriptive materials, although Baoyu, as a mere visitor without rank or duty, lacks the authority to disseminate official messages and can only receive semiofficial documents such as visiting cards and name cards. On the whole, Baoyu's encounters with documents in the Civilized Realm evidence his dramatic metamorphosis from an observer of media to the technical medium of the narrative. The two inscriptive worlds of *New Story* do not collide somewhere between barbarity and civilization, but between humans and their technical counterparts. In Wu Jianren's imagination, information flows traverse both humans and technologies as hitherto overlooked, inscriptive surfaces to evoke the language of cybernetics and information theory that I have elsewhere discussed.[47]

Hence, more intellectually and commercially driven documents in the first half of the novel contrast with the bureaucratic paperwork of the second;

and yet it is Baoyu's observations of them that produce a difference between the two kinds of writings in the first place. As a cognizant, third-person center of consciousness who perceives the inscriptions around him, Baoyu cannot be dissociated from the nonhuman form on which his human experiences are engraved. In *New Story* as it is throughout this book, text, context, and media materiality hold equal importance. All three—or rather, the dynamic and yet unpredictable relations between them—require interpretation and close reading. This is how the *form* of *New Story* as received by its dramatized reader, Old Youth, toward the conclusion, mutually constitutes its content: how the engraved stone in all of its stoniness shapes its account of other technologies and the institutions and practices to which they belong. Everything that Baoyu perceives of his surroundings, which he then processes and arranges into a legible narrative engraved on his mythical, stone form, does not exist apart from him insofar as it also constitutes *New Story* on every page. On the one hand, the received text is a record (*ji*) of the protagonist's adventures in semicolonial China and its sovereign opposite. On the other hand, it is a fulfillment of the original stone's fate of helping the Goddess Nüwa to "mend Heaven," here translated as the "serious business" of "nation-building." This tension between the life of a man and questions of statesmanship, between private and official histories, has a long antecedence in the Chinese biographical tradition, explored in the next chapter, beginning with *Shiji* by Sima Qian (ca. 145–86 BCE).[48] The inherent capaciousness of the genre drives the traffic of personal and commercial writings in the first half of *New Story*, and the more prescribed chains of government exchanges in the second. As a symbol of their intersection, Old Youth, whose exact official role in the utopian state remains ambiguous, copies the text by hand during his spare time only when he is not at work. More, as in Wu Youru's depiction of the Dianshizhai printing room, therefore lies behind the scenes before both "collected tidbits [of writing]" and "official documents" come to be transferred to the "smooth stone."[49]

BAOYU, MEDIA OBSERVER

The diverse records, papers, and mediatory processes that Baoyu encounters cannot be understood apart from the loose, digressive manner with which the narrator casually embeds them along with questions of cultural and national identities in thinly plotted, descriptive episodes. In an early scene from *New Story*, a bewildered Baoyu is introduced to the telegraph and telegraph codes by Bohui, a learned companion, and Xue Pan, Baoyu's cousin from the original classic, who now dabbles in the book-selling trade in Shanghai (201).[50] The conversation jumps, as the novel frequently does, from the world's first binary signaling communication system to print, when Baoyu asks to be taken to Shanghai Polytechnic Institution and Reading Room, headed by Fryer at the Jiangnan Arsenal, to purchase translated volumes of English-language books. In anticipation of their trip to the reading room, the trio debate the best way to transport their purchases back home and decide that they will do so with a small cart (*xiaoche*).

We can dismiss this transporting of translated books from one of the late Qing's most preeminent institutions of new learning as a banal and rather tedious bit of banter, or we can take seriously the combination of telegraphy, translation, and the book cart to raise the larger question of how technologies surmount cultural, and not only physical, distances. The Chinese verb for telegraphing, *chuan* ("to send or pass," which forms *chuanbo*, "to broadcast") and the action of *fan* ("to turn over") in the term for translating *fanyi* ("to turn over in interpretation") have similar etymological resonances with distance as the Greek and Latin prefixes *tele-* and *trans-*. Telegraphic codes require translations, and the latter, in turn, need decoding. To derive such meaning from this modest conveyance is not about digging too deep into an otherwise superficial narrative episode, but in fact to partake in its literal or plainspoken quality. Indeed, the book cart is *only* a vehicle, but no more or less so than the new knowledge in translated books on science and technology that the characters are using it to transport (*zai* 載). Physical functionality only *appears* more instrumental than the uses of knowledge. Which saying captures better—that is, more literally—the need for conveyance (*zai*) than the neo-Confucian influential precept of Zhou Dunyi (1017–1073), *wen yi zai dao*, commonly translated as "writing as a vehicle to convey the *dao*"?[51]

Certainly, the books that Baoyu ends up reading ought to be more significant than how he carries them back home. At the same time, it is this question of the instrumentality of conveyance (*zai*), which problematizes the role of *wen* in the Chinese philosophical tradition. Are writing and its specific genres ends in themselves or simply means to a greater end? The above scene in the novel raises the stakes of how to categorize or cognize new texts such as telegrams and foreign instructional materials on science and technology. Baoyu's deliberation over the book cart suggests that writing, refined or otherwise, always calls for a vehicle or material component *qi* 器, which the philosophical tradition following *The Book of Changes* has distinguished from *dao* 道, the noncorporeal "way." Defined as the everlasting origin of the universe and society, *dao* undergirds the Confucian moral essence of virtue and self-cultivation.[52] The *dao-qi* distinction lent itself to the Self-Strengthening Movement's negotiations of Chinese and Western learning: just as the spiritual *dao* harnesses the material *qi*, Chinese culture and tradition—emblematized by *wen* or refined writing—could buttress the import of Western technical knowledge without the latter superseding indigenous identity.[53]

Thus, to unravel the *dao-qi* distinction in the Confucian philosophy of writing, from a mere car or vehicle (*che* 車) and its corresponding action of conveyance or transportation (*zai* 載), far from indulges in the clichéd literary faux pas of "reading too much" or "too deep." On the contrary, mine resembles more of a literal or denotative reading, which in Cannon Schmitt's postcritical stance necessitates that we "account for what is hidden in texts in conjunction with what is plain to see."[54] Joining recent attempts to move criticism away from paranoia and its suspicious hermeneutics, while avoiding the pitfalls of surface reading, Schmitt urges that we tend to the literal or the plainly spoken without forsaking "deeper" and "ideological resonances of texts."[55] Such a literal harnessing of the vehicle or conveyance (*zai*) in *wen yi zai da* dialogues productively with *New Story*'s digressive structure instead of simply dismissing it, and regards the otherwise trivial book cart in the friends' chatter as "a phenomenon to be engaged with."[56]

By the time of the publication of *New Story* in the first few years of the twentieth century, the Self-Strengthening Movement had lost political momentum. Subsequent reformers saw the need for more thoroughgoing changes in thought, education, and "the indigenous intellectual system in general."[57] If the new and the foreign could not be limited to the status of the purely material or technical without also seeping into the essential or the substantial, then the distinction between the vehicle and its content is generative rather than constrictive: a medium can always be the content of another medium.

The world of vernacular fiction and the unfolding of printed ephemera outside it, moreover, foreground the question of media forms at the heart of the original myth's metafictional and intertextual concerns. At the very opening of the novel, for instance, Baoyu, in true form to the original *Dream of the Red Chamber*, where he leaves home to become a monk (and subsequently regain his original form as Nüwa's stone), decides to return to the mortal world. To set the tone for his serious recommitment to "mending Heaven" as contrasted with his "previous" dalliances with women (152)—hence the novel's intertextuality—he immediately comes across the sixteenth-century *Fengsheng bang* (*Investiture of the Gods*) and Li Baichuan's eighteenth-century *Lüye xianzong* (*Traces of Immortals in the Wild*), both vernacular novels about demons and immortals. Less interested in these two titles, which Zhou Zuoren (Lu Xun's younger brother) will in a famous essay denigrate as "hindrances to the growth of human nature," Baoyu is drawn instead to the paper wrapping them. The fragment of modern newspaper, unfamiliar to Baoyu with its incomprehensible format and the heading of "news" (*xinwen*), delivers its striking blow by stating in both the Chinese dynastic and Gregorian calendar that its reader is now in the twenty-sixth year of Guangxu, or 1900 (156). Comically, the time-traveling hero and his page Beimin (an original character from *Dream of the Red Chamber*) will not stop marveling over a humble matchbox printed with the logo "Xiechang," one of the largest matchstick manufacturers in Shanghai at the time (157).[58] Subsequent mechanical ingenuities that the duo encounter include the steamship and the equally unfamiliar custom of rendering the ship's name visible on the vessel (165). But it is the blurred line between fiction and nonfiction that decisively adds to Baoyu's confusion about his identity and whereabouts. After reliving his "real" life as recounted in Cao's *Dream of the Red Chamber* (162), and attempting to find himself in *Lidai mingren nianpu* (*Biographical Chronology of Famous People*), Baoyu, who belongs comfortably to neither the eighteenth century nor the present, concentrates his efforts instead on figuring out the cacophonous, material world of urban Shanghai.

More so than the printed books and newspapers that the protagonist actively seeks out, however, it is the inventory of ephemera both printed and written that most vividly accounts for Baoyu's "development" beyond that of a "critical intellectual" to an "independent evaluator" of semicolonialism and Western learning.[59] Because his character functions not just as a third-person center of consciousness but also as the stone-jade inscribed with the text of the narrative, his media environment is more than the sum of intelligent, enlightening readings. If a cognizant protagonist espouses ideological and political opinions shaped by the views around him, a stone engraving all the more cannot observe, discern, judge, and write by itself without other texts, their engravers, readers, and copyists.[60] It is thus not for fear of anthropomorphism that I hesitate to attribute to the stone, even a sentient one, the same characteristics of a person; rather, it is because such an attribution risks mystifying inscriptive media by abstracting them from larger mediatory processes that constitute their history. In contrast to the enthusiastic text accompanying Wu Youru's 1884 illustration of the Dianshizhai printing room, which extracts lithographic printing from all human labor, the stone, either as a stele or as the printing surface in lithography, does not inscribe, impress, and print by itself. To ignore the role of labor risks some of the theoretical overreach practiced by post-hermeneutic media studies, which affords the nonhuman so many human characteristics as to rob it of its precise distinction and value as nonhuman.[61]

Baoyu's interest in contemporary newspapers such as *Qingyi bao* and *Shiwu bao* and their reformist messages may mark him as an informed citizen of turn-of-the-century China (191). But what "identity" does the novel's more haphazard accumulation of textual artifacts, of which Baoyu-as-stone/jade counts as one, offer in turn? The cognizant character Baoyu observes a media environment—which his nonhuman counterpart subsequently chronicles—constituted by media objects that do *not* outwardly serve any intellectual or mass-entertainment purposes. Not unlike the media sensorium composed from Guo Songtao's laborious diary entries, Baoyu's experience juxtaposes one document with another, thereby gathering otherwise disconnected situations and meanings, as does the abovementioned association of telegrams, translations, and book cart. In another instance right after Baoyu consults the *Biographical Chronology of Famous People* to check if his name is included, Xue Pan and Baoyu receive a paper card of sorts (*pianzi*) from Xue Pan's good-for-nothing friend, Bu Yaolian (literally "shameless"), whom Baoyu immediately detests for his undiscerning embrace of everything foreign (187). Xue Pan then instructs the reluctant Baoyu to send a similar slip of paper (*tiaozi*) with their names on it to announce their visit to Yaolian's place, where Baoyu meets the more intellectually compatible Bohui, who will be his informal mentor.

This sequence thus links the metafictional question of Baoyu's *documented* existence—whether he is a "real" person properly chronicled or a character in fiction—to the practice of sending and receiving visiting or calling cards on which the inscription of one's name enacts the rules of social etiquette. The ontological nature of Baoyu's identity thus carries over to what can be best described as an autological or self-referencing function of documents since "visiting cards" and "name cards" perform their functions through what is inscribed on them. Baoyu's self-searching, perhaps even soul-seeking, quests to find out who he really is thus overlap with the routine exchanges of visiting cards wherein it matters just as much who one knows. Names on papers are everywhere; yet a name can serve so many different genres, printed in various formats, and signify multiple social relations.

The history of visiting cards or name cards in China dates back to the Qin and Han dynasties and flourished during the Tang.[62] Such cards (*jian, mingce, tiezi,* and *shoubeng*) were handwritten on wood or bamboo before they were printed in larger quantities with woodblocks during the late imperial period. The earliest visiting cards primarily functioned to establish relations at court and quickly became a more popular form of communication among the upper class for social calls. It is for this later, more informal, purpose that the characters send and receive visiting cards in the Barbaric Realm. Baoyu's acquaintance with Bohui through such a social setting proves decisive. From Bohui, who used to work as an accountant in a foreign-owned shipping company, Baoyu learns about the telegraph code and the Chinese code book *Dianbao xinbian*, the 1880s edition of S. A. Vigeur's 1871 *Dianbao xinshu*, by the merchant-reformer Zheng Guanying (1842–1922). It is also Bohui who acquires for Baoyu specific Chinese-English dictionaries, discourages him from reading other, more dubious, language instruction books, and teaches him English (217). Alternating each day between translated volumes and original materials in English, Baoyu jumps at every chance of learning, even looking up English words he finds on random scraps of paper (217).

Paper fragments occupy the lowest rung of Shanghai's kaleidoscopic world of print. But as Des Forges shows, "almanacs, textbooks, guides to writing examination essays, novels, collections of verse, and even handbills and posters" became increasingly difficult to ignore with the rise of literacy in the Qing era.[63] As printed words became more readily available, often to advertise brand-name products, they were abandoned and misused only to be picked up by word-cherishing societies whose members rescued paper fragments with writing on them and destroyed them through ritualistic burning.[64] These material fragments appear less substantial only after the birth of an "organic" and "whole" "concept of the book" and likewise constitute "'disposable' media" when abandoned only because of the invention of printing on paper.[65] Baoyu's interest in scraps with English words on them, however, varies from the reverence of the Chinese written character since it is neither "literary value" nor "civil service career advancement" that preoccupies the protagonist, but the sheer practicality of expanding his English vocabulary. Yet rather than reinscribe nonbook paper ephemera into forgotten histories of the book, it makes sense to release material fragments from the dominion of the "literary-critical project" into the daily lives of Shanghai urbanites, not all of whom, like Baoyu, were invested in holding onto inscriptions for the pursuit of knowledge for knowledge's sake.

Xue Pan, for one, makes his money as a trader, including book-selling, and somewhat tellingly, the textual objects he attaches importance to illuminate a financial rather than intellectual orientation. After receiving a letter from a former acquaintance in Beijing luring him to the capital to join the Boxers, Xue Pan plans his trip, leaving Baoyu his luggage along with a luggage tag (*xingli dan*), and his Western-style bank passbook (*yangshi shouzhe*). As he explains to Baoyu, the latter needs the passbook in order to wire some money to Beijing from Shanghai through the Hongkong and Shanghai Banking Corporation (*Huifeng yinhang*) (218). Established in 1865 by Thomas Sutherland with investments from the Hong Kong international merchant community, the Hongkong and Shanghai Banking Corporation (HSBC) strengthened its foothold through extending major loans to the Chinese imperial government between 1874 and 1890.[66] From then on, the bank catered to demands from a distinguished trio of clientele composed of the British Empire, the Manchu Empire, and its shareholders. With a majority of its businesses concentrated in Shanghai's import-export trade, wire transfers, bills of exchanges, and money orders made up two-thirds of its Shanghai transactions in the 1870s.[67] The advent of telegraph communications expedited transactions such that remittances changed hands before commodities did. The bank thereby lived up to its Chinese name *Huifeng*, literally translated as "abundant remittances." In addition to circulating bank notes and the selling of bond certificates, the foreign bank profited immensely from its ability to attract private deposits from Chinese elites.[68] HSBC's repute as the "custodian of Chinese funds," in the words of an economic historian, continued until the Central Bank of China assumed the role of state bank after the currency reform of 1935.

Xue Pan's trusting of his bank passbook to Baoyu along with his luggage tag thus reflects more than his financial standing in turn-of-the-century Shanghai society. The act details a constructed relation between individuals and financial and state institutions, highlighting the symbiotic nature between foreign commercial interests and the Manchu state's dependence on a private banking institution for the financing of indemnity loans after the First Sino-Japanese War.[69] That the author inserts this episode in the brief section of the novel dramatizing the Boxer Rebellion, which resulted in huge indemnities made out to the Eight-Nation Alliance, only underscores the indispensable role that modern banking practices played in China's geopolitical context.[70] The humble passbook, like commercial bookkeeping, bank ledgers, and international finance records, records the invisible movement of money. Yet unlike these other more mercantile bookkeeping methods,[71] it has not received comparable scrutiny even though the increasing abstraction of national boundaries, geographical distance, and human relations directly impinges on the cultural imagination of personal trust and credit. The passbook, like other financial documents under capitalism, not the least of

91

which is money itself, thus materializes through writing what is essentially, as Marx has demonstrated, the mystical immateriality of value.

It is no exaggeration, then, that the bank passbook, as a French economic historian puts it, doubles as a kind of "moral passport" for nineteenth-century *citoyens* since each transaction had to be signed off by the bank's trustees to verify the cashier's entries.[72] The document became a "mediating device" of high communicative significance between working-class depositors and trustees who were business elites in nineteenth-century France. It was this second group of signatories who in turn ensured the bank its respectability. As a kind of contract, the passbook's list of transactions thus "expressed the abstractions of financial writing in concrete form."[73] In the nineteenth-century United States, banks marketed their opening hours and carried messages promoting the virtues of thriftiness in their passbooks.[74] As a conduit between the state, the depositor, and the private financial institution, an 1870 passbook in New York City stated in "English, German and French" that the United States government backed the issuing bank's good standing.

However, in nineteenth-century China, it was not only foreign banks that issued passbooks. According to Cheng Linsun, the Chinese *qianzhuang* or private banking institutions employed runners who sent passbooks to existing and prospective customers in order to extend to them "specific line[s] of credit" or overdrafts.[75] In these cases, passbooks were privy to how confident the runners were of their receivers. The document, in other words, was not just a "moral passport" but proved the intimacy and importance of personal relationships and local runners. This model of doing business by word-of-mouth personal credit soon proved to be unsustainable, and modern banks drifted away from the traditional *qianzhuang* model based on personal credit toward a reprioritization of material guarantees. With this financial streamlining, we can speculate that the previous promissory nature of passbooks was also brought in line with its modern-day function as a factual record of transaction values.

BAOYU, MEDIA OBSERVED

After extricating himself from the mess that his involvement with the Boxers creates, Xue Pan journeys to an idyllic Liberty Village (*Ziyou cun*), inviting Baoyu to join him and to bring along his passbook. Before setting off, Baoyu rationalizes to Bohui his decision to join his relative up north: the popular trend of leaving China to see the world should come second to actually learning about one's own country (174). Rather than produce volumes of diplomatic and travel diaries of Western countries, Baoyu pontificates, why not send officials to live in various parts of China, and award them posts based on who produces the most detailed diaries proposing the best laws of governance? This suggestion, while acerbic, fittingly describes *New Story* as a diary written from the perspective of an eighteenth-century literati who finds himself in utopia at home. While the observer's tone in the first half is critical, at times aggravated, his outlook after stumbling into the Civilized Realm located somewhere in Shandong (Confucius's birthplace) while looking for Xue Pan can best be described as passive admiration. How does a "media observer"—to borrow an anachronistic term from the twenty-first century—in one become an observing medium in another?

If even banal banter around a book cart troubles the distinction between essential knowledge and the material mode of its conveyance in the Barbaric Realm, one would expect a more "civilized" society preoccupied with scientific excellence and innovative gadgets to do away with the implied *dao-qi* hierarchy in the first place. Yet, everything about the Civilized Realm, in its buttressing of Chinese science and technology by Chinese culture and tradition, unimaginatively recapitulates to the Self-Strengthening Movement's dictum of Chinese learning as essence, which had long been discredited by the time the novel was published. While everything desirable in Shanghai is made overseas, so much so that, to Baoyu's chagrin in the first part of the novel, foreign insurance companies dare not insure Chinese-manned ships (188), Chinese traditional philosophy and even its fictional imagination undergird all scientific inventions in utopia. When Baoyu first enters the so-called Civilized Realm, he sees an impressive gateway demarcating utopian China from its decrepit counterpart (280–81). Not everyone, however, can enter the gate at will, Old Youth explains. The character-assessment mirror, as we have seen, denies entry to those whose "extreme barbarity" (*yeman touding*) "cannot be improved" (*bu neng gailiang de*). Using a chemically altered glass, the mirror reflects a crystal-clear image for civility and a smoky hue for barbarism (282). The invention stems from both the "advance of science" (*kexue zhangjin*), which makes visible everything previously invisible to the naked eye, as well as from unscientific "ideas" (*lixiang*) associated with traditional notions of "vital life force" (*qi* 氣)—not to be confused with *qi* 器, the "material substance" discussed earlier. Contemporary doctors and scientists, in other words, actualize what previous writers of gods and ghost stories only dreamed up. The character-assessment mirror thus relies on an ephemeral vitality that further generates divisions between ideas or theories and produced realities, fictions, and truths.

In a reversal of the Barbaric Realm by way of the mirror as both technical medium *and* narrative device, Chinese inventions in the second part of
the novel are now models for foreign imitation and learning. Hence gadgets
ranging from human-like robots to the artificial creation of the four sea-
sons are introduced less as scientific breakthroughs in and of themselves
and more as means to ridicule existing Western practices (284, 288). Identity
politics asserts itself in the form of techno-ethnocentrism and often veers
toward pure mockery, as for example when the utopian host and his atten-
tive guest make fun of the clumsiness of the Western hot air balloon (307). In
another episode, Baoyu follows an underwater expedition to Australia in a
whale-shaped submarine so advanced beyond its time that upon shining its
bright light onto a foreign submarine, the latter rushes home frantically to
report the Chinese technology to its scientists and scholars (346). Without
actually coming into contact with such foreigners, the characters' encounter
with exotic wildlife outside China turns into a retreat back to its mythical
past. As Nathaniel Isaacson points out, the giant bird *peng* and the *shu* fish,
which Baoyu and his utopian guides hunt down, respectively originated in
the *Zhuangzi* (ca. third century BCE) and the *Shanhai jing* (*Classic of Mountains and Seas*, ca. fourth century BCE).[76]

Closed off to differences to the point that all foreign inventions and practices are flatly dismissed, Wu Jianren's utopian imagination reproduces the
kind of intentional isolation and inaccessibility depicted in Tao Qian's fable,
Tao hua yuan (*Peach Blossom Spring*, 421 CE) and in Thomas More's *Utopia* (1516), in which the ideal country is separated from the mainland by
a wide trench. *New Story* and the nearly 400 other titles of utopian fiction
(both translated and original texts) published in China between 1900 and
1919,[77] however, share more affinities with their North American predecessors. Scholars unfailingly point to Edward Bellamy's 1888 utopian bestseller
Looking Backward: 2000–1887, first serialized in a Shanghai missionary publication, *Wanguo gongbao* (*Globe Magazine*) in 1891 and subsequently published as a single volume in 1898, as having greatly influenced Kang Youwei,
Liang Qichao, and Tan Sitong.[78] Like Bellamy's protagonist, who wakes up
from deep hypnosis to an already perfected United States, Baoyu walks into
the Civilized Realm after the fact; Liang's incomplete *Xin Zhongguo weilai
ji* (*The Future of New China*, 1902) assumes a similar structure by omitting
processes detailing the actual establishment of the perfect society.[79]

94   Literary utopia's intercultural and intertextual connections notwithstanding, the utopian segment of *New Story* excludes print culture—whether
newspapers, novels, or paper ephemera—from a general reading public.

The Chinese term for civilization, *wenming*, as Lydia Liu observes, highlights the technology of writing more so than the Latin root of the English equivalent.[80] Despite its other futuristic innovations, the Civilized Realm's celebration of writing, hearkens back to the ancient past. Hence books in its museum are displayed more as fetishized relics than, as they are in the Shanghai bookstores, available for anyone's "investigation and study" (213). In the utopia's museum, Baoyu learns that out of the numerous volumes of Chinese and foreign books from the past and present that stand for all the world's knowledge, none is as important and foundational as a rope from the prehistoric Chinese method of rope-tying (*shanggu jieshen*), also known as "the ancestor to the written word" (*zi de shizhu*) (318). Accompanying this display are first editions of Confucian classics and pages recovered from the first emperor of Qin's book-burning campaigns. Having seen the very ancient (*jigu zhiwu*), Baoyu does ask his hosts for the new. Yet, when he is given a book entitled *Scientific Inventions* (*Kexue faming*) published that very day, he barely glances at it before hurrying out of the museum to survey other treasures (320). This seems to be a far cry from the Shanghai Baoyu, who attends to even the most insignificant of inscriptions such as a matchstick factory's logo (170).

The utopia of *New Story* stands as antithetical to Kittler's hyperbolic claim in *Gramophone, Film, Typewriter* that the "writing monopoly" gave way in the nineteenth century to advances in photography and phonography.[81] In the technologically advanced Civilized Realm, newer representational media far from replace older ones. Rather, it would be more accurate to suggest that utopian communications rely on noticeably simplified models whereby the material bodies of information—that is, information's media— either stagnate in older and existing forms like the ropes kept in museums described above or naively incline toward human likeness in appearance.[82] This design simplification can be taken as either cause or effect of the overarching political message of Chinese superiority; manifest on the technical level, communication focuses on direct transmission rather than on the storage and possible manipulation of messages.

Earlier in Shanghai, Baoyu hears the phonograph's muffled recording of a human voice for the first time, scrutinizes its yellowish wax cylinder, and complains that the recording more resembles an animal (177). Interestingly, utopia's revamped version of the audio device comes in the form of a time-announcing robot, who instead of producing sound through friction between a needle placed in a groove, uses air passing through a diaphragm box to produce clear, human-like voices, thereby eradicating the phonograph's unwanted noises (283–84). The ability to customize the robot's appearance as either a wise, old sage or cherubic boy seems to be more important than the actual recording. As to how the robot clock is programed to tell time, Old Youth fails to mention. The fact that he and Baoyu are even comparing it with the phonograph, however, shows the limits of their grasp of the recording mechanism. Yet, like Guo Songtao's account examined in chapter 1, uncertainties toward what a recording and a transmission do vigorously reorder the relation between information and its perceived other. From the perspective of the utopian inventors of the Civilized Realm, insofar as information can be distinguished and made independent of noise and mechanical ingenuities appear more human-like, all that is made in China surpasses other nations' machines.

In *The Noise of Culture*, William R. Paulson argues that noise, understood as "anything that arrives as part of a message, but that was not part of the message when sent out," is not simply a theme in fictional narratives but the very redefinition of literature.[83] If literature is "noise," it is because it is more than a "transmission channel" but rather a "perturbation or source of variety in the circulation and production of discourses and ideas."[84] Yet, any claim that literature is "more than" communication faces the conundrum that communication is already in excess of itself. According to Claude Shannon and Warner Weaver's mathematical study of information, noise accumulates with the increase in signal transmitted through communication channels, akin to the disorder of closed thermodynamic systems over time.[85] All communicative channels are subject to random fluctuations that contain noise, and therefore uncertainty. Nonetheless, just as thermodynamics theory eventually shows how entropy is not antithetical to energy, we may advance an understanding of noise as a "productive ambiguity" that too is information. However, ambiguity and its opposite imply a message's meaning. Information, on the other hand, exists as a signal or "pattern" without meaning until it is coded as a "message" by physical carriers such as "newsprint or electromagnetic waves."[86] Noise is thus not noninformation but information's necessary correlation or "supplement"; it can even reorganize the signal "at a higher level of complexity."[87] Hence while a new medium like the robot clock emits clearer sounds without the phonograph's muffles, it does not mean that what is sent as signal or pattern exists without noise, but that the mechanical components that make up its, quite literally in this case, "body" has reduced its complexity when encoding information as message.

On the surface, Baoyu's disengagement with print in either book or nonbook forms may suggest that the Civilized Realm is relatively less mediated

96

by communicative technologies than its "barbaric" counterpart, but this is not the case. Messages are sent and received frequently in the second half of the novel, only they do not concern the visitor. To further accentuate the theoretical terms above, information has no "dimensions," "materiality," and "necessary connection with meaning."[88] However, the material medium, which encodes a sent signal into a message with these qualities, is always situated and specific, thereby structuring its users, their lives, and the spaces they inhabit. In utopian China, communication takes place between different officials in various organizations, including with the emperor himself. Telegrams are sent by a museum director to inform the government and the state newspaper of his team's finding of the mythical *peng* bird from the *Zhuangzi*. The director drafts the letter before passing it to his secretary to translate into telegraph code (318). Old Youth suggests to Baoyu that they stay at the museum while awaiting the government's reply, since the latter will likely include an award recognizing their achievements. Subsequent wireless telephone calls and telegrams are mobilized for similar purposes, as the exploring team, having completed their submarine adventures, reports to those higher up about the rare sea creatures and corals they have retrieved (351). At the same time, traditional writing formats remain in vogue. In addition to telephone calls and telegrams, the team engages another clerk to draft a *qi* 啟, a letter usually sent by subordinates to superiors, to send to the emperor (358). The emperor writes in Classical Chinese, not vernacular, when he honors the explorers' contributions in the newspaper and issues imperial edicts when conferring a formal title on an accomplished air force general (392).

Visiting cards, which circulate among Baoyu's social circle in the Barbaric Realm, here appear in the form of name cards that designate the sender's official status rather than mark informal calls between friends. This function dates to the court's use of such cards (*ye* or *ce*) during the Qin-Han period, on which cards usually indicated one's official title and county of residence.[89] Needless to say, a household name such as the late Qing viceroy Li Hongzhang did not need much elaboration.[90] According to Qing practices, usually only subordinates had to present their cards to higher-ranked officials through servants and receivers, and not the other way round. Whereas visiting cards serve the function of social calls in the first part of the novel, utopian inhabitants only exchange name cards for official and semiofficial business. In *New Story*, Old Youth makes clear that he has "applied for leave" in order to show Baoyu around (291). At the same time, we are told that his job is to receive foreign guests who visit the land (287). This ambiguity surrounding the momentary lapse in the tour guide's official duty will persist

97

until the end of the novel. Thus when we first see him present his name card to a hospital staff member in order to announce their visit to the leading medical officer (293), Old Youth may be playing utopian guide to Baoyu in his spare time. Nonetheless, his name card casts him in an official role rather than as a private individual, and Old Youth's interactions with various administrators touch on their various ranks. Baoyu and Old Youth's outings, moreover, do not resemble social visits since they entail inspections of the state's functional sites from its hospitals to military training grounds (375). When the naval officer Wu Shuqi in turn pays his visit to the duo, he similarly sends a name card (325). Baoyu's tour of the land culminates in his visit to the nation's founder, Dongfang Wenming (literally "Eastern Civilization"), to whom Old Youth announces their arrival in the same way (395).

Formal and informal state communications involving letters, telephone calls, telegrams, and name cards are scattered inconspicuously around the Civilized Realm. In addition to Old Youth and other high-ranking officials who participate in these exchanges, there are also the unnamed clerks (*shuji*) and servants who help draft letters, translate writing into telegraph code, and pass along the visitors' names to their masters. Through their seamless efforts, the imagined China stands out as an effortlessly efficient technocracy wherein a minimal layer of paperwork connects the different government organizations to each other and to the people. When three of the land's top scientists devise an unprecedentedly powerful cannon, all they have to do is write a letter to the army commander detailing the invention's smokeless, soundless, and powderless projection, and they receive the go-ahead to test and manufacture the new artillery (389). When debating a state agenda, the emperor considers propositions from all, and he invites people's opinion through official publications (*xingwen*) (377). Some Chinese scholars, after Max Weber, define late imperial Chinese government in terms of "patrimonial rule" mixed with a "minimalist" state apparatus.[91] Its high "despotic power," in Michael Mann's formulation, works hand in hand with a low "infrastructural power."[92] The Civilized Realm is such an authoritarian state, where the efficient relaying of messages over distances buttresses the people's faith in the emperor's mandate to rule.

During one leg of Baoyu's tour, Old Youth explains that between constitutionalism, republicanism, and authoritarianism, the land has adopted the third system, the least popular among reformers worldwide (307).[93] Through the practice of "moral education" (*deyu*) based on Confucian teachings,[94] however, authoritarian rule has eradicated all crime and along with it the need for official legal administrators and law enforcement. Gone are the terms for "robbers and thieves" (*daozei*) from the land's "civilized" (*wenming*) dictionary (307). Even the *yamen*s, local administrative offices, are replaced with warehouses. This radical bureaucratic cut further minimizes the state apparatus and its infrastructures. Without the formal court system or the existence of crime to require informal mediatory functionaries at the local level, there is really no "third realm" between state and society in the way that Philip C. C. Huang proposes.[95] State and society, for better or worse, merge into one. As outlandish as this vision of moral perfection sounds, the minimization of the bureaucratic machinery exudes pragmatism. Historically at least, this model offers the benefit of ensuring that individual officials remain loyal to the emperor and that what Huang calls "local patrimonial satrapies" do not gain too much power.[96]

The more utopian this government structure appears, the more the novel exposes the contradictions, anxieties, and fantasies that undergird existing paperwork and bureaucracies.[97] Nowhere are these contradictions more apparent than in the state's continuing reliance on the faceless clerks and runners drafting and handling official and nonofficial documentation for the realm's top scientists, organizational directors, and military personnel. With the abolition of the *yamen* institution and its ranked officials, it would be fair to ask under whose control these administrative staff on the lowest rung of the hierarchy fall. From the text, there is little indication besides the immediate issuing of orders as to whether Old Youth, the many other scientists, medical officials, and military men have equal authority over the clerks and runners.

Historically, the administrative and judicial functions of Chinese government lack formal separation. In his study of Qing dynasty clerks and runners of the county *yamen*, Bradly Reed argues that only "ranking officials" and not unranked *yamen* staff were subjected to "formalized regulation of administrative behavior."[98] Clerks and runners fell under the control of the magistrate, whose authority stemmed neither from his official position nor management skills but from his "identification with the highly personal Confucian moral ideals underwriting both the authority of the imperial state . . . and social elites at the local level."[99] Without the magistrate, utopia's sole authority similarly lies with the abovementioned Confucian moral idea of *deyu* and its ideal embodiment in Dongfang Wenming, his three sons, daughter, and a large extended family, even though the founder himself has long retired and it is unclear who is now the emperor (287).

Paperwork strewn in the novel's background thus amplifies Confucian anxieties about the shadowy administrative body that managed it in real life. This is yet another instance where recording (*ji*), one of the keywords of this media study, accurately captures an inherently historical conundrum rather than imposes an anachronistic, unrelated theoretical concern. Through the Qing dynasty, clerks and runners, who devised and enforced their own "customary procedures" outside "the body of official regulations," and organized themselves by "nonrational forms of association" such as "kinship bonds, patron-client ties, and factional formations," held the status of, to borrow Reed's term, an *illicit legitimacy*.[100] No other administrative class was as heavily associated with corruption. Imperial officials as early as the Song dynasty (960–1279) viewed clerks and runners with suspicion and regarded their services as menial and socially degrading as opposed to the culture of the elite literati associated with office holding. Yet clerks and runners were indispensable to the imperial government, performing "rudimentary and critical tasks" from the "drafting, copying, and filing of documents and records" to the transmission of messages, as well as all the "sundry duties associated with the magistrate's court" like "arrest and detention" and "the collection of taxes."[101] So vast were their job scope and possible spheres of influence, and yet so excluded from the system of laws and control, that the imperial government consistently made efforts to curtail the negative influences of such "corrupt and venal scoundrels."[102]

In the sixth month of Guangxu 27 (1901)—around a year after Baoyu finds himself in Shanghai at the beginning of the novel—Empress Dowager Cixi (1835–1908) issued the following edict: "The affairs of all yamens great and small are to be managed personally by the officials in charge," the sovereign proclaimed. "Clerks will be limited to *copying and drafting* and under no circumstances should they be allowed to supervise matters on their own authority."[103] While details of this exact ruling is irrelevant to my study, the edict's limitation on clerical work to "copying and drafting" is monumental for understanding one of the final enigmas of Wu's novel. Not only do the clerks in the second half of *New Story* appear efficient and trustworthy, their work indeed "only" consists of copying and drafting in addition to occasionally receiving guests and their name cards. A strictly historicist reading will likely relish the novel's expression of the court's concerns over unchecked power and corruption, which led to legislative reductions in clerks' influence and the scope of their work.

Yet insofar as *New Story* encloses its protagonist's experience of media devices and processes with his own recording as a stone-inscription, the clerks' jobs exceed any superfluity otherwise associated with mere copying and drafting. In other words, the seemingly mundane tasks carried out by the utopia's nameless and forgotten clerks more than reflects historical reality.

Instead, copying and drafting thematically intimate the narrative form of the novel itself such that representations of such inscriptive acts are inseparable from material media. As I elaborate below, the text may appear marvelously through Baoyu's transmigration back into Nüwa's stone, but its reception by Old Youth lacks any mythological connotation, consisting instead of the laborious process of copying out by hand with ink and paper. While copying and drafting help illuminate the historical context of Qing clerks and runners, it is the interweaving of content or context and form, and of media theory and history, rather than any either side in isolation, which highlights the ineluctably material basis of writing. Rather than study paperwork as evidence undergirding broader political, social, and economic patterns,[104] I excavate otherwise discrete mentions of the manual, thankless tasks of drafting, translating, sending, and delivering of both formal and informal state communications, so as to comprehend what paperwork performs in the novel. Precisely because the clerks and runners "only" copy, draft, and relay messages, *New Story* puts what Ben Kafka calls "the *bureau*" with all of its "pens, papers, and other raw materials of power" back "in bureaucracy."[105] For, what better way to approach Wu Jianren's twentieth-century rewrite of *Dream of the Red Chamber,* than as a copy of copies?

WORLDS WITHIN WORLDS

Toward the end of the narrative, Baoyu appears unable to digest more of the details fed to him about the advances and superiority of this perfected regime. So abundant are the "newly invented" and the "never-before-seen" that he "cannot even begin to ask what they are" (321). His last request to his guide is to be introduced to Dongfang Wenming, the nation's now-retired founder. When they finally do meet, the dignified, still-youthful statesman addresses a bewildered Baoyu as if they already know each other. Later, the utopian guest learns that Dongfang Wenming is really Zhen Baoyu from the original *Dream of the Red Chamber* (406), whom the current Baoyu of the unofficial sequel has earlier in the story rationalized to be his "real-life" doppelgänger (184). Indeed, Zhen Baoyu—whose surname is a homophone for "real," unlike Jia's own, which sounds like "false"—is meant to be Jia Baoyu's alter ego in Cao's original novel. The late Qing protagonist's ambition to "mend Heaven," which lands him in the thick of China's turn of the century turmoil, is thus ultimately an "illusory wish" (*xuyuan*) already accomplished by a more authentic version of himself twice over (407)—once, intertextually, in Cao's classic, and again, in Wu's rewrite. With this ultimate setback,

101

Jia Baoyu leaves the Civilized Realm. Prior to his departure, he gifts Old Youth his birthstone. The precious jade and its subsequent metamorphosis into a large rock at the foot of a mountain record less their alter ego's enlightenment than they do the failed wish of nation-building, which the unnamed narrator has hoped at the opening of the novel that his revival of *Dream of the Red Chamber*'s original protagonist will accomplish.

It is at this point in the narrative that Old Youth, hitherto utopia's unofficial guide and expert authority on its history and accomplishments—not unlike our modern-day public relations expert—discovers a new calling. Amazed at the twelve or thirteen thousand-odd words of "marvelous writing" (*qiwen*) legible in Baoyu's transformed namesake, now in a remote part of the Civilized Realm, Old Youth commits himself to sharing the text with the world (408). Without pen or paper on him, he rushes back on his flying car to purchase some from the market only to find, upon returning, that a verse, which serves as the text's prologue, has appeared. This verse laments the stone's origin and failure to mend Heaven despite its ordained sentience and powers. At home with a full copy of the text, Old Youth fears that its erudite language may escape most readers and mislead Confucian stalwarts to impute to it erroneous interpretations. He thus spends his quiet evenings after work studying the text and rewriting it as "historical fiction" (*yanyi*) in vernacular language for "enjoyment by the refined and the unsophisticated alike" (*ya su gong xiang*). As a final touch, Old Youth names the text *New Story of the Stone*.

Baoyu is thus not the only character who undergoes some kind of transformation. At the end of the narrative, his utopian guide moonlights as a copy editor with skills surpassing those of an ordinary clerk, and polishes and rewrites the received text. Following *Dream of the Red Chamber*'s narrative structure, Old Youth, like Vanitas or Kongkong Daoren in the original classic, is the novel's first and final reader, whose engagement with the text, according to Anthony Yu, performs the "act of proleptic reading."[106] *New Story* is thus mediated not twice but three times: first, as Baoyu in the story; second, as an engraving on stone; and lastly, as an edited and more accessible manuscript now with a title. Just what kind of text emerges from the editor's desk, and how much has changed? We are thus led back to the original problem: does the engraved text in stone capture Baoyu's personal history or, more objectively, the spirit of his time? Is *New Story* a biography in the rich tradition inaugurated by Sima Qian, or even a kind of epitaph engraved on stone, if we read Baoyu's disappointment at the end of the narrative as a symbolic death? Old Youth's choice of historical fiction speaks to the complexities of genre. In fiction as in biographical writings, accuracy almost plays second fiddle to liveliness. On the matter of "recording speech [of historical figures]," the philosopher of history Zhang Xuecheng (1738–1801) demands of the historian that he "must convey what was in the speaker's mind at the time, even if it requires adding a thousand words."[107]

The difference between *Dream of the Red Chamber*'s Vanitas and *New Story*'s Old Youth, moreover, underscores the materiality of the unofficial sequel's many editions and formats. The former is a Buddhist monk who after reading the stone's text a second time finally awakens to the "Truth" of "Void," and having arrived at "Truth by way of Passion," renames himself Brother Amor.[108] Old Youth, on the other hand, experiences no such profound awakening in the Buddhist Nagarjuna tradition. His worldliness, hospitality, and efficiency—all in all, he is an administrator perfect for the peculiar demands of the utopian regime—also makes him an ideal reader and copyist for the unofficial sequel. The late Qing novel, after all, has transformed Cao's original protagonist into someone who envies rather than shuns traditional public office. *New Story*'s solution to China's turn-of-the-century, semicolonial predicament is not any idyllic utopia but a technocratic, autocratic state with a minimalist approach to bureaucracy dependent upon infallible moral authority. To excel in this environment, little wonder that Old Youth, a modern reincarnation of Vanitas or Brother Amor, has enough good sense to keep his copy editing separate from his day job.

I will leave the question of work—of the culture of work and work of culture—and its relation to automation for chapter 5, though my discussion of Nüwa's stone and the evolution in technologies of writing from stone rubbings and lithography from the beginning of this chapter has already broached these matters. Between 1856 and 1936, industrial development in China's coastal regions noticeably increased the wages of skilled workers relative to unskilled and low-skilled workers before they declined again during the 1920s. Based on Se Yan's research using data from the Imperial Maritime Customs Service, writers and copyists topped the category of skilled labor, with their median pay higher than engineers and pilots.[109] Considering too the frequency and ease with which Old Youth could take leave, the free time, and the cordial colleagues with whom he keeps company, one can truly make a comfortable living in the Civilized Realm. *New Story*, despite its mythological roots and utopian wish fulfillment, contravenes contemporary promotions of lithography as an innovation that dispenses with the "craftsmen with the heavenly gift and the carvers with uncanny skill."[110] Instead, it has taken a whole lot of observing, questioning, interacting with, reading, copying, editing, simplifying, and not a little supernatural intervention of

103

the human-nonhuman variety to "transfer" a variety of textual artifacts—newsprint, translated books, paper ephemera such as bank passbooks and luggage tags, traditional imperial edicts, name cards, wireless telephone and telegraph messages—"to the smooth stone."[111]

By tracking the novel's many media including the *ur*-medium of the stone, the present discussion, in continuation from the preceding chapter, shows how narrative form—format, genre, and reception—reflexively registers the question of older and newer records both real and imagined. *New Story*'s metafictionality performs the operation of mediation defined throughout this book as the back-and-forth between the social and signifying processes of mediation and technological media, between the historical specificities of turn-of-the-century Shanghai print culture and the period's more overlooked paper trails, as well as the theoretical implications therein of the distinction of culture from so-called noise. What does Baoyu's transformation from media observer to the novel's medium bode, however, for the task of China's political reform at the heart of Wu's work? Has Baoyu, as "late spectator to what will 'already have happened'"[112] or a symbol of a "belated modernity" who can only witness or record what has already been accomplished by a "true" version of himself,[113] completely surrendered whatever agency he has at the beginning of novel to become a writing technology? In raising such questions, this turn-of-the-century proto-science fiction imagination wedges the nonhuman, which has inspired so much recent media theoretical scholarship, into the nation-building problem archetypal of the late Qing.

Just as this book's treatment of media exceeds the thematic, a nonhuman rethinking of Chinese nationalism is more than a topical intervention. Few records better assume media as a method than Baoyu's birthstone and namesake in its interweaving of history and form, materiality and signification. The point of distinguishing the two halves of the novel with the kinds of writing (and reading) they produce is not to stereotype Baoyu as a critical intellectual in the first instance and his exclusion from utopian governance in the second, but to integrate the novel's political critique and ideological implications *into* the question of its very material form. The waning of Baoyu's attention to print and nonprint media in the Civilized Realm syncs with his nonhuman metamorphosis insofar as he will become, at the end of his journeys, the record (*ji*) par excellence. As the physical form on which a world of different technologies, media, *and* their historical and social relevance are carved, the stone documents both the intensities of embodied experience and the nuances of discursive representations.

New Story, after all, challenges any clear line between reality and utopia, civilization and barbarism. Right before Baoyu stumbles into utopia, his page, Beiming, suddenly turns into a decrepit statue of an immortal boy. As someone who does not believe in ghosts and spirits, Baoyu lacks an explanation for Beiming's mysterious transformation.[114] In this "civilized, enlightened age," the unnamed narrator interjects, such a plot twist is indeed ridiculous; regardless, readers must probe deeper into its "hidden allegory." The statue's symbolism for the mimetic functions of art and literature may be a tired trope, and Beiming's posthuman transformation but another play on *Dream of the Red Chamber*'s blurring of ontological distinctions between the true and the illusory, the authentic (*zhen*) and the fake (*jia*). Yet since Beiming's transformation occurs more than once, the human/statue doubling more than complicates *New Story*'s formal structure, something which has already been suggested by the character-testing mirror. The latter, as narrative device and reflective surface, reverses the first and second halves of the novel.

At the beginning of the novel, master and page, newly reunited, take shelter in an abandoned temple and meet an old priest who jumps at the sight of Beiming, whom he claims resembles a statue he had just seen. Baoyu assumes that the priest, not a little mad, must have been confused by Beiming's soot-covered face.[115] This is the "hidden allegory" suggested by the unnamed narrator, that the Civilized Realm, instead of being seen as outside the Barbaric Realm, overlaps with it, signaling Baoyu's itinerary as an unfolding of worlds *within* worlds. Baoyu originally stumbles upon the utopia after being persuaded by Xue Pan to join him in a paradisiacal place north of China (174). When Baoyu later asks Old Youth about this destination, the guide remarks that there is also a Liberty Village where they are, and the one where Xue Pan is must refer to another place that is more appropriately known as Barbaric Liberty (*yeman ziyou*) Village (286). If there is no one distinct utopia, perhaps there are also multiple dystopias.

At the end of the novel, after Old Youth completes his rewrite, the unnamed narrator interjects again to invite readers to visit the stone themselves if they do not believe his tale, and adds one final admonition (409). The marvelous text will only reveal itself to "men of high moral standing" (*zhangfu*) and not those with a "slave mentality" (*nuli sixiang*), to "gentlemen" (*junzi*) and not "petty persons" (*xiaoren*). For the second group of readers who lack patriotism and betray the nation to foreigners, they will only see on the stone an English verse chastising anyone who "oppress[es]" their own "countrymen" and "worship[s]" foreigners for financial gain (408–9). Baoyu himself might have written this message, as he has occasionally engaged in

105

similar didactic admonishing when he was in the Barbaric Realm. Besides, with all the hard work, his English would have been adequately proficient by now. While the protagonist as an actor in the story has long exited the scene, his pedantry remains stupendously legible. The by-now exhausted slogan of media studies finds its unlikely resonance in the inscribing (corner)stone of classical Chinese fiction, adapted by Wu Jianren for turn of the century tastes and concerns: Baoyu's body is also the message. His very name, after all, attests to the indissociability between a material object (*yu* or jade) and its social value (*bao* or precious).

A WOMAN'S TOOL

The legends of the Goddess Nüwa, mythical stones, and the Gaomei deity are emblematic of women's mastery of technology. Yet gender and sexual differences are strikingly muted in *New Story* aside from the characters' superficial debates about foot-binding in Shanghai (195–96), or when Baoyu and Old Youth discuss the importance of female education in the Civilized Realm (377–79). Published a few months after Wu Jianren's *New Story*, *Nüwa Shi* (*The Stone of the Goddess Nüwa*, 1904), penned by the pseudonymous Haitian duxiao zi (Lone Howler of the Sea and Heaven) similarly adapts the ancient creation myth to address China's dynastic decline. Unlike *New Story*, *The Stone of the Goddess Nüwa* stresses less the tool and more the identity of the goddess, who first used the mythical stones to mend Heaven. Its ten chapters depict a group of clandestine female assassins who, in their zealous goal to eradicate corrupt officials and prove women's superior heroism, willingly marry into the imperial court or work as courtesans in a brothel equipped with advanced scientific instruments and fantastic technologies. But not all women, its author suggests, are key to China's salvation. The novel opens with a lavish ceremony honoring Empress Hu, a thinly veiled satire of the Empress Dowager Cixi, during which a large stone mysteriously crashes at the palace. The stone exudes brilliant light and an air of auspiciousness, and inscribed on it are three ancient words unidentifiable to anyone.[116] The court urgently sends telegrams to all corners of the empire inviting wild speculations until a scholar of ancient stone inscriptions finally manages to identify the primeval scribblings as "Nüwa's stone" (*Nüwa shi*). Its mysterious descent from Heaven surely has but one purpose: to affirm Empress Hu's mandate to rule. Unsurprisingly, the tyrannical sovereign revels in this interpretation, a flood of congratulatory telegrams ensues, and celebrations proceed for months.

As later assassination attempts on the monarch and members of her court indicate, Empress Hu far from possesses the mandate to rule. If the novel thus suggests that she cannot lay claim to Nüwa's stone, any association of the goddess's symbol with the female assassins is just as problematic in light of the narrative's exploitation of female sexuality and violence as justifiable means to achieve radical political heroism. These militant women belong to a hierarchical political party with strict rules that prohibit them from having romantic relations, interests, and external loyalties.[117] Such restrictions lead one rebellious member to describe the party as a "nonsensical organization" (*wuhui wudang*) with its equally "nonsensical rules" (*wu zongzhi*). Boastful of their possession of powerful weapons and fancy gadgets, including artificial reproductive technologies, it is the bodies of female revolutionaries, however, that are ultimately subsumed under the greater ends of the nation-state. Nüwa's stone, originally the mythological tool of human salvation, proves that its metamorphosis into an inscriptive surface is open to gross misinterpretation. Whether or not the stone refers to the corrupt Empress Hu or the enemies of her state, the eponymously titled text embodies the inherent manipulability of women underlying the period's nationalistic, anti-Qing fictional imagination.

The Stone of the Goddess Nüwa transforms what is primordially a woman's instrument into the instrumentalization *of* women. To put it differently, the narrative retools femininity for a stronger, more scientific Chinese future by recording it, as we have seen with Baoyu's tale, on a stony surface. For the case of *The Stone of the Goddess Nüwa*, moreover, the instrumentalization of women is also inscribed behind an ostensible message about women's emancipation. Early Chinese feminism, Amy D. Dooling points out, took on an "unusually dominant male tenor."[118] The author Lone Howler, who was also one of the earliest translators of Japanese science and adventure fiction into Chinese, stood among other male writers who similarly celebrated the image of the revolutionary Chinese woman and promoted the usefulness of modern science to radicalize her.[119] Jin Tianhe, in his early treatise *Nüjie Zhong* (*Bell for the Women's World*), encouraged women to rid themselves of folk magic and superstition since modern craniometry showed that women were as clever as men. Once educated in modern science, he argues, women could accelerate China's progress, especially if they were willing to resort to violence.[120] According to Jing Tsu, other male writers of "women's fiction" (*nüzi xiaoshuo*) produced even more sensational works, sinicizing European models of female assassins whose "adroitness at technological manipulations" make them a "harbinger of a more scientific than moral civilization."[121]

Yet, such feminine techniques are far from innocent; women, once liberated from their traditional roles, risk being manipulated by the period's unprecedented embrace of individual sacrifice and social Darwinian approach to science and technology.

When Lone Howler repurposes Nüwa's stone into a medium for inscribing the categories of the "woman" or the "feminine," his unfinished text firmly delivers a lesson in the gender politics of media and mediation in early twentieth-century China. While it is certainly not the case that only women can produce feminist texts, we will have to ask whether women can communicate—no, more than that, actually engage with inscriptive media, including writing about their experiences using said media—*without* being reduced to the twinned ideological tools of scientific progress and national renewal. It is to this debate that the following chapter turns.

PART II
傳 *CHUAN/ZHUAN* | TRANSMISSIONS

LYRICAL MEDIA | TECHNOLOGY, SENTIMENTALITY, AND BAD MODELS OF THE FEELING WOMAN

The first proclamation of a poetic revolution was conceived rather befittingly onboard a steamship. Leaving Tokyo, where he had spent a year in exile for his involvement in the abortive Hundred Days' Reform movement, Liang Qichao traveled to the United States in 1899 in a campaign to gain support for the restoration of Emperor Guangxu. Liang wrote in his diary—as he was recovering from bouts of seasickness—that the fate of Chinese poetry was doomed without a "poetic revolution" (shijie geming).[1] Such an assertion was in line with his call for a "new fiction" (xin xiaoshuo) a year later in 1900. As the reformer strove in his personal journey to become both a "national subject" (guoren) and "world citizen" (shijie ren),[2] political exigency steered aesthetic innovation.

But there is another context in Liang's modern global imaginary: the vessel of his trans-Pacific ruminations that carried both the political and the poetic. An emblem of China's treaty-port system since the end of the First Opium War (1839–1842),[3] the steamship here occasioned the declaration of a new literary aesthetic in the last year of the nineteenth century, running the question of technological or instrumental form full steam into the highly idiomatic, but no less confounding, issue of "poetic medium." In chapter 2, I explained how the book cart in *New Story of the Stone* unravels the supplementary logic of "writing as a vehicle to convey the *dao*" (*wenyi zaidao*), such that what is driving writing, itself a conveyance for *dao*, is quite literally another vehicle. The same urgency with which mediation operates between the discursive or signifying and the technical or material—between the aesthetically formal and the physical form—resurfaces with the setting of a new Chinese poetics *qua* medium inside a literal vessel, and henceforth a novel representational form altogether.[4] As I perceive traces of mediation from Liang's journey upon a conveyance built by modern technology, new issues of ontology come to the fore—such as the inseparability of medium from message and the tension between the literal and the figurative—as well as the researcher's own methodological question of how to approach those relationships. The steamship carrying Liang to the New World, or what he calls "the first advanced republic," is another instance of a material metaphor—but also a literal medium—for poetry whose medium, language, is arguably no less material.[5] The knotty problem of the figurative and the literal, which I examined in the previous chapter, and which has more famously preoccupied scholars of Chinese and Western comparative poetics, is already coming undone, as will become clear, for reasons not unrelated to the technological.[6]

Poetic "medium," after all, assumes the potency of the literal when it registers technology as its content. In return, the "mere" theme of technical media informs the materiality of poetic form. The present chapter, in keeping with the book's attentiveness to media's formal representations in texts and images, as well as to their materiality as communicative devices, directs the question of the dynamics between content and form, and between form and history, to the most stylized of refined writing, poetry (*shi*). Certainly, Liang's proclamation bestowed upon poetry both "conceptual coherence" and "[national] identity."[7] I evoke Liang's poetic revolution, however, in order to broach my larger concerns here: what are the formal elements of poetry in this historical period that enable it to become an instrument or a means to a higher end, and where lies the place of women in this instrumentalism?

Lyricism (*shuqing*), as a characteristic feature of Chinese poetry and its evocations of the feminine, provides just the opening for these questions. Women's growing prominence in this period of intense political and sociocultural reform saw the specific reconstruction of feminine lyricism as mediums or instruments of social change, particularly in the genre of life writing (*zhuan*) celebrating virtuous and patriotic women. This is one definition of the female medium as a channel or conduit for the nation-state. Overlooked, however, are alternatively lyrical depictions of the Chinese woman and her engagement with the new media technologies of her time, which mobilize another, more literal, understanding of media as a means or an intermediary in material, communicative processes.[8] This chapter will begin by tracing this second, less moralistic, definition of the female medium and her feelings in the series of poems "Jin bieli" ("Modern Parting," 1899) by Huang Zunxian (1848–1905), which Liang singles out in his 1899 proclamation as an exemplar of new Chinese poetry. I then scan the period's didactic use of feminine sentimentality for the nation-building project through late Qing feminist writings and the construction of exemplary women's lives (*zhuan*) in the popular press, and locate in "Ziti xiaozhao" ("Self-Inscription on a Photograph," 1906), the autobiographical verse of Qiu Jin (1875–1907), less instrumental and more unorthodox feminine lyricisms. Despite being one of the—or, arguably the most—celebrated anti-Qing martyr of her time, Qiu Jin short-circuits the conventional biographical practice of female exemplarity and its codification of female sentimentality when poetic form crosses paths with the photographic medium. Such a feminist mediation of technical devices with the technics or mechanics of feelings, paradoxically, recovers a noninstrumentalized femininity historically subsumed by nationalist agendas. By refocusing the "woman" question in early twentieth-century China on the intersecting medialities of lyrical verse and photography, this chapter refracts the historical situatedness of gender politics through the prism of media theory, and vice versa.

The question of how a gendered subject conducts or transmits meanings for others structures the book insofar as the concept of a lyrical medium guiding this chapter serves too as a conduit between the first and second parts of my study. Chapters 1 and 2 contrasted traditional and novel ways of recording in the literary genre *ji*, and chapters 4 and 5 will explore, through public telegrams (*gongdian* or *tongdian*) and the intersection between neurology and electricity, the potentials and limits of "interconnectivity" (*tong*), which also evokes the historical writing known as *tongshi*, a form of cross-dynastic history as opposed to dynastic history. *Ji* and *tong* thus operate as distinct genres while also signifying a communicative action or larger mediating principle not specific to the literary genre in question. Chapter 3 similarly revolves around a single character 傳, pronounced either as *zhuan*, meaning "biography," or *chuan*, translated as "to transmit or express." The two meanings of 傳 clearly split the written genre from the larger communicative action or mediating principle, a distinction that is less apparent in the other keywords *ji* and *tong*. This central chapter thus aims to unite the biographical (*zhuan*) and various modalities of emotional "expressivity" or "transmissibility" (*chuan*) under larger communicative processes and technical media by rethinking the genre of life stories, which most directly speaks to this doubled sense of transmission. The biographies and autobiographies (*zhuan*) of typically male inventors of media machines, which typically inform a cultural history of inscriptive devices and processes, will not suffice here. To pursue a more experimental notion of lyrical media experienced and documented by lesser-known "users" and "transmitters," we will have to look into more unconventionally mediated situations resplendent with the "lives" of technical objects themselves.

At the same time, this chapter divides as much as it bridges. Whereas chapters 1, 2, 4 and 5 excavate the mediated effects of "recording" (*ji*) and "interconnectivity" (*tong*) primarily in prose writing, chapter 3 concentrates on verse. Interrupting the dominance of male voices in parts I and II, the present discussion embodies the spirit of its main subject matter, the female medium, and her uneasy status as a channel or conduit during a time of dynastic decline and renewal. While both genders, in embodying the need for radical political and social change, mediate between textual representations of communicative media and technical formats, devices, and processes, women and the proper transmission of their feelings were especially appropriated as a means to an end in early twentieth-century China. Whereas mediation has been regularly invoked as a metaphor for late Qing China's relations with other nations in multiple aspects of the linguistic, cultural, and socioeconomic save for the techno-scientific, the gendered nuances of technical mediation are even more sharply politicized, and all the same occluded. This intermediary chapter—one that also fails to connect—thus recovers women's relationships with technology in ways not necessarily co-opted by nationalist ideologies. I will revisit, in the conclusion to this book, a different evocation of the female medium in Chen Qiufan's science fiction novel, *Huang chao* (*Waste Tide*, 2013), updated with contemporary developments in augmented- and virtual-reality technologies and cloud computing. In the meantime, women's writings about media and mediation will serve as ground zero for the lively commutations between material media forms and the forms of media in texts and images.

A POETIC REVOLUTION

Liang in his travel diary explains that new Chinese poetry must have three components: new artistic "imagery" (*yijing*) coupled with a new "lexicon" (*yuju*) in accordance with the "style of the ancients" (*guren zhi fengge*).[9] Without the restraints of classical form, Liang continues, sheer novelty in subject matter and expressions would cause any poetry simply to resemble alien creatures from Neptune, nonsensical and absurd. Liang's version of a "poetic revolution" was therefore, in J. D. Schmidt's evaluation, "not a violent rejection of the entire Chinese literary heritage but merely an extensive reform of Chinese poetry."[10]

Of contemporary poets, Liang singles out Huang Zunxian, whose works best exemplify this infusion of European imagery and a new lexicon into the ancient style. Huang, who was born in Meizhou, Guangdong, to a Hakka gentry family, was a precocious poet who in his adolescence developed an interest in politics.[11] After suffering initial setbacks at the provincial examinations, which contributed to his preference for foreign affairs over eight-legged essays, Huang settled into a minor official position in Beijing, where he finally obtained the degree of provincial graduate in 1876 and began an illustrious diplomatic career, first as a counselor to the Chinese ambassador to Japan and later in 1882 as consul-general in San Francisco.[12] Far from stifling his creative output, Huang's official duties provided the poet with diverse subjects for his work, ranging from the Eiffel Tower to the London fog, the extreme humidity of tropical Southeast Asia, to the 1884 US presidential elections.

Huang's "Jin bieli" (1899), or "Modern Parting," is a series of four poems in the tradition of parting poetry that draws on his panoramic range of experience.[13] As such it tests the delicate balance between tradition and innovation that for Liang Qichao typified the new Chinese poetry.[14] The lyric subgenre of parting poetry (*songbie shi*) dates back to the first millennium BCE.[15] Typically, these poems took the form of a woman pining for her departing husband or lover. Later, the Tang poets' lachrymose sentimentality and the Song masters' wit and humor, best represented by Su Shi in his parting poem to his brother Su Zhe, set the pattern for practically all subsequent works in this genre, such that critics often judge the genre by its derivativeness rather than originality. The title *Jin bieli* is itself a reference to "Bieli" ("Parting"), a series of poems by Cui Guofu (678?–755?). Indeed, even Huang's turn-of-the-century exploration of modern science and technology is not without precedent: Yang Wanli (1127–1206), for example, wrote widely about mechanical inventions, such as his personification of a water-powered pounding device.[16] Fittingly, Huang intends for his 1899 poem to explicate the bearings of classical forms on the modern world, and for literary expression to meld with historical reality. As he explains in the preface to the collection of poetry in which "Modern Parting" was published, *Renjing lu shicao (Poems from a Hut within the Human Realm)*, "there are events outside poetry, just as there are men within it" (*shi zhi wai you shi, shi zhi zhong you ren*).[17] That is, verses that allude to the ancients are no less relevant or innovative. Huang appeals to the ancients' employment of "*bi-xing* in the *shi* form of poetry," and yet prefers the unrestrained spirit of Qu Yuan's *sao*

115

style and nonparallel writing, both of which have more in common with prose than with poetry. For every classic that the poet follows—the Confucian classics, Sima Qian's histories, and other Zhou and Qin philosophers—he also lists unconventional sources: "compilations of regulations, regional dialects, and vulgar maxims . . . realms previously unexplored."[18] Hence, Huang's addition of the character *jin*—indicating "now," the contemporary, or the modern—to Cui's original *bieli*, or "departure," ostensibly invites his readers to judge for themselves how references to the contemporary world can rejuvenate the lyrical tradition in which parting poems operate.

Each poem in "Modern Parting" consists of twenty-six lines in classical pentasyllabic parallel verse, and is uttered by a woman longing for her faraway lover. The first of the series contrasts carts and boats journeying through "ancient" mountains and rivers with the "cars and ships" of today, whose tight schedules forbid drawn-out goodbyes; the woman's beloved has disappeared beyond the horizon without her even realizing it.[19] The second poem recognizes that telegrams allow for more frequent correspondence, but that every elliptical, telegraphic exchange is also less personal. In the third poem, a couple's photographic portraits hang beside each other: photographic realism brings to life the face of one's beloved at the same time as it augments the realities of separation. Whereas these first three poems dramatize the modern efficiency of trains, steamships, telegrams, and photography, the last of the series focuses on a drastically different technique found in traditional parting poems and popular literature—namely, the meeting of souls in dreams. As the female speaker laments, this fantasy is now also obsolete because, with the difference in time zones, she may be awake when her lover's soul visits her in his sleep. The first poem is the only one that names the technical innovations in question, while the second, third, and fourth are literary riddles. As clues to their readers, these poems offer exaggerated physical resemblances, as when the speaker of the second mistakes telegraph poles for trees, and linguistic polyvalences, as in the third poem, where a Chinese word like *jing* refers to both the mirror and camera lens. Such befuddlement and homophony thus exploit the confusions that new technologies and their neologisms generated around the turn of the twentieth century.[20]

Huang was not the only late Qing poet who waxed lyrical about new media technologies. Ten years before "Modern Parting," a series of mourning poems bemoaned receiving news of a husband's death via a telephone call.[21] The Kinmenese poet Xu Zili, who went by the pseudonym Dianhua shizhu, "Master of the Telephone Room," published a set of riddles on the telephone, the telegraph, electric light, and photography in *Lujiang bao* in 1904 while studying in Japan.[22] In the same year, a pair of quatrains on the phono-graph and telephone, in direct imitation of "Modern Parting," appeared in the journal *Guomin ribao huibian*.[23] Such verses, scant in comparison with prose writings that deal with the theme of technology, perhaps underscore a certain intransigence of the poetic medium with regard to other media devices.

As is often the case, the most guileless of questions—What are the poems really about?—warrants an elaborate response. Does "Modern Parting" directly communicate the changes effected by new infrastructures, the telegraph, and photography? Alternatively, does it primarily execute one of the lyrical tradi-tion's main concerns, the speaker' melancholic longing for her faraway lover, to which the new technologies merely serve as accessories—or in Liang's words, "new artistic imagery" and a "new lexicon?"[24] Once again, the entan-glement of medium and message, of the literal with the figurative, which I first raised with regard to the vessel of Liang Qichao's trans-Pacific journey, comes into play. To put the question differently: Do new transportation networks and innovations such as the telegraph and photography actually constitute the *substance* of a new poetic culture, or do they, like the steamship, serve merely as technological *form*, vehicle, and occasion for poetic creativity? And, if it is feminine sentimentality that Huang specifically retools to depict the techno-logical conditions of modernity, what new conceptions of the self in relation to technology can we glean from the poem's formal ruptures? What reconfigura-tions of lyricism and technical media emerge as a result?

In a continuous movement between the roomy vessel of poetic form and its vast outside, we must not overlook the historical fact that feminine sub-jectivity in classical-language lyric poetry has been a predominantly mas-culine construction. Maureen Robertson, in her study of medieval and late imperial poetry, argues that the distinction between the actual subject posi-tion and dramatized speaking voice is explicit when male authors depict "passive, narcissistic women" with their "romanticized suffering" through a voyeuristic lens.[25] Such poems often amplify the hopeless solitude of the fe-male speaking subject longing for her absent lover, whereby the woman, as a "non-referential, iconic image and projected voice," stands as an "empty sig-nifier into which the male author/reader may project his desire."[26] Schmidt implicitly censures Huang for depicting the female speaker in "Modern Parting" as a "hilariously ignorant heroine," although he adds in her defense that the particular scenario of mistaking telegraph poles for trees, to which I will return, can occur to "anyone ignorant of telegraphic technology."[27] Nonetheless, a laughable naivety is not the same as the eroticized voyeur-

117

ism Robertson detects in earlier parting poetry. What is novel in Huang's reconstruction of the iconic woman in "Modern Parting" is her role as a *user* of new technologies—albeit an unimpressed one—whose femininity makes her particularly sensitive in registering older and alternative forms of communication.

Lyricism's gender politics thus reveals more than just the individual poet's proclivities. David Wang, in his analysis of lyricism (*shuqing*) in a period of Chinese literary production most concerned with national crisis, expands the term beyond poetry to include prose, film, and painting.[28] For Wang, "lyricism" more generally designates "a set of concepts, discourses, or values regarding the poetics of selfhood," which nonetheless "inform[s] the intellectual and literary culture of a historical moment." Yet lyrical feelings also complicate our very understanding of history when they engender their own "disavowal" or "irony."[29]

"Modern Parting" similarly produces such disavowals or ironies, I argue, by exteriorizing traditional lyricism's feminine interiority via new communicative technologies. This, then, is what the poems are *about*: the lyrical medium's ironic mediation, which far from simply "reflecting" the female speaker's position vis-à-vis her historical context, thoroughly interrogates the sense of contemporaneity—the "now" (*jin*) in the poems' title—through the technical imageries produced and circulated *by* the poetic form. By questioning the contemporaneity of the technologies represented vis-à-vis older media including the poetic form itself, "Modern Parting" shows that another set of oppositions between technics and poetics can dismantle the trite dichotomy of tradition and innovation. If, in other words, we can define "tradition" by the evolution of handwritten letters, mirrors, and ships and carts, and move "innovation" from the prerogative of technical devices and scientific inventions to the realm of poetic revolutions, we would then be able to perform a "chiasmus on the predicates" of tradition and innovation, to borrow Saussy's term for his deconstruction of Western theory and Chinese reality,[30] which I discussed in addition to my own reassessment in the introduction to this book. Instead of distilling essences of "Chinese reality," Huang's "Modern Parting" intimates a different theory of poetics through the female speaker's amalgamation of communicative devices and processes both old and new, indigenous and foreign. The poems' success in updating traditional lyricism's sentimentality—and whether, indeed, the identity of the poet matters in upending the masculine construction of feminine subjectivity—will in turn depend on their confrontations with a certain technics of gender.

"Modern Parting" does not simply represent new technologies but conforms poetic devices such as the metaphor (*bi*) and stimulation (*xing*) to specific technical functions. The first poem of "Modern Parting" depicts the sadness of departure by comparing the churning of one's "intestines" (*chang*) with the "turning of the [steamship's] wheel" (*zhuan ru lun*), whereby a "single moment" (*yi ke*) feels like "ten thousand weeks" (*wan zhou*).[31] Several lines down, a bodily organ is equated with a mechanical part once again, where the female speaker likens the steamship's "rudder (*jun duo*) of thirty thousand pounds" to the effortless "twirling of one's finger around the hand" (*dong ru rao zhi rou*). Each action is analogous to the other, signaled by the Chinese character *ru* ("to liken"), and so while the churning of the intestines is already a metaphor for the speaker's lovelorn state, the comparison highlights the technical context in which both organic and inorganic signifiers cohabit and so generate other signifiers. (An analogy, as a literary device, has its technical counterpart in the analogue, a continuous signal representing another time-varying signal, in contrast to the digital.) Such a comparison of the organic and intimate with the inorganic and external calls to mind Michele Yeh's study of metaphors or "comparison" (*bi*) in Chinese poetics, wherein she emphasizes the "affinity or intimacy" with which the metaphor conjoins "the human subject and the external world, or feeling and scene, . . . creating a unified experience."[32]

In addition to the comparative *bi*, Huang's poetry also employs the ancient technique of "stimulation," *xing*.[33] Comparison/*bi* and stimulation/*xing* are two of the six "song methods" of *Zhouli* (*Rites of Zhou*), and they reappear in *Shijing* (*Classic of Poetry*) as two of the six principles of poetry.[34] Confucian scholars have argued variously about the difference between comparison and stimulation, since the stimulation of a situation affords comparisons of one object with another, and vice versa.[35] According to Pauline Yu, if what distinguishes stimulation from comparison is the former's ability to "evoke something" in the reader, little consensus has settled on "what precisely is 'stimulated' or evoked."[36] The classic case in this long exegetical tradition is *xing*'s evocation of nature, specifically the ospreys in the *Guan ju* poem of the *Classic of Poetry*. One school of thought favors the interpretation that the stimulation of the imagery of ospreys serves the didactic purpose of illustrating "proper conjugal relations" and thus the moral and political order of the marriage institution.[37] A later view contends that the poet simply wrote what they saw that happened to move them, and that stimulation/*xing* operates spontaneously with the power of emotive evocation, which does not need to imbue proper meanings at all. A more radical version of this interpretation argues that the poet did not even have to see such an image. According to Zhu Xi, a proponent of this third position, both comparison/*bi* and stimulation/*xing* emphasize some kind of analogical relationship between a natural image and the human situation, which is "affective" and "technical" rather than moralistic or empirical.[38]

Comparison/*bi*, as discussed above, involves substitution, while stimulation/*xing* works through juxtaposition.[39] But whereas the external world or scene in Yeh's study of traditional Chinese poetics depicts nature, "Modern Parting" sets the human subject in scenes where technical imageries predominate. Poetic devices are literally that: devices. Whereas ancient vehicles and ships "caused [literally, *zai*, "transported"] departures," they at least allowed one to get on or off at will.[40] Modern steamships and trains, on the other hand, "join forces to increase sorrows" (*bing li sheng li chou*). In contrast to the passivity of previous transportation modes, the ships and vehicles of Huang's time actively "join forces" to create an entirely distinct pace of life, forbidding drawn-out goodbyes with the ringing of departure bells (*zhong sheng*). The imagery produced conforms to the documented effects that modern railway journeys have had on perceptions of time and space.[41] "Modern Parting," however, elaborates on this phenomenon through a lyrical self who does not only feel the compression of modern, industrialized time, but the regulated durations of feeling itself. If the era of steamships and trains leaves little time for parting sorrows, the intensity of which increases nonetheless, how can the poetic medium, as the "affective" and "technical" relation linking the human situation and the outside world, effectively communicate technical imageries?

Riddles presented in consecutive poems heighten this reflexivity between poetic form and technological content. The female speaker in the second poem, unimpressed by the frequency and speed with which her lover's messages arrive, complains of their impersonality. The poem clues its readers in on the technical innovation in question in its sixth line: "it seems to have been translated three or four times" (*kuang jing san si yi*).[42] Translation (*yi*) here refers to the multiple decoding process in the Chinese telegraph code designed by a Danish professor of astronomy, H. C. F. C. Schjellerup, and a French harbormaster, Septime Auguste Viguier, which had been in use since 1871.[43] The code first organizes about 6,800 commonly used Chinese characters according to the Kangxi radical-stroke system, and then assigns each character a series of "distinct four-digit numerical codes" from 0001 to 9999. The 1871 code, Thomas S. Mullaney explains, "was premised upon an additional or double mediation of Chinese" that does not occur in alphabetic and syllabic scripts: "a first layer mediating between Chinese characters and Arabic numerals, and a second layer mediating between Arabic numerals and the long and short pulses of telegraphic transmissions."[44] The female speaker, as if in anticipation of this later interpretation, thus grasps the "technolinguistic" rules undergirding the Chinese script's adoption into the language of international Morse code. But in counting "three or four translations," the poem also draws our attention to the more elementary sense of translation captured by the character *yi*—namely, writing (*wen*)'s expression of the composer's intention or heart/mind (*xin*). This primary sense of *yi* thus precedes the "double mediation" of telegraph codes, at the same time as it refers to the process.

In the context of the riddle, translation signifies the poem's rendition of the unnamed technology into elusive and yet adequately recognizable imageries, this time by manipulating the shapes of its physical infrastructure. "In front of my gate two rows of trees, / reach far to the horizon (*menqian liang hang shu, lili dao tianjie*). / In their center hangs a string (*si*), / strings attaching one end of the tree to another (*zhong yang yi you si, you si liang tou xi*)."[45] A Chinese reader will recognize the two meanings of *si* as electric wires (as in the neologism for "electric fuse," *baoxian si*) as well as its older symbolic reference to heartstrings (*xinsi*).[46] These double meanings emphasize how telegraph communications employed, at least before the wireless, a point-to-point or person-to-person model of communication, not unlike the tugging of lovers' heartstrings. While it is laughable to mistake telegraph poles for trees, what matters more is the distance between sender and receiver, the relaying of one "heart" to another. The humor when conventional nature imageries are used to represent unfamiliar man-made infrastructure is unmistakable; at the same time, logic resides in the speaker's perplexity.

Are heartstrings metaphors for electrical wires, and trees for poles, or does the poem suggest an essential seamlessness between ontologically distinct realms, between the self and the world, nature and technology? In the former case, the more conventional imageries found in traditional lyric poetry would refer to modern communications as something "*fundamentally other*—belong[ing] to another plane of existence," just as allegories do.[47] Here, it is about time we address the longstanding controversy in comparative poetics over the difference between Chinese metaphor and the operation of the Western mimetic tradition of allegory. Indeed, this very controversy has been lurking in the background—or rather, in the infrastructure.[48] According to Yu, the Chinese imagistic devices of comparison/*bi* and stimulation/*xing* do not allegorize but rather contextualize.[49] That is, traditional scholarship on the *Classic of Poetry* does not see its imageries as "fictional works composed ad hoc to create or correspond to some historical reality or philosophical truth, but as literal vignettes drawn from that reality."[50] In this regard, Yu's claim resounds with Huang's own account of his craft in his preface to *Poetry from the Hut within the Human Realm*, that there are "events outside poetry just as there are men within it."[51] Whether or not the poet was inspired by actual trees when he compared them with telegraph poles is secondary to the fact that the telegraph was an existing innovation, which radically transforms the poetic imagery of lovers' heart-to-heart communications. The emphasis on contextualization allows the reader to perceive new communicative technology as something in line with both the poetic process and the conventional imageries of nature. At the same time, the representations of these technologies do not aspire "to some historical reality or philosophical truth," but are simply "literal vignettes drawn from that reality."[52] That heartstrings and trees help "contextualize" the visual and affective experience of new media technologies foregrounds the definition of mediation that this book has been tracing so far, as the simultaneous cleaving and bridging between technologies' textual and cultural significations and their irreducible materialities.

Mediation therefore defines an active rather than a passive process. This operation of the term places limits on certain questions of ontology, particularly that of an essential monism in Chinese philosophy and poetics as articulated variously by Yu, Michelle Yeh, Andrew Plaks, and Stephen Owen.[53] I share these critics' position that Chinese poetics operates on an irreducibly different register from Western metaphor and allegory only to the extent that it underscores the specifically referential nature of the relationship between poetic form and technological content. Ontology, whether within Chinese monism or Western dualism, is of lesser importance than the genesis or development of being. For this reason, Saussy's magisterial deconstructive analysis takes away as much as it offers. By exposing the abovementioned critics' prescriptions of alterity as being premised on the "very logic of sameness and difference" that allows one to separate a metaphor from a synecdoche, or figurative from literal sense, he also extracts alterity from the historical context that Yu's argument affords.[54] It matters little, indeed, whether trees "occasion" or figure as telegraph poles, whether heartstrings "stimulate" or figure as wires. Both Chinese monism and Western dualism maintain a relation between imageries and their referents. When such imageries evoke technical objects and not just nature, they simply highlight, even more readily, the constructivism or genesis of the poem. Telegraph poles and wires are patently man-made; by rendering these heterogeneous material dimensions into meaning, the poem reveals how it itself comes into being, how its medium is also forged. The poem, in other words, does not exist prior to its imageries.

The theme of technology, like any other theme, informs the aesthetic form that carries it. But *unlike* other content, technology, particularly media, has the added advantage of being analogous to the genesis of its own form. By conveying the shifts brought about by the telegraph, the poetic medium demonstrates its own flexibility and even experimental nature. "Media content," a now ubiquitous phrase revamped in light of late nineteenth-century Chinese poetics, thus adds more than just "new artistic imageries" and a "new lexicon" to lyric poetry.[55] Rather, by adapting the formal devices of comparison-stimulation (*bi-xing*) to shore up the conditions of its own poetic making, "Modern Parting" updates the "style of the ancients" according to technological change. The poems' predominant lyricism, contrary to their effusions of saccharine melancholy, is one that mediates the poetic and the technical. To return to my earlier question of what exactly "Modern Parting" is about—Is it really about technology? Or is it more revealing of sentimentality?—the answer is patently both, for it is no longer possible to determine whether it is new technological content or theme that mediates traditional poetic form or the other way around. Technologies, as Csongor Lörincz reminds us, are always metaphorical, either "as their own metaphors in another medium, or that other medium as their metaphor."[56] "Modern Parting" registers the encounter between lyricism and technical media, once more, with feeling.

Like the preceding verse, the third poem exploits the double meanings of *jing*, which can refer to a mirror as well as a camera lens, to pun reflexively on image-making and medium specificity. The mirror image, a classic motif in Chinese literature, functions as a narrative device complicating the status of fictionality.[57] For a lyrical poetics of the self, the linguistic ambiguity of *jing* as both mirror and camera lens suggests that the reflected subject relates to her lover's photograph as one image to another. At the beginning of the poem, the female speaker gazes at a photograph of her lover that she has just received while holding up a mirror to herself.[58] Both images perform different relations to the original that call into question the notion of referentiality. In the photo, he is wearing the coat she has made for him as a going-away memento—his image thus accentuates their separation. Her mirror reflection, on the other hand, shows a countenance of someone who, despite being worried and lovesick, turns rosy as a peach tree's blossoms at the sight of his portrait. The speaker's mirror image is thus produced at the instant of the perception of the photographic image, whose temporal and

123

spatial distance from its original, and its basic condition of reproducibility, prompts the speaker to hold a mirror up to her face.

Self-portraits, like all writings of the self, encourage mimicry, multiplicity, and replaceability.[59] The female speaker proceeds to "open a small case" and send her beloved her "portrait inside it" (*kaiqie chi zengjun*).[60] Schmidt's translation retains the riddle's original ambiguity of the object gifted thanks to the word *portrait*, which is not limited to photographic portraits. Given how the speaker has just contemplated herself in a mirror, the gift could signify a mental image of her reflection instead. To physically send one's reflection—whether by post or telegraph—is of course an absurdity, but to grant the absurdity poetic license is to conceive of the mirror and photographic images as embodying the two contradictory dimensions in Charles Sanders Peirce's concept of indexicality.

Mary Ann Doane, in an essay prompted by contemporary digital media's redefinition of print photography and in her introduction to a special issue of the journal *differences* on indexicality, scrutinizes the uneasy coexistence of the index as deixis and as trace.[61] A mirror image by definition does not leave a trace or imprint of the object reflected; it captures the reflection only in the duration of the object's presence in front of the mirror. Like Peirce's example of the pointing finger or the "this" of language, a mirror image assumes the deixical aspect of an index.[62] It loses its referent once the latter exits the path of reflected light. The mirror surface implies ephemerality, a "hollowness that can only be filled in specific, contingent, and always mutating situations."[63] In contrast, the photographic portrait of the speaker's lover partakes in the indexical as a trace. The photochemical imprint proves a material connection to the object and attests to the "reproducibility of a past moment."[64] A mirror image cannot leave a residue, whereas a photographic image "remains as the witness of an anteriority."[65] By gifting her lover a copy of her mirror image, the speaker contests the permanence of the photograph and its claim of abundance. The index as deixis *and* as trace circulates in the poem's imagistic economy. The lines "Face to face, the pictures will not know what to say, / As if separated by a thousand mountain ranges" (*duimian bu jieyu, / ruo ge shan wangchong*), after all, does not bemoan the lovers' separation.[66] Instead, the "as if" (*ruo*) underscores how the mirror and photographic image are in fact *not* "separated by a thousand mountain ranges" and captures the opposing elements of Peirce's notion of the index as *both* deixis and trace: ephemeral, contingent, and yet flush with presence and historicity.

124

Like the "vehicles and ships" of yesteryear in the first poem, and handwritten letters before the advent of the telegraph in the second, the mirror is a crude technology compared with the camera, a mere surface that creates no durable images, a medium on which no "words of light" can be stored.[67] Yet the poem insinuates that both produce images, which, detached from the living body, similarly authenticate and diverge from the self. In offering the fantastic imagery of a mirror's reflection hanging side by side with a photograph without either of the lovers present in person, "Modern Parting" shifts the register of a lover's discourse to a lyricism of mediated images, a poetics of the self shaped by specific mediums that detach and connect to varying degrees. When the photographic image of a distant lover does not bring him closer to home, what can one do but reciprocate in the form of a reflection whose very impossibility of reproduction spells the desire for an irrefutable "thereness?"[68]

Little wonder, then, that the female speaker in the fourth and final poem, frustrated with all technologies, finally attempts an out-of-body rendezvous with her beloved. Entering his bedroom and finding an empty bed, her soul realizes that her lover must have gone to bed at a different hour, living as they are now in different time zones.[69] The oft-evoked image of the moon, to which the heroine looks, becomes a reminder of how global travel makes obsolete the trope of lovers' souls meeting in dreams. The spotlight falls less on the female speaker's romantic foolishness than on the poem's conscious-ness of its dissipating aura in the age of global travel made more accessible by oceanic liners, not unlike the one which took Liang Qichao from Japan to the United States.

What distinguishes "Modern Parting" from previous parting poems is not that it generates feelings *about* machines, but that it exposes the *mechanism of* feeling—that is, the technical condition that makes possible sentimental longings, including the transmission and preservation of such sentiments. I expand on Ina Blom's notion of "mechanism of memory" to include feelings or sentiments not in order to recuperate a psychological account of memory but to emphasize the "event-like character" of sentiment.[70] That is, feelings can encourage or prohibit memory's capacity for action: there are memories, and there are feelings around such memories—and often it is nearly impos-sible to disentangle them. In each of the four poems, the woman recollects technologies past in tandem with her longing for her departed lover and reminiscing of their time together. Yet there is a strong sense in which one cannot return to the days of ancient carts and boats, or to handwritten let-ters. The poems' mechanism of feeling, in other words, leaves no room for nostalgia. Hence despite complaining of steamships and trains, the speaker wishes for her lover to return hastily via air travel in a hot-air balloon. For

125

all of her dissatisfaction with telegrams, she hopes to transform herself into "electric light" (*dianguang*) so she can appear by his side in a flash.[71] What more authentic alternative is there to the photographic image, when even a mirror reflection can fantastically divorce itself from its original? Insofar as the "vastness of the Earth cannot be reduced" (*dichang bu neng suo*), the last poem harbors no illusion: the meeting of souls in dreams is a defunct device.

Modes of transportation, postal communication, and portraiture constitute reflexive subjects of history, which, in the words of Lisa Gitelman, embody the "sense of pastness" responsible for any historical representation in the first place.[72] In "Modern Parting," the time before steamships and trains, telegraphs, photographs, and the standardization of Greenwich Mean Time symbolizes the sentimentalized time of togetherness and proximity. Nostalgia may tinge the latter, but on its own it is too weak to reverse technological change, to cancel out what is "modern" (*jin*) about Huang's refashioning of traditional parting poetry. Precisely with this heterogeneous temporality, this desire for a past time (and a lover) petrified in technical developments cannot, from the speaker's perspective, be halted.[73] For our poet, technical ingenuity is what gives a sense of the past *and* of the physical present. The poetic devices of comparison-stimulation (*bi-xing*) are not the only affective and technical links relaying the subject's interiority to her external circumstances since technical objects perform the same function—and with qualitatively different effects. In memorializing older and newer media, the poetic—specifically, lyrical—medium communicates developments in communicative technology. More than conventional, anthropocentric narratives of how new media impact modern lives, lyrical transmissions (*chuan*) double up to express the lives of communicative technologies.

The same Chinese character for "biography," *zhuan*, when pronounced differently as *chuan*, also means "to transmit or communicate." A life, to quip, is only known through its transmissions. Correspondingly, the technological content of "Modern Parting" allows it to comment on its own mediatic status. I thus locate in Huang's poems an "autobiographical reflexivity" and "self-memorizing" capabilities, which Blom, adapting French philosopher Gilbert Simondon's notion of the individuation of technical objects, identifies in early video art.[74] Individuation or ontogenesis shows that a technical object is never "such and such a thing, something given *hic et nunc*," but one that creates its own conditions and environment as a result of its specific operations.[75] I do not for a moment imply that a poem about technology can be the same thing as a technical object. Rather, Simondon's philosophy makes possible a thinking of a "technical mentality" *of* the technical object, one that,

126

contrary to a purely cognitive notion of mentality, is, according to Brian Massumi, "immanent to a material event of taking-form."[76] The model inside an inventor's head in the process of the making of the technical object is not a "cognitive form imposed from outside" but a realization of the form from the actual functioning of materials, which can only come from the "future" when specific materials and their functions will already have been in place.[77] An invention seeks to solve a technical problem, yet the problem presupposes that certain technical conditions of the invention already exist.

Lest it still needs to be stated: poems about technologies are not the technologies themselves. To nonetheless grasp the affinities between the signified forms of media and media devices, however, requires seeing that both retain a notion of mentality immanent, not external, to its relevant operations.[78] This is what I mean by the analogous relation between the content of technological change in "Modern Parting" and its poetic form. For Simondon, "the dynamism of thought" operates analogously to the circular causality of technical objects: "Mental schemas react upon each other during invention in the same way the diverse dynamisms of the technical object will react upon each other in their material functioning."[79] This analogous dynamism does not capitulate to what Mark B. N. Hansen, whom I discussed in the introduction, criticizes as the reduction of technology to discourse. In alluding to the telegraph and to photography in the first and second poems, "Modern Parting" far from assumes their realities, but represents their technical functions—namely, the "double mediation" of Chinese script for the telegraph code, and the likeness of photographic reproduction—as imageries in the formal language available to it. The poems' "material functioning" proceeds not via telegraphic signals and light-sensitive receptors, but with the arrangement of imageries whose juxtapositions and substitutions give the poems their meanings, "ornamentations" that inform the poetic medium itself.[80]

THE FEMALE MEDIUM

As to what lies between the poetic medium, lyricism, and communicative media—to raise the perpetually resilient question of the relation between signifier, signifying form, and referent—there are, as the jocular expression for the unmoved mover goes, mediums all the way down. When this medium, however, names the "woman," when the history of the lyric mode of parting poetry is tied to the masculine construction of feminine sentimentality 127 and authorship, and when Huang remakes this poetic medium through new technical media, woman is never just "another" medium. "Modern Parting" communicates through a gendered speaker. Human agency and subjectivity remain central, not peripheral, to its (auto)biography of technical objects.[81] I have been hesitant in my interpretation to conflate the poems' female speaker with passive, narcissistic figures found in classical poetry, and have claimed instead that her feelings toward her lover and contemporary technologies alike interrogate the poems' relation to tradition. Nevertheless, the speaker's agency does not cancel out her imposed instrumentality. It is not insignificant that it has to be a feeling woman, and not a man, who operates the "mechanism of feeling." Schmidt is not wrong in charging Huang for equating femininity with a disdainful ignorance of new technologies.[82] At the same time, there is something charming in "Modern Parting" about the depiction of the female speaker's sensitivity toward the changing conditions of inscription and communication.

Jill Galvan foregrounds similarly contradictory traits attributable to the female medium's phenomenal rise in the popular imaginations of nineteenth- and early twentieth-century Europeans and North Americans: woman's alleged sensitivity or sympathy, attributed to her delicate nervous system, and a propensity for losing all feelings and consciousness.[83] While a woman is supposedly endowed with an ability to "reach out feelingly to others," nevertheless, insofar as "such self-extension would *only* be a matter of feeling," it is easy for her to be reduced to a state of automatism, to become a neutral party to other people's conversations.[84] Women were perfect "go-betweens because they potentially combined the right kind of presence with the right kind of absence."[85] Because of these paradoxical characteristics, Galvan argues, the "female medium" is susceptible to being manipulated as "the tool of another's, usually a man's, design of gaining information or social power."[86] Therein lies the other, more "metaphorical" use of the word *medium* that accompanies Galvan's "literal" study of women both as telegraphers and telephone operators and as spirit mediums in Spiritualist séances. The heroine of "Modern Parting" is no less ideal as a conduit: she displays a Luddite-like aversion to new technologies alongside a sensitivity toward the technics of communication and image reproduction borne from a steadfast loyalty to an absent lover. Hers is a lyricism that shuttles to and fro, led not by industrial employment or supernatural forces as in Galvan's study, but by late Qing intellectuals' reluctant embrace of foreign technologies, and the period's lyrical reconstruction of the feminine voice. We therefore find ourselves back where we started: the literal vessel of Liang Qichao's proclamation of a "poetic revolution" driving the metaphorical "vehicle" that is the writing of *dao*, figured as the "weaker vessel" to man.

Robertson's analysis of the male construction of the feminine voice in the Chinese literati tradition leads her to ask whether, when women authors compose in the lyrical mode, they can "represent their own gendered consciousness in a medium already scripted."[87] When the themes of technology and of changing media forms inform traditional poetic form, and the latter informs technological content, then the expression "poetic medium" assumes a technical meaning not always dominant in its idiomatic usage. The challenge, then, is not whether women can represent their gendered consciousness "in" a medium, but whether it is possible to posit gendered consciousness radically *as* a lyrical medium, and one that no longer serves as mere instrument or tool for another.

Late Qing literature and criticism catalogue a plethora of emotions (*qing*), often expressed by men rather than by women. Readers of this period would be familiar with Liu E's histrionic preface to *The Travels of Lao Can*, where incessant weeping measures the quality of a man's spiritual nature and his concerns for the crisis of the Chinese nation.[88] Wu Jianren, the author of *New Story of the Stone*, titled a series of fifty-seven observations *Wu Jianren ku* (*Wu Jianren Weeps*), wherein he cries over an assortment of issues ranging from societal woes to personal tragedies.[89] According to one anecdote, the prolific translator Lin Shu (1852–1924) and his collaborator Wang Ziren were so moved by their reading of *La dame aux camélias* that their bawling could be heard from another room. This anecdote almost exceeds in fame their translation of the French novel itself. In Rey Chow's psychoanalytic reading, the two Chinese men's identification with Marguerite's self-sacrifice constitutes a moment of "masochistic identification with the Other" whereby her perceived suffering is transposed to the viewers.[90] Marguerite, instead of being seen as a mother, the figure of self-sacrifice, takes on the role of a "powerless infant to whom the reading subject becomes the understanding mother."[91] Lin Shu and Wang Ziren's excessive crying, instead of eliciting powerlessness, occupies a "position of narcissistic power in implying an Other who will respond."[92] For all of its feminist illumination of popular fiction grouped under the late Qing, early Republican school of "Mandarin Ducks and Butterflies," however, female authorship of Chinese literary sentimentality is absent from Chow's examination of the parodic function of feminine emotions.

The "politics of male sentimentality," David Wang's term for the target of Chow's analysis, takes for granted that late Qing male writers mobilized a wide range of emotions other than sorrow such as laughter, anger, vengefulness, cynicism, "the whimsical, or downright silly."[93] Zeng Pu's *A Flower in the Sea of Sins* and Wu Jianren's *Eyewitness Reports* infuse characters with "mismatched" displays of patriotism and promiscuity, or heroism and buffoonery that are symptomatic of the contradictions of their time. Literary criticism, instead of moderating such emotional excess, affirms it for didactic purposes—Liang Qichao's discussion of the four powers of fiction to excite one's mind in "On the Relationship Between Fiction and Government of the People" being a perfect case in point.[94] Even Wang Guowei's critique of the excess of *qing* in the form of *yu* manifests a desire for a "transvaluation" of desires, one which circumvents lust and the impossibility of its fulfillment.[95] Emotional excess permeates so much of late Qing fiction that it is difficult not to suspect a coincidence between form and content—or, rather, what David Wang identifies as "narrative (anti-)typology and libidinal turbulence" such that the more the plots, characters, and scenes multiply without being resolved, the more abundant the emotional registers become.[96] Yet if Wang detects in the heavy-handed emotional ornamentation of late Qing fiction "a desperate effort to fill in" for essential formlessness, whereby form stands for "the Object that is ever elusive,"[97] one wonders if such analysis of late Qing emotions in prose writing might not also revolve around another empty center—namely, women's agency of their own sentiments in verse.

This silencing of feminine sentimentality is ironically a historical legacy of the birth of Chinese feminism, which, under conditions of colonial modernity, subsumed the "woman" question under the "national" question.[98] At the same time, the advocacy of national progress, as we saw, far from impeded male poets of the same period from enlisting a spectrum of emotions ranging from the personal and the romantic to the heroic. According to Joan Judge, Chinese woman feminists on the other hand rejected the "talented women (*cainü*) of the past," who, excluded from the official realm of civil service, devoted their literary capabilities to the writing of "emotional and purposefully apolitical" verse in contrast to male scholarly prose.[99] These modern women, most of whom studied in Japan, established their newfound roles as national subjects by founding their own journals and contributing articles to overseas student organizations, writing essays and poems advocating for reform in the classical style and occasionally in vernacular Chinese. In so doing they opened a new chapter in Chinese women's writing in modern mass media, while closing what they saw as overly "feeling and flowery diction" employed by their literary predecessors.[100] From the perspective of these patriotic women, past women poets churning out "sounds of lamentation" to "fill the inner chambers" had no regard for the nation, and were thus as ineffectual as illiterate women.[101] They also derided other Chinese classics and the popular novel for their weak female characters, but in censuring the lyrical tradition seen to be most indulgent of typically feminine sentimentalities, they helped erase, in Judge's assessment, "the feminine aesthetic in national culture."[102] An anarchist like He-Yin Zhen, in sharp contradiction to her contemporaries, wrested women's rights from under the weight of patriarchal, nationalist concerns; nevertheless, she did not consider aesthetics as part of her radical project to bring about equality between men and women.[103] Later critics, in reconstructing the subject of woman from their own historical vantage points, inadvertently extend early Chinese feminism's obscuration, or in extreme cases "elimination," of femininity's "lyrical traces."[104]

A paradox akin to that found in Galvan's study of the female medium and my interpretation of "Modern Parting" thus perturbs the politicization of the Chinese woman at the turn of the twentieth century. This is a period, as Hu Ying points out, before the term *new woman* (*xin nüxing* or *xin funü*) gained momentum.[105] During this historical juncture, the idealized woman is easily stirred to nationalistic zeal, and yet her passions must not approach the lyrical pathos associated with the talented women of the past. As an avatar of a new people, she must not stop feeling, but instead learn how to control her emotions. She must, in short, surpass Huang Zunxian's heroine in "Modern Parting" in becoming a more "conducive" female medium, one who is more adept at channeling her feelings for the greater good. While Huang asserts what Amy D. Dooling calls traditional "male 'authority' over women's images," it is often the period's feminists who overwhelmingly contribute to the derision of traditional feminine aesthetics.[106]

Since the Chinese woman is already a conduit for nationalistic zeal, we merely need to follow such a perverse mediality to the letter in order to bring her implicit instrumentality to the fore. An alternative woman of feeling whom this chapter is tracing would therefore not shy away from harnessing novel technologies since it is through complex processes of social technologies that her gender comes into being in the first place.[107] Adapting Michel Foucault's study of sexuality, Teresa de Lauretis defines a notion of gender that is related to but not "virtually coterminous" with sexual difference in its representation and self-representation.[108] Yet, since de Lauretis's engagement with technology remains indebted to Foucault's discursive lens, *Technologies of Gender* begs the question of the relation between gender as the "differential solicitation of male and female subjects" and technical media.[109] The "medium" through which gender both represents itself and is represented constitutes communicative technologies, and not just state and social institutions and discursive constructions.

Representation, of course, matters, but so too do its means. A radicalized female medium communicates through narrative representations of technologies as well as the specific material forms that make possible such representations. I thus expand on de Lauretis's work on the self-representation of gender to include, as I have done with "Modern Parting," the self-representation of the *technologies* of gender. The poetic medium is once again our vehicle of choice, carrying the woman, who is this time its author, to finesse literary writing for political causes. Here, Galvan's study of telegraph and telephone operators, and spirit mediums in nineteenth- and early twentieth-century Great Britain and the United States offers a materialist guide. Espousing a similar historical focus, I mine from Chinese nationalism's exploitation of femininity another, more literal, notion of instrumentality: women's sentimental evocation of technical media.

Contemporary scholars such as Joan Judge, Tani Barlow, Amy D. Dooling, and others have thoroughly criticized the subsumption of femininity within the national question without at all relating this phenomenon to women's use of technical media. But the first, more figurative sense of female mediality overlaps with its second, more literal and, interestingly, more obscured counterpart. The idealized female medium-and-model is someone whose navigation between linguistic signification and competing formats of inscription hinges upon the proper transmission of her feelings within the conceptual confines of the nation-state. There is thus an *analogous* relationship between how she restrains private sentimentality from seeping into her passions for the nation, and how she distinguishes and separates the poetic medium from newer modes of inscription. The woman, as a conducive channel between the individual and the nation, has to construct a poetics of the self with the technical media available to her, all the while keeping them separate. Yet once poetry and newer media meet and address each other, the feeling woman begins to shake the ground on which her identity as the perfect go-between is built. The moment at which she acquires a relationship to technology that does *not* reproduce the orders of instrumentalization which engender her in the first place, an alternative version of the female medium emerges, one who ceases to feel solely for her idealized brethren.

QIU JIN: BETWEEN PHOTOGRAPH AND POEM

Qiu Jin's patriotic fervor as revolutionary martyr, women's rights advocate, educator, and poet has struck contemporaries and later critics alike. Lu Xun provides one of the most memorable accounts of her fiery public persona when recounting how she threw a knife onto a table in the middle of a speech given in Tokyo in December 1905.[110] There are indeed many ways to remember Qiu

Jin. Nevertheless, her role as a female medium in the more technical or literal way I am defining it has hardly been a chief reason for her posthumous fame being tied to the making of a collective Chinese identity.[111] In what follows, I analyze her poem "Self-Inscription on a Photograph" and so sidestep the revolutionary passion for which she is so famed in order to highlight Qiu Jin as an astute commentator of the relationship between poetry and photography.

"Self-Inscription on a Photograph" belongs to a late Qing hybrid genre that combined images with inscriptions (*ziti xiaoxiang*). It can be seen in the same category as another contemporaneous trend in women's journals: photographic portraits accompanying short biographies (*xiaozhuan*) of famous women. Despite her own contribution to this journalistic fad of famous women's biographies, to which I will return, Qiu Jin's self-inscription in this hybridized media departs from hagiography. Rather, it constructs an autobiography of past, present, and future selves as models for both emulation and denigration. As Qiu Jin's poem bleeds into her image, referencing the other medium's physical properties as well as its limits, the female go-between becomes an unwieldly example. To the extent that the photographic index-as-trace also points to the contingencies and arbitrariness of language, thereby showing the cohabitation of the index as trace and deixis in both photo and text, the female medium challenges the prescription of women's feelings and the erasure of femininity's "lyrical traces."[112]

The photograph, taken in 1906 in the Jiang Liutang Photographic Studio in Shaoxing after her study in Japan, presents Qiu Jin dressed in a traditional Han Chinese man's vest and gown (figure 3.1). With her hair braided in conventional male style, she stands beside a potted plant, right arm partially hidden behind her, while her left arm holds the handle of a folded umbrella, its index finger extended in full view horizontally across the handle. Of the four extant photographs of Qiu Jin all taken in various professional studios (three in China, one in Japan), this is the only one with her accompanying inscription. The earliest existing image of Qiu Jin was taken around 1902 where she sits placidly in the traditional outfit of a Yangtze Delta gentlewoman.[113] A second, more flamboyant image, taken circa 1904 after her time among intellectuals in Beijing, shows her dressed in a dark Western man's suit, holding a cane and grinning theatrically for the camera.[114] The third, perhaps the most iconic, picture of Qiu Jin was taken in 1905. It is a half-body portrait of her in a kimono, hair up in *nihon-gami* style holding a dagger in her right hand.[115] Together, the four photographs map Qiu Jin's journey from being a wife and mother to two children to her gleeful flouting of conventional gender norms and familial obligations; from her embrace of the swordsman

133

3.1 Qiu Jin, ca. 1906. Source: Guo Changhai and Qiu Jingwu, eds., *Qiu Jin yanjiu ziliao: wenxian ji* [Research material on Qiu Jin], 2 vols. Yingchuan: Ningxia renmin chubanshe, 2007.

persona and Japanese reformism to her return to China.[116] In this last photo, Qiu Jin's sartorial choice of traditional Han Chinese male dress scarcely veils her anti-Manchu, revolutionary resolve. Compared with the swashbuckling, more exotic version of herself in Japanese kimono, this image, together with the inscribed verse, evince more solemnity and distance.

"SELF-INSCRIPTION ON A PHOTOGRAPH, DRESSED AS MAN"

Who could this person be, looking, looking so sternly ahead?
The martial bones I bring from a former existence regret the flesh
that covers them.
The physical form that I now inhabit is but a phantom,

134

But in a life yet to emerge, I trust it will be more real.
To my regret I met you late—feelings overwhelm me;
As I look up and sigh over our times, my energy is stirred.
Some day when you see my friends from the old days
Tell them I've scrubbed off all that old dirt.

自題小照 （男裝）
儼然在望此何人？俠骨前生悔寄身。
過世形骸原是幻，未來景界卻疑真。
相逢恨晚情應集，仰屋嗟時氣益掙。
他日見余舊時友，為言今已掃浮塵。 [117]

Qiu Jin's seven-syllable, regulated verse opens with an apostrophe addressed
to her barely recognizable other. This is because her masculine self resides
in a woman's body as "martial bones" (*xiagu*) concealed by a "phantom" or
"illusory" (*huan*) female exteriority. In a "future vista," the speaker continues, may her physical form assume more authenticity (*zhen*). The poem's
plaintive tone continues as the speaker regrets having met her other self
so late, the stirring of her emotions intensifying as she looks up, presumably from the photo, toward the ceiling above (*yangwu*). The last lines of
the poem deepen the Buddhist message contemplating truth and illusion
and the transmigration of souls in the earlier lines. The speaker informs
her male form that should he run into her "friends from the old days," he
ought to pass along the message that she has "scrubbed off all that old dirt"
(*jinyi sao fuchen*), which stands for the illusory nature of physical forms. In
a cycle back to the opening apostrophe where the speaker fails to recognize
the photographic image, her friends may also need some explanation of her
radical transformation. This implied address introduces a conundrum in
the belief in the illusory nature of all existence. After the first two lines, the
speaker continues to denounce her female, physical form, lamenting in the
third line that she has taken so long to encounter her other self in the photograph before alluding, in continued apostrophe form, to the illusory nature
of all bodies at the end of the poem. [118] Whereas her feminine self has transcended this world, it is up to the relative permanence of the photographed
self, implies the poem, to articulate the former's departure.

In terms of Peirce's understanding of the index, the poem partakes of the
symbolic in its use of the explicit pronoun "I" (*yu*) in the possessive form
when encountering old friends. Implicitly, the subject of line 7 refers to the
second-person self in the photographed image, who, running into "my old

friends" (*yu jiu shiyou*) someday in the future, is tasked with explaining the poet's transmigrated identity.[119] The concluding line reveals an enlightened "I" no longer caught up in the dust of existence, thus establishing the disjuncture not just between two but three entities: the first-person I (*yu*) whose former acquaintances the photographed image encounters; the photographed image; and the "self" who is no longer present in any physical sense. These three selves in turn move between different temporalities. While the image of Qiu Jin in male dress comes from a "former existence," it persists for an indefinite time in to the future when it encounters "friends from the old days." The speaking self or the first-person "I" belongs to the present moment as observed, fleeting and transient compared with the final self who has transcended the earthly realm. Out of the trio, it is the photographed Qiu Jin in male dress who plays witness to—and, paradoxically, escapes—the Buddhist ideal of spiritual transcendence.[120] Qiu Jin's masculine image has to inform those who used to know her that the old Qiu Jin has since departed from the material world. In so doing, it uncannily embodies Peirce's definition of the photographic index as trace: a material residue formed by a photochemical reaction, whose mechanical reproduction of a past moment, unable to be scrubbed off as dust, finds itself back in the eternal cycle of wretched existence.

"Self-Inscription" thus assumes the dual dimensions of the photographic index as both a permanent, iconic trace and as a more arbitrary deixis. Deixis, which Peirce identifies as "shifters" in language, here corresponds to the form of classical Chinese pronouns.[121] While the photograph, according to Doane's elucidation, "partakes in the iconic"—and indeed, what better icon of pre-Republican Chinese feminism than Qiu Jin?—"the index as shifter (or deixis) forces language to adhere to the spatiotemporal frame of its articulation."[122] Yet in its limited frame, the arbitrarily defined symbolic sign manages to endow Qiu Jin's photograph with its iconic longevity. In Wu Shengqing's study of this relatively new practice of "writing about a photograph of the self," the form "engage[s] with the issues of *zhen* (real) and *huan* (illusion) and the conceptions of the self."[123] Yet Qiu Jin's poem accomplishes more as it gives voice to the very specificity of the photographic medium. Unlike traditional Chinese painted portraiture, which preferred that the subject did not sit for the painter since priority was placed on transcribing the subject's "essence" or "spirit" instead of on verisimilitude through direct observation, a topic I examined in chapter 1, photography attests to its subject's having been there.

136   That Qiu Jin, dressed as a Han Chinese male, stood in front of the camera in a studio in Shaoxing in 1906 was an unassailable fact with an aesthetic-theoretical afterlife when photographic indexicality intersects with lyrical

address. The poem's inscription of photographic legibility through the interplay between the speaking self, photographic image, and the transient, eternal "I" thus complicates Doane's understanding of medium specificity, a concept that she develops from Rosalind Krauss to refer to the medium's departure from its material conditions on which it nonetheless relies, thereby reinventing and transgressing itself.[124] "Self-Inscription" likewise surpasses its own materiality, except that it also employs its medium's specificity and rules to indicate the materiality of the verbal medium.

What, then, does the photograph do in return for the poem? Whereas language's symbolic sign can allude to the photographic image as something that existed in a physical reality, the latter elucidates, quid pro quo, the poem's more ephemeral and ambiguous relation to its referent, to a decentered self in its process of observing itself. Doane's interpretation of the indexicality of the pointing finger in Fritz Lang's *M* (1931) helps to illuminate the formal, visual language of Qiu Jin's portrait. Here, the self-styled Swordswoman of Mirror Lake (*Jianhu nüxia*) gazes straight at the camera, her eyes directed ever so slightly to her left. With her upright, standing posture perpendicular to the folded umbrella in her left hand and the potted plant placed on a tall, decorative stand to her right, her left index finger extending horizontally across the umbrella handle marks a horizontal plane matching that of the surface of the decorative stand. The finger, as Hu not inaccurately suggests, evokes the "restrained move of a sword dance," suggesting the care with which Qiu Jin curated this image of herself that later gained such an iconic status.[125] Whether or not this can be reduced to the Swordswoman's intentional self-fashioning, the resulting image is such that her finger points to a space away from, while still contiguous to, the subject's bodily form. Unlike Doane's examination of the blind man, Heinrich, in *M*, whose pointed finger grazes the left edge of the cinematographic frame and so directs "the spectator to look here, now,"[126] Qiu Jin's gesture implies a more tentative deixis. While the pointing finger in the former instance depletes itself in the moment of its signification, being contingent upon a specific situation that may shift the very next second,[127] Qiu Jin holds her finger so close to her body that it could be well touching it. Thus, the finger neither fully embodies the exhaustibility of the symbol nor the abundance of the icon, yielding instead the tension between the two instances of the index.

It is this same tension that commands Qiu Jin's poem inscribed at the back of her photograph. The finger in her iconic image directs the viewer to the poetic medium and its power to supplement the physical integrity of the photochemical residue. Yet its proximity to the body reminds us that the photographic self in Qiu Jin's poem perseveres, paradoxically, in order to attest to the transience of forms. Rather than see the poem and its speaking female self as wishing to emulate the male self in the photograph, it would be more accurate to view both sides as highlighting, allegorically, what the other is *not*, at least not completely.[128] The photographed self fails to fully signify permanence. Similarly, the poetic speaking self does not only stand for transience. In their mutual referentiality, photograph *and* poem outline the physical shape of Qiu Jin's identity, only to obscure it together.

Self-obscuration runs contrary to the late-Qing construction of exemplary women in the popular press that relied on the hybridized medium of photographic portraits and accompanying texts. The new genre of inscribed poems on photography with which Qiu Jin experimented followed closely upon the heels of another prominent feature in women's journals, the photographic portraits accompanying short biographies (*xiaozhuan*) of famous women.[129] Women's biographies known as "accounts of conduct" (*xingzhuang*) date back to China's long biographical (*zhuan*) tradition and were traditionally formulated to mythologize "stories of women who commit suicide in the name of chastity or who dedicate their lives to serving their parents-in-law in the name of celibate widowhood."[130] Such biographies are usually commissioned by a deceased woman's relative for the purpose of eulogizing conventionally feminine virtues. The shorter biographies in late Qing journals, on the other hand, often portray contemporary women from all over the world known for their professional and political acumen. Qiu Jin's own *Zhongguo nübao* (*Chinese Women's Newspaper*, 1906) introduced readers to fearless women such as Russian anarchist Sophia Perovskaia (1853–1881) and the French revolutionary Madame Roland (1754–1793), who laid down their lives for the nation. Features on Florence Nightingale and on Margaret Fuller, the American feminist journalist, appeared in the feminist Tokyo-run journal *Zhongguo xin nüjie* (*New Women's World of China*, 1907). Similarly, *Nüxue bao* (*Journal of Women's Education*, 1898–90) published biographies of women heroes of the world, and *Qingyi bao* (*Journal of Disinterested Criticism*) printed Liang Qichao's biography of Kang Aide, "the first woman doctor of China" in 1898.[131]

Gender difference became an indispensable touchstone for the nation-building project. As Xia Xiaohong shows, pronouncements of "the men surrender, but not the women" (*nan jiang, nü bu jiang*) circulated frequently in late Qing periodicals between 1903 and 1905.[132] Driving the rhetoric of women's self-sacrificing heroism was the revolutionaries' intense anti-Manchu hatred, and the stories themselves can be traced to those of courageous women who defended the Ming dynasty from the invaders' barbaric

138

conquest. It is as if, so overwhelmed by her emotional intensity, the feminine figure cannot avoid becoming an exemplary patriot for others. Sianne Ngai, in a deft rereading of Freud's classical essay on group identification, detects a "correlation between femininity and exemplarity" that is strengthened by a "shared principle of transmissibility."[133] Women, unlike their male counterparts, cannot help but imitate each other to the extent of being compelled to—or, in Freud's own words, "infected" with a need to—identify with each other. Feminine identifications, therefore, follow a structure of exemplarity that is far from gender "blind." How can women overcome the binds of such a "feminization of exemplarity?" In other words, how can the new woman of feeling feel otherwise? How can she use media to communicate feelings that no longer serve the ends of the nation-state?

Photography, in visualizing the physical images of women models for public consumption, fueled the cycles of feminine imitation and exemplarity. In Qiu Jin's case, however, the new visual medium helped to materialize physical form only to index its evanescence with the aid of the accompanying verse. Her finger in the photograph points both to the passing "now" of signification *and* the permanence of her body clothed in male dress. While the latter played a social, even pedagogical, function in encouraging Chinese women to assume a more masculine posture, the close encounter between the poetic medium and newer inscriptive technologies disrupts the compelling force of exemplarity. Certainly Qiu Jin's image functions as a model for the female speaker of the poem in both the temporal sense of having preceded the poem that is written in response to the image, and also in the normative sense. The female speaker, at least at the beginning of the poem, venerates the "martial bones" of her other self. Yet she quickly chooses the promise of spiritual transcendence over earthly pursuits of this more spirited, visual exemplar. The poem thus first exudes regret in encountering the ideal too late (*xiangfeng hengwan*), before resigning itself to the meaninglessness of all modeling. At the last instance, even the visual example, for all of its concrete materiality, is too unreliable.

Qiu Jin's resignation proved to be prophetic. When in death Qiu Jin was exulted as a martyr, she had to live up to different, at times conflicting, ideas of exemplarity and their respective emotions. As Hu Ying shows in another essay on her posthumous commemoration, the restriction of women's virtue to chastity (*zhen*) in the writing of her eulogy endows the female martyr with an allure that differs from that of her male counterpart. This moral demand marks the first phase of Qiu Jin's layered commemorative history. Dramatic scripts and poems heighten the sense of "wrongful death" (*yuan*) in her execution by appealing to supernatural signs such as "snow in June."[134]

139

The sense of grievance pervades accounts of events immediately leading up to her death. The play *Xuanting yuan* (*Tragedy at Xuanting*) depicts Qiu Jin as "fainting and crying" when Xu Xilin (1873–1907), a fellow revolutionary, was executed for his assassination of a Qing official. She remains overcome with grief until her own capture and sentence, thus evoking conventional stories of faithful widows "dying of passionate sorrow."[135] By casting Qiu Jin in such a familiar "widow-suicide model," such commemorative works controversially highlight her "transgressions," as Xu, after all, was not her husband. An excessively emotional Qiu Jin on stage weeping over another man's death smears the martyr's moral character so much so that her close friend and chief mourner Xu Zihua (1875–1935) felt the need to redress Qiu Jin's unconventional womanhood. In the epitaph Xu composed for a stele inscription (*mubiao*), a public monument for the martyr, Xu emphasizes that despite Qiu Jin's "careless" tendencies to "give free expression to her emotions," and her weakness for "wine and swords," she was in "true essence . . . exceptionally upright and prudent." "Although she loved freedom," Xu stresses, the heroine "never transgressed."[136]

In contrast to the dramatized pathos of wrongful death caused by a corrupt government, other male revolutionaries highlighted Qiu Jin's valiant "self-sacrifice," substituting the earlier feeling of wrongful death for the theme of "martyrdom for an explicitly nationalist cause" (*lie*).[137] This second wave of commemorative efforts thus recoded Qiu Jin as masculine, only to have what Hu calls its "laudatory masculinization" backfire to a reassertion of femininity by default. Uncomfortable with Qiu Jin's cross-dressing and aspirations toward swordsmanship, Zhang Binglin (1869–1936), for one, attributed her ultimately limited success as a revolutionary to her gender transgressions. She was too unfeminine in her embrace of public speech-making, Zhang suggested. This strand of criticism resurfaced in the May Fourth period with Lu Xun's description of Qiu Jin as being "clapped to death."[138] Here, the faulted emotion appears less to do with excessive sorrow and more with hubris. The woman becomes a bad role model for the Chinese nation once her feelings go awry. Undue distress prevents Qiu Jin from living up to the feminized "widow-suicide model"; too much pride distances her from the "honorary male."[139]

The gendered politics of Qiu Jin's martyrdom thus enforced the strong grip that early Chinese feminism had on the communication of women's feelings. Emotional transmissibility (*chuan*) is made possible by the many biographical (*zhuan*) accounts of Qiu Jin after her death, which are themselves not unrelated to the martyr's own promotion of exemplary women, both traditional and modern, during her lifetime.[140] To detect less grand effusions of feminine sentimentality, we have to look elsewhere in more intimate recollections of Qiu Jin where the biographical betrays, in its affective and technical registers, an "autobiographical reflexivity" and "self-memorizing" capability perceptible in her "Self-Inscription," discussed earlier.

In an informal memoir (*yishi*) of Qiu Jin published in *Xinwen bao* (*Daily News*) on July 24, 1907, Wu Zhiying (1868–1934) depicts a Qiu Jin who did not just die an unjust death, but led a misunderstood and tragically lyrical life. Inspired by a now lost photograph of Qiu Jin in a "sword-dance pose," and her numerous poems devoted to swords, Wu conjures an image of her friend performing a sword dance in Shanghai after her return from Japan about a year before her execution.[141] As Hu notes, Wu's wistful description of Qiu Jin's singing and dancing, as if a last solemn performance before her death, recapitulates the "lyrical ethos of 'The Biographies of Assassins'" by Sima Qian, in particular Jing Ke's singing before departing for his "doomed mission" to assassinate the king of Qin. Like Jing Ke, Qiu Jin died for her country, but more significantly, both embodied for posterity strains of "tragic lyricism, the ephemeral traces of a unique and spirited presence that disappeared too quickly."[142] By modeling Qiu Jin after the figure of the knight errant (*xia*) following her self-styled persona Swordswoman of Mirror Lake, Wu's personal memoir underscores a less glorious side to Qiu Jin: her propensity to being misunderstood, and therefore her loneliness, which punctuates her search for the perfect "soul mate" (*zhiyin*).

This motif of the inability to find one's confidante was pervasive in the wider "lyrical ethos" cultivated by the cult of feelings (*qing*) during the Ming dynasty.[143] Ideally, but rarely so, one finds one's match in marriage, and the failure to do so generates its own archetypical lament in poetry, opera, and fiction, often expressed by talented women literati frustrated by their marriages. Wu Zhiyin, in the same memoir, draws from this lyrical tradition to emphasize Qiu Jin's inability to find her *zhiyin* in her husband as the heroine's personal tragedy.[144] Wu's echo of the martyr's regret would be unremarkable if it were not for the fact that Qiu Jin, in a poem gifted to her later biographer, celebrated finding her perfect *zhiyin* in Wu herself.[145] The two friends first met in the spring of 1903 when Qiu Jin and her family leased an apartment from Wu's husband, Lian Quan.[146] Qiu Jin characterized her friendship with Wu as a "union through words," and compared this union with classic models of sworn brotherhood, as "intimate" as that which bound the legendary warriors of classical literature.[147] On February 22, 1904, Qiu Jin and Wu, despite political differences—Wu described herself as a "conservative"—became sworn sisters.[148]

By omitting this episode of sworn sisterhood in her informal biography, Wu Zhiyin amplifies Qiu Jin's solitude and failure to be understood by those around her. Moreover, Wu detaches the search for one's confidante from the pursuit of an ideal self advanced in late Qing biographies of exemplary women. Not only is the search for the perfect *zhiyin* by nature elusive, it also emphasizes the irony of composing a poem about the lack of true friends that is neverthe-less addressed to a valued friend.[149] The tragic lyricism that accompanies such a search, moreover, revives the "talented women" (*cainü*) sentimentality that Chinese feminists at the turn of the twentieth century had attempted to stifle. Instead, by reaffirming Qiu Jin's complaint that "My songs find no one to ac-company them"—which was "the ultimate lament for anyone brought up on the lyrical aesthetic of *zhiyin*"[150]—Wu's recollection makes legible again women's expunged "lyrical traces."[151] The ruminating, solitary Qiu Jin is remembered less for her overwhelming patriotism easily roused for ideological ends, and more for her tragic lyricism, which is now "useless" for the nation-state.

Elsewhere in a more formal memoir, Wu notes the popular press's over-enthusiastic promotion of Qiu Jin as a normative model. "Some compared [Qiu Jin] to Sofia [Perovskaia] and Madame Roland. She would answer [to such appellations] without much thought."[152] And yet, even Wu herself can-not help but compare the swordswoman with celebrated generals in the sixth-century work *Xiaoxuan*. If Qiu Jin's life was indeed exemplary *for* others, it was also *like* many others. For this reason, her biography's norma-tive exemplarity paradoxically underscores Qiu Jin's function as a "model" *tout court*: a reproducible representation. Such a "model" would resemble less the idiomatic role model, but more of a technical prototype from which subsequent models may emerge simply as one version or design within a se-ries without conscious, moralized emulation. A merely reproducible repre-sentation of Qiu Jin, a photograph or a biography for instance, does not need to—though it certainly can—muster feelings surrounding her death for a greater good. Counterintuitively, the more technical the model becomes, the less instrumentalized and normalized it may be.

I have shown how Qiu Jin's "Self-Inscription on a Photograph," through the hybridity of poetic and photographic media, eschews the conventional bio-graphical mode of feminine exemplarity for more technical and less morally prescriptive definitions of the female medium. Poetic form, by not imitating the photographic medium but by granting the latter only a partial, iconic lon-gevity (since a photograph also abides by the other definition of the index: its exhaustible, contingent deixis), allows *the* model or medium of exemplary fem-ininity to reemerge as merely *a* model, a type or version among many others.

142

To return to Wu's 1907 informal memoir of Qiu Jin, we witness a no less lyrical exchange between poetic and photographic form. A casual glance at the martyr's photograph on the wall, the surviving confidante explains, brings forth "acute pains" and immense "sorrow." It is unclear which image of Qiu Jin is being referred to by Wu—whether the photograph in question depicts her sworn sister in male dress, perhaps with a sword or a cane, or if it simply captured a less iconic Qiu Jin in everyday clothing as a late Qing woman literati. In all likelihood, Wu was viewing a lost image; more important is that its photographic imprint as indexical trace interacts with Wu's written elegy. Both the visual medium and the less perceptible emotions it inspires coalesce to constitute the writer's aesthetic process as she goes on to explain how her tears wet the ink stone, and she "writes out the couplet on a yard-long piece of cloth."[153] Emotional expression hastens the flowing of one inscriptive medium into another. Human and mechanical senses, too, meld with inscriptive surfaces: from the eye that sees to the camera aperture that allows in the light subsequently recorded on photographic film, and from the tear on Wu's skin forming a line akin to calligraphic strokes on cloth. Echoing the recursive indexicality between poetry and photography in Qiu Jin's "Self-Inscription," the durability of different media forms—that is, their mechanisms for the event-like characteristics of both memory and feeling—reconstructs the exemplary woman as little more than simply a reproducible representation of her former self. The interactions between poem and photography emphasize each medium's "autobiographical reflexivity" and "self-memorizing" capability. Rather than further glorify Qiu Jin as the model revolutionary, poet, or friend, the photograph on Wu's wall signifies, first and foremost, the dead's passing, an absence that was once a presence, as well as the reminder and physical imprint of her having been present.[154]

POSTSCRIPT ON AN INTERREGNUM

A study of pathos in the writing and reading of biographies still needs to be written. The dissemination (*chuan*) of an extraordinary life (*zhuan*), as David Wang observes of Shen Congwen's reading of Sima Qian's biographies, "came into existence as a result of the sedimentation of pain."[155] In Qiu Jin's "Self-Inscription," an ironic awareness of the meaninglessness of all modeling undercuts the poet and revolutionary's more famous valorizations of exemplary women elsewhere. Posthumous biographies of the martyr, in turn, reveal more about her mourners' obsessive, albeit conflicting, investments in notions of female exemplarity than any irreducible truths about

Qiu Jin's life itself. And it is with Wu's informal commemorations—at once more reflexive and less assuming—that Qiu Jin's elusive search for a soul mate breaks the cycles of feminine imitation and exemplarity. By the same token, when the female speaker of "Modern Parting" bemoans the passing of technologies alongside that of her departed lover, she moves away from a more conventional feminine lyricism to focus on the mechanisms of feelings, registering the poems' own sense of contemporaneity vis-à-vis new transportation networks, the telegraph, the telephone, and international travel. Huang Zunxian's reform of Chinese poetry may lack Qiu Jin's revolutionary fervor, but these two late Qing mediators find common ground when the mechanisms of feeling in their lyrical verses enliven the representation and self-representation of femininity.

When feelings of others swerve inward to reflect more on the self, which simultaneously prompt subjective feelings to reenter the external world of social relations and the technical media that help make them possible, what we have is none other than the unified meanings of *chuan*, to transmit, and *zhuan*, biography, in the single character 傳. The Chinese word's semantic doubleness allows for the reconstruction of feminine mechanisms of feeling, of women's feelings about themselves as well as their regard for older and newer inscriptive media, feelings which break out of the prescribed molds of women's biographies that serve to illustrate and admonish.

As emotions, feelings, and sentimentality—words that I have been using interchangeably when referring to the Chinese term *qing*—now come into sharper focus through their material carriers and specific historical contexts, they also converge, to a certain extent, under the study of affect. Yet while influential theories of affect over the past decade have predominantly emphasized the physiological, bodily impact of felt sensations that escape such sensations' correlation in words, I locate the signs of affect's communicability within narration instead of without. Affective dynamics, instead of being regarded as "intensities" that are entirely unhinged "from meaningful sequencing, from narration," as Brian Massumi has argued, operate between discursive representations of media (the semiotic or symbolic) and their physical forms (the visual or iconic).[156] Not unlike Rey Chow's search for "formal and cognitive ruptures" in sentimentality's "mood of endurance," the textual communication of technological form demands our interpretation.[157] Insofar as the mechanisms of feelings in "Modern Parting" and in writings by Qiu Jin and Wu Zhiying help communicate early twentieth-century gendered consciousness, lyricism ceases to operate apart from the technologies it represents, thereby emerging *as* lyrical media, simply put.[158]

144

Figurations of technology—that is, their poetic renditions—inform media's material structures or actual, physical existence; conversely, literal vehicles convey figurative and even lyrical connotations. Like Jia Baoyu's book cart transporting foreign books in chapter 2, the steamship carrying Liang's proclamation of a poetic revolution is literally poetry's medium.

It is no historical coincidence that Liang singles out Huang's "Modern Parting" as heralding the future of Chinese poetry, and yet, unexpectedly, the poems' focus on new ways of recording and communicating over long distances unmute late Qing nationalism's silencing of traditional feminine lyricism. Precisely because the exemplary woman is only one technical model among others, gender is more than simply one example or metaphor among other technologies of representation. That a literal or technical meaning can be more subversive than its figurative employment does not simply ring true for the verse, prose narratives, and photographs I examine in this chapter, but is one that guides the overall ethos of this book.

PART III
通 *TONG* | INTERCONNECTIVITY

1900 | INFRASTRUCTURAL EMERGENCIES OF TELEGRAPHIC PROPORTIONS

Heaven has no rain, the land is scorched dry, all because foreign devils have blocked the sky.... Lift the [railway] tracks, pull down the telegraph poles, let's all rush to wreck the steamships. —BOXER DOGGEREL

The situation will soon be dire. Please send an official telegram. I am pressured; we absolutely must wire (*bu de bu dian*). —SHENG XUANHUAI, TELEGRAM, JUNE 12, 1900

New communicative devices, as we saw in chapter 1 with Guo Songtao's vacillation between phonographic recordings and telephonic transmissions, are often lost in translation. At the same time, language can be effectively telegraphic in incorporating new foreign media into its vocabulary.[1] The noun *dian* 電 for electricity, like the English use of the verb "to wire," serves as a shorthand for the action of writing or sending telegrams. Hence someone like Sheng Xuanhuai (1844–1916), chief of the Imperial Telegraph Administration (ITA), could appeal for a telegraph edict at the height of the Boxer Rebellion (1900)—over a telegram, no less—with the terse imperative, "we absolutely must electrify" (*bude budian* 不得不電), or less literally in common English parlance, "we absolutely must wire" or "telegraph."[2]

The crisis of connectivity and blockage, which is the concern of this chapter, begins *in media res* in 1900. By 1899, the ITA, a commercial business under official supervision, had laid down a comprehensive telegraph network consisting of 50,478 kilometers of landline after three decades of intense disputes between Qing policymakers, villagers and local officials, and

4

foreign governments and merchants over whether China had any need for the new technology, and who ought to be in charge of it.[3] As early as the 1860s, rejections of telegraphy took the violent form of the dismantling of telegraph poles and attacks on engineers and workers, attributable to the lines' disruption of *fengshui* as much as to local officials' manipulation of such beliefs for their own negotiating purposes with the central government and foreigners.[4] If the destruction of telegraph lines in the second half of the nineteenth century in concert with other factors delayed the establishment of telegraphy, the same phenomenon that escalated during the Boxer Rebellion and the Siege of the Legations of 1900 did not stop communications but helped expedite it.

Neither a comprehensive study of the telegraph in China nor the Boxer Rebellion, this chapter examines novel and conflicting representations of interconnectivity or *tong* 通 in telegrams, letters, eyewitness reports, newspaper articles, and visual media leading up to and during the tumultuous events of 1900. Chapters 1 and 3 showed how the genres of the written record (*ji*) and biography (*zhuan*) grappled with new inscriptive devices and their impacts on textual reproduction, circulation, and temporal economies. My focus there was intermedial. In this chapter, I turn to a wider range of both Chinese, and now non-Chinese, textual genres and pictorial mediums that represented infrastructure breakdowns at a time when the telegraph promised to revolutionize connectivity. My inquiry here is thus both intermedial and transmedial. The telegraph, for all of its transformative impact on communication in late nineteenth and early twentieth-century China, was, as in many other places, expensive, inadequately maintained, inefficiently managed, and restricted to urban areas and official usage. Yet exactly how other media communicated Chinese telegraphy's technical limitations, which in turn illuminates complexities of interconnectivity between technologies, is less well understood.

Another way of foregrounding the telegraph as a transmedial phenomenon is to adapt and revise a media infrastructural approach. This more expansive view of media goes beyond the focus on relatively distinct techniques of recording (*ji*) and transmitting (*chuan*) in the previous chapters, and it anticipates Xu Nianci's imagination of an all-encompassing communicative medium and energy source, as I will discuss in chapter 5. As a burgeoning interdisciplinary field that views technology as a complex relational formation, media infrastructural studies delineates technical mediation as processes that span different macro and micro "scales," and takes into account the differences in labor and "affective relations," as well as environmental concerns across different geographical locations.[5] Thinking about media technologies as infrastructures rather than as individual devices and processes requires examining the unexpected and sometimes haphazard networks intersecting the telegraph and other forms of inscriptive media when the former stopped working during the height of the crisis of 1900. Existing scholarship on the telegraph in China has largely focused on issues of technological modernization, political sovereignty, language reforms, and civil participation related to the early history of the new technology, without also reflecting on where such issues were debated—that is, in print and other visual media—and also the fundamental entanglements between the technical context and nontechnical questions.[6]

Networks, moreover, are not entirely legible "under the sea, across lands, or 'in the cloud.'"[7] Insofar as print and photography represented the telegraph and in so doing produced textual and visual forms of the medium as well as its incommunicability, these various technologies mediated each other in ways that generated surprising meanings. Textual and visual significations of telegraphy express and make possible wired communications' promise of interconnectivity: telegram reprints, newspaper articles, photographs and lithographic renditions do not simply represent but also constitute the different material components of a robust telecommunicative network. Certainly, physical sites such as "data centers, mobile-telephone towers, and undersea cables" highlight "the unique materialities of media distribution."[8] But the contents of telegram reprints themselves, for instance, attest to the extent to which turn-of-the-century telecommunications depended on couriers and the postal system. Feelings about new technologies conveyed through these discursive significations, to continue the previous chapter's scrutiny of the mechanism of feelings, moreover, constitute media's "affective relations."

In what follows, I study writings and images of telegraph technology together with actual telegrams. Roland Wenzlhuemer, in his "micro-study" of the contents of a series of Bala railway (North Wales) telegrams, questions the dominance of a "structural perspective" in telegraph scholarship for its "almost exclusive focus on the structures and access patterns of local, regional, and global communication networks," which overlooks the actual content of telegrams except for some cursory nods to their "brevity and limitations."[9] Telegram messages, after all, are "short and poor on context," lack "literary quality," and when studies link them to larger historical events, "their significance seemed to rest more in the fact that they were sent at all."[10] Such a tendency to value structure over content in early telecommunications history is symptomatic of the more popular theoretical move in posthermeneutic, postcritical studies away from interpretation and toward the technical and situational conditions of meaning-making. Unlike Wenzlhuemer, I resist "leav[ing] the structural level" completely and focus solely on the hermeneutics of "the telegrams themselves."[11] Content, after all, both constrains and reconstitutes structure. Rather than isolate the structure of media forms—letters, newspapers, stereographs, and illustrations circulated or archived in print—from textual specificities and formal representation, this chapter observes meanings behind telegrams and writings about telegraphy and other intersecting technologies as equally important effects of the poles, wires, codes, translators, engineers, policy makers, and documents that constitute a telegraph network.

I share with critics of posthermeneutic research a healthy skepticism of "the reality of the material or the materiality of the real."[12] At the same time, there are what K. Ludwig Pfeiffer diagnoses as "underlying constraints whose technological, material, procedural, and performative potentials have been all too easily swallowed up by interpretational habits."[13] Therefore, in order to truly inhabit "the dimensions in between" "the cult(ure) of interpretation" and "reductive technologisms,"[14] we need to update Pfeiffer's evocation of the "in between" from a common figure of speech to a more rigorous—that is, immanently mediating—analysis that takes as its method of inquiry both the materiality and the textual and visual forms of media. The nineteenth-century Chinese telegraphic imagination was no stranger to the entanglements of the ineffable spirit and bodily matter; when actual telegrams passed through to print as public or circular telegrams (*gongdian* 公電 or *tongdian* 通電), moreover, spirit and matter conjoin materially in the form of print-and-electronic hybrids. Before the political crisis during the summer of 1900 put to test the first binary signaling system in China, the different circuits that separated the political from the media-technological and cultural systems were already beginning to fuse.

A ROMAN GOD WITH CHINESE WIRING

Nineteenth-century North American and European receptions of telegraphy were, as Hayles puts it, Janus-faced: Writers and users celebrated its spiritual quality of defying temporal and spatial bounds on the one hand, and cursed its "resistant materiality" of broken cables, defective conduits and poles, fragile glass insulators, and wonky wiring on the other.[15] Janus, the Roman god of beginnings and transitions, is famous for looking both to the future and to the past. One wonders, though, what he would see looking elsewhere to both "East" and "West." Certainly, no two histories of telegraphy could have the same two faces.

Chinese perceptions of the supernatural aspects of telegraphy were fused to the materiality of the medium in question. This is reflected in early names for the telegram in Chinese used before the term *dianbao*, imported from Japan, was popularized around 1880: *tongxian* 铜线 (bronze wire), *tiexian* 铁线 (metal wire), *dianqi xian* 电气线 or *dianxian* 电线 (electric wire, sometimes also translated as "lightning wire") variously emphasized the wire and its materiality.[16] Less frequently used variations such as *tongxian* 通线 (connecting wire) and *feixian* 飞线 (flying wire) conjured telegraphy's more abstract qualities of sending messages through space and connecting far-flung places in time. Electricity, after all, is invisible to the naked eye, but everyone can see telegraph lines. The Chinese, moreover, were especially apprehensive about the sight of poles and wires upsetting the harmonious balance of the landscape or *fengshui*, the geomantic principles that organized Chinese living spaces. Auspicious places are those containing *shengqi* (life breath), a key criterion for the choice of burial grounds since it is believed that an ancestor buried there will ensure good fortune for their descendants.[17] The idea that telegraph wires made for bad *fengshui* combined both metaphysical beliefs in the afterlife and ancestor worship with very physical concerns, as we can see in an 1875 memorial written by Chen Yi, a conservative official, in opposition to the introduction of telegraphy into China.

> the installing of lightning wires (*dianxian*) deep into the earth penetrates horizontally and vertically (*hengchong zhiguan*) and extends to all directions (*sitong bada*). With the pulse of the earth (*dimai*) stopping, and the wind and water entering, how could descendants (*zisun*) feel calmly about such an intrusion?[18]

Fengshui's role in delaying the introduction of telegraphy into China may be overstated. Many officials dismissed such ideas as "sheer nonsense" (*wuji zhitan*) and for "spreading devilish words and inciting the masses" (*yaoyan huzhong*). When Qing officials did support superstitious beliefs against the telegraph, they did so either as an "excuse for popular resistance" against foreigners' import of telegraphy or as a means to mobilize local masses when they failed to negotiate with foreign engineering companies.[19] More important and less discussed, however, is how this traditional belief system contributes an organicist dimension to the technology's Janus-like existence as "dematerialized information" on the one hand and "resistant bodies" on the other.[20] The telegraph's mysteries lie less in its annihilation of time and space "on Earth" and more in its underground "traffic," which anticipated later underground lines and submarine cables. Wires interfered with the notion

153

of the bloodline in Chinese ancestral worship; the awe it evoked came not from the notion of dematerialized information but the wires' running amok underground. Physical wires, Chen protested, clashed not with the spiritual soul (*hun*) but with its corporeal counterpart (*tipo*), which remained with the ancestor's corpse after death.[21] Others believed that electronic signals obstructed bodily functions: in many cases, residents complained to authorities how the telegraph poles caused unexpected illnesses and sudden deaths.[22] The telegraph's induction of one of the nineteenth century's most popular metaphors, the "social nervous system," and other bodily metaphors connecting the individual and society with the unseen forces of electricity—the focus of my next chapter—demonstrated, in the case of *fengshui*-related fears, a kind of organicism gone haywire.[23]

In light of the above, an 1867 article in the *New York Times*, which named Chinese superstitions rather than the country's landscape as the main obstacle to the laying of telegraph and railway lines, clearly did not know how *fengshui* worked.[24] Surely, it was tricky to fathom that the new media's spiritualism was rooted in such "earthly" matters, in wooden poles and electrical wiring. Yet this is precisely the kind of materiality that Hayles advances in *Writing Machines* and *My Mother Was a Computer*. Chinese spiritual beliefs in the telegraph emerged through, to borrow her words, "dynamic interactions between physical characteristics and signifying strategies," a product of both the "physical reality" of telegraph lines and burial grounds as well as "human intention."[25] As I will discuss later, popular imaginations of the telegraph's mystical-because-material properties would intensify during the Boxer Rebellion not because the movement encouraged superstition, which it certainly did, but, paradoxically, because it helped reinforce the telegraph's material infrastructure.

The Janus-faced metaphor of looking toward the past and the future turns out to be a spatial metaphor as well. As James Carey and others have clarified, the telegraph did not so much annihilate time and space as speculate on and distort them.[26] How such speculations of time and space played out in the telegraph's intimate relation with the press, however, warrants more study. Needless to say, I am not concerned with the customary delays that early telegraphed news experienced due to incomplete coverage.[27] Nor am I contesting the fact that with later extensions of the telegraph network, the latter, in tandem with modern newspapers, accelerated the rate at which news within China, especially that concerning official political information, traveled.[28] Instead, I ask what exactly was communicated when newspapers printed telegrams days *after* they were sent in the form known as public or circular telegrams (*gongdian* or *tongdian*)—that is, opinion pieces "sent to publicize specific positions, opinions, or statements on a particular issue by individuals, groups of people, organizations, or government organs."[29] If, to risk stating the obvious, all printed news exists *post festum*, there is in fact no difference between papers that publish a letter, edict, or any public announcement and those that reprint a telegram. What these published materials share in common is the shift from point-to-point or one-to-one communication (a letter or telegram, of course, can be addressed to, but not received by, multiple addressees at the same time) to a one-to-many model where there are no predesignated recipients and anyone can potentially read them.[30] The lack of difference *was* the point: when the press reprinted a telegraph message, it absorbed and abstracted from the technology its regimen of speed. Time was simply, in Carey's formulation, "an aspect of space, a continuation of space in another dimension."[31] In other words, the telegraph, after it changed medium and assumed another life as a public or circular telegram (*gongbao* or *tongbao*) in late nineteenth-century Chinese-language newspapers, emphasized spatial expansiveness and diasporic identity over temporal urgency.

The late Qing development of the public telegraph helped construct and was in turn shaped by overseas "Chinese" or Sinophone consciousness and their positions in the South Seas (*Nanyang*). According to Zhou, the first public telegram appeared in *Shenbao* on May 25, 1895, with a reprint of a telegram sent by the Taiwanese twelve days earlier on May 13 protesting the court's ceding of the island to Japan in the Treaty of Shimonoseki.[32] In this telegram, signed by "the whole people of Taiwan," the writers "abandoned by the court" with "nobody to rely on" declared their intention to "establish an island country, a country that will revere the emperor from afar and be a protective shield in the South Sea." The next day, *Shenbao* published telegraphic news of the establishment of the Republic of Taiwan received by Shanghai foreign newspapers. While *Shenbao* was unable to ascertain the validity of this news immediately, it only managed to affirm it on June 3 by printing another public telegram, again in the name of the Taiwanese people, declaring the island to be independent and not subject to Japanese rule. An editorial appeared on the same page that very day titled "On Adopting a Protracted Strategy to Defend Taiwan," which addressed the island as the "Republic of Taiwan," while printed on the next page was the text of the Treaty of Shimonoseki.[33] Given that nearly two months had lapsed since the signing of the hugely unpopular treaty on April 17, 1895, its publication on the same day as the telegram declaring Taiwan's independence served to justify, or at least provoke sympathy for, the Taiwanese people.[34]

155

Taiwan's short-lived sovereignty as an "island country" in Nanyang when it fell to Japan on October 21, 1895,[35] did not spell a break in its telegraph traffic with the mainland. Together with other overseas Chinese communities in Singapore and elsewhere, the Taiwanese made themselves heard through a series of circular telegrams protesting Empress Dowager Cixi's telegraph edict on January 24, 1900, instating Fujun, a member of the imperial family, as a foster son of the previous emperor, Emperor Tongzhi. Empress Cixi's announcement caused public uproar over the implication that Fujun would then replace Emperor Guangxu, who had lost his power after the failed One Hundred Days' Reform of 1898. On the very next day, Jing Yuanshan (1840–1903), chief (*zongban*) of the Shanghai Telegraph Administration, co-authored a joint telegram signed by 1,231 Shanghai elites appealing to the Ministry of Foreign Affairs (*Zongli yamen*) to petition the emperor not to step down. The telegram's statement of probable foreign intervention might have aided the petitioners' cause, but it was its wide circulation in newspapers, nationwide and beyond, that forced Cixi to reconsider her case. Befittingly, the cosigned telegram was celebrated as a "lightning remonstration, electrifying the world" (*feidian zujian diandong quanqiu*).[36]

On the front page of its first issue after the Chinese New Year, on February 9, 1900, the Singapore Chinese newspaper *Thien Nan Shin Pao* (1898–1905) compiled special telegrams from various countries pertaining to the attempted dethronement. As the article explained, local readers might have seen flyers related to the event, but they were mostly likely unfamiliar with the "emergency telegrams" (*jidian*) the newspaper had been receiving.[37] What followed was almost as informative about the global, not to mention unreliable, nature of telegraphic communication as it was about the order of events that transpired since the court's succession announcement on January 24. According to the report, *Thien Nan Shin Pao* received a special telegram from fellow Shanghai patriots (*tongbao zhongyi shi*) at one o'clock on January 26 conveying Empress Cixi's plan to designate Fujun as the next emperor. The telegram also urged overseas Chinese (*huaren*) in Nanyang and the Americas to telegraph Beijing opposing the dethronement. Notices, however, were also sent to individuals separately. Earlier that same morning, a merchant in Singapore had received an official telegram from Shanghai of six words; at twelve thirty in the afternoon, a telegram from Japan of eight words; and finally a telegram from Hong Kong stating that, as of January 25, Emperor Guangxu had already stepped down. Rumors confirming the dreaded news continued over the rest of the month, until a telegram received on February 2 finally denied the dethronement. Telegraphed statements of loyalty from different parts of the world convinced Cixi that Emperor Guangxu could not be replaced.

This transnational civic engagement reached its height in late January and February 1900, during which Empress Cixi was already backing off from her decision to appoint Fujun as heir.[38] It is therefore remarkable that two months later, on April 23, 1900, *Thien Nan Shin Pao* was still reprinting protest telegraphs from the Chinese in Kuala Lumpur, Hong Kong, San Francisco, New York, Honolulu, Thailand, Burma, and Japan.[39] Such reprints were clearly not aimed at being headline "news"; their belatedness nonetheless registered the geographical effect of public outcries. It mattered little that the protest telegraphs were printed after the fact; that the Qing court reversed its earlier decision to replace Guangxu evidenced the extent to which the newspaper successfully exploited the new technology to close the distance between Beijing and overseas Chinese, and helped consolidate a transnational identity. An article in *Thien Nan Shin Pao* on March 5, 1900, for example, reprinted a protest telegram sent by a group of Chinese merchants in Thailand after receiving news about Emperor Guangxu being poisoned. That the Thailand telegram was relatively late compared with those sent from the rest of Nanyang and the Americas did not prevent the paper from printing it anyway.[40]

If, according to a contemporary observer, Chinese-language newspapers were now comparable with the telegraph network for spreading ideas akin to "wild electrical currents,"[41] we must interrogate the very category of terms such as Chineseness, which presumably facilitates such rapid connectivity. The authors of the telegrams published in *Shenbao* who identified themselves as "the people of Taiwan" did not use racialized or ethnic terms as Chinese (*zhongguo ren* or *huaren*), while still proclaiming their political loyalty to the Qing dynasty. On the other hand, the writer of a February 9 report in *Thien Nan Shin Pao* referred to himself and his readers as "overseas Chinese" (*waiyang huaren*), bemoaning how the dethronement crisis gravely affected "our China" (*wo zhongguo*).[42] Chineseness, as Shu-mei Shih rightly points out, reveals the limits of the diaspora paradigm for excluding all other ethnicities, languages, and cultures from the category of ethnicity.[43] "Overseas Chinese," as employed in the Singapore newspaper's February 9 report, rallied behind a statist interest, and in so doing complemented the Han's internal hegemony within China that would be increasingly significant after the fall of the Manchu state. And yet the Taiwanese authors' identification as Taiwanese cited earlier shows that, historically, the late Qing project of a unified state did not have to leverage upon an ethnic or racial identification. Consequently, the diasporic paradigm, which Shih targets for its racist misrecognition, can variedly function.

157

The events of the Boxer Rebellion later in the same year would eclipse Empress Dowager Cixi's attempted appointment of Fujun as heir to Emperor Tongzhi, also known as the *Jihai jianchu* in historical memory. The less remembered event, however, played a role in the second. According to Zhou, Empress Cixi and her faction in court became more distrustful of foreigners due to their alleged interference, and Fujun's father Zaiqi, who came close to seeing his son become the next emperor, was an outspoken supporter of the Boxers.[44] Both *Jihai jianchu* and the Boxer uprising, moreover, stood out as transnational media events. The earlier crisis connected overseas Chinese elites to their reform-minded compatriots elsewhere over jointly signed public or circular telegrams in newspapers. The subsequent upheaval was so well documented in narratives that circulated beyond China that the British adventurer and writer Peter Fleming dubbed the event as "part of the iron rations of general knowledge that everyone carries in his head."[45] This section momentarily moves away from telegraphy to examine several foreign visual representations of immobility, which helped sketch a vivid picture of the telegraphic imagination on the eve of its breakdown.

International press coverage of the Boxer Rebellion was extraordinarily rapid and widespread. Chinese scholar Yiqian Wang-Fan counts articles concerning the event in sixty-six Chinese language and eighty-one non-Chinese language newspapers worldwide.[46] These reports were quickly accompanied by an immense material and discursive network made up of missionary narratives, architectural memorials, adventure stories for boys in English, organizations for foreign legation veterans, the development of Boxer tourism, and German figurines, mechanical toys, and military tin miniatures.[47] Such networks, James L. Hevia argues, not only archived the crisis and spread Allied propaganda, but also instructed the world on the necessary punishment and reeducation of imperial subjects.[48] New mimetic devices such as the camera, in conjunction with print technology, made photography "ubiquitous" in and outside China.[49] Cinematic reconstructions of the uprising in England, the United States, and Japan were presented, all within the year of its occurrence, to their respective home audiences as authentic footage.[50] The Boxer Rebellion, in short, aided the making of transnational media history.

Thanks to the 1900 uprising in China, the global informational infrastructure, rather than simply convey images and texts about the event, increasingly became a subject matter in its own right. To put it slightly differently, because it was difficult to obtain accurate information about the

Boxer upheavals, any media coverage inevitably drew attention to its own communicative process. Moreover, because we can neither ignore nor take for granted the sustained reciprocity between infrastructural materiality and representative meaning, both of which undergird the network of print and nonprint media, we have to theorize and complicate their interdependence. And such work requires the analysis of both written texts as well as visual materials, lest one kind of historical document is reified at the expense of another. Similarly, Hevia challenges the receptive "precedence and ontological priority" given to the image isolated from its production process, and claims instead that we give equal attention to both human and nonhuman actants that make up the photography complex.[51] Extending Latour's actor-network theory, Hevia includes the camera, optics theory, negatives, chemicals, the technologies that reproduce the photographs in print, the archive, and light itself as intricate agents in the construction of the photographic real. This is not to say that the photographers themselves and what they photograph are unimportant, but simply that we cannot ignore "the transportation and communication networks along which all of these parts travel, and the production and distribution networks that link faraway places to end-users."[52]

In fact, one such "photography complex" to emerge from the Boxer Rebellion was made possible because of and not despite the breakdown in transportation and communication networks, which impeded the journey of a photographer and in so doing became his vital subject matter. On May 29, 1900, the American traveling photographer and war correspondent James Ricalton (1844–1929) was sent by his employer, Underwood & Underwood, from Shanghai northward to the Dagu forts to cover the intense fighting between the Qing court, in alliance with the Boxers, and the Allied fleet.[53] Before departing from Shanghai, Ricalton wrote of how Boxers attacked the railway and telegraph lines near Beijing and isolated the capital from Tianjin and the "outside world." The first image in his travelogue captured the sense of impending war, and attempts at escape (see figure 4.1). A bare-chested Chinese man stands alert in one of the several sampans stationed at Zhifu (Chefo), while his passengers, mostly missionary families in sun-hats and umbrellas await with children in tow. It is unclear whether the passengers are alighting or embarking. As Ricalton explains, "many of the Europeans kept sampans in readiness" so that in case of a surprise attack, they could "make for the warships" stationed at Dagu, two hundred miles away.[54] Ricalton and other correspondents seemed to have worse luck trying to obtain passage to the front. The Chinese wooden boat must have been in high demand. In his words, "Every one sought information, but could find none;

(44) Missionary Refugees fleeing from the "Boxers"—landing at Chefoo, China. Copyright 1901 by Underwood & Underwood.

4.1 Missionary refugees fleeing the Boxers, landing at Chefoo, China, 1901. Source: James Ricalton, Underwood & Underwood. Purchased 1999 with New Zealand Lottery Grants Board funds. Te Papa (O.040969).

there was a perplexing mystery about all movements, and mystery always increases apprehension."[55]

When he did finally get to Dagu on July 4, Ricalton witnessed the aftermath of Chinese gunners' attack on the harbor (see figure 4.2). His stereograph shows the defeated USS *Monocacy*, with the Stars and Stripes on its masthead. The warship was only one of many other "crippled ships," we are told, "strung along the river in different stages of convalescence," functioning as temporary refuge for refugees from Tianjin.[56] Outside Dagu, Ricalton found all railway communication severed; only after persuading the locals was he able to depart for Tianjin on a tugboat.

With the help of extensive commentaries accompanying his stereographs, we can uncover the neglected and silent "actant" in Ricalton's photography complex: the transportation and communication networks of 1900. Stereographic technology provides viewers with an exaggerated illusion of depth via side-by-side double images viewed through a stereoscope. Ricalton's collection of one hundred stereographs, originally published as *China through the Stereoscope* in 1901, with maps, diagrams, guidebooks, and viewing apparatus, was marketed as part of Underwood & Underwood's popular "virtual tours" to exotic locations.[57] Together, images and texts "offered up the world

160

4.2 "USS Monocacy, at the landing with a hole through her bow made by a Chinese shell, during the burning of Tongku, China, circa June 1900." Photo printed on a stereograph card, copyrighted in 1901 by Underwood & Underwood. Source: Commander Donald J. Robinson, USN(MSC), 1982 US Naval History and Heritage Command Photograph.

in a kind of hyperreal mode of presentation" through "an active and interactive experience."[58] Even the thread that brought Ricalton to China makes for an interesting "material metaphor."[59] Ricalton was originally a schoolmaster from New Jersey whom Thomas Edison sent to India, the Malay Peninsula, China, and Japan in search of a filament fiber most suited for the early incandescent lamp. However, his employment with Edison ended in 1899 when the inventor found that cellulose and subsequently tungsten burned much better than bamboo.[60] This early termination launched Ricalton's two-decade journey as a traveling photographer and war correspondent with

161

Underwood & Underwood; and the latter by 1891 was producing nearly 25,000 stereographs daily.

The combination of text, stereographs, and maps in *China through the Stereoscope* transported contemporary viewers outside China to scenes that often feature mobility as their elusive subject. As Rosalind Krauss's study of stereography's reality effect shows, the stereograph viewer could not, paradoxically, test the image's reality since any movement through the scene is denied.[61] But prior to the viewer's experience, to stay within the photographic form itself, many of the historical actants—the trains, ships, passengers, and the photographer himself—that appeared in Ricalton's account were similarly immobile within the frames, having been included there by virtue of their lack of movement. Here, I introduce Ricalton's text-image relation into Hevia's assembling of human and nonhuman parts in the photography complex. One of the first stereographs Ricalton made upon his arrival in Tianjin was of bodies of dead Chinese floating in the Pei-Ho river along with debris of a shelled bund foregrounding semi-derelict Western-style buildings. According to the accompanying text, even though the stereograph only revealed "four or five" corpses, the photographer had witnessed, on other occasions, larger numbers of dead bodies including more gruesome details of severed body parts.[62] Even the bombed buildings in the photograph were not as scarred as the ones he saw elsewhere along the same bund. So why did Ricalton feature a toned-down version of what he saw? This is what the photographer had to say:

> A hundred sights in Tien-tsin [Tianjin] alone would give you a fuller conception, but even the greatest number could not tell you all. It is impossible to picture the apprehension of faces on the street—the roar of bursting shells and deadly smaller missiles that filled the air. Subterranean housekeepers cannot be "sculptured by the sun" nor can pale, fear-stricken faces peering out of cellar windows; nor the measured tread of soldiers at all hours of day and night; nor the thrilling bugle-calls in every direction. Just across the way, too, is a full hospital, and the stillness about it is solemn and awe-inspiring. These things cannot be portrayed by any cunning of the camera. The number of troops is daily increasing. The transportation of commissary stores for all the different troops fills the streets with every form of nondescript conveyance—army wagons, carts, "rikishas," wheelbarrows, pole-coolies, confiscated carriages.[63]

What Ricalton did not photograph, namely the "apprehension of faces" and "the roar of bursting shells and deadly smaller missiles" and so forth, he

162

nonetheless fully described in his text. In her essay on Ricalton and other American photographers of the Boxer Rebellion, Jane Elliott rejects Allied sympathies and the technical incompetence of the camera as reasons for Ricalton's withholding of visual evidence.[64] Instead, she attributes his hesitance to a universal, humanist "dilemma": "no less than that of war itself."[65] While alluring, this ascription of a modernist sentiment toward the "shattering experience" of death and destruction explains little of why Ricalton's sense of photography's "impotence" did not carry over to his writing. What "any cunning of the camera" cannot capture, Ricalton spent quite a few sentences elaborating. As Elliott does not fail to point out, this was the same man who also wrote that "Photography is merciful and does not portray the blood-smeared garments and the blood clots on the ground where the wounded have lain overnight."[66] Indeed, why spare one medium and not the other from the ineffable blood, smeared or clotted?

A plausible response is to foreground the material circumstances that undergird this apparently existential dilemma. The fact that the graphic details in Ricalton's text do *not* appear in his photographs fully captures the peculiar coexistence of traffic and immobility central to the crisis of 1900. The Tianjin in Ricalton's description quoted above bustles with both action and inertia: the soldiering mass marches with "measure"; the hospital works at full capacity, and yet appears absolutely "still." In emphasizing the "nondescript" nature of the "conveyances"—the wagons, carts, and rickshaws—which have escaped the "cunning of the camera" (but not his pen), Ricalton shows how nothing that moves, not even the most rudimentary form of vehicle, would be left idle in a disaster of this proportion.[67] There was then in Tianjin little difference between a carriage or a wheelbarrow: when the conveyance of military provisions was consistently interrupted, more and less reliable forms of transportation became equally "nondescript" in writing. Since text and photography corroborate each other in *China through the Stereoscope*, that one fails where the other succeeds rather faithfully communicates the juxtaposition of movement and blockage, a juxtaposition essential to what Hevia underscores as photography's "production process."[68] For the very formal disjuncture between texts and images—the interruption of conveyance on a discursive, significatory level—replicates the photographer's physical experience of abeyance. If the episode of the book cart in *New Story of the Stone* analyzed in chapter 2 signals how writing always calls for another vehicle or medium, Ricalton's observation highlights how language and meaning cannot fully rely on photography precisely when what moves *and* fails to move lie at the heart of the matter. This is not to say, however,

4.3 "Old Teintsin showing terrible destruction caused by bombardment and fire, 1900, China." Source: James Ricalton, Underwood & Underwood. Purchased 1999 with New Zealand Lottery Grants Board funds. Te Papa (O.041002).

that visuality therefore took a backseat: the respective technical languages unique to each medium communicate at the point where the two mediums precisely fail to connect.

In light of the above interpretation, the photographer's diary fully encapsulates the paradoxical drama of interconnectivity (*tong*) in the Boxer Rebellion of 1900. By exposing this tension between text and image, Ricalton's diary more than accessorizes Underwood & Underwood's commercial product—namely, the stereograph and all of its accompanying gadgets. Yet the individual stereographs too rise to the occasion by instantiating the gap between foreground and background. Both Sarah E. Fraser and Andrew F. Jones have analyzed Ricalton's foregrounding of Chinese figures who, as racialized "specimens" of the "menacing 'yellow poor,'" help to mark the background setting as Chinese and alien.[69] I join these criticisms of foregrounded racialism by turning my attention to Ricalton's photographed backgrounds, beginning with that which is perhaps most perfectly synonymous with background: infrastructure. Ruined and deserted cities, burned city walls and gates, empty palaces, and panoramic views of broken rooftops featured in Ricalton's works, and many other stereographs and photographs of the time archive the pained movement of people and things. Another of

164

Ricalton's stereographs exposes a deserted and badly burned Tianjin with three desolate figures (figure 4.3). We learn, again from his written observation, that only a day after Ricalton took the stereograph, "a slow-moving line of homeless, weeping human beings" crowded the same thoroughfare.[70]

By photographing an empty city and supplementing this image with his account of the "homeless, starving" Chinese, Ricalton allows for the visual to convey more neutral moments of stillness, and language the more problematic pathos of movement. To grasp the communication crisis of 1900 means grasping the indissociability of information from movement. "Every one sought information, but could find none; there was a perplexing mystery about all movements, and mystery always increases apprehension."[71] Does this lack of information about movement have something to do with the "inscrutable Chinese"? Certainly so, if even the physical infrastructure through which information travels can appear politically and racially charged. In the foreground of another image, a ragged-looking Chinese woman holding a child stands facing Ricalton's camera (figure 4.4). Behind her, in the middle ground, Ricalton's Chinese porter poses next to a semi-destroyed telegraph pole. His shadow parallels the left-leaning pole; in contrast, the woman's shadow slants forty-five degrees to the right. Aside from narrow depressions in the road and shelled buildings in the background, the thoroughfare is, thanks to the Eight-Nation Alliance's, and not the Boxers', retaliations, "macadamized and sewered."[72] The accompanying text explains that prior to the cleanup, explosions had blown up this corner of the French legation, causing numerous casualties. Stereographers, according to Jones, composed their images around "a vertical marker in foreground or middle-ground," usually a human figure, who "works to center the space, forming a representation within the visual field of the eyes' convergence at a vanishing point."[73] Here, it is the half-standing telegraph pole in visual juxtaposition to the two standing Chinese figures and their shadows that gathers the visual field, reminding us that it took both sides of the conflict to image the infrastructural breakdown.[74]

Whereas Jay Bolter and Richard Grusin's influential analysis of remediation focuses on newer and older media,[75] I show that the contemporaneous advances in print, photography, telegraphy, and the railway remediate between technology, cultural essence and national identity.[76] Images of broken telegraph and railway lines are not uncommon in Chinese and international illustrations of the Boxer Rebellion. When the Boxers' destruction of infrastructure was seen as, in Paul A. Cohen's description, "Luddite-like attacks" on Western-style modernity and its conveniences, such visual representations

4.4 "Ruins of the French Legation, Peking." Source: James Ricalton, *James Ricalton's Photographs of China during the Boxer Rebellion*, plate lix.

inevitably perpetuated the image of backwardness, ignorance, and violence.[77] The illustration "Les Boxers" in the "Evénements de Chine" series of *Supplément illustré du Petit Journal* depicts a group of Chinese civilians, presumably Boxers, threatening another Chinese, most likely a Christian convert, with knives and bayonets (figure 4.5). Two Westerners lay trampled on the ground along a railway line. The middle ground of the illustration depicts a Boxer near the top of a telegraph line tugging at its wires with bare hands. Burning buildings flank the right and background of the colored lithograph. The telegraph-hating Boxer, elevated to a height, emerges as menacing as his fellow Christian-bashing pagans.

CHAPTER FOUR

4.5 "Les Boxers" in the "Evénements de Chine" series of *Supplément Illustré du Petit Journal*, no. 501, June 24, 1900. Source: gallica. bnf.fr/BnF.

Another lithograph in the *Illustrated London News* depicts British officials and Sikh soldiers looking onto collapsed trains on a severely destroyed railway line leading to a derelict city gate in the picture's background (figure 4.6). The direction that the wrecked trains point to suggests that they were heading for the gate, which is marked by what appears to be a foreign legation's flag. Boxers are absent. Their presence by virtue of their destructive act, however, amplifies the extent to which they have disconnected the foreign settlement from the outside world.

The destruction of railway lines by the Boxers can be found in Chinese sources too. In Li Di's *Quan huo ji*, circa 1905, rebels dressed in uniforms inscribed with the characters *Yihe tuan*, "Boxers United in Righteousness," dismantle a railway with pickaxes (figure 4.7).[78] In the background, a Boxer pulls at a telegraph line, its falling position almost perpendicular to the

167

4.6 "The Crisis in China." *Illustrated London News*, November 24, 1900, 762+. Source: *Illustrated London News* Historical Archive, 1842–2003.

4.7 "Quanfei chai tielu" [Boxers destroying railway]. Source: Li Di, *Quan huo ji*, preface dated 1905.

horizontal railroad. Given the absence of foreigners and expressions of menace on the figures, the Boxers' raised arms and collaborative effort, funnily enough, almost made them appear, if the viewer lacks the historical and linguistic knowledge, to be workers assembling the tracks.

These images go beyond typical observations about the destructiveness of the Boxer Rebellion. Nor are they intended to encourage their viewers here to take a side on either Chinese or foreign historical accounts of the contentious upheaval in 1900. As visual representations of technological media, they extend—without jettisoning—the framework of political and social critique to highlight the visual forms of media relations, made possible by both the technical conditions of photography or print and the discursive representations of the technologies. One of Carey's most significant insights into telegraphy was how it effectively separated communication from transportation.[79] Ricalton's stereographs with their accompanying texts as well as the printed illustrations in European and Chinese sources reveal that infrastructural breakdowns and fears of immobility recoupled *both* communication and transportation, not to mention communication *about* transportation. This is how media infrastructure, Susan Star argues, becomes visible upon breakdown.[80] Operating at multiple levels and scales, infrastructure intersects with other industrial, physical, organizational, and belief and cultural systems.[81] Any one malfunction highlights the relational nature of infrastructure not because everything then starts to break down, but rather because some aspect of communication, including discursive representations, continues to function, at times even more effectively, through both existing and emergent technologies.

Despite the impact that the *Jihai jianchu* had on the court's actions during the Boxer Rebellion, the two watershed events of 1900 reflect different aspects of interconnectivity that guide this chapter: whereas the earlier crisis connected overseas Chinese elites to their reform-minded compatriots overseas over jointly signed public or circular telegrams in newspapers, the events of the summer of 1900 rigorously challenged different media's representation of communicative failures. Rather than simply acknowledge how photography, travel writing, and print illustrations constitute part of the media infrastructure around the Boxer Rebellion, it would be more productive to assert that the upheaval helped bring to light these various mediums' self-representation. What a stereograph, a piece of travel writing, or a printed illustration is able to variously foreground or downplay depends on its technical specificities—that is, its material form. At the same time, infrastructure also informs, often as an in-*form*-structure that retraces ethnocentric lines.

Like the February 9 compilation of telegrams situating the Empress Dowager Cixi's attempt to dethrone Guangxu *in situ*, a June 15 article in *Thien Nan Shin Pao* pointedly situated the Boxer Rebellion as a "Crisis in Beijing" (*Beijing bianluan*).[82] This time, however, the telegrams that the Singapore paper received from readers specifically expressed anxieties over the movement of people and information. These telegrams asked questions ranging from "How could foreign troops get to China so quickly?" to "Why did the military in Beijing and Tianjin not block the Boxers coming from the North?" and "Why is there no news from Beijing and Tianjin at all?" Such queries echo Ricalton's exasperation, worth citing again: "Every one sought information, but could find none; there was a perplexing mystery about all movements, and mystery always increases apprehension."[83] Yet when we consider information as intertwined with movement, and blockage as requisite for interconnectivity, these questions—themselves having traversed between photography, telegraphy, and print—appear somewhat less mysterious.

COMMUNICATION'S MANY-HEADED DRAMA

This chapter has so far traced the communications crisis during the Boxer Rebellion from the material-spiritual topographies of the telegraphic imagination prior to the summer of 1900 to the American photographer James Ricalton's, and others', visual depictions of movement and immobility. The constant interplay between different physical infrastructures and their cultural significations reveals the materiality of media forms *in* the discursive afterlives of communicative technologies in texts and images. Such an understanding of mediation through the interface of technology and culture has no doubt a theoretical or epistemic thrust. Yet media theory here, as it is practiced throughout this book, does not leave untouched the historical context in which it is grounded. To truly grasp the conceptual key term *interconnectivity* (*tong*) that unites this chapter and the next means viewing the 1900 crisis in terms of both connectivity and blockage. Maintaining such tensions between materiality and meaning, history and theory, this section returns to the protagonists with which I opened the chapter: the Boxers and the Qing officials, who were caught between their warring compatriots, the equally vexed foreigners, and their frantic telegrams.

Those hostile to the Boxer movement called them "Boxer bandits" (*quanfei*); sympathizers preferred "Boxers United in Righteousness" (*Yihe tuan*). Their anti-foreign, anti-Christian aggressions initially targeted missionaries, Chinese converts, and churches, until, in late May 1900, the Boxers turned to the destruction of railway and telegraph lines.[84] However, as they spread southward from northwestern Shandong toward the capital, they did not just leave behind wrecked communications infrastructure. Boxer notices, announcements, and proclamations posted publicly or passed around by hand began wide circulation from early 1900 onward as a counter-medium. Like the one quoted at the beginning of this chapter, such notices often blamed the drought and famine that hit north China after the winter of 1898–1899 on "foreign devils," their religion, architecture, and technologies. At the same time, these messages, often written in doggerel or jingles for easy memorization and oral circulation, offered their readers a clear course of remedy, or what historian Paul A. Cohen calls "a full-blown religious structuring" of drought, unemployment, and economic crisis brought about, ironically, by the development of the railway and telegraph industries.[85]

It becomes tricky at times to fathom whether communication was the cause, effect, or the very content of the 1900 crisis. Boxer followers were to pit direct communication with gods via bodily possession against the foreigners' railway tracks, telegraph poles, and steamships. Moreover, the notices themselves, as chain letters, claimed the magical power of multiplication. As one broadside circulating in late spring 1900 in Beijing warned, "pass on one copy [of this notice] and avert calamity to one family; pass on ten copies and avert disaster to a whole area. If you read [the notice] and don't disseminate its contents, calamity will surely strike you."[86]

The Boxer Rebellion was and continues to be many things. Commentators situate its historical significance on a diverse spectrum, from being mocked as the "last feeble challenge of traditionalism" (Harold Issacs and G. G. H. Dunstheimer) to being hailed as a patriotic, anti-imperialist watershed in Chinese revolutionary history (Li Shiyu and Zhou Enlai).[87] Both positions go "fairly far," Cohen claims, "in the direction of mythologizing the Boxer experience."[88] Precisely so: neither position grasps the historic uprising as a communicative disaster, one that nonetheless advances a notion of "media" before the term as it is commonly understood gained popular usage in either English or Chinese. Insofar as the Boxers' "streamlined, easy-to-master possession ritual" was a most effective form of "religious communication in undermining authority,"[89] certainly some precepts of authority they helped to challenge included how people read and received messages, who may be believed, and what constituted religious or spiritual and technical communication in the first place.

Earlier, I suggested how *fengshui*-related fears about the telegraph since its introduction into China in the 1860s encouraged a materialist rethinking

171

of the new medium's spiritual qualities. Here, I argue that the Boxers' magic and invulnerability rituals intensified the codependency between religious significance and the materialities of communication, so much so that this late Qing episode urgently rethinks what it is that media do—namely, mediate. Consequently, this "Chinese" context more than passively augments Bernard Dionysius Geoghegan's reconstruction of North American Spiritualism in the second half of the nineteenth century, which in itself disputes culture's supplementary role to understanding existing communicative technology. Previous studies of Spiritualism have characterized the movement as a "cultural interpretation or 'fiction' for reflecting on the period's dominant information and communication technologies (electricity, telegraphy, photography)," and in doing so reaffirmed the strict separation between a "durable media-technical base and its supposed cultural reception or interpretation."[90] What happens instead, Geoghegan asks, if we grasp Spiritualism not as "a fiction for thinking about media" but a "technology in its own right" with its "bricolage" of diverse techniques?[91] It would then be possible to view the movement's encounter with "the incomplete and partial features of communication—its gaps and its delays" in terms of the infrastructural uncanny, defined as "a range of unsettling phenomena that tend to emerge in periods of rapid expansion in the means of technological conveyance."[92]

I will leave the question of historical influence—specifically, the impact on Chinese writers and intellectuals of Spiritualism's cousin, the New Thought movement—for the next chapter. My elicitation of Spiritualism here mobilizes a comparative heuristics with which to grasp the Chinese movement as more than a historical case study corroborating theories of media developed elsewhere.[93] Like Geoghegan, I understand the Boxers' techniques—their notices and placards, communication between the physical and supernatural worlds, invulnerability rituals, possession by fighting deities such as Sun Wukong (the Monkey King) or historical figures such as Liu Bei and Zhang Fei, rhymed incantations during combat, and powerful incendiary techniques—as technologies in their own right. Unlike the study of Spiritualism, however, the turmoil in China in 1900 adds a complicated dimension insofar as Boxer technologies resisted so-called bona fide technologies associated with modern science and Western innovations.[94] Eyewitnesses reported that Boxers managed to avoid burning down non-Christian Chinese people's homes when targeting the nearby homes, shops, and churches of Christians.[95] When they destroyed the section of the Beijing-Baoding railway running from Liulihe to the capital on May 28, they only had to point sticks of sorghum (*gaoliang*) at the tracks while chanting "burn, burn," for

172

the tracks to catch on fire. According to another first-person account, a senior Boxer (*dashixiong*) simply had to face the sea and chant with his finger pointing, and he would immobilize an incoming steamship carrying foreign troops. The Red Lanterns (*Hongdengzhao*), a sect of adolescent females associated with the Boxers, were also known for "flying and controlling the strength and direction of the wind."[96]

It is not adequate to simply supply such accounts of magic with the ethnographic seriousness they rightly deserve. Instead, that Boxers' magic complements to "the 'world-shrinking' magic implicit in the telegraph, powerful weaponry, and steamships of the foreigners,"[97] exposes the summer of 1900 in all of its mediatized glory. Abundant literature has documented the shock, unease, and sheer awe that accompanied the arrival of railways in nineteenth-century Europe and North America.[98] A sense of the infrastructural uncanny occurs, after all, not just when a technology fails to work but also when it works *too* well. The Boxers' infrastructural destructions inadvertently exposed the uncanniness inherent in the accelerated movements of information and bodies, which in turn betrayed the sense of righteousness, not to mention the national and geographic boundaries to which believers and enemies of the movement appealed. This is exactly what Arthur H. Smith, the American missionary, recorded in his account of the crisis. He observed with astonishment that a London evening newspaper announced on June 16 "the murder [in Beijing] of the German minister" Baron Clemens von Ketteler "four days before the event" actually occurred on June 20.[99] Given that Smith dedicated many of his entries immediately preceding this one to accounts of wrecked lines disconnecting Beijing with the rest of the world, and the foreigners' increasing sense of isolation, a piece of telegraphed "news"—or more accurately, prognosis—occurring *before* the event itself must be nothing short of fantastic.

The Hydra in Greek and Roman mythology, with which Joseph E. Esherick and Cohen compare the Boxer's ability to magically multiply and reproduce itself,[100] therefore makes for an equally powerful symbol of China's contesting and heterogeneous media network. On May 27, the Beijing-Baoding line ceased to function. Around two weeks later, on June 13, the Beijing-Tianjin line was cut, along with Beijing's connection to Manchuria to the north and Shanghai to the south.[101] Only a day earlier, on June 12, Sheng Xuanhuai wired Liu Kunyi (1830–1902) and Zhang Zhidong (1837–1909), instructing them to telegraph the court and request the return of Li Hongzhang to Zhili 173 province to help quell the Boxers. The urgency of his demand to "absolutely wire" (*bu de bu dian*) serves as one of the two epigraphs of this chapter; the

Boxers' imperative, naturally, contributes to the second. Over the next two days, the Boxers destroyed the Tianjin-Jinan line and China's link to Russia. Lines along the borders between Shanxi, Kaifeng (Henan), and Shandong, and routes running between Baoding and Tianjin to the east, were disconnected. Sheng's message captures this desperate state of affairs while suggesting ways to mitigate it. "The Beijing-Tianjin lines may be broken," Sheng advised, but they could still send telegrams to the Tianjin office as long as the "North-South lines" still worked.[102]

In his position as chief officer of the ITA in Shanghai, Sheng, along with other provincial officials, served as a conduit between the Qing court, regional governors such as Liu and Zhang, and foreign ministers. Their "transfer telegrams" (*zhuandian*) could still pass through functioning lines connecting Beijing, Dagu, and Shanghai, supplemented by mounted express couriers, whose practice of relaying telegraphic court letters from the Forbidden City to the Ministry of Foreign Affairs and other parts of China was in place before 1900.[103] The specific "transfer network" managed by the Ministry of War redirected telegrams from Beijing via two stations in Zhili (Baoding and Shanhaiguan) and one in Shandong (Jinan), though this was restricted to only the most important messages.[104]

On June 21, Empress Cixi declared war on all foreign powers.[105] Sheng immediately ordered local telegraph branches to ensure the transfer of the edict to its designated recipients and not leak the news to the public, especially to newspapers. On June 24, Sheng telegraphed Li Hongzhang, Liu Kunyi, and Zhang Zhidong, proposing the "Mutual Protection of the Southeast" (*dongnan hubao*) scheme, an informal pact with foreign consuls in Shanghai who, in return for the governors' protection of foreign lives and property, agreed not to send troops into southeast China. Prior to the declaration of war, these powerful southern governors had acted as a de facto foreign ministry and used the still-functioning network outside north China for lateral communications, thus bypassing the central seat of power.[106] Each side, even foreigners who insisted on communications access, exploited the breakdown of infrastructure to its benefit: Allied troops seized control of three major railway stations between Tianjin and the Dagu forts, and in the process cut telegraph lines preventing the court from monitoring Allied naval activities "in real time." Qing officials posted in Tianjin, already isolated from Beijing, were now unable to contact Manchuria. Unfortunately, this meant that foreigners in north China were cut off from their contacts in the south as well.

174   Sheng's collection of telegrams, letters, and newspaper reports made possible by China's hybrid courier-telegram network functioned as both an

"information-collecting device" and media infrastructure.[107] An analysis of the content of these exchanges reveals an image of Sheng different from typical accounts emphasizing his masterful choreography of the "Mutual Protection of the Southeast" scheme. On one level, we can detect Sheng's lack of confidence and imperfect knowledge of the situation because his messages meaningfully communicate what broken wires and half-destroyed telegraph poles cannot. This is what Marvin means when she claims that "the early history of electric media" rests on "negotiating issues crucial to the conduct of social life."[108] Yet whereas Marvin downplays "the evolution of technical efficiencies in communication" so as to prioritize the "drama" over the "instrument,"[109] I underscore moments when much of the "drama" revolves precisely around the "instrument." The content of "transfer telegrams" received and sent under Sheng's charge makes legible the technical processes and material structures of this telegraphy and express-courier network, which in turn shapes "who is inside and outside, who may speak, who may not" and "who has authority and may be believed."[110] This is how we grasp mediation as that which determines the valences between the "instrument" and its "drama" in their full complexity.

At the earlier stages of the crisis, telegrams, letters, and excerpted news in Sheng's files mainly tracked missing foreigners. With damage mostly concentrated on railways, Sheng sought protection for foreign railway engineers and servicemen (*lugong*), in particular those in the Baoding area.[111] In contrast to the railway, telegraph communication, as evidenced by Sheng's rare reliance on letters, seemed to be working even in early June 1900. According to a summary of reports from *Zilin xibao* between June 5 and 8, telegrams evidence the extent to which "Boxers are destroying railroads and train stations," leading to the disconnection of the Tianjin-Beijing line.[112] A June 9 telegraph sent by Sheng to Tianjin still exuded confidence that foreign settlements would be able to protect telegraph stations within his jurisdiction.[113] With increasing casualties over the next few days, however, Sheng's tone became more uncertain. Wiring Tianjin on June 11, he now indicated that outgoing telegrams would now need to be carried by postal relays.[114] Even then, the chief of the ITA had little clue as to how to deliver letters when trains were not in operation since, as he put it, no one knew where the trains stopped.[115]

Toward the middle of June, as the number of letters sent and received by Sheng increased and telegrams began to lag, Sheng and his circle attempted to maintain control over other more social aspects of the communicative infrastructure. In a rare telegram mixing both the official and the personal, he admitted to being out of the loop because of his location in Shanghai, and

175

requested daily updates via post from the court as well as information on his daughter's impending labor.[116] When even the location of blockages was left to speculation, the most Sheng could do was to call on Yantai officials to send soldiers to protect the students and engineers in charge of repairing damaged electrical lines.[117] The previously efficient and fast transmission of telegraph edicts, which since 1898 had replaced the courier delivery system, was blocked for ten days.[118] Even at this tense juncture, Sheng did not neglect to reprimand a telegraph officer for lacking proper social etiquette in his telegram—a validation of the "drama" of authority that interests Marvin.[119] Access to information, moreover, is always a privilege and political tool: Fei Nianci (1855–1905), Sheng's cousin, wrote to him on June 27 in support of the banning of reformist newspapers such as *Jiebao*, *Subao*, and *Dulibao*, which supported "rebels" such as Kang Youwei and Liang Qichao.[120] With the disconnection of the north-south line and the court's sole reliance on the western line, Sheng ordered that all official telegrams receive a 50 percent discount, while the cost of commercial telegrams was to remain the same.[121] "The boundary between the court and the merchants must remain clear."[122]

The escalation of the Siege of the Legations redrew political and geographical boundaries and introduced new complications. Communication's "drama," to evoke Marvin's term once again, intensified between the Boxers, the court, foreign powers, and provincial governors. As his cousin Fei cautioned Sheng toward the end of June, international troops had always been more wary of northern China than they were of the south, but this situation might soon change.[123] Despite the Boxers' alliance with the court, Sheng's urgent missives to provincial officials to protect telegraph lines from their destruction did not stop.[124] Indeed, "if the Boxers are helping the country," Sheng asked rhetorically, "they ought to protect the telegraph lines."[125] Here, he switched from the more derogatory "Boxer bandits" (*quanfei*) to the more favorable term "Boxers United in Righteousness" (*Yihe tuan*). In the meantime, the court began to loosen its grip on telegraphic sovereignty. While Sheng had abided by the International Telegraph Convention to reject any foreign coded telegrams during national crisis, much to the chagrin of foreign diplomats,[126] the chief of the ITA, in his August 8 telegram, allowed coded telegrams between diplomats and their respective countries.[127] Even more significant was the change in rules on transferring telegrams from foreign personnel to Beijing: no longer was it necessary for them to be redirected via Sheng's office.[128]

176   The gradual decentralization of the telegraph network accompanied an increasing perception of immobility as the 1900 crisis dragged on. Analogous to Ricalton's stereographic witnessing of the same crisis, Sheng's dispatches

highlight the paradoxical generation of movement in the midst of blockage. As the tide turned against the Qing armies in July and August, Sheng's messages increasingly focused on his limited access to available resources, placing him on the receiving end of information access and mobility. In rather frantic-sounding letters dated August 18, August 23, and August 30, Sheng requested foreign ambassadors in their respective legations to allow the ITA's technicians access to broken telegraph lines in Tianjin and Beijing.[129] Without a passport issued by the foreign embassies, Western and Chinese technicians with their cumbersome tools, lumber, and electrical wiring were stuck.[130] Even though the repaired lines would benefit all foreign nations, that those foreign nations' representatives repeatedly ignored Sheng's requests proved once again that access to information was a privilege and not a right. Chinese telegraphy's exposure of its own uses and limitations after the court signed the Boxer Protocol on September 7 could not be more dismal. As Sheng advised a provincial official in Baoding in a September 14 telegram: "if foreign armies arrive, send someone to hold a white flag and present this telegram, written in both English and Dutch, to the officers in charge. It will protect your life, property, and the railroad."[131] A successful wire at a time of blockage saves lives by providing, as Ricalton would certainly appreciate, movement and escape.

CHINESE WALLS

The ITA managed to repair most of the telegraph lines in Beijing and north China after the end of the Boxer Rebellion. Nevertheless, they could not rebuild China's telegraphic sovereignty, which the Allied forces gradually dismantled in their occupation of north China and Manchuria. By August 22, an Anglo-American military landline was built to connect the Dagu forts and Beijing.[132] Around the same time, Western forces laid claims to the empire's submarine cable network, whose first cables extended between Dagu to Zhifu in northern Shandong, and from Zhifu to Shanghai, as well as connecting to overland cables in southern Manchuria and Shandong. Russian and German submarine cables were strung between their respective areas of influence. In a series of agreements signed by Sheng on August 4 and September 27, foreign powers would manage and supervise these cables until "peace returned to China."[133]

The signing of the Boxer Protocol did not see the foreign powers fulfill their promise, even though the Qing court began the process of nationalizing the ITA in 1902 under the Ministry of Posts and Communications

(*Youchuan bu dianzheng zongju*).[134] Lines of communication in north China remained in foreign hands until the Republic of China established after 1911 fully recuperated the telegraphic network.

Landline and submarine cables formed only part of a larger communicative infrastructure, alongside early names for the telegraph, *fengshui* beliefs, and public or circular telegrams' spatial construction of diasporic consciousness in Chinese-language newspapers. Poles and wires were easy targets for destruction, which, counterintuitively, also fueled the telegraphic imagination of infrastructural breakdown. While stereography and pictorial illustrations of the Boxer Rebellion were not electronically transmitted, they nonetheless connected China with the rest of the world over distances, and in so doing *tele*-graphed the very failures of transportation and communication. Certainly, the widest distances the telegraphic imagination helped bridge remain what I have been tracing throughout this book: distances that traverse textual and visual representations of the new communicative network in order to uncover its technical capabilities as well as weaknesses; gaps that expose media's mechanical functions and physical conduits *without* shortchanging the "readability" of wires, poles, electrical signals, and so forth. After all, a half-toppled telegraph pole in a photograph encapsulates the formal dimension of the medium as lines, and a telegram that relays messages about communicative breakdowns demonstrates the medium's contradictory self-referentiality. Such interpretations are not meant to reduce the telegraph and its workings to language and to figurations; on the contrary, media formalism intensifies technological, material forms.

Sheng's telegrams and letters representing the progressive faction of the Qing elite thus vied with the Boxers' spiritual beliefs and with the foreign legations' technologies and communicative strategies in a Hydra-like network. The issue is not who won, when clearly all heads of the metaphorical serpent were severed at some stage during the crisis of 1900–1901. Interconnectivity or *tong* is, to leverage Pfeiffer's redefinition of communication, less about "understanding, coming to terms, mutuality, exchange" and more about "an open dynamic of means and effects."[135] Mutuality of connectivity *and* blockage proved to be as indispensable for the Boxers as it was for their adversaries. This chapter inducts the mysteries of information and movement—their blockages, disruptions, and breakdowns—into *tong*, and mobilizes the Chinese term for a historical redefinition of what media means in the wake of the Boxer Rebellion. The next chapter will analyze interconnectivity or *tong*'s other necessary counterparts: the divisibility of the self and the other, and its practical effects on industry and labor, which shape and are in turn shaped by an early science-fictional imagination.

4.8 "First train passing through the wall of Peking." Source: Arthur Henderson Smith, *China in Convulsion*, vol. 2, title image. Source: Internet Archive.

A parting image, this time illustrating the Boxers' facilitation of infrastructure rather than its destruction, can be found in the frontispiece of the second volume of Arthur Smith's *Convulsion in China*.[136] In "The first train passing through the wall of Peking" (figure 4.8), a train penetrates the outer wall of Beijing headed toward the Temple of Heaven, where the British army was stationed during its occupation of the capital. Smoke from the stacks blurs the upper left edge of the once-mighty wall. To the right of the train stand some soldiers. In the middle ground, facing the direction of the oncoming train, is a well-dressed, male Chinese. Their positions serve as a subtle counterpoint to the illustration found in the *Illustrated London* (figure 4.6), which depicts British officials and Sikh soldiers looking onto col-

179

lapsed trains, and that in Li Di's *Quan huo ji* of Boxers dismantling railways with pickaxes (figure 4.7). While the image reprinted in Smith's book highlights British reconstructive efforts in semicolonial China, the other illustrations discussed earlier stress Chinese barbarism and regression. In both sets of images, the hierarchy of progress and backwardness remains perceptible. Hevia encapsulates the significance of the photograph in Smith's book and its composition when he writes that "no trains had ever entered Beijing before."[137] Not only are the tracks newly laid, with signs of their construction, as contrasted to the destruction visible in the image, their rupturing of the city wall could be seen as "striking at the pride of the city's wall-obsessed inhabitants."[138]

It is not difficult, Jones reasons, to see why Chinese walls—indeed, that favorite emblem of its people's preference for isolation over the benefits of the "global village"—were "targets of Allied retribution" during their campaign.[139] And yet it falls on Smith, the same contemporary observer who also muses on the uncanniness of the telegraphic news reporting of an event before it occurred, to give credit to the Boxers where credit is due.

> The first instinct of the Occidental on taking possession of a Chinese city is to provide facile means of ingress and egress. The Chinese seldom make gates except in the middle of walls on each face of the city, to the great inconvenience of traffic and with a waste of time almost intolerable to Westerners. Peking had not been occupied three days before the hole already mentioned had been blown through the walls into the Imperial City, at the head of the canal above the British Legation, and this has ever since been an important thoroughfare. . . . Directly in front of the Temple of Heaven was the new terminus of the Tientsin and Peking Railway, formerly at Ma Chia P'u, a mile or two outside the southern city, through which the trains enter, reminding the traveler of Old York in England—*an innovation for which, but for the Boxers, we might have waited long.*[140]

Smith's critique of the foreign legations' "facile means of ingress and egress" undercuts the premium otherwise placed on technological breakthroughs. Breakdowns, on the other hand, can often signpost alternative views of connectivity and progress that are no longer seen as contradictory to isolation and barbarism. If not for the Boxers, infrastructural destruction and the foreign legations' occupation of China would not have happened. But if not, too, for such disasters, the particular connections and inroads that early Chinese telegraphy took would have looked very different.

180

A MEDIUM TO END ALL MEDIA |
"NEW TALES OF MR. BRAGGADOCIO" AND
THE SOCIAL BRAIN OF INDUSTRY AND INTELLECT

In a series of advertising campaigns launched in major Shanghai newspapers between 1904 and 1907, medicinal entrepreneur Huang Chujiu (1872–1931) speaks through pseudonymous versions of himself to promote his latest product, Dr. Yale's Brain Tonic (*Ailuo bunaozhi*). In one installment of the multipart advertisement titled "Yale Brain Tonic Guarantee" (*Ailuo bunaozhi baozhang shu*), Huang purports to have sampled the wondrous concoction on the recommendation of his friend Huang Guoying, whose name literally means "national talent or elite."[1] Within ten days of consuming Dr. Yale's brain tonic, the first-person narrator completely recovers from his nervous ailment (*naojin bing*). When asked for the formula, however, Guoying insists that the medicine should serve a nobler cause beyond individual cure. Since "the study of chemistry in China is still in its infancy; merely obtaining the formula will only harm our people. . . . You and I have no control over political reform. Perhaps this brain tonic could awaken the Chinese spirit?"[2] Enlightened, the narrator devotes himself to the study of Western medicine with Dr. Yale. This is how, according to the advertisement, Huang Chujiu's drugstore began to import Dr. Yale's Brain Tonic into Shanghai, starting a business so successful that the modest bottle of liquid can be found "wherever there is a Chinese person with a brain."[3]

Beginning in the mid-nineteenth century, medical, commercial, and political discourses coalesced around an interest in neuroanatomy. A translation of *New Theory of Anatomy* by Benjamin Hobson (1816–1873) was published in

5

1851 as *Quanti xinglun*, and was particularly influential in China for advancing the centrality of the brain as well as the extensive reach of nerves, the latter translated into Chinese as *nao* ("brain"), *jin* ("nerve"), *naosi* ("brain thread"), *naoqi* ("brain essence"), or some combination of the above.[4] "The brain may be the master of the body," Hobson declared, but it is the "nerves (*qijin*), divisible as ropes, thread, and wires, known collectively as brain nerves (*nao qijin*), which surround the entire body and its senses, connecting every muscle, tendon, and bone to the inside and outside of the internal organs."[5] Divisibility, paradoxically, advanced the national project of collective unity. When both Yan Fu and Liang Qichao compared the human body with the nation, it was anatomy—arteries, veins, and organs and their interrelations within the individual body—that made such a figuration possible.[6] The introduction of the New Thought movement into China around the same time with John Fryer's 1895 translation of Henry Wood's *Ideal Suggestion through Mental Photography* (1893), a work that I will return to, sealed the period's fascination with ether and electricity. Together with the nervous system and electrical wiring, a neuroanatomical psyche worked together to connect the nation through the fields of advertising, science and technology, social criticism, and biology. Tan Sitong (1865–1898), martyr of the 1898 failed reform, and whose work deserves further analysis, perfectly encapsulated the mediation of the biological and the technical when he compared the brain with "electricity materialized" (*nao wei youxing zhi zhi dian*) and electricity to a brain "without form" (*wu xingzhi zhi nao*).[7] The historical entity that is "late Qing China" is not simply a case study for the transnational reach of these early twentieth-century intellectual and popular interests, but a conceptual realm for connecting advancements in communicative media technologies with both philosophies and more general discourses reflecting on what it means to connect.

From the politics and aesthetics of inscription (*ji*), and the dissemination and circulation (*chuan*) of women's biographies (*zhuan*)—two inscriptive genres and modes of mediation that organize the first two sections of this book—we arrived at the dream of interconnectivity (*tong*) made possible by disrupted and disruptive communicative networks in chapter 4, before turning in this chapter to the converging divisibility of the physical body. Nerves join the self to the other by first linking together different parts *within* the self. The dialectics of the one-to-the-many *and* the many-in-the-one takes on biological, socioeconomic, and technological significances as biologic or bio-medium. Vividly illustrating Eugene Thacker's definition of biomedia as "novel configurations of biologies and technologies,"[8] my opening example shows how such a biologic or bio-medium also manifests narratologically as character. In real life, the King of Advertising, as Huang Chujiu's contemporaries called him, knew nothing about Western pharmacology and lacked a business partner who did.[9] Moreover, he certainly did not receive any education in Western medicine. Both Huang Guoying, the patriotic friend in the advertisement, and Dr. Yale were Huang's alter egos.[10] To help connect and strengthen China, the creator of Dr. Yale's Brain Tonic first needed to present a split or fragmented persona.

In a similar vein, the first-person narrator in "Xin faluo xiansheng tan" (1904–1905), or "New Tales of Mr. Braggadocio," by Xu Nianci (1875–1908), speaks through multiple selves while traversing diverse fields of knowledge dramatized by the brain motif.[11] At the beginning of the story, the first-person narrator, "inclined to the words of religious superstition," languishes in his frustrations at the limits posed by the empirical research of "mineralogy, botany, and zoology," and that there is no "knowledge" outside the "purview of science."[12] The narrator, out of obsessive frustration with these constraints, flees to the top of a mountain peak, where, caught in an immense gravitational pull, he finds himself split into two halves: the "immaterial" part he calls "soul" (linghun), and the material unit he refers to as the "body" (quke).[13] At one point in "New Tales," Mr. Braggadocio's soul-self journeys to Mercury, where it witnesses the macabre process of cerebral transfer where the dead can be revived by scooping out their brains and replacing them with new cerebral matter.[14] If he "learn[s] the method of this art," he will be able to "amass the necessary capital to open a brain matter renewal company in Shanghai," driving the makers of Dr. Yale's Brain Tonic out of business while ridding the country of its "outdated, polluted, and contemptible customs."[15]

Huang Chujiu paid writers (including Wu Jianren, the author of *New Story of the Stone*) to place his product in their stories, and Xu Nianci's satire of the brand's practices foregrounds the increasing role played by private capital in Shanghai businesses.[16] The narrator's entrepreneurial aspirations return toward the end of the story, when, inspired by animal magnetism and hypnosis, he develops and sells methods of perfecting brain electricity on campuses established in major Chinese cities. The formidable product produces light that replaces man-made light, heat that makes redundant the need for heating, and communicative and transport networks that drive telegraph, telephone, and railway companies out of business.[17] "There cease[s] to be revenue for annual repairs, and dilapidation sets in."[18] Ultimately, brain electricity forces one-third of the world's population into unemployment, and the story concludes with the narrator having to go into hiding.

183

What is remarkable about brain electricity is that it is both a natural energy source and a communicative device that fails at perfecting universal connectivity. Xu's description of brain electricity's detrimental effects on industry and employment takes up only two pages, but it is plenty to rethink the roles that a fictionalized medium and the knowledge required for its operation play in production and labor. The gradual opening of trade under the treaty systems set in place from the First Opium War (1839–42) to the First Sino-Japanese War (1894–95) tied literary production inextricably to economics, as changes in the latter drove not only the expansion of printing as a means to create text, but also determined the content of print matter. Despite this clear connection between culture and economics, criticisms of representations of commerce in late Qing fiction seldom scratch beneath the thematic surface to examine the *formal* relation between these two fields in order to pose the larger historical problem of material production.[19] In "New Tales," the brain serves as more than a motif or trope—rather, it plays a global or organizing role. Neurology and narrative subjectivity within the text speak to the period's ostensible preoccupations with political and technological connectivity on the one hand, and with less palpable or at least less clearly defined concerns of economic productivity and livelihood on the other. In so doing, this early example of Chinese science fiction envisions the production of subjectivities beyond the modern nation-state under burgeoning industrial capitalism. Insofar as Mr. Braggadocio's educational conglomerate presciently stages a knowledge economy centered on the servicing of brain electricity and abstracting of information from its users, the science-fiction fantasy casts a long shadow over late-capitalist formations of immaterial labor.

THE MASSES: A MINOR CHARACTER

Nathaniel Isaacson offers a compelling analysis of Mr. Braggadocio as a character "literally torn between fields of knowledge for whom double consciousness is a leitmotif in terms of narrative style, voice, and plot."[20] That is, the protagonist's dual identity develops not only as a plot point, but as a way to structure the entire work. As I will show, the brain with its extensive nerves and connective faculties even more fundamentally underpins Mr. Braggadocio's double consciousness such that his sheer divisibility manifests conversely as an ideal indivisibility and interconnectivity. Beyond the leitmotif of double consciousness, the protagonist's cerebral transformations technically mediate between the literary and the extra- or para-literary, the material and immaterial, the individual and the collective, and science and non-science.[21] "New Tales" first appeared in the journal *Xiaoshuo lin* (*Forest of Literature*), edited by Xu himself, under the label "science fiction" (*kexue xiaoshuo*). Xu, writing under the pseudonym Donghai juewo, filled the story with references to scientific terms, numerical details of weight, speed, and quantity, and point-by-point observations of empirical evidence that often distract from the main story. At the same time, the author, not unlike his character, expressed interest in "discoveries and inventions of the immaterial world" (*xuekong jian de faming*) such as the soul and quasi-scientific trends of hypnosis and animal magnetism.[22] The mix of literary (*wenyan*) and vernacular (*baihua*) Chinese in "New Tales" buttresses its thematic blending: the classical tale, rooted in the fantastic (*chuanqi*) and the strange (*zhiguai*), now filters through a worldview increasingly dominated by scientific rationality.[23]

As in my analysis of *New Story of the Stone* in chapter 2, the hybrid genre of "New Tales" is significant, but even more so is the transformation of its main character from an observer of media processes into a communicative medium. For the case of Mr. Braggadocio, his process of becoming a medium is more gradual than Baoyu's more mythological transformation, and it needs to be grasped as a problem of representation quintessential for the individual-and-collective or part-to-whole tension germane to early twentieth-century Chinese nationalism. Seo-Young Chu proposes a science-fictional theory of representation as a "translucent process that necessarily involves greater similitude than dissimilitude between referent and representational text."[24] Rather than define science fiction as a genre outside or even antithetical to mimesis, she argues that all representations are to an extent science-fictional since the distance that a representation poses between reality and itself are cognitively estranging, at once familiar and yet overwhelming.[25] One such cognitively estranging and not explicitly science-fictional referent in "New Tales" is the large unit of social existence, known in sociological terms as the collective, masses, crowd, or group; in bio-evolutionism as the species or race; the "swarm" as appropriated by design robotics and culture; intersubjectivity in philosophy and psychology; the Marxist notion of social totality; and most commonly as the people, community, citizens, or the public, with their various points of origin in political discourse.[26] However we call them, such sizable human groups are at once knowable and commonplace, and yet strangely obscure and abstract, occupying what Chu calls the "middle" of the "referent-spectrum."[27] It may also be fruitful to regard the narrative representation of the largest units of our social existence as resembling a computational problem, defined less as digital manipulations and binary codes but, according to Katherine Hayles, as a "process that starts with a parsimonious set of elements and a relatively small set of logical operations."[28] Fiction can then be viewed as a simulation of some of "the most complex phenomena on earth, from turbulent flow to multiagent social systems."[29]

As liaisons between the familiar and the unfamiliar, the "human race" and "Chinese people" appear frequently and interchangeably in "New Tales," indexed but not fully represented.[30] The text points to their presence, in fact, by either signaling their inevitable demise or by depicting them as symptoms of moral degeneration. When Mr. Braggadocio, realizing that his soul-self wields an incredible light source, shines upon Earth, only European and American scientists rush to investigate the light. The Chinese, disappointingly, are either asleep or indulging in other pleasures, unperturbed by the disturbance.[31] Mr. Braggadocio, revolted by the contrast between Chinese and Euro-Americans, is tempted to set himself on fire and smash into the eastern half of the Earth to exterminate the Chinese race so that its land may be discoverable by a future Christopher Columbus.[32] When the narrator next encounters the human race (*renlei*) via a panoramic "external viewing lens," he fails to actually "see" them.[33] As the inventor of this visual medium, who turns out to be the ancestor of the Chinese race (Huang Zhongzu, literally "Yellow Racial Ancestor") explains, a thickening smoke reflecting human ills such as lack of ambition, superstition, arrogance, and indecision is threatening to engulf the human race.[34] No society is inherently bad; only when the propensity for evil overpowers that for good—represented by other chemical substances—will a society decay.[35] Note too the equivocal result: the external viewing lens supposedly reveals the entire human race, but concerns over its diagnosis are obviously directed specifically toward the Chinese. Mr. Braggadocio's duty, as he announces elsewhere in the narrative, is to "awaken the citizens of the country."[36]

Diseased minds and bodies as metaphors of an ailing social polity feature prominently in modern Chinese literature from the mid-nineteenth century onward. Since "the mind and body" make up identity, Howard Y. F. Choy explains, "discourses of disease probe into the psychosomatic politics of subjectivity by speaking about the sick person's mental and physical conditions in the socio-historical context."[37] The *yan* 言 "speech" radical accompanies the Chinese character for "diagnose" (*zhen* 診), thereby highlighting the discursiveness of diseases and the significance of discourse for diagnosis and disease.[38] Fiction is not the only kind of discourse to symptomatically diagnose Chinese totality; social criticism goes one step further to task fiction directly with the rejuvenation of the citizenry. No piece illustrates this better than Liang Qichao's influential "On the Relationship between Fiction and Government of the People." Much attention has been given to the essay's reevaluation of fiction, and my introduction touched on a little-studied aspect—namely, the problem of immediacy. Here, I attempt another reassessment of the essay's opening rhetoric of "the people" (*qun*) as readers over whom fiction "has the most profound power."[39] From there, Liang expounds on generalized characteristics of human nature, singling out discontentment with the world and the limits of self-expression as the basis for the appeals of the idealistic and realistic schools of fiction. The relationship between fiction and the people, as stated in the title, turns out to take the form of a one-way street, whereby fiction actively shapes society through its powers of "thurification" (*xun*), "immersion" (*jin*), "stimulation" (*ci*), and "lifting" (*ti*), adapted from Buddhism, leaving the people or society with no positive impact on fiction except in influencing the popularity of certain genres. Although Liang observes that an author's character can determine how these powers are put to use,[40] the essay continues to construct the Chinese as avowedly passive readers who cannot control their "spontaneous psychological" fondness for fiction. Collective passivity, as in the case of "New Tales," allows the author to both generalize and specify his referent. While the attraction of fiction is a universal trait, Liang implies that the Chinese, in particular, suffer from its negative influence. Even those who do not like novels—neglecting entirely the question of literacy—are indirectly influenced by the popularity of their ideas.

Interestingly, Xu, in his 1908 article "Yu zhi xiaoshuo guan" ("My Views on Fiction"), provides a view contrary to Liang's: fiction cannot produce society because only society can create fiction.[41] Yet this view is equally unsatisfying since it merely reverses Liang's position to emphasize fiction's passive role as a reflection of societal mores. A more nuanced position between the two requires reintegrating this large unit of social totality into fiction instead of excluding it from the storyworld, and representing its cognitive estrangement as something both familiar and yet overwhelming. A more rigorous approach to this ubiquitous and yet cognitively abstract referent in "New Story" would have to examine the "the Chinese" as a minor, fictional character.

Alex Woloch argues that literary characterization intervenes between the "discrete representation of any specific individual" and a text's distribution of attention to "different characters who jostle for limited space within the same fictive universe."[42] Minorness takes on two corresponding forms: either as a flat character who lacks interiority and is therefore easily "absorbed" into the

187

narrative, or as one who is unable to restrain their interiority and so suffers from fragmentation and needs to be expelled from the narrative.[43] For the most part, the masses in "New Tales" resemble the first type of minorness. The narrative denies any perspective on the Chinese as a whole, evoking them only to advance its didactic message. The static, unvaried, and emotionless "people" contrast with the agitated protagonist of most late Qing fiction who, like Mr. Braggadocio, feels a range of emotions from anger, disgust, helplessness, and despair at the state of his country.

But not entirely. Toward the end of "New Tales," social totality reemerges as the other version of minorness in Woloch's typology, as uncontrollable masses whose interiority exceeds the narrative framework. After the narrator's invention of brain electricity, "people in industry, commerce and in the world in general who had lost their jobs began to pile up like sands upon the banks of the Ganges."[44] Indivisible like sand, their collective discontent grows as brain electricity replaces more and more existing industries, until "a great storm of derisive laughter, curses, condemnation, hatred, and ridicule began to stir which, within a week, had reached a crescendo."[45] For this reason, multiplicity in Xu's story refocuses Woloch's theory to examine larger, more abstract units of social existence, instead of the latter's study of multiple but nonetheless individualized characters such as the Bennet sisters in *Pride and Prejudice*.[46] Existing at the periphery and subjected to caricature and instrumentalization in order to foreground China's urgent need for reform, the "people," depicted as asleep, drugged, and unconscious, nonetheless reemerge at the narrative's end with excess emotions to chase the narrator, quite literally, off the page. With the unemployed now amounting for more than one-third of the world's population, "the masses rose up in attack" (*qun qi er gong zhi*).[47] Mr. Braggadocio is "compelled to hide away for a while," announcing an abrupt and definite closure to his personal history.[48]

Woloch situates his study of nineteenth-century European novels at the crossroads between "form and history."[49] It demonstrates how the structure of "omniscient, asymmetric character-systems . . . can imaginatively comprehend the dynamics of alienated labor" to the extent that "minor characters are the proletariat of the novel."[50] The mass unemployed in Xu's striking blend of science fiction with the classical tale, on the other hand, stand out as a character right at the moment when the text shifts its focus from national rejuvenation to the effects of technological innovation on labor. What light does this shift shed on this period of Chinese literary production? On the one hand, the Chinese classical short story at the turn of the twentieth century, which Sheldon Lu characterizes as having a "last blooming" of its kind,[51] cannot be more at odds with the development of nineteenth-century European realism.[52] On the other hand, due to the very multiplicity of genres at this particular historical juncture of literary production, of which "New Tales" is a prime example, the science-fictional classical tale both exemplifies and contradicts Woloch's analysis. If the importance of minor characters lies precisely in their disappearance, and "in the tension or relief that results from this vanishing,"[53] what happens when it is the first-person, involved narrator instead of the minor character who vanishes? Woloch stresses that "*every* minor character does—by strict definition—disappear."[54] Her disappearance elicits our feeling of "interest and outrage, painful concern or amused consent,"[55] and becomes part of how we remember them. In doing so, the fate of a minor character draws attention to the relationship between story and discourse crucial to all narrative form, between the actual depiction of events within the story and the arrangement of that story by the narrative's discursive structure. This mirrors exactly Mr. Braggadocio's end, whereby he does not simply retreat from the narrative discourse but also from an "imagined space within the story itself,"[56] presumably China, where his educational conglomerate is based.

Before the nameless masses erupt as minor characters contesting the structural unity of the narrative universe, the boasting and potentially unreliable first-person narrator alone shoulders the burden of multiplicity. Like Huang Chujiu's multiple personas promoting Dr. Yale's Brain Tonic in the name of curing the nation, Xu's short story splits the narrative first-person consciousness in order to eventually connect, via brain electricity, the individual and the collective, indexed as the unemployed masses. If the power of Mr. Braggadocio's brain insinuates the power of fiction made fashionable by thinkers such as Liang Qichao, it is one that envisages interconnectivity only through fragmentation. Before virtual reality and the uploading of consciousness onto a computer database became popular platforms for simulating large social systems in later science fiction, themes which I will revisit in the conclusion, "New Tales" relies on depictions of out-of-body experiences drawn from both Chinese popular beliefs and Judeo-Christian understandings of body and soul.[57]

The majority of the story chronicling Mr. Braggadocio's soul-and-body split, its spiritual connotations notwithstanding, can be interpreted as groundwork for the subsequent remaking of his own brain into a mass communicative medium in the finale. "After my trip around the Sun, when I had been reunited with my body," the narrator realizes, "a mysterious transformation had occurred in my brain."[58] This "mysterious transformation" is none other

189

than the externalizing of the *first*-person narrative voice as a *third*-party commentator observing the two parts of his disintegrated self during his soul-and-body split. This is how his two selves are described: his soul takes the form of a one-inch, gaseous sphere which, without eyes, ears, nose, or tongue, nevertheless has extraordinary sensory perception; without hands or feet, can move without inhibition; and without circulatory, respiratory, digestive, and central nervous systems nonetheless still carries out their functions.[59] His physical body has all the abovementioned organs and systems that his spirit lacks. Curiously, everything seems to be in place—except for a brain.

The absence of his brain from either his spirit or physical self resembles a mere sleight of hand, and yet it is one absolutely crucial to the eventual reappearance of the unemployed masses as an explosive minor character. For where can the brain be except "in" the narrative perspective of the first-person "I," an "I" who cannot be positioned either within his soul or bodily self because it speaks interchangeably and at times simultaneously *for* both of them as the center for all biological functionality, capable of both affect and reason? After realizing that his bodily self lacks a brain, Mr. Braggadocio fears that even with a central nervous system, he will be "non-thinking," "non-functioning," and thus "no different from a dead person."[60] Comically, he spends the next twenty-four hours weeping over such misfortune before realizing that if he is truly dead, he cannot possibly be crying. Suddenly, Mr. Braggadocio has a revelation:

> At this moment I clearly had two selves (*mingming you er shen*), one my soul-self and the other my bodily-self, and in the future, I would make good use of these two selves to study all the world's phenomena and invent all manner of things. I was but one (*shi yu zhi yiren*), but my contributions would be far greater than those of any single person (*qi gongxiao bu chi beiyu ren zhi yishen ye*).[61]

With enhanced capabilities, the speaking "I" (*yu* in the Chinese original, one of the earliest Chinese first-person pronouns that include the now-default first-person pronoun *wo* 我) therefore addresses his spirit and physical bodies in the third-person plural "they." Mr. Braggadocio's new powers reach far beyond those of a single individual because he is, quite literally, *more than one*. What is more fantastical than his out-of-body *and* out-of-spirit experience is the first-person narration that functions simultaneously as a third-person reference to his "selves," an "I" who surveys his disparate selves as he transitions from panic to tempered reason, and back into hysterics. Delighted by this discovery of his increased powers, Mr. Braggadocio proceeds to laugh hysterically for another twenty-four hours.[62] Even as the narrator goes on to explain that he is able to combine his physical body and spiritual self into one or split them at will in various permutations, the grammatical imposition of the "I" who continues to address his physical and spiritual halves in the third person prevents any clear unification of the subject. Instead, the grammatical disjuncture between the speaking "I" and the "they" whose experiences the "I" narrates raises questions about the cognizant subject who exists outside any reliable notions of the self. The complexity of the third-person "I" in "New Tales," through which the first-person narrator simultaneously acts as a third-person narrator, moreover enhances the sense of disunity and disorientation characteristic of the late Qing malaise, which critics Jiang Jing and Dorothy Ko point out.[63]

The narrator's perspective or gaze into his split consciousness, however, necessitates an attention to form insofar as the latter will shed light on the larger questions of connection and disconnection that undergird this present discussion. Milena Doleželová-Velingerová argues that despite "long-overdue theoretical attention" given to Chinese fiction of this period, indifference to narrative mode persists, perhaps due to the fact that the distinction between first- and third-person narrations "is less conspicuous in Chinese than in any Western language."[64] Chinese verbs have no indication of person, and traditionally the language tends to leave out sentence subjects and pronouns altogether. All the same, first-person personal narrations are well established in Chinese literary language (*wenyan*). Indeed, it was Wu Jianren, author of *New Story*, who made the first attempt at first-person narrative in the vernacular language with *Ershinian mudu zhi guai xianzhuang* (*Strange Events Observed over the Past Twenty Years*, 1903–10).[65] There were earlier first-person narratives in the literary language, such as Shen Fu's *Fou sheng liu ji* (*Six Chapters of a Floating Life*, 1808), which is a work of confessional prose (strictly speaking, a memoir) that focuses on the narrator's private life, marriage, and emotional experience. Nevertheless, according to Doleželová-Velingerová, Wu pioneers first-person narration in vernacular literature, which emphasizes the narrator's observation of the society around him and relegates his personal life to the background, including his feelings and emotions.[66] Unlike Shen's *Six Chapters of a Floating Life*, Wu's *Strange Events* engages with political and social issues unique to China. Given the lack of deeper psychological introspection, the former cannot be said to be copied from the Western first-person novel or the modern Japanese autobiographical novel. In short, "the basic question 'Who am I?' prevalent in Western fiction is in the Chinese context overshadowed by the query 'Who am I in society?'"[67]

This tension between the self and society complicates Woloch's distributional matrix of literary characterization.[68] As suggested earlier, Mr. Braggadocio's positioning of a third self capable of addressing an already doubled consciousness injects multiplicity into the representation of an individualized narrator such that the dialectics of the one versus the many reflects the many-in-the-one or the social "I." The distinct narrative voice of "New Tales" contemplates singularity and totality simultaneously; it is fair to say that the narrative enacts a social or cultural mediation of the individual and the collective. Cultural mediation alone, however, stands incomplete without technical media. From literary characterization I thus turn to the concept of biomedia to foreground the persistent entanglement between biology, technology, and the social production of subjectivity made possible by Mr. Braggadocio's discovery and commodification of brain electricity. Once narrative dimensions of the self and subjectivity assume bio-material, informatic functions undergirding the distinction between intellectual and machinic labor, which constitute the material basis of the social whole, brain electricity emerges as a fitting solution to the narrator's search for the perfect medium. In the final instance, "New Story," by extending an unlikely bridge between late Qing fiction and Marxist critique, puts a somber spin on early twentieth-century Chinese literature's pursuit of nationhood, industrialization, and progress.

SOUL-MEDIUM

At first glance, the notion of "biomedia" brings to mind stem cell research, DNA coding, and computational biology and biological computation as it advanced in the mid-to-late twentieth century, all things far removed from the early twentieth-century preoccupations of "New Tales." Eugene Thacker's definition of biomedia, however, suggests otherwise.

> Put briefly, "biomedia" is an instance in which biological components and processes are technically recontextualized in ways that may be biological or nonbiological. Biomedia are novel configurations of biologies and technologies that take us beyond the familiar tropes of technology-as-tool or the human-machine interface. Likewise, biomedia describes an ambivalence that is not reducible to either technophilia (the rhetoric of enabling technology) or technophobia (the ideologies of technological determinism). Biomedia are particular mediations of the body, optimizations of the biological in which "technology" appears to disappear altogether.[69]

192

A technical recontextualization of the body on both "biological or nonbiological" fronts is possible because biomedia does not assume a pure constitution of the physical self.[70] "New Tales" indeed begins with the narrator doubting the limits of scientific biology, reframing the question of "what can a body do" in terms of "what can the soul do *as* a body." In so doing, he presents his divisible selves as biomedia exploiting the tensions between textual and media forms. Recall that Mr. Braggadocio's soul-self takes the form of a gaseous state invisible to the naked eye, but with the biological functions of the five senses and working circulatory, respiratory, digestive, and nervous systems.[71] While it lacks biological materiality, the soul-self nonetheless carries what Thacker calls "the informatics capacity to enhance biological materiality," a "lateral transcendence" or "the recontextualization of a 'body more than a body.'"[72] In this regard, Mr. Braggadocio's ability to produce and emit light independently translates into a technical remediation *sans* the taint of technological or biological determinism that Thacker rightly cautions against.

Upon discovering that he is able to further divide half of his soul-self to meet half of his physical body and make new configurations without "los[ing] the slightest bit of function,"[73] the first thing the narrator accomplishes is to have his soul- and bodily-selves cooperate to forge the former into a fantastic source of light. The imagery of the bodily-self holding up the soul-self above its head while standing on top of Mount Everest indeed evokes a physical, if not comical configuration. The result is nothing short of miraculous in this light source's superiority over sunlight in three specific ways: first, light from the soul-self bends with an even distribution so that "one can look directly at it without the eye suffering from the glare," and second, it possesses a bioluminescence effect such that one hour of exposure to the light illuminates the whole world for three hours.[74]

Third, and most wondrously, such an energy source, like Mr. Braggadocio's subsequent invention of brain electricity, doubles as a communicative device. As the narrator continues to brag, everything including "mountains and rivers, plants and animals" that comes into contact with this light turns into images on a screen.[75] The latter "also served to magnify, so it was as if the whole thing were covered with eyes, and even an object of just a few square centimeters in size could be seen in minute detail."[76] Certainly, any reflecting surface can double as a screen, but the metaphor of a screen covered with eyes emphasizes how Mr. Braggadocio's light transforms the physical world into both the seeing and the seen. The transformed soul-self, far from immaterial, operates as a medium powered by its own energy source.

193

Dazzled by this marvelous illumination, European and American "astronomers, physicists, chemists and naturalists" clamor to "observe it through a telescope," while "others tried to experiment with light sensors," and the rest "tried to capture images of it with cameras," only to remain ignorant of the exact light source.[77] While Mr. Braggadocio succeeds in ridiculing Western science, his effort to lead his own people out of the dark, symbolically speaking, nevertheless falls flat. It is fair to say that his is a light that observes but accomplishes little in enlightening either a race or a civilization.

Mr. Braggadocio's light is neither a result of "machine-body hybridity" by prosthetics and artificial organs nor "fantasies of 'uploading' the mind into the disembodied space of the computer."[78] The extraneous application of technology to the body does not apply here because the soul-self manifests its inherent technicality *as* light, literally making visible what Thacker calls the "optimization" of the biological.[79] For this reason, biomedia resists any ontological separation between the body and technology since it is "the components of the body, along with their range of uses," and not techniques external to or qualitatively different from the body, that give it the quality of being a medium.[80] Mr. Braggadocio's division of his self into the physical body and the soul, as well as their subsequent ability to recombine in various proportions, thus transforms the act of narration into a technology of "internal organization and functioning."[81] After all, what better way to prove the redundancy of the "technical metaphor of the 'interface'" than with the body-soul relationship, which, as the narrative proceeds, becomes less dichotomous and more connective and combinatory? Like the modest book cart of *New Story* discussed in chapter 2, Mr. Braggadocio's bodily- and soul-selves undercut their own espousal of national and individual salvation by showing that such an end goal, however, lofty, is but a technical content in need of a vehicle, mode of conveyance, or expression.

And light is but one of the more moderate means with which the narrator hopes to reeducate his countrymen. There is also heat that could have allowed him to ignite himself and set the "eastern half of the globe" on fire, thereby establishing a clean slate for a new China.[82] When he is shown further evidence of the Chinese's degeneration by Huang Zhongzu, the ancestor of the Chinese, Mr. Braggadocio wishes to unite his soul- and bodily-selves in order to transform into a "miraculous device of sonic emanation" (*buke siyi zhi fasheng qi*).[83] Not to be overshadowed by Huang Zhongzu, Mr. Braggadocio, upon traveling to Venus, considers staying on the planet so he can "become the primal ancestor of humans on Venus!"[84] It is as if the narrator is driven by his failure to reform the Chinese national character to desire

194

the more extreme scenarios of extinction and evolution. Such visions of creation, as Jing Jiang points out, dominate late Qing nationalist discourses and science fiction including and not limited to Wu Jianren, and Lone Howler of the Sea's readaptation of Goddess Nüwa's stone, discussed in chapter 2.[85] The making of a new race in "New Tales" arises from the reordering of the narrator's soul- and bodily-selves *as* technologies. The narrative, similar to Jia Baoyu's recursive transformations from a stone inscription or recording medium of the story to its central protagonist thus weaves a kind of creation myth premised upon the creator's self-inventions. Interpreting the story through the lens of biomedia—that is, through the inherent informatics of Mr. Braggadocio's biological self—the more complicated question to ask is if the message of national revival is transferrable from one material substrate to another—from light, to heat, to sound—such that the message remains the same. Certainly, it *matters* which medium communicates the historical period's prevalent desire to create a new people and new body politic.

Indeed, our egoistic narrator does not always deliver the information he promises. His supreme light source cannot replicate sunlight's heat.[86] When he fails to produce sound to awaken his countrymen, a quarter of his soul-self attempts to raise temperatures instead.[87] By experimenting with the continued material reprocessing of biological information across different material substrates, "New Tales" allegorizes the role of technical media in the reimagination of the Chinese state. Buttressing its titular rhetoric of newness—counting too Wu's New Story of the Stone (chapter 2) and Liang's call for a "new fiction" (*xin xiaoshuo*) (chapter 3), among other examples of the period—is its self-conscious juxtaposition of traditional and innovative forms of communication.

Mr. Braggadocio embodies an unreliable medium, even more so than the reincarnated Jia Baoyu. He questions his own account through a far-flung episode on Venus, which pits an earlier record in the form of a diary and relatively conventional travel narrative against his subsequently stupendous experiments communicating with light, sound, and heat. After finding himself on the strange planet and discovering precious gems and prevertebrate life-forms at different stages of evolution, he recovers his lost diary, which "nearly drove [him] crazy with overjoyed surprise."[88] The journal records his exploration of the North Pole five years prior to the events of "New Tales." Cited in excerpted form, the events there are strikingly tame compared with his adventures leading up to the present moment of narration. To summarize: Mr. Braggadocio made a solitary expedition by hydrogen balloon. Strong winds landed him on a glacier, where he gained a polar bear as a

195

companion. After journeying farther north, Mr. Braggadocio's balloon was shot down by other explorers, leaving him unconscious. After coming to, he rode on the bear to return to safety.[89] While the tone of the journal assumes some of the same comical effect as the larger narrative in which it is embedded, absent are the exaggerations of scientific precision or metaphysical concerns. What the "history of this North Pole exploration" (*tanji zhi lishi*) foregrounds vis-à-vis Mr. Braggadocio's present account is the materiality of its "record" (*zai*) in journal form, as inscriptions of self-writing.[90] After all, the narrator has never been to Venus before, and it is confounding that the book could have made its way there. Its unexplainable recovery corroborates Mr. Braggadocio's fantasy of being the origin of a new human species on Venus expressed earlier. Eventually, Mr. Braggadocio decides that he shall leave his journal as a "memento" for future archaeologists to discover "when human beings proliferate there."[91] Since the narrator subsequently gets caught in a gravitational whirlpool and eventually returns to Earth, the linguistic record evidences an antecedent life-form, an "*arche*-fossil"[92] more advanced than the mollusk and related organisms, as well as other strange minerals on the planet.

Compared with the narrator's recovered diary, light, heat, and sound are more ephemeral, nonrecording media that double as natural energy sources, hence their potential, however ineffective, to literally enlighten or totally annihilate the masses. Whereas the journal of his North Pole expedition constructs a subjectivity external to the subject, the transformational effects of Mr. Braggadocio's body-soul split are innately biological and technical. It is the more abstract technique that, as I will show, structures a new kind of social relationship and anticipates brain electricity.

Nonetheless, the narrator's present journey in outer space echoes the journal of his North Pole expedition in that both exhibit the colonial ambitions of exploration narratives. After leaving Venus and hurtling through space, he comes up with the idea to "establish routes of navigation between the Earth and all the planets" (*ge kaitong wanglai zhi hanglu*) so that even "ten Columbuses" cannot rival his accomplishment.[93] Ultimately, both the more conventional linguistic record and his interplanetary soul-self signify abortive forms of communication. The hope that mankind will proliferate on Venus is as much wishful thinking as Mr. Braggadocio's failed attempts to reform the Chinese citizenry by transforming himself into pure light, heat, and sound. The "people," as such, never receive the message. Whatever connection (*tong*) there is within the narrative as story—as distinct from narrative as discourse—occurs thus far between multiple versions of

Mr. Braggadocio, as I have argued in the earlier section. Until the advent of brain electricity, the narrator, except for his brief conversation with Huang Zhongzu in his underground abode, quite literally talks to him*selves*.

BRAIN ELECTRICITY, INC.

In "New Tales," brain electricity connects all of the issues that this book raises *with regard to mediation*: different fields of knowledge grappling with the distinctions between the body (or matter) and the spirit (or the mind); the relation between specific individuals and different characters (the self and the other) that constitutes large units of social existence; and last but not least, the technical recontextualization of the body as biomedia in contrast with more conventional inscriptive mediums. It would not be remiss to characterize brain electricity as the form with which both technology and its myriad cultural forms, to evoke Raymond Williams's terms, converge. The various articulations that I have been tracing overlap and feed into each other, and brain electricity, as the symbol for their interconnectivity or *tong*, repeats these overlaps, beginning with the short story's intellectual influences. According to Mr. Braggadocio, the technique of brain electricity belongs to the "subfield" of animal magnetism, which he learns from a symposium on mesmerism in Shanghai after his trip around the Sun.[94]

Around the last decade of the nineteenth century, writings on hypnosis, mentalism, and other practices associated with the mind's power appeared in Chinese journals and newspapers. A Shanghai newspaper, *Dalu bao*, reported on a lecture on hypnosis organized in 1905, the year in which Xu published "New Tales." Xu was a member of the Chinese Education Society, with which the conference was associated, and it was very likely that he attended the hypnosis lecture and drew on its proceedings.[95] In 1896, John Fryer translated Henry Wood's *Ideal Suggestion through Mental Photography* (1893) as *Zhixin mianbing fa* ("A method for the avoidance of illness by controlling the mind"), and a new science of mental or psychic force (*xinli*) gained traction among intellectuals such as Liang Qichao and Tan Sitong looking to reform the nation by first reshaping the individual mind.[96]

Wood, like many other Americans and Europeans involved with the New Thought movement and Spiritualism between the mid-nineteenth and early twentieth centuries, relied on the notion of ether, the all-permeating medium, to explain how the power of thought can travel through space in a manner akin to sound, light, and electricity.[97] Experimental spiritualities' appeal to scientific theories and technologies such as telegraphy and telephones,

197

Geoghegan argues, was not just a "cultural interpretation or 'fiction' for reflecting on the period's dominant information and communications technology" but a medium in its own terms.[98] The conundrum, however, is the extent to which psychic force is immediate if it is first mediated even by something so elemental and omnipresent as ether. Bolter and Grusin's double logic of remediation in terms of the simultaneous affirmation and denial of mediation operates with full force in the title of Wood's work, "mental photography." Insisting on the one hand that immaterial energy produces all phenomena, not materialism and outward forms, Wood admits on the other hand that human thought always seeks embodiment. The latter gives rise to Wood's comparison of the human body with "a grand composite photograph of previous thinking and mental states."[99] Neither "scalpel" nor "microscope" can discover the power of thought, and yet ideal suggestion is a "plain scientific application of well-understood means to ends."[100] The form of the instructional manual embodies this very conundrum: while thought has to shut itself off from "all physical sensation and imperfection,"[101] *Ideal Suggestion* encourages readers to focus their eyes on its pages, often written with enlarged letters in upper case, to reform their minds.

In a letter to his teacher Ouyang Zhonggu dated August 31, 1896, Tan Sitong praised Fryer's translation of Wood's work and expressed "great joy" upon learning more about the power of the mind (*xinli*).[102] Tan's posthumously published *Renxue* (*An Exposition of Benevolence*, 1898–1901) proposes a thorough mutuality between the mediating medium and mediated substance. In his explication of the Confucian principle of benevolence (*ren*), the ever-changing and everlasting rule of life called *tong* 通 ("mutuality or communication") is a fundamental principle without which benevolence cannot be transmitted.[103] Ether (*yitai*), electricity (*dian*), and mental forces (*xinli*), concepts culled from a mixture of Indian, European, and Chinese traditions, are all interrelated ways through which *ren* manifests itself, and the three in turn generate other phenomena and relations. Take for instance ether's most "spiritual" function in the human brain, which Tan further divided into six components: "main brain (*danao*), cerebellum (*xiaonao*), brain stem (*naodi*), pons (*naoqiao*), spine (*jinao*), and nerves (*naojin*)."[104]

Like Huang Chujiu's advertisements for Dr. Yale's Brain Tonic with which this chapter opened, Tan's philosophy was a product of the period's fascination with neuroanatomical connectivity and media devices and processes. Insofar as "man knows that nerves connect man's 'five features' (*wugua*) and 'hundred bones' (*baiha*) as one body," Tan argues, "surely he knows that electricity pervades heaven and earth and a ten thousand things as one."[105]

Elsewhere, he also compares the brain with telegraphy, stressing that "good thoughts . . . like sending a telegram," travel far with "no obstruction for 10,000 *li* (5000 kilometers)."[106] *Tong* is the ultimate communicative principle *and* machine lying both inside and outside the body.

Given the many affinities between electricity and brain activity, it is difficult to overstate the influence that Wood's psychic force and Tan's *Renxue* played in Xu's conception of brain electricity. The latter is technically not a product that Mr. Braggadocio "invent[s]" (*faming*) but "the most efficient use of natural energy," which he simply regulates, manages, and commercializes.[107] Whereas the telephone, telegraph, and wireless technology are "mechanical" applications of electricity, the brain provides people with a "natural capacity for electrical response" (*ziran you ganying li*) between themselves.[108] In practice, however, precisely because the brain is an "organ possessed by all," unregulated communication will send the world into chaos.[109] There are other technical issues as well, such as the initiating of responses between strangers, coordinating sending and receiving simultaneously, and the effects of such complex operations on the human body. After researching and experimenting on these problems for "two or three years," the narrator comes up with the following solutions. A regularly updated ledger containing users' photographs will be sold at a low price so that users initiating responses recognize one another by sight. Mr. Braggadocio assigns the brain's left hemisphere to be in charge of "incoming transmissions while the right would handle outgoing transmissions," with the cerebellum serving as an "archive." To ensure healthy equilibrium, energy expended in sending messages balances energy gained in receiving them.

For this is in fact the narrator's true discovery: the regulation and management of information access, storage, and content. The power of thought may be invisible, abstract, and virtual, yet it is only accessible through print (the photographic ledger) and person-to-person interaction. Gathering students in his first Shanghai campus, he teaches them how to produce brain electricity through meditation. Only after having grasped "the rules of solemnity" are they taught the remaining procedure of "encoding messages, memorization, and analysis."[110] The course lasts a mere six days, and with forty teaching weeks in a year, Mr. Braggadocio's Shanghai campus graduates 200,000 students per year. The narrator needs quite a few words to delineate the global reach of his educational conglomerate.

In the first year, relatively few students from Western countries came, but by the second year, because of our remarkable success, students came in such droves that by the beginning of classes, there were eight times as many, totaling 800,000. They travelled back across the Pacific Ocean to San Francisco, through Southeast Asia and the Indian Ocean to Africa; through Southeast Asia to the Indian Ocean and on to the Red Sea and the Mediterranean, then westward to the Atlantic Ocean from whence they spread throughout all of Europe. New steamship companies sprang up by the dozen all over, and in a single week I would watch them come and go in a crowded mass. It became necessary to open additional campuses—one e-c⁻ Tⁱ antai, Ningbo, Fuzhou, Guangzhou,

by means of brain electricity could learning education system. Instead, aching in residential campuses. His his behalf, and smaller institutions Here, the sheer number of students f "minor minor characters."[113] So quantifiable in terms of Mr. Brag- eople in the world to come to me s, 100,000 tongues, and 100,000 ing them all."[114]

both American and Chinese ad- o's instruction in brain electricity fishly preoccupied as he is with ... ᴜᵢ ɑ̣ᴛ᷅ ᴛime."[116] His schools are technical institu- tions along the lines of practical education established under the *yangwu* or Self-Strengthening Movement, promoting subjects like astrology and mathematics for their practicality (*shiyong*).[117] Over the last three decades of the nineteenth century, technical education institutions multiplied, in- cluding such prominent officials schools as the Fujian School of Shipbuild- ing (*Fujian chuanzheng xuetang*, 1866), School of Artillery at the Shanghai Jiangnan Arsenal (*Shanghai Jiangnan Zhizhaoju fushu caopao xuetang gon- gyi xuetang*, 1874), Fuzhou School of Telegraphy (*Fuzhou dianbao xuetang*, 1876), Tianjin Naval School (*Tianjin shuishi xuetang*, 1881), and Shanhai Pass Railway School (*Shanhai guan tielu xuetang*, 1895).[118] While these in- stitutions taught the *Four Books* and *Five Classics* (*Sishu wujing*) alongside foreign and less traditional curricula, Mr. Braggadocio's educational empire focuses narrowly on the perfection of a technical skill. Over time, with the increasing momentum of educational reform after the First Sino-Japanese

200

War (1894–95) and the abolition of the imperial examinations in 1905, Chinese practical education likewise concentrated on the acquisition of new skills for the restructuring of the national economy.[119] Hence Yan Fu excluded traditional economies such as agriculture from his idea of technical education, limiting the category of industries (*shiye*) to "matters having to do with science, applied manually to the use of machines to grow profit, which benefits the people and increases their livelihood"—in short, to what we know as industrial capitalism.[120]

There has been no lack of fictional works envisaging an economically developed China: the Shanghai of Baoyu's dream in *New Story of the Stone* flaunts numerous Chinese factories and businesses, and similar images of prosperity can be found in Liang's *Xin Zhongguo weilai ji* (*The Future of New China*) and *Xin Zhongguo* (*New China*) by Lu Shie (1878–1944).[121] Xu's "New Tales," in contrast, pulls such proud images from the realm of utopian vision to dwell instead on the commonplace, specifically the realm of work related to telegraph, telephone, and transportation networks threatened by the powers of brain electricity.[122] The last two pages of "New Tales," in other words, illuminate capitalism's Other, or what David Harvey calls the "industrial reserve army" of unemployed workers caused by capital's "accumulation by dispossession."[123] Brain electricity, as a natural energy source, posits an alternative to older forms of production that include both manual labor and existing technologies. Whereas knowledge of brain electricity encourages the naturalization of a machine within the body, the unemployed masses are now estranged from their own bodies.

BRAIN WORKERS OF THE WORLD . . .

For reasons outlined above, "New Tales" offers much more than a literary dystopia of modern China in which its protagonist's experience of failure and humiliation paradoxically signifies an expression of national strength.[124] The narrative, by problematizing the role that machines or at least augmented sources of energy play in the collective production process, reconfigures the otherwise familiar ethos of the period as a technically mediated experience. And yet, Xu's story interrogates the materiality of communication less from a technomaterialist perspective but more from a Marxist one. It is able to do so because its science-fictional imagination breaks China out of the confines of its preindustrial present, even to the extent of anticipating post-Fordist theories of intellectual labor that emerged in the late twentieth century. Of course, such a proposition far from dilutes the historical context of semicolonialism, including the importance that European and American scientific beliefs assert on Xu's uncanny story. What "New Tales" does is to project the long-term outcomes of early twentieth-century Chinese educational policies and economic restructuring. In this sense, the last two pages foretell and condense the future of the global political economy as seen from Shanghai in 1904–5.

Marx's seminal, not to mention prescient analysis of machinic labor in the *Grundrisse*'s "Fragment on Machines" is familiar to scholars of late capitalism.[125] There, he distinguishes between fixed capital—that is, raw materials and machinery—from circulating capital, the reproduction of the relations of capital that make up workers' consumption and maintenance of themselves as living labor capacity.[126] This distinction, Marx adds, is based on fixed capital's use in the production process and not by some inalienable "mode of their being." A machine's "durability, or its greater or less perishability" is determined by the amount of time during which it can continue to perform its function, whereby its use value becomes a "form-determining moment, i.e. a determinant for capital as regards its form, not as regards its matter."[127] Since nothing is "natural" or "mechanical" in and of itself but only in its use value in the production process, brain electricity can be seen as circulating capital, which becomes mechanical and fixed in its use as a communicative medium, subsuming labor under an alternative form of "natural" machinery.

Mr. Braggadocio's education empire, moreover, emphasizes the significance of knowledge objectified in the operating of this machinery. The perfection of the art of brain electricity into an all-permeating medium is that which the principle of interconnectivity (*tong*) in Tan Sitong's *An Exposition of Benevolence* attempts to achieve. Automation—that is, the free associative powers of brain electricity *en masse*—transforms the skill into a system and achieves the idea of *tong* in practice.[128] The result that automation has on the worker, however, far from achieving Tan's vision of mutuality and communion, produces alienation and abstraction. In explicating this process, Marx employs metaphors that resonate uncannily with the imagery of the brain in late Qing discourse as a natural organ connecting each person to every other. Since machines "act upon workers like an alien power," labor "appears, rather, merely as a conscious organ, scattered among the individual living workers at numerous points of the mechanical system."[129] The organic and the mechanical cross over in Marx's description of the "living (active) machine" confronting the individual worker's "insignificant doings as a mighty organism."[130] Finally,

The accumulation of knowledge and of skill, of the general productive forces of the *social brain*, is thus absorbed into capital, as opposed

202

to labor, and hence appears as an attribute of capital, and more specifically of fixed capital, in so far as it enters into the production process as a means of production proper.[131]

Mr. Braggadocio's invention of brain electricity is quite literally—continuing the literal or denotative reading I have practiced throughout this book—the accumulation of knowledge and skill by the "social brain" of new Chinese capital. While primitive accumulation in Marx's original study entails the privatization of traditional assets such as land, the narrator's educational conglomerate foresees the future postindustrial or information society where technological knowledge of brain electricity creates surpluses of capital and labor, which can then be seized upon for profitable use in the future.[132] Herein lies Marx's foresight into the post-Fordist mode of production while writing in 1858, and Xu Nianci's science-fictional foray into a postindustrial society in 1905 before China embarked on full-scale industrialization.

Over time, knowledge required in the operation of machinery, according to Marx, becomes a direct force of production. He calls this the "general intellect," general because "the conditions of the process of social life itself have come under" its control "and been transformed in accordance with it."[133] As Paolo Virno explains, Marx's original expression of "general intellect" in English counters Rousseau's *volonté générale*, and in some ways serves as a "materialist" version of Aristotle's *nous poietikos*, "the impersonal and separate 'active mind.'"[134] Transposed to Xu's fiction, brain electricity's materialist take on social production confronts the uneasy relation that mental healing and psychic power, the story's intellectual influences, have with the material world. As I have repeatedly emphasized, it is with the *effects* of unemployment—namely, what Marx terms the presentation of "general social labor" in capital—that the multitude resurfaces toward the end of the narrative as a minor character.[135] And it is by manifesting the uncontrollable, excessive aspect of minorness that the mass unemployed expels the egoistic narrator.

What, then, becomes of the self-other relationship under this condition of the general intellect? How does the narrator's metamorphosis into biomedia translate to the accumulation of knowledge and skill in the (social) brain electricity? Extending Marx's notion of the general intellect, autonomist Marxists such as Antonio Negri, Michael Hardt, and Maurizio Lazzarato show how post-Fordist economies prioritize communication and subjectivity in the production process, placing increasing emphasis on the informational, cultural, or affective elements of the commodity.[136] Manual labor now involves "intellectual" activities, and "new communicative technologies

203

increasingly require subjectivities that are rich in knowledge."[137] Whereas an earlier division lay between physical and intellectual labor, the new "management mandate" demands that all workers, not just highly skilled ones, "become subjects of communication."[138] Even a worker's personality and subjectivity are calculated in the production of value. Because of this communicational model premised upon networks and flows, immaterial labor presupposes "immediately collective" forms. Consumption is now about the consumption of information.[139] The latter, in turn, does not simply terminate at the act of consumption but continues to shape the ideological and cultural environment of the consumer. For these reasons, it is important to insist that "immaterial labor produces first and foremost a 'social relationship.'"[140] As Marx already demonstrates, knowledge and skill belong to the general productive forces inherent in labor, and are absorbed into capital only when it enters into the production process as a means of production.[141] Thus industry does not originate this social labor power, which forms the basis for immaterial labor, but simply "takes it on board and adapts it."[142]

Mr. Braggadocio's third-person reference to his soul- and bodily-selves does not place him outside the process of social communication and the production of subjectivity in the narrative, but in fact initiates them. His technical recontextualization of the body as the biomedia of light, heat, and sound further emphasizes the importance of the production of subjectivity, signaled by the recovery of his lost journal, for the purposes of communication. These communicative processes are not productive in the economic sense, however, until the narrator's discovery of brain electricity, thereby dramatizing the process by which, in Lazzarato's words, the "social" becomes "economic."[143] Nestled in this early Chinese work of science fiction is thus a study of "the production of subjectivity defined as the constitutive 'process' specific to a 'relation to the self,'" which *also connects to* "the forms of capitalist valorization."[144] Without Mr. Braggadocio's establishment of worldwide campuses, the sending of instantaneous messages from mind to mind will not become so successful that it replaces existing forms of communication. The teaching of brain electricity merely exploits, as in late twentieth-century industry, what everyone already has—namely, the social basis of communication and the production of subjectivity—as *the* medium for interconnectivity or *tong*, now revealed, simply, as capital.

Evaluating "New Tales" as a literary response to the restructuring of the Chinese economy, moreover, also occasions a rethinking of the role of late Qing intellectualism. In "Lun shengli fenli" ("On Production and Consumption"), Liang Qichao distinguishes between direct and indirect producers, and

204

physical (*tili*) and mental labor (*xinli*).[145] He further divides mental labor into intellectual (*zhili*) and ethical labor (*deli*). The essay outlines six kinds of productive labor (*shengli*), thirteen categories for people who are unproductive because they only consume, and seven types of people who are simultaneously producers and consumers. Typical professions considered as mental laborers fall within the last category, and they include scholars (*dushu ren*), teachers (*jiaoshi*) and certain officials (*guanshi*).[146] Consumption is patently normative and profit-driven: producers of harmful goods such as opium are denigrated as consumers who do not produce, and failing to use machinery (*qixie*) such as the railway and mining technologies properly for cost-efficient practices makes one a consumer rather than producer.[147] Liang ends the essay, as he routinely does, by calling for reform, which raises the question as to whether the work of reform and self-renewal (*zixin*) is production or consumption, or both, and whether it can be identified as intellectual or ethical labor.[148]

Like Jia Baoyu in *New Story of the Stone*, Mr. Braggadocio starts out in the narrative as a particular late Qing intellectual archetype: caught between Western learning and indigenous traditions, the idealist narrator is also particularly aware of the delusions of grandeur in which patriotism often indulges. Similar to Baoyu's transformation in Wu's novel, the narrator of Xu Nianci's text increasingly manipulates his own body as the medium for transmitting messages of reform. His discovery of brain electricity after the incredible transformation of his brain, however, appears to be a solely commercial enterprise with no echoes of the kind of ethical labor that Liang alludes to. On the one hand, it is possible to read this commercial focus as an illustration of how "intellectual labor has become subjected to the norms of capitalist production."[149] On the other hand, the new medium that is brain electricity blurs the lines between manual and intellectual work, and the ethical and the commercial. The leveling of labor and the closing of different spheres of social production accomplish the goal of universal connectivity (*tong*).

Uses of "medium" to refer to a distinct device, according to Raymond Williams, abstract the word from societal practices.[150] In contrast, early uses of medium to refer to mass communications such as a newspaper or advertising referred to "a social organ or institution" rather than an "intermediate communicative substance."[151] The latter meaning similarly began to dominate discussions of the visual arts as the material in which the artist's work overtook the practice. Accompanying this "reification of the medium" was the distinction of art from mechanical work or manual work, and thus a division of labor and class. The substitution of medium as the working process itself worsened as the capitalist system of material production for

205

the market grew in size. Artists—painters, sculptors, dramatists, musicians, and writers—remain manual workers insofar as they produce works with manual skills, and with "physical and material consciousness."[152]

With Williams's insight, I would recast Thacker's work on biomedia and Mr. Braggadocio's brain electricity, the most direct manifestation of intellectual and mental work, in terms of such materiality. After all, it is commodity production and not the materiality of the working process that is degrading, warranting the need for art to be elevated into "abstracted 'higher' or 'spiritual' forms."[153] Within this working process, Williams singles out communication, language, and the production of subjectivity for evoking "many of the most intense and most significant forms of human experience."[154] Here, Williams and Lazzarato would agree on the same point. If immaterial labor and the technical medium of its transmission are premised on social relations and specific material means of production, "New Tales" tracks the mediation of the technological and the socioeconomic through its narrative characterization of the one and the many. What becomes obsolete at the end of Xu's story is less traditional forms of labor and existing communicative technology, and more the division between intellectual and manual labor—namely, the totality of social production itself. The work of reform and self-renewal that Liang calls for at the end of his essay "On Production and Consumption" is *both* physical and intellectual: it consumes as well as produces.

This is how the novel economy alluded to in "New Tales" circles back to Huang Chujiu's multipart advertisement "Yale Brain Tonic Guarantee" with which this chapter opened. They bring together the distinct genres of advertising and fictional narrative, as well as the intellectual contexts of neurology, psychology, technology, and nationalism, in order to jointly reinforce interconnectivity (*tong*) as the ends of social production. Neat divisions of labor—whereby scientists study the brain and the nervous system, writers exploit the symbolisms of human anatomy for the nation-state, technophiles adapt the brain's innate psychic powers for technical contexts, and entrepreneurs profit from selling magical cures to rejuvenate the citizen's slackened nerves—no longer hold. With the enigmatic ending of "New Tales," the question of the self with which the narrator begins his adventures ceases to be a strictly philosophical or narrative problem. Instead, the self enters the social world of economic production to emerge as the "general productive forces of the social brain."[155]

Stone, Woman, Wireless

Whither Jia Baoyu's stone and Mr. Braggadocio's proto-wireless imagination today, two seemingly contrasting contrivances mediating turn-of-the-twentieth-century China? One self-identifies as an ancient Chinese mythological tool to convey early twentieth-century visions of techno-utopian governance. Another is a fantastic energy source and messaging device poised to replace intellectual and manual labor through practical education. Both pace the interminable relays of history, technology, and culture: the stone and the wireless imbue the historical weight of Qing society with timeless appeal, and infuse the materialities of inscriptions, transmissions, and interconnections with literary conventions and cultural traditions. Throughout this book, the stone and the wireless serve not as tokenistic symbols of what the Chinese term for communicative media, *meiti*, was and could be before its popular usage. Instead, they actively reconstruct what inscriptions, transmissions, and interconnectivity *do*—namely, mediate between physical devices and techniques on the one hand, and their discursive significations as forms of media on the other. As bookends, the two objects also exceed themselves by stepping over thresholds of the technological to invite in the more ephemeral and the allusive, and vice versa. More than simply an argument for the politics undergirding technological innovations and communicative devices, *The Stone and the Wireless* gathers both familiar and lesser-known documents of late Qing intellectual and cultural history to recast the historical period through the problem of the forms of relation between technology "itself" and its "softer" equals.

The stone *and* the wireless—and not *from* the stone *to* the wireless—sketch a media archaeology of nonlinear Chinese modernity.[1] At their core, my chapters mobilize the Chinese terms for recording (*ji*), transmission or biographies (*chuan* or *zhuan*), and interconnectivity (*tong*) to contribute to mediation's revival in contemporary media theory. One impetus for this renewed attention toward mediation comes from Marxist and post-Marxist scholars seeking to prioritize certain inflections of the "social, aesthetic, technical, and (not least) critical" roles of mediation that were nominally "suspended by Kittler."[2] Another strand of media theory strives to recuperate more experimental workings of mediation unbridled by the normative drive to assess media in terms of their potential for social change as practiced by the Frankfurt School, cultural theory, and continental philosophy.[3] It appears that, the mercurial landscape of media notwithstanding, mediation is here to stay.

Having said that, I do not intend *ji, chuan* or *zhuan*, and *tong* to substitute perfectly as mediation. Insofar as each Chinese term refers to a distinct literary genre or social practice as well as a communicative function, it consolidates the abovementioned efforts to reintegrate social and cultural processes of mediation, in which linguistic translation plays an essential role, with studies of material media. At the same time, these keywords, which structure the book's five main chapters, surpass "the operationalization for a native method" or "a genealogy of native concepts" with which we can then safely attain a "pure equivalence" between Western media theory and local Chinese context.[4] Instead, I marshal *ji, chuan* or *zhuan*, and *tong* as "the specific conditions through and in which concept and history"—along with their affiliated binaries of the foreign and the Chinese, and technology and culture—are first rendered legible and then problematized.[5]

The Stone and the Wireless examines the discursive media forms represented in diaries, newspaper and magazine articles, telegrams, photographs, letters, and fictional prose and poetry without losing sight of the technical and material contours of these very media documents, which in turn represent other communicative devices and practices. The practice of media formalism this book advances therefore differs from Lev Manovich's practice in *The Language of New Media*.[6] Instead of treating media technologies as formal devices with their *own* language—that is, with distinct techniques and modes of operation—I return media *to* language and, most of all, to the vicissitudes of meaning and interpretation. Far from harboring a tenuous relation to history, I align my understanding of media forms with Frederic Jameson's investment in "the poetics of social forms," Bao Weihong's "politics of media" as the "strategic and rhetorical positioning of cinema vis-à-vis media old and new," and Xiao Liu's notion of "precarious mediation" tied to technological failure and social upheavals.[7] Following Williams's critique

CONCLUSION

of McLuhan's work as "a development and elaboration of formalism" from other disciplines to the letter,[8] I bring recent invigorations of historically inflected formalism in literary and film studies to overlap with media theory's re-enchantment with politics and the social. In turning next to contemporary Chinese science fiction's exploration of the problematic intersection of gendered subjectivity and technological form, this study concludes by showing how the work of mediation still has a long way to go.

As the road to an immanently mediating inquiry—whereby "media" marks both the subject and method of my study—winds down, the yoking of structure and argument risks coming apart in the middle, and could use some final stitching. Chapter 3, led by the double-meaning character 傳, examines various life writings (*zhuan*) of femininity through the technical transmissibility (*chuan*) of lyricism. Like the figure of the exemplary female conduit on whom it dwells, this chapter connects the first and second halves of this book while also turning away from them. The woman-as-intermediary has her own stories about technology to tell; and yet, most of the voices in this study are admittedly masculine. Contrast, if you will, Qiu Jin's ambivalent femininity as a lyrical medium with Mr. Braggadocio's pompously universal recontextualization of both his soul- and physical-selves into light, heat, an illuminating screen, and finally, brain electricity. While the woman's self-presentation in the hybridized media format of verse and photograph chips away the iconicity of her legacy as a female martyr, the man's multiple subjectivity is seldom questioned until he is expelled from his empire of infinite energy and perfect communion. We would not detect Qiu Jin's mediated lyricism in the patriotic verses that stupendously appear on the stone, which Jia Baoyu gifts Old Youth at the end of Wu's novel: nowhere are the feminine origins of Nüwa's tool inscribed on its stony surface.

Is it even necessary to point out that whereas Qiu Jin's legacies have thrived in modern Chinese history, the bombastic narrations of Mr. Braggadocio or Baoyu are seldom celebrated in modern Chinese fiction? I do not think so. Indeed, that the midpoint of this study monumentalizes autobiographical and biographical feminine obscuration, and ends with a fantastical story of masculine self-adulation, only accentuates the troubling intersections between genre and gender. If my intermediary chapter—one that also fails to connect—attempts to retrieve women's relationships to technology in ways that have not been co-opted by masculine-nationalist ideologies, it is only appropriate to conclude this book by tracking once more the cultural appropriation of women's affinity to communicate and connect in our present moment.

As a generative, natural, and uncostly communicative device to end any need for media writ large, brain electricity in the last chapter unexpectedly reintroduces the laboring masses displaced by capital. The point of mining Xu Nianci's 1904–5 text for a Marxist critique is not, contra Galloway, Thacker, and Wark, to determine media "normatively as either good influencers or bad influencers,"[9] but to highlight how we need an understanding of mediation to untie the Gordian knot of technology, communications, and the social relations of production. Xu's late Qing story's remarkable conclusion stages the inevitable clashes between more traditional physical labor and the new knowledge economy. Occluded there, however, is how practical advances in the education and industries (*shiye*) of the early twentieth century also prompted women's liberation movements on the grounds of national-industrial development.[10] Historically, advanced technologies intensified, rather than erased, the complexities of women's work, a critique similarly directed to theories of immaterial or cognitive labor for obfuscating post-Fordism's continuing reliance on traditional forms of wage labor from the Global South.[11] The portrayal of a male entrepreneur and his invention of brain electricity in "New Tales of Mr. Braggadocio" therefore begs the question of what a feminine repossession of media technology would look like.

While late Qing reformers' quest for wealth and power fueled the period's utopian imagination, growing inequalities accompanying the postsocialist state's rapid ascension to late global capitalism steer contemporary science fiction from the PRC toward dystopian waters. The 2012 Hugo Award–winning novella *Folding Beijing* by Hao Jingfang (1984–) revolves around a third-class citizen in a city where physical space is unevenly allocated, by time, among different economic classes.[12] The short story "Lijiang de yuermen" ("The Fish of Lijiang," 2006) by Chen Qiufan (Stanley Chan, 1981–) similarly dramatizes the technological manipulation of time and its perpetuation of class divides. In his only full-length novel to date, *Huang chao* (2013), translated as *Waste Tide* (2019),[13] Chen sets the complex interplay of information communicative technologies, environmental degradation, and labor conditions on the dystopian Silicon Isle (*Guiyu*), a fictional town loosely based on the real Guiyu in Guangdong, known for being one of the world's largest and most polluted e-waste sites. On this post-2020 island, three powerful local clans (the Luos, Lins, and Chens), foreign investors, and even environmental activist groups variously profit from unregulated e-waste processing industries. The underpaid and contaminated migrant workers (aptly referred

210

to as the "waste people") in turn indulge in black markets, electronic hallucinatory drugs and cheap prosthetic enhancements, while the Chinese government controls the flow of digital information by designating the island as a low-bitrate zone. *Waste Tide* exposes the codependent logic of neoliberal free market ideologies, state control, and traditional clan governance; global capital flows and economic sabotage; technological sophistication and animism; and environmental degradation and activism, all immersed in a "high-tech, low-life" atmosphere characteristic of the cyberpunk tradition.[14]

More crucially, the story centers on a young electronic waste–processing worker, Xiaomi, her disturbing endowment with a powerful split consciousness, and her eventual path toward martyrdom in order to rescue an apathetic human race from self-destruction. She first develops significant brain alterations after coming into contact with a mysterious silicon-biotechnology e-waste virus. After being raped and buried alive by small-time thugs from the Luo clan, Xiaomi's consciousness (*yishi*) escapes her body (104). Although her consciousness lacks physical form, it "recalls" her suffering and "sees" her perpetrators right in front of her, and yet is unable to touch them (104). Not unlike Xu's description of Mr. Braggadocio's mind-body split, Chen augments Xiaomi's quasi-mystical, out-of-body experience with physiological details. Xiaomi's consciousness, too, lacks eyes, ears, nose, and tongue, but nonetheless has extraordinary sensory perception, and without hands or feet is able to move at will. It takes control over an abandoned, damaged robot by entering into its half-burned exoskeleton, and the union of human consciousness and robot acts out both the primitive choreography of a "shamanistic ritual," and the neurological visualization of electrical waves sweeping over countless neurons in a "three-dimensional field" (105).

Whereas Mr. Braggadocio's metamorphosis is a result of self-discovery and the pursuit of knowledge, that of the *Waste Tide*'s female protagonist is plotted with gratuitous violence. The figure of the female medium whom I evoked in chapter 3 assumes here a cyborg form, and also, unfortunately, cyberpunk's notorious sexism. Chen's original draft had graphic details of Xiaomi's rape; in our email correspondences, the author explained to me that these details were censored by his mainland publisher, Changjiang wenyi, for fears of "causing negative effect[s] on the youth."[15] The author tried to reinsert the censored scenes for the North American English translation of the novel, but the editor of Tor Books similarly felt the "unnecessary violence" untoward. In response, Chen rewrote the original rape scene into one "with more tech involvement to soften the violence," which the American-Chinese award-winning author Ken Liu then duly translated for the 2019 publication.

211

What this complex censorship, editorial, and rewriting process reveals is the sexual politics behind science fiction's depiction of new media and their promises of disembodiment.[16] In the published English translation, Xiaomi's rapist puts on a helmet joined to an "augmented sensing device shaped like a six-tentacled octopus," whose electric pulses, unbearably painful for the victim, delivers to the perpetuator "an experience richer, more encompassing, more addictive than that of any drug in the history of mankind."[17] With two entire pages graphically depicting this "otherworldly . . . tech of nightmares" absent from the published version of the Chinese text, it is difficult to resist the sense that Chen's rewrite, while kindly intended to "soften the violence" of a "conventional" rape,[18] ends up functioning as a "literary" augmentation of sorts to amplify the novel's science-fictional, prosthetics-filled qualities. Even if one were to spare the depicted tentacled device from phallic interpretations of the most superficial kind, it is quite impossible to accept without question Chen's equation of "high-tech" with "softer violence." The florid English prose—I do not have access to the Chinese rewrite with which the translator worked—describing the rapist's ecstatic reactions to Xiaomi's biofeedback signals gathered from the augmented sensing device could be allegorically interpreted as symptoms of contemporary Chinese science fiction's global ascendance.[19] The exorbitant "cost for the next hit,"[20] to borrow the narrator's description of drug addiction in the novel, falls disproportionately on women.

By highlighting the false distinction between so-called mediated and immediate violence, the above, "augmented" scene also redraws the intersection between more literal or technical meanings of a medium and its more figurative or instrumental usages. I argue in chapter 3 that the more literal meaning of a model or an example as merely one technical model among many others paradoxically rescues the woman from the strait-jackets of moral conventions and national goals. The becoming-technical of the female medium, however, suffers from opposite repercussions in *Waste Tide*. The disturbingly technical "recontextualization" of Xiaomi's rape, to borrow a term from Thacker's theory of biomedia, in addition to her further recontextualization in a robot's exoskeleton, would multiply the female protagonist—not unlike the tentacled device to which she was subjected— for the sake of, as we will see, resolving the novel's portrayal of class conflict and moral degradation.

Whereas Mr. Braggadocio very quickly aspires for his soul- and physical-selves to accomplish something great for China and for himself, *Waste Tide* is slow in revealing the higher purpose of Xiaomi's split consciousness. We are told that there are two versions of herself, Xiaomi 0, the naïve and yet curiously resilient waste girl, and Xiaomi 1, the "unfathomable existence" (*wufa kaikuo de cunzai*) who has unexpectedly possessed Xiaomi 0 like a spirit (153). Xiaomi 0 fears Xiaomi 1, yet hers is a fear bordering on the sublime admiration of a more powerful entity (154), who can intercept information and control other peoples' minds at will (144, 151). Nonetheless, it will only be too confusing, in an already dense plot, to refer to the two Xiaomis; most of the omniscient narration after her metamorphosis refers to Xiaomi plain and simple, without a numerical tag. Like the first-person narrator of "New Tales" who speaks *for* while speaking *as* his soul- and physical-selves, *Waste Tide* suggests that the need for narrative focalization alone engenders a multiplying perspective that the science of a dissociative consciousness brought about by neurological mutation tries to explain. Xiaomi, as the third-person "she," thus stands over and above her two selves in ways even more enigmatic than the commands that Xiaomi 1 wields over other characters in the novel.

While the "0" and "1" suffixed to Xiaomi's name evoke the binary logic of computational calculations, Xiaomi "as such" pits the narrative representation of the one and the many against the computational. The latter essentially constitutes, according to Katherine Hayles, any "process that starts with a parsimonious set of elements and a relatively small set of logical operations."[21] For this reason, if Xiaomi's confounding neurological anomaly renders her like a computer that processes and communicates information beyond human capabilities, it far from celebrates post-humanism and the disembodied virtuality of information. Instead, *Waste Tide* pulls its readers headlong into violent representations of women's bodies and the struggle with capital—problems that only prove to be magnified in the age of computation. Though the "0" and "1" may allude to computational data, Xiaomi, as the third-person "she," signals limits to the textual representations of digitality. The very form of address with which the novel relays her split consciousness thus undercuts the narrative's digital exploits. This, then, marks the exorbitant price of Xiaomi's "mediated" violence: her assault via a devious prosthesis affords her with both the literal and more figurative meanings of the female medium. She serves as the necessary grammatical intermediary between her original and psychic selves without which the narrative would not make sense; she is also, upon gaining advanced computational capabilities, the perfect go-between for bringing together China's haves and have-nots.

Whereas the working masses only appear toward the end of "New Tales of Mr. Braggadocio," they prop up Guiyu's nouveau riche as victims of uneven development and digital fetishization. In *Waste Tide*'s early pages, we are introduced to the island's nightmarish waste processing sites, where metal casings, damaged display screens, circuit boards, plastic parts, and wires are piled like manure, and around which migrant workers hover like flies (32). The workers are in turn consumers of the electronic goods on which their livelihoods depend, though they can only afford *shanzhai* (a Chinese term for counterfeit goods) augmented-reality glasses and illegally downloaded programs for entertainment purposes. Only when pursuing Xiaomi's rapists do we see the waste people transform their cyber addiction for individual forms of escape into a collective countersurveillance network against their exploitative employers who control the island's CCTV system.[22]

As the e-waste workers proclaim in underground fliers, a "war" has now begun between labor and capital (118)—and clearly, we must add, gender. After Xiaomi returns home from her near-death experience, the waste people go on strike to force the Luos to hand over her rapist and murderer (175). In retaliation, the Luo clan cuts their water and food rations, and a total shutdown of the migrant workers' communication channels looms (197). The backstory to the island's restricted-bitrate status is then revealed: the Chinese central authorities clamped down on Guiyu after another rape case of a young e-waste worker some years ago—recorded on camera and subsequently circulated—agitated a series of network violations. Xiaomi's attempt to circumvent Guiyu's bitrate restrictions in order to upload the e-waste workers' consciousnesses to a low-orbit server station to form a fast-connecting network between them (197–98) thus more than short-circuits internet protocols. The technically detailed descriptions of how Xiaomi skillfully bypasses local network proxies in the third part of the novel barely masks the two incidences of violence against women. For all of the narrative's baroque dedication to algorithmic functions, data tracking, and augmented reality scenarios, it is the traditional figure of the female medium who exposes the true cost of *Waste Tide*'s "high-tech" overdrive.

THE LONG MARCH OF THE LABORING MASSES

Early Chinese science fiction imparts a few lessons from a distance: if Mr. Braggadocio's invention of brain electricity hinges upon his split consciousness such that the narrative form of the many-*in*-the-one undergirds the principle of perfect communication, it is Xiaomi's disturbing dissociations after her assault which endows her with frequency-hopping skills to aggregate the waste people's consciousness. Even passages portraying the workers' uploaded minds as they are digitally transmitted to the nearest unrestricted bitrate zone, Shantou, resemble the brief depiction of the laboring

214

masses in "New Tales." In *Waste Tide*, metaphors typically used to depict the physical mob apply to the virtual realm: their consciousnesses are "scattered" like "floating spirits" (*youling ban fupiao*). Like "tourists," they "cannot contain their excitement" (*chuchu yu dong*), while their guide, in contrast, combs through Shantou's surveillance system, an observer scrutinizing the city as an unfolding, self-organizing fractal structure (*zizhu ji fengxing jigou*) (210). After finding what she is looking for, a "very small aperture terminal" (VSAT) on a television station's van, and with only two minutes or so before her hacking will be detected by the authorities, Xiaomi 1, in an effort to turn on the VSAT system, lets loose the waste people's consciousnesses, which like "feral horses" that have just been unrestrained, run amok (213). At first they rush about erratically, but they finally reach agreement and head in the same direction. With code-cracking tools provided by Xiaomi 1, they rush to break the digital locks of the city's prison, releasing prisoners who, like the waste people's consciousnesses, clumsily regain their freedom of movement. The station that owns the van rushes to report the prison break, thus activating the VSAT system, which searches for a satellite signal.

Here, the crowd manifests as an uncontrollable minor figure, which, to return to my extension of Alex Woloch's analysis in the previous chapter, is unable to restrain its interiority.[23] Class consciousness in *Waste Tide* appears as a force to be reckoned with, but so disorderly that the class needs to be reined in by a more rational leader. Yet, Xiaomi is only slightly more in control than the masses whom she commands, as she inwardly remains destabilized. Xiaomi 0 disagrees with Xiaomi 1's action of first breaking open the prison, and then wreaking havoc on the traffic control system. When asking her more impulsive self whether she has killed anyone in the process, Xiaomi 1 replies nonchalantly that *she* has not, but, shifting the blame to the rest of the waste people, "*they* have" (214, emphasis added). In both "New Tales" and *Waste Tide*, "minorness" manifest as larger, far more abstract units of social existence. The two novels, from otherwise contrasting eras of Chinese-language science fiction, attempt to represent social totality first by challenging the "discrete representation of any specific individual."[24] Neither Mr. Braggadocio nor Xiaomi are singular units in juxtaposition to the whole, but relate to their respective crowds instead as heterogeneous selves that are bound to multiply.

Xiaomi's multiplicity, moreover, echoes my assessment of the instrumentality of female lyricism in chapter 3, which examines how a woman's emotional sensitivity makes her especially ideal as a martyr for collective causes in late Qing women's journals and early feminist writings. In this instance, data storage and cloud computing intensify the problem of feminine instrumentality. After gaining access to a low-orbit server called Anarchy.Cloud, Xiaomi 1 asks the organization to disrupt the existing network in Guiyu and grant the waste people a communicative channel of their own. Toward the end of the novel, Xiaomi 1 finally reveals to Xiaomi 0 the moral reason behind her elaborate hacking. She has planned the shutdown of Guiyu's entire network just as a catastrophic storm is about to hit. The waste people are then presented with two options: either choose between doing nothing while the rest of the Guiyu residents die, or to help the very people who have subjugated them (227–28). They choose the second option; much to Xiaomi 1's relief, there is still hope for humanity. Long-term addiction to dopamine and technological augmentations have, she explains, damaged the physiological basis for the survival of the human race—namely, neural patterns that control feelings of sympathy, shame, fairness, and morality (236). The entire effort to bypass the firewall and cause damage along the way was meant to remind the waste people of the basic values of empathy and cooperation that they are in danger of losing. Mr. Braggadocio, who, after being repeatedly disappointed with the Chinese people's moral corruption, is tempted to terminate the entire race. Xiaomi 1, on the other hand, turns out to be less cynical than she appears, as she only manipulates the "technical recontextualization" of her former physical body in order to cease the acceleration of human extinction brought about by other biomedia reconfigurations.[25]

Despite pompously branding Xiaomi 1 as the "unintentional whirlpool" in the "self-organizing deluge of modern technology" (235), the narrative abruptly writes her off; the protagonist, after a violent struggle, loses all her cognitive functions and is left with the intelligence of a three-year old. At least Mr. Braggadocio receives a less demeaning send-off at the end of "New Tales" as his proto-wireless invention makes obsolete existing forms of work, causing labor unrest that hints at a possible crisis of capital. In contrast, the waste people, after saving the well-to-dos of Guiyu, return to their posts at work. The clans agree to promote modern management practices in the waste processing industry, including a freer movement of labor and better working conditions (250). As a reward for their collective efforts during the typhoon, the government relaxes their monitoring of Guiyu's network and bitrate restriction. All in all, the dirty work of manually sorting out the different categories of e-waste remains to be done. Should Xu have continued his story after Mr. Braggadocio's abrupt exit, perhaps the same process of labor's reabsorption into capital might have befallen the unemployed masses.

From the tremendous change in Mr. Braggadocio's brain that leads him to discover brain electricity, to Xiaomi's own neurological mutation and eventual martyrdom, the late Qing proto-wireless imagination finds a problematically gendered sequel in Chen's *Waste Tide*.

If imaginary media and fantastic communicative channels in "New Tales" foreground the problems of labor and political economy in early industrial, turn-of-the-twentieth-century China, *Waste Tide*, by momentarily turning a female migrant worker into the "social brain" of Guiyu's underclass, raises the specter of sexual politics and gender difference in the PRC's phenomenal economic ascent and its technological innovations since its market reforms in the late 1970s. The contemporary novel rethinks what media do via the female body, not only because Xiaomi's neurological mutations and subsequent leadership among the waste people magnify contemporary debates over the dominance of information control over traditional categories of class and labor,[26] but also because the English version of the text attempts to mitigate, with effects to the contrary, her assault through augmented-reality technologies. This most distressing technical mediation generates new forms that must be read for: just as Mr. Braggadocio's mind-body split provides a glimpse into future class conflicts, Chen's rewritten scene of "high-tech" sexual violence jars uncomfortably with his "low-tech" depiction of the e-waste workers' uploaded consciousness. Literary fiction entangles different representations of technical, social, and cultural mediations in surprising ways. In any case, both early and contemporary Chinese science-fictional imagination reinforce the idea that communication is never simply the transmission (*chuan*), whether successful or not, of information between peoples, but also the problem of connectivity (*tong*) *within* each individual. Such an instance of interconnectivity as both a technological theme and narrative form shows that devices, objects, and processes, as well as their larger social and cultural significations, continue to grapple with the problems of the one-in-the-many and the many-in-the-one.

Needless to say, the twenty-first century offers an exhausting (and yet inexhaustible) range of issues for anyone interested in global China: from the domestic costs of the PRC's economic restructuring, such as its impact on migrant workers, to the country's global role as both producer and recycler of information communication technologies. The urgency of environmental degradation in particular push *Waste Tide* toward a didactic resolution not dissimilar to late Qing nationalist discourses, which sought moral exemplars in the feminine propensity to feel. Contrary to the earlier historical impulse, however, the contemporary novel shows that the global ecological crisis exceeds any call for a national solution, let alone ethnocentric claims to technological innovations. In this regard, Chen's commendable use of the Shantou-Guiyu dialect in Waste Tide is not insignificant

The Stone and the Wireless has prioritized less overtly political aspects of late nineteenth- and early twentieth-century writings, not because nation-building and the search for the perfect citizen are uninteresting or unimportant, but because these issues have often appropriated other mediums both figurative and literal, and technical and political-ethical, to achieve their ends. Until we understand the complex interplays between the signi-fied forms of media and their physical, material forms, starting with the de-ceptively simple question of what it is that media *do*, the work of mediation will continue to be unevenly and unjustly distributed.[27]

218

NOTES

Introduction: The Forms of Media

1 Liu, *Translingual Practice*, 266, 351. *Tongxin xianji*, a neologism derived from English missionary texts, was used to refer to "communication device." A similar neologism from Japan, *dianqi tongxin xue*, refers more specifically to the modern usage of "telecommunications." Unfortunately, this resourceful appendix does not indicate the dates of these new Chinese terms.

2 Li Gui, *A Journey to the East*, 119.

3 Li Gui, *A Journey to the East*, 119.

4 Mullaney, *The Chinese Typewriter*, 24.

5 Li Gui, *A Journey to the East*, 121–22. It is not difficult to detect in Li's troubled hearing in the Machinery Hall allusions to twentieth-century studies of noise. Claude Shannon and Warner Weaver's 1949 book *The Mathematical Theory of Communication* has canonized the inclusion of noise, as informational entropy, into the consideration of information (see Bruce Clarke, "Information"). Drawing diversely from fables, physics, information theory, anthropology, music, art, and political economy, Michel Serres contends that only noisy, noncommunicative channels mediate, and that the parasitical relation, or nonrelation, spells the essence of relations (Serres, *The Parasite*, 78).

6 Li Gui, *A Journey to the East*, 119.

7 Desnoyers, "Translator's Preface," in Li Gui, *A Journey to the East*, vi.

8 Galloway, Thacker, and Wark, *Excommunication*, 9–10.

9 The phrase "when old technologies were new" evokes the title of Carolyn Marvin's seminal book.

10 An Haibo, "Wan Qing de 'guang yu chengxiang.'"

11 Tang Hongfeng, "Huandeng yu dianying de bianzheng."

12 Baark, *Lightning Wires*.

13 Karl, *The Magic of Concepts*, 12.

14 Liu, *Information Fantasies*, 15.

15 For an assessment of these historical demarcations, see the introduction in Starr's *Red-Light Novels of the Late Qing*.

16 Xiao Liu, *Information Fantasies*, 15–16.

17 For a helpful encapsulation of New Qing History, see Rawski, "Reenvisioning the Qing"; Waley-Cohen, "The New Qing History."

18 Karl, *The Magic of Concepts*, 13.

19 Zhang Longxi, "Western Theory and Chinese Reality," 116.

20 Zhang Longxi, "Western Theory and Chinese Reality," 128.

21 Saussy, "Outside the Parenthesis," 854. For other works that more indirectly confront this issue common in global or comparative Chinese literary studies, see Bush, *Ideographic Modernism*; Bachner, *Beyond Sinology*; Hayot, *Chinese Dreams*; Hayot, Saussy, and Yao, *Sinographies*; Klein, *The Organization of Distance*; Stalling, *Poetics of Emptiness*; Yao, *Foreign Accents*. For a link between the "container" model of historicizing and contextualizing to the posturing of suspicion in critical reading, see Felski, "Context Stinks!"

22 I borrow the phrase "chiasmus on the predicates" from Saussy, "Outside the Parenthesis," 853.

23 For an overview of these views, see Huters, *Bringing the World Home*, chapter 1, 23–42, wherein the author defends the second position.

24 Chen Depeng, "Wenhua jiegou," 35. For a reappraisal of Zhang's *Quanxue pian*, see Hon Tze-ki, "Zhang Zhidong's Proposal." For a discussion of the mapping of "Chinese learning as essence, Western learning as application" onto the *dao/qi* distinction by the merchant-reformer Zheng Guangyin (1842–1922), see Wu Guo, "Gailiang de di xian."

25 Chen Depeng, "Wenhua jiegou," 35. See also Huters, *Bringing the World Home*, 31–32. In the 1867 memorial by Woren (1804–1871) rejecting the progressive proposal of Prince Gong (Yixin, 1833–1898) to teach Western techniques to Chinese students, he insisted that "skills and crafts" are "trivial," not "fundamental," and that "reliance on technical skills" would fail to "raise [a country] out of weakness" (quoted in Huters, *Bringing the World Home*, 31–32). Philosophical precepts' superiority over technical skills is thus something that opposing factions of the Qing court mutually agreed upon.

26 Fraser, "Heterosexism, Misrecognition, and Capitalism," 286.

27 Karl, *The Magic of Concepts*, 13.

28 In his seminal *Chinese Intellectuals in Crisis*, Hao Chang calls this adaptation of more radical change after 1895 "a crisis of orientational order" (5).

29 Yan Fu, "Lun shi bian zhi ji."

30 Lu Xun, "Wenhua pianzhi lun."

31 Doleželová-Velingerová, "Literary Historiography." The Imperial Edict of January 4, 1904, introducing the new university curriculum, helped give rise to an expanded use of the term *wenxue*, "literature, belles lettres," to cover the broad meaning of "humanities." While humanities curricula excluded Neo-Confucianism and economics, it included historiography, early Chinese philosophy, archival studies, and stylistics. Literature was further divided into the "exegesis of script and prosody," "stylistics and creative writing," "literary

style and grammar," "and propaedeutics." Other new fields of study instituted by the edict included political science (*zhengzhi*), natural sciences (*gezhi*), agronomy (*nongxue*), industrial studies (*gongyi*), business (*shangwu*), and medicine (*yixue*).

32 Snow, *The Two Cultures*. Snow first critiqued the division of Western intellectual life into the sciences and the humanities in the Rede Lecture of May 1959.

33 Latour and Woolgar, *Laboratory Life*; Latour, *We Have Never Been Modern*.

34 Latour, *We Have Never Been Modern*, 81, 48.

35 Felski, "Context Stinks!," 578.

36 Tsu Jing and Elman, *Science and Technology in Modern China*.

37 Tsu Jing and Elman, "Introduction," 7.

38 Guillory, "Genesis of the Media Concept," 354. The under-theorizing of the concept of mediation in media and communication studies is all the more peculiar, Guillory suggests, given how relatively uncontroversial it has been to infer "modes of social mediation" from the operation of technical media, as in the work of John B. Thompson and others.

39 Guillory, "Genesis of the Media Concept," 354.

40 For instance, we could view the concept of *biantong* or dialectics, and the *dao* and *qi* debate, as executing comparable operations of mediation through the reconciliation of conflicting epistemologies, entities, processes, peoples, and domains. See Tian, *Chinese Dialectics*; Mao Zedong, *Mao Zedong on Dialectical Materialism*; Wang Qian, *"Dao" "ji" zhi jian*; Hui Yuk, *The Question Concerning Technology in China*.

41 Marvin, *When Old Technologies Were New*, 4.

42 Galloway, *The Interface Effect*, 17.

43 Rajagopal, "Communicationism," 355.

44 Larsen, "Literature, Immanent Critique, and the Problem of Standpoint"; Ma Shaoling, "To Compare Otherwise."

45 Jones, *Yellow Music*, 11. According to Jones, this slip reveals an ahistorical, analytical oversight, one which mires Chinese media culture in an anxiety of influence.

46 McLuhan, *Understanding Media*.

47 See Gitelman, *Scripts, Grooves, and Writing Machines*. On new media histories and theories that similarly focus on European and American contexts, see Acland, *Residual Media*; Chun and Keenan, *New Media, Old Media*; Gitelman and Pingree, *New Media*; and Wardhip-Fruin and Montfort, *The New Media Reader*. On the branch of German media studies focusing on cultural techniques (*Kulturtechnikforschung*), which is starting to attend to cross-cultural analysis, see Geoghegan, "After Kittler"; Siegert, "Cacography or Communication"; and Vismann, "Cultural Techniques and Sovereignty." 221

48 Jones, *Yellow Music*, 10.

49 The reverse impulse has similarly struck comparative philosophical studies, which accord materiality a Chinese orientation while tracing signification

and form to their provenance in European concerns with mimesis and transcendence. See Saussy, "No Time Like the Present."

50 Lydia H. Liu, to give but one prominent example, proposed more than two decades ago "the idea of 'translingual practice' in [her] book to raise the possibility of rethinking cross-cultural interpretation and forms of linguistic *mediation* between East and West," where mediation does not just operate across linguistic difference but also spans other "cross-cultural" relations between China and other nations (Liu, *Translingual Practice*, xviii).

51 Since David Wang's 1997 *Fin-de-Siècle Splendor*, scholars have successfully unsettled the narrative of decline and stagnation associated with Chinese literary historiography before the May Fourth period. Nevertheless, disagreements arise over the degrees to which such modernity is incipient, transitory, or simply unfixed, which imply that other mediating positions continue to nuance the modernity debate. Hence Starr suggests that rather than overdetermining the late Qing according to one terminology, we ought to "widen the debate by finessing definitions. . . . The new modernity debate needs to acknowledge the continuum of change in literary practices through the nineteenth century and on into the May Fourth era" (*Red-Light Novels*, 14). See also Schwartz, "The Limits of 'Tradition versus Modernity.'"

52 See Tsu Jing, *Failure, Nationalism, and Literature.*

53 Huters, *Bringing the World Home*, 6. Rather than take modernity as his central concept, Huters claims that Westernization, which he defines as "the thorny accommodation between China and the incoming rush of Western ideas and practices," gives the period 1895 and 1919 its "own unique character." Elsewhere in the book he refers to this process of accommodation as a "dialectic" of "Sino-Western relations" whereby the West had been admired and yet disdained at the same time (3).

54 Liu, *Translingual Practice*, xviii. Michael Gibbs Hill's focus on translation as labor, however, risks exposing a lack of mediation between labor and culture insofar as the latter is deemed to be less tangible and material (*Lin Shu, Inc.*, 12).

55 Reed, *Gutenberg in Shanghai*; Wagner, *Joining the Global Public*; Zhang Xiantao, *The Origins of the Modern Chinese Press.*

56 Bao Weihong, *Fiery Cinema*; Liu Xiao, *Information Fantasies.*

57 Saussy, *Great Walls of Discourse*, 2–3.

58 Saussy, *Great Walls of Discourse*, 3. I will further discuss Saussy's deconstructive logic in chapter 3.

59 For a discussion of Pierre Bourdieu's use of the term *praxeology*, see Everett, "Organizational Research." For a political economy approach, see Caldwell, "Praxeology and Its Critics."

60 Galloway, "What Is New Media?," 380.

61 Williams, *Television*, 127.

62 Jones, "The Technology Is Not the Cultural Form?," 6.

63 Jones, "The Technology Is Not the Cultural Form?," 6, emphasis added.

64 Williams, *Television*, 130.

65 Quoted in Jones, "The Technology Is Not the Cultural Form?," 7.

66 Jones describes Williams's use of homology and correspondence as an "embrace" of the "methodological legacy of aesthetic modernism" within a "sociological frame" ("The Technology Is Not the Cultural Form?," 7).

67 An important contribution to this formalist renewal is the March 2000 issue of *Modern Language Quarterly*, which was republished as a book in 2006. See Wolfson, "Reading for Form," and also Wolfson and Brown, *Reading for Form*. Caroline Levine argued for a notion of "strategic formalism" in her 2006 article of the same name, which generated a wave of responses in the subsequent issue of *Victorian Studies*. Levine continues her investigation of literary forms' destabilizing relation to social formation in her most recent work, simply titled *Forms*. Outside the field of literary studies, a most representative defense of cinematic form—and not just form, but also continental theory—can be found in Eugenie Brinkema's *The Forms of the Affects*, 36. There, she argues for a "radical formalism" in film and media studies to counter the dominant fashion of treating affects according to models of expressivity, embodiment, and lived intensities. She also distinguishes her approach from David Borwell and Kristin Thompson's neo-formalism in film studies.

68 Brinkema, *The Forms of the Affects*, 36–37, 39.

69 David Wellbery in 1990 first devised the phrase *post-hermeneutic criticism* to describe the work of Friedrich A. Kittler (Wellbery and Kittler, "Foreword," xiv). Since then, the phrase has been associated with posthumanism and names a subfield of media studies.

70 Geoghegan, "Mind the Gap"; Parks and Starosielski, *Signal Traffic*.

71 Mullaney, *The Chinese Typewriter*, 19. Mullaney develops the phrase *techno-linguistic* to account for the linguistic and infrastructural significance of the typewriter beyond what he calls the "sound-meaning-shape triad."

72 Kittler, *Gramophone, Film, Typewriter*, i.

73 Kittler, *Gramophone, Film, Typewriter*, xxxix–xl.

74 Wellbery and Kittler, "Foreword," xiii.

75 Winthrop-Young and Michael Wutz, "Translator's Introduction," xxxiv.

76 Kittler, *Gramophone, Film, Typewriter*, 33.

77 Kittler, *Gramophone, Film, Typewriter*, 56.

78 Kittler, *Gramophone, Film, Typewriter*, 133.

79 Kittler, *Gramophone, Film, Typewriter*, 155.

80 Kittler, *Gramophone, Film, Typewriter*, 163.

81 Kittler, *Gramophone, Film, Typewriter*, 163.

82 Kittler, *Gramophone, Film, Typewriter*, 200.

83 Kittler, *Gramophone, Film, Typewriter*, 200.

84 Sebastian and Geerke, "Technology Romanticized."

85 Kittler, *Discourse Networks*.

86 See Anker and Felski, *Critique and Postcritique*; Felski, *The Limits of Critique*; Latour, "Why Has Critique Run out of Steam?"

87 Rooney, "Symptomatic Reading," 129–30.

88 Rooney, "Symptomatic Reading," 137–38.

89 Rooney, "Symptomatic Reading," 139–40.

90 Best and Marcus, "Surface Reading," 15.

91 Schmitt, "Tidal Conrad," 13.

92 Schmitt, "Tidal Conrad," 15.

93 Schmitt, "Tidal Conrad," 15.

94 For a non-exhaustive list of scholarship devoted to refining the basic assumptions of what media and mediation are, see Galloway, Thacker, and Wark, *Excommunication*; Guillory, "Genesis of the Media Concept"; Hartley, *Communication, Cultural, and Media Studies*; Kafka, "Media/Medium"; Lacey, *Image and Representation*; Lacey, *Narrative and Genre*; Mitchell and Hansen, *Critical Terms*; Ouellette and Gray, *Keywords for Media Studies*; and Peters, *The Marvelous Clouds*.

95 Rooney, "Form and Contentment," 29.

96 Parikka, "New Materialism as Media Theory," 95–96; see also Allen-Robertson, "The Materiality of Digital Media."

97 Guillory, "Genesis of the Media Concept," 322.

98 Luo Dajing, *Helin yulu*, vol. 6, 109.

99 Williams, *Marxism and Literature*, 187.

100 Williams, *Marxism and Literature*, 97.

101 Williams, *Marxism and Literature*, 99.

102 Li Gui, *A Journey to the East*, 119.

103 Latour, *We Have Never Been Modern*, 81.

104 Hansen, *Embodying Technesis*, 7.

105 Hansen, *Embodying Technesis*, 3.

106 Hansen, *Embodying Technesis*, 8.

107 Hansen, *Embodying Technesis*, 19.

108 Hansen, *Embodying Technesis*, 19.

109 Hansen, *Embodying Technesis*, 21.

110 Hansen, *Embodying Technesis*, 34.

111 Hansen, *Embodying Technesis*, 82.

112 Hansen, *Embodying Technesis*, 85.

113 Hansen, *Embodying Technesis*, 85.

114 Brinkema, *The Forms of the Affects*, xiv.

115 Hansen, *Embodying Technesis*, 248.

116 Gitelman, *Scripts, Grooves, and Writing Machines*, 6.

117 Hayles, *Writing Machines*, 25–26.

118 Hayles, *Writing Machines*, 25.

119 Hayles, *Writing Machines*, 30.

120 Stiegler, "Derrida and Technology."

121 Hansen, *Embodying Technesis*, 8.

122 Thomas Bartscherer, Review quote, The University of Chicago Press Website, https://press.uchicago.edu/ucp/books/book/chicago/E/bo14413838.html.

123 Williams, *Marxism and Literature*, 6.

124 Williams, *Marxism and Literature*, 159.

125 Jones, "The Technology Is Not the Cultural Form?," 12.

126 Williams, *Marxism and Literature*, 188.

127 Williams, *Marxism and Literature*, 189–191.

128 Williams, *Marxism and Literature*, 191.

129 Williams, *Marxism and Literature*, 191.

130 Huters, *Bringing the World Home*, 74.

131 Huters, *Bringing the World Home*, 103.

132 Huters, *Bringing the World Home*, 113–14.

133 Williams, *Marxism and Literature*, 191.

134 Liang Qichao, "Yin bingshi ziyou shu," 23. Liang published this short essay in *Qingyi bao* in 1899 under the name Rengong.

135 Liang Qichao, "On the Relationship," 78.

136 Liang Qichao, "On the Relationship," 79.

137 See Huters, *Bringing the World Home*, 114. Liang's marriage of Buddhism with an increasingly vulnerable Confucian-based ideology fulfills a national outlook, but it is one undoubtedly ambiguous about how exactly to "pursue the understanding, the representation, and the transformation of the outer world."

138 Liang Qichao, "On the Relationship," 77.

139 Williams, *Marxism and Literature*, 159.

140 The first translated work of science fiction was an abridged serialization of the American writer Edward Bellamy's *Looking Backward: 2000–1887* in 1884 in *The Globe Magazine* (*Wanguo gongbao*) by Timothy Richard. Huangjiang Diaosou's 1904 *Tales of the Moon Colony* (*Yueqiu Zhimindi*) is generally believed to be the first Chinese science fiction story. Qian Jiang, "Translation and the Development of Science Fiction."

141 Isaacson, *Celestial Empire*, 7–8. The very term *science fiction* (*kexue xiaoshuo*) is a portmanteau of two major developments in early twentieth-century China: Western science and the novel.

142 Suvin, *Positions and Presuppositions in Science Fiction*. Suvin's authoritative definition of science fiction as "a literary genre whose necessary and sufficient conditions are the presence and interaction of estrangement and cognition, and whose main formal device is an imaginative framework alternative to the author's empirical environment" (66) has been adopted by many studies of Chinese-language science fiction, including Isaacson's, with some variation. See also Isaacson, *Celestial Empire*, 27–28. For problems of generic identification, see, in addition to Starr's *Red-Light Novels*, Des Forges, *Mediasphere Shanghai*; Isaacson, *Celestial Empire*; see also Keulemans, *Sound Rising from the Paper*; Yeh, *Shanghai Love*.

143 Zhang Zhi, "Wan Qing kexue xiaoshuo chuyi." The ten types of fiction, listed in a 1902 article published in *New Citizen* (*Xinmin congbao*), are "historical" (*lishi*); "political" (*zhengzhi*); "philosophical-scientific fiction" (*zheli kexue*); "military" (*junshi*); "adventure" (*maoyan*); "detective" (*zhentan*); romance (*xieqing*); stories of the strange (*zhiguai*); diaries (*zaji ti*); and tales of the marvelous (*chuanqi ti*). Specifically, "philosophical-scientific fiction" held "noble ideals and scientific observations" that were seen as being able to

bring "progress to the world, encourage imaginative thought" (69). Conse-quently, it became an important category featured in most late Qing fiction journals. According to Zhang, the transition from philosophical-scientific fiction to its latter-day designation as "science fiction" reflected a general sense of confusion over literary genres and the need to distinguish between scientific and political-societal ideals (69).

144 Williams, *Marxism and Literature*, 190–91.

145 McDermott, "The Ascendance of the Imprint in China."

146 *Ji* also names various types of historical chronicles (*dashi ji, shiji, jichuan, jidie, jifu*) and other forms of writing (*jishu*, a general biographical or family record; *youji*, travel journals; *riji*, diaries; *zaji*, miscellaneous notes; and more generally *jishu wen*, written narrations or belles lettres).

147 Regarding thoroughness, the second-century Chinese dictionary *Shuowen jiezi* defines *tong* as "extension and infinite reach" (*tong, da ye*). All etymolo-gies and their sources in this section are excerpted from *Handian* online, https://www.zdic.net/, accessed November 7, 2017. With regard to penetrabil-ity, *The Classic of Filial Piety* (*Xiao jing*) uses *tong* to define filial piety as some-thing that penetrates (*tongyu*) spiritual intelligences (*shenming*) and radiate all within the four seas (*wusuo butong*). In the *Daode jing*, the *dao* subtly and ex-quisitely penetrates (*weimiao xuantong*). I will discuss the significance of the *dao*'s relation to its perceived other, *qi* 器, for late Qing politics in the follow-ing chapter. Finally, regarding exchangeability, the *Comments of the Recluse* (*Qianfulun*) (102–67 CE) uses *tong* in *tonghuo*, the exchange and trading of goods.

148 This sense of communication is at once earlier than and at variance with the above noted *chuanbo* ("to propagate") found in the appendix of Liu's *Translingual Practice*. See also *The Commentary of Zuo* (*Chunqiu zuozhuan*), the chapter on "Lord Ai," 1826–1994.

149 Liu Guanglei, "Wan Qing chuanbo guannian," 15.

150 Liu Guanglei, "Wan Qing chuanbo guannian," 15.

151 Liu Guanglei, "Wan Qing chuanbo guannian," 15.

Chapter One. Guo Songtao's Phonograph

1 Fryer, "Chinese Education," 332, emphasis added.

2 Fryer, "Chinese Education," 334.

3 Hayles, *Writing Machines*, 22.

4 Taussig, *Mimesis and Alterity*, xviii.

5 It is well known that phonograph playbacks exhibit a low fidelity to the orig-inal sound because of scratching sounds produced by the needle following the groove created by the recording process. Rather than credit, or in Fryer's case deride Edison's invention, together with the woodblock and typewriter, for making perfect copies, it would be more accurate to associate them with more efficient information retrieval at a later stage. Misunderstandings over what related media can and cannot do, as Gitelman illustrates, can be very

"revealing both in their misapprehension of technology *and* misapprehension of textuality" (*Scripts, Grooves, and Writing Machines*, 16, emphasis added).

6 Elliott, *Some Did It for Civilisation*, 409. Prototypes of the typewriter appeared before 1872.

7 Elman, "Naval Warfare," 292.

8 Chinese, Anglophone, and Japanese scholarship of the 1950s and 1960s characterized the low standards of arsenal production as premodern or technologically backward, which, in Allen Fung's view, contributed to the "failure narratives" or a scholarly "witch hunt" of the period (quoted in Elman, "Naval Warfare," 284). For other revisionist accounts of the Self-Strengthening Movement, see Yue, "Hybrid Science versus Modernity"; Elman, *On Their Own Terms*.

9 Elman, "Naval Warfare," 293. See also Wright, "John Fryer and the Shanghai Polytechnic," 7.

10 It is not difficult to see why a year before he resigned in 1896 from his post as head of the translation department, Fryer organized a public contest for new fiction attacking what he saw as the three main ills of Chinese society: opium, foot-binding, and the examination essay. See Hanan, *Chinese Fiction*, 124–43.

11 After China's loss to Japan, Fryer, the once "tireless" translator of foreign texts, lamented that efforts to translate all the "arts and sciences of the West" would only "succeed up to a point" (quoted in Elman, "Naval Warfare," 325).

12 Originally titled *Shixi jicheng* (*An Account of My Embassy to the West*), Guo's diary was later compiled and edited as *Lundun yu Bali riji* (*London and Paris Diaries*) in the "Walking into the World" book series (*Zou xiang shijie congshu*) edited by Zhong Shuhe, the version used here.

13 Liu Xihong, *Yingyao siji*.

14 Zhang Deyi, *Suishi Ying E ji*.

15 Yi, *Donghai xihai zhi jian*, 32.

16 Yi, *Donghai xihai zhi jian*, 20.

17 Yi, *Donghai xihai zhi jian*, 10, 30–31. The next chapter will examine a novel's treatment of paperwork and bureaucracy.

18 Rudolph, *Negotiated Power*, 135.

19 Rudolph, *Negotiated Power*, 138.

20 Quoted in Yi, *Donghai xihai zhi jian*, 30.

21 Rudolph, *Negotiated Power*, 135.

22 Yi, *Donghai xihai zhi jian*, 30.

23 Yi, *Donghai xihai zhi jian*, 26–27. Even though the ministry did not issue the same order to the Burlingame mission of 1868 to 1870, it received the diary of one of its officials, Zhi Gang, upon his return. See also Rudolph, *Negotiated Power*, 136.

24 Yi, *Donghai xihai zhi jian*, 27. After the murder of British translator Augustus Raymond Margary on the Yunnan-Myanmar border in 1875, Thomas Francis Wade, the British ambassador, negotiated the Yantai Treaty, which stipulated that China must appoint an ambassador to Great Britain.

25 Quoted in Yi, *Donghai xihai zhi jian*, 31.

26 Hevia, *English Lessons*, 124.

27 Young, *Colonial Desire*, 252.

28 Hayles, *Writing Machines*, 22.

29 Galloway, *The Interface Effect*, 44.

30 Galloway, *The Interface Effect*, 31. Although Galloway is here referring specifically to Marshall McLuhan's influential claim in *Understanding Media* that new media serves as "a container for a previous media format," McLuhan's remediation thesis can also be found in the subfield of media archaeology's practice of reading the "'new' against the grain of the past" in order to resist "a telling of the histories of technologies from past to present" (Lovink, *My First Recession*, 11). For other literature on media archaeology, see Parikka, *What Is Media Archaeology?*; Huhtamo and Parikka, *Media Archaeology*.

31 Galloway, *The Interface Effect*, 53, 47. It is important not to judge coherence and incoherence as "good or bad" but rather in terms of "aligned or unaligned," "fixed or not fixed." To the latter two sets, Galloway also proposes to add the parallel terms of "territorialization" and "deterritorialization" found in Deleuze.

32 Galloway, *The Interface Effect*, 53.

33 Quoted in Yi, *Donghai xihai zhi jian*, 31.

34 Plaks, "Towards a Critical Theory," 313.

35 Plaks, "Towards a Critical Theory," 313.

36 Yi, *Donghai xihai zhi jian*, 151.

37 Plaks, "Towards a Critical Theory," 351.

38 Kluitenberg, "Introduction," 8. Other scholars associated with this offshoot of the larger field of media archaeology include Siegfried Zielinski and Bruce Sterling.

39 Felski, "Context Stinks!," 587.

40 Kluitenberg, "Introduction," 9, 14.

41 Quoted in Zhong Shuhe, "Lun Guo Songtao," 2.

42 Zhong Shuhe, "Lun Guo Songtao," 20.

43 The introduction discusses this movement in greater detail.

44 Quoted in Yang Xiaoming and Zheng Yaofei, "Guo Songtao keji guan chu tan," 76.

45 Xiao, "Xiyang zazhi," 258.

46 Yu Cuiling, "Riji fengbo," 76.

47 Yu Cuiling, "Riji fengbo," 77.

48 Ryan, *Narrative across Media*, 347.

49 Yi, *Donghai xihai zhi jian*, 17, 20.

50 Fuller, *Media Ecologies*, 14.

51 Fuller, *Media Ecologies*, 15, 2. Media ecology's materialist approach to media systems and information is not unique. The term *ecology*, often used interchangeably with *environment*, offers a conceptual tool to highlight the maximal intensity of relations between "processes and objects, beings and things, patterns and matter."

52 Fuller, *Media Ecologies*, 15.
53 Guo Songtao, *Lundun yu Bali riji*, 131, 166–67. All dates refer to the Chinese calendar.
54 Guo Songtao, *Lundun yu Bali riji*, 202–3.
55 Guo Songtao, *Lundun yu Bali riji*, 535.
56 Guo Songtao, *Lundun yu Bali riji*, 534.
57 For a representative study of *wen* as marks found in nature, see Lewis, *Writing and Authority in Early China*. On *wenzhang*, see Cai, "*Wen* and the Construction of a Critical System," 11–12. *Wenxue* traditionally referred to humane letters, one of the four Confucian categories of learning. See Huters, *Bringing the World Home*, 77; Liu, *Translingual Practice*, 273; Zhang Longxi, "What Is Wen?," 26. According to Liu, seventeenth-century Jesuit translations used *wenxue* to translate "literature," though its modern sense of literature to refer to works of fiction was not used until the nineteenth century by Protestant missionaries, and it became popular via the "round-trip diffusion of Japanese *bungaku*" (273). The translingual aspect of *wen* as *wenxue* may be overdrawn, as Zhang Longxi claims that even before Liu Xie, *wen* has already taken on "the specific meaning of literature as the art of writing" in the Wei and Jin dynasties (26).
58 Cai, "*Wen* and the Construction of a Critical System," 17–22.
59 Unsurprisingly, it is the mind, for Liu Xie, which has the boundless imagination to traverse time and space. Zhang Longxi, "What Is Wen?," 27.
60 Menke, "The Medium Is the Media," 214.
61 Guo Songtao, *Lundun yu Bali riji*, 538.
62 Fuller, *Media Ecologies*, 15.
63 Liu Xihong, *Yingyao siji*, 71, 75.
64 Yi, Donghai xihai *zhi jian*, 125.
65 Yi, *Donghai xihai zhi jian*, 125–26.
66 Zhong, "Lun Guo Songtao," 20; Zhong, "Yong xia bian yi," 15.
67 Zhong, "Yong xia bian yi," 16.
68 Liu Xihong, *Yingyao siji*, 50. For a background on the Gezhi shuyuan established by Fryer with the help of other Chinese and foreign scientists, officials, and merchants, see Vittinghoff, "Social Actors in the Field of New Learning."
69 Wang Hui, "The Fate of 'Mr. Science,'" 11–12.
70 Wang Hui, "The Fate of 'Mr. Science,'" 14–15. From around 1898 to the early years of the Republic (1912–1949), writers used *science* and *gezhi* interchangeably; the latter was more traditional in focus while the former emphasized new ways of categorizing knowledge and changes in the educational system.
71 Liu Xihong, *Yingyao siji*, 50.
72 This is also Yi's view in *Donghai Xihai zhi jian*, 144.
73 Fuller, *Media Ecologies*, 15.
74 Yi, *Donghai Xihai zhi jian*, 14.
75 Yi, *Donghai Xihai zhi jian*, 151.
76 Guo Songtao, *Lundun yu Bali riji*, 100.
77 Liu Xihong, *Yingyao siji*, 73.

78 Tong, "Guo Songtao in London," 8.

79 Zhang Deyi, *Suishi Ying E ji*, 312; Liu, *Translingual Practice*, 332. Liu attributes her entry on *chuanbo* to Federico Masini, who tracks "the use of the noun *chuanbo* in modern Chinese to a 'round-trip diffusion via Japan'" (*Translingual Practice*, 332).

80 Whereas I have been defining *wen* in Guo and Liu generally in terms of writing, language, and cultural refinement, Zhang's specific manipulation of the Chinese written character (*wenzi*) is more distinct.

81 Zhang Deyi, *Suishi Ying E ji*, 382.

82 Zhang Deyi, *Suishi Ying E ji*, 525.

83 Zhang Deyi, *Suishi Ying E ji*, 495.

84 Zhang Deyi, *Suishi Ying E ji*, 389.

85 Zhang Deyi, *Suishi Ying E ji*, 373.

86 Zhang Deyi, *Suishi Ying E ji*, 595.

87 Zhang Deyi, *Suishi Ying E ji*, 647.

88 Bachner, *Beyond Sinology*, 89.

89 Morton, *Sound Recording*, 18.

90 "Xin chuang ji sheng qi tu shuo," 47.

91 Gitelman, *Scripts, Grooves, and Writing Machines*, 1.

92 This undoubtedly refers to Alexander Graham Bell.

93 Guo Songtao, *Lundun yu Bali riji*, 576. The editor's note specifies that by *meng* 萌, Guo meant membrane *mo* 膜, as in *zhumeng* 竹萌, which names the thin membrane in a bamboo plant.

94 Guo Songtao, *Lundun yu Bali riji*, 577.

95 Scholars who have made this identification include Xu Chenchao, "Wan Qing shi qi guoren yu liushengji," 14–15; Zhong Shuhe, the editor of Guo's diaries in his notes in "Lun Guo Songtao," 30; and Andreas Steen, *Zai yule yu geming zhi jian*, 40.

96 Liu references *chuansheng tong* in her appendix of neologisms, and tellingly, includes a question mark to signal uncertainty over the original English term, *megaphone* (*Translingual Practice*, 275).

97 Quoted in Dong Huining, "Feiying ge huabao," 106.

98 "Liusheng xinji," 26.

99 Compare the accounts in Preece, "The Phonograph," and Edison, "The Latest Offerings of Science." Whether it was Edison or Preece who demonstrated the new device was not insignificant for the two inventors, whose personal relations were already strained. Preece was a "co-adjutor" of a certain Professor Hughes in claiming the latter to be the inventor of the microphone, carbon telephone, and heat measurer. Edison felt personally betrayed by Preece, whom he made agent for the presentation of the carbon-improved telephone and the phonograph in England on account of having, in Edison's words, "always manifested a great desire to be the means of presenting discoveries to the British public" (Edison, "The Latest Offerings," 663). That Preece in his demonstration of the phonograph on May 8, 1878, attributed the microphone, telephone, and heat measurer to Professor Hughes was nothing short of "an

infringement of rights and violation of confidence of friendship" (Edison, "The Latest Offerings," 663).

100 Quoted in Yi, *Donghai xihai zhi jian*, 31.

101 "The Principles of the Telephone Applied to the Phonograph."

102 "There is no doubt," confided Edison in his experimental notebook, "that I shall be able to store up and reproduce automatically at any future time the human voice perfectly." Disputes over nomenclature are no stranger in the history of inventions. In 1878, when another inventor, E. J. Houston, called the telephone relay really a "speaking telegraph," which he claimed to have invented the year before, Edison was quick to fire back the response that "change of form and name appears to be an easy and favorite method nowadays of making discoveries and inventions" (quoted in Gitelman, *Scripts, Grooves, and Writing Machines*, 2, 163).

103 Rooney, "Form and Contentment," 37.

104 Chen Zhanbiao, "1878 nian Guo Songtao," 18; see also Guo Songtao, *Lundun yu Bali riji*, 576, 787. In an entry around a year after his account of "Edison's" demonstration, Guo mentioned again the two machines, this time using the transliterated terms *delüfeng* for telephone and *fangluogenaifu* for phonograph. Transliteration here has the advantage of avoiding the earlier confusion that arises from neologisms.

105 Gitelman, *Scripts, Grooves, and Writing Machines*, 3.

106 Gitelman, *Scripts, Grooves, and Writing Machines*, 3.

107 Gitelman, *Scripts, Grooves, and Writing Machines*, 3.

108 Gitelman, *Scripts, Grooves, and Writing Machines*, 4.

109 Ernst, *Sonic Time Machines*, 94.

110 Guo Songtao, *Lundun yu Bali riji*, 575.

111 Ernst, *Sonic Time Machines*, 95.

112 Ernst, *Sonic Time Machines*, 93.

113 Quoted in Iovene, *Tales of Futures Past*, 10–11.

114 Iovene, *Tales of Futures Past*, 10n20.

115 Edison, "The Phonograph and Its Future," 535–36.

116 Sayers, "An Archaeology of Edison's Metal Box," 40.

117 Sayers, "An Archaeology of Edison's Metal Box," 41.

118 Sayers, "An Archaeology of Edison's Metal Box," 41.

119 Edison, "The Phonograph and Its Future," 535–36.

120 Sayers, "An Archaeology of Edison's Metal Box," 41.

121 Pang, *The Distorting Mirror*, 4.

122 Pang, *The Distorting Mirror*, 21, 39, 46.

123 Pang, *The Distorting Mirror*, 21.

124 Pang, *The Distorting Mirror*, 78. The lithograph's accompanying text, Pang adds, challenges the progressivism associated with lithographic visuality by exposing, in this case, its exploitation of gender relations.

125 Zhang Deyi, *Suishi Ying E ji*, 600.

126 Peng, "Lingering between Tradition and Innovation."

127 Zhang Deyi, *Suishi Ying E ji*, 600–601.

128 Gu, "What's in a Name?," 126.

129 Adding to *chuan*'s conjoined inflections of the material, the spiritual, and the spatial would be the role of temporality or historicity, which I will discuss in relation to women's biographies in chapter 3.

130 Gu, "What's in a Name?," 126.

131 Hung, "Inventing a 'Chinese' Portrait Style," 80. Thompson based his account on an interview with an explicitly fictive Hong Kong photographer, Ah-hung, an interesting juxtaposition to *Shenbao*'s reportage insofar as the latter claimed to have derived its source from British newspapers, which in turn cited Goodman.

132 Hung, "Inventing a 'Chinese' Portrait Style," 81.

133 Zhang Deyi, *Suishi Ying E ji*, 608–10. In subsequent entries, Zhang describes Guo's anger after reading the *Shenbao* article, and that the ambassador blames Halliday Macartney for erroneous translations between himself and Goodman during the painting process, which might explain *Shenbao*'s misreporting. Both Macartney and Goodman published notices in the *Chinese Telegraph* and the *London Chinese Daily*, two English-language newspapers in Britain, to clarify that they had never mocked Guo and did not speak to any British newspapers about the ambassador's portrait (Zhang Deyi, *Suishi Ying E ji*, 663). In the end, we learn that *Shenbao* copied its report from *Zilin bao*, an English-language paper based in Shanghai. The latter asserted that they had failed to check their sources because they assumed that it is common for Western newspapers to make light of even government officials.

134 Bazin, *What Is Cinema?* This is not to say that spatial media are void of temporal dimensions, given photography's well-studied ability to "embalm time," as André Bazin puts it, and painting and sculpture's function in memorializing historical events. Similarly, it is common knowledge that the so-called temporal arts such as theatrical staging, novel settings, and film significantly portray space. Nonetheless, I share W. J. T. Mitchell and Mark B. N. Hansen's opinion that these mark secondary or minor elements, and not the formal qualities of spatial and temporal media. See Mitchell and Hansen, "Time and Space."

135 For a summary of the philosophical and aesthetic tradition that prioritizes time and the temporal arts over space, see Mitchell and Hansen, "Time and Space."

136 See Crary, *Techniques of the Observer*; Elsaesser and Hagener, *Film Theory*; Mannoni, *The Great Art of Light and Shadow*. For a recent study of visual culture and its entanglements with other media forms in nineteenth-century North America, see Clark, *City of Second Sight*.

137 Cheng Xiuhua, *Zhongguo dianying fazhan shi*.

138 Tang Hongfeng, "Huandeng yu dianying," 42.

139 Pang, *The Distorting Mirror*, 21.

140 Guo Songtao, *Lundun yu Bali riji*, 534.

141 "Aidisen xin chuang jisheng jixing qi shuo," 46.

142 "Aidisen xin chuang jisheng jixing qi shuo," 46.

143 Altman, *Silent Film Sound*, 157–58.

144 Williams, *Marxism and Literature*, 99–100.

145 Said, *Culture and Imperialism*, 66.

146 Wilson, "Edward Said on Contrapuntal Reading," 267.

147 Liu Xihong, *Yingyao siji*, 141. The school of "wealth and power" is famously associated with Yan Fu's thinking beginning with his early writings in the last decade of the nineteenth century. For an authoritative study of Yan Fu, see Schwartz, *In Search of Wealth and Power*.

148 Liu Xihong, *Yingyao siji*, 141–42.

149 Liu Xihong, *Yingyao siji*, 141–42.

150 Liu Xihong, *Yingyao siji*, 62.

151 See Fang et al., *Zhongguo jindai minzhu sixiang shi*. The origins of Chinese democratic thought can be traced to the *Shi jing, Shang shu, Zuo zhuan* and other early works, which espouse notions of equality and "the people" (*min-ben, zhongmin, aimin*, etc.). The nineteenth century in particular witnessed the actual dissemination of democratic thought in China, notably in the post–Opium Wars period with Wei Yuan's *Haiguo tuzhi*, Feng Guifen's "*Jiao-binlu kangyi*" ("Protest from the Jiaobin Studio"), and Hong Xiuquan's writings during the Taiping War. Western missionaries, missionary newspapers, and Chinese travelers and emissaries such as Guo, Zhang, and others played essential roles in popularizing more concrete understandings of democracy in the form of *Junmin gongzhu* (shared governance by the sovereign and the people). See also Judge, *Print and Politics*. It is notable that Judge attributes the first use of the term *people's rights* (*minquan*) to Guo Songtao's *Lundun yu Bali riji*, dated May 19, 1878 (*Print and Politics*, 64).

152 Liu Xihong, *Yingyao siji*, 83, 127.

153 Liu Xihong, *Yingyao siji*, 102.

154 Liu Xihong, *Yingyao siji*, 111.

155 Quoted in Yi, *Donghai Xihai zhi jian*, 147.

156 Chapter 5 explores how Xu Nianci's short story "New Tales of Mr. Braggado-cio" constructs labor in general and the division of labor as a "final frontier" of technical media and cultural mediation.

157 Liu Xihong, *Yinyao siji*, 50.

158 Zhong, "Lun Guo Songtao," 24.

159 Galloway, Thacker, and Wark, *Excommunication*, 2.

160 Galloway, Thacker, and Wark, *Excommunication*, 2.

161 Galloway, Thacker, and Wark, *Excommunication*, 10.

162 Quoted in Tong, "Guo Songtao in London," 8.

163 Galloway, Thacker, and Wark, *Excommunication*, 16.

164 Zhong, "Lun Guo Songtao," 43.

165 Latour, *We Have Never Been Modern*, 11.

166 Latour, *We Have Never Been Modern*, 11.

167 Latour, *We Have Never Been Modern*, 12.

168 The term *incipient modernities* is taken from Wang, *Fin-de-Siècle Splendor*, 1. This influential study revives the messy, unfinished, and not fully Westernized

qualities of late-Qing fiction from its suppression by the dominant discourse of the May Fourth paradigm. For a classic study that complicates the characterization of Confucianism as the obstacle to modernization, see Wright, *The Last Stand of Chinese Conservatism*.

169 Latour, *We Have Never Been Modern*, 11.
170 Latour, *We Have Never Been Modern*, 81.
171 Galloway, *The Interface Effect*, 46.
172 Galloway, *The Interface Effect*, 46–47.
173 Yi, *Donghai Xihai zhi jian*, 31.
174 Galloway, *The Interface Effect*, 52.
175 Latour, *We Have Never Been Modern*, 47. Unlike the anti-modern, which reacts against modernity by defending values such as spirit, universality, and nature without realizing the role that modernity played in their construction, the non-modern attitude that Latour espouses does not "subtract" or "denounce" but "adds" and "fraternizes" (47)

Chapter Two. Stone, Copy, Medium

Some of the research presented in this chapter was published in "Stone, Jade, Medium: A Neocybernetic New Story of the Stone (1905–1906)." *Configurations* 26, no. 1 (2018): 1–26.

1 For a classic representation of discourses of posthumanism around the development of intelligent machines, see Hayles, *How We Became Posthuman*.
2 Stiegler, *Technics and Time*, vol. 1. Hui Yuk discusses the creation myths of Nüwa, Fuxi (her brother and later husband), and Shennong and their resemblance to the Greek Promethean myth of granting technology to humankind (*The Question Concerning Technology in China*, 14–29). However, because there was no sharp distinction between the world of gods and the world of humans in Chinese mythology, the latter gave rise to a different philosophy of technics, one based on "correlative thinking" and the "dynamic relation between Qi and Dao" (*The Question Concerning Technology in China*, 29).
3 Liu Zhimin and Li, "Lun Nüwa de chuangxin gongde," 193–95.
4 To avoid possible confusion between Cao's *The Story of the Stone* and Wu Jianren's *New Story of the Stone*, I will refer to the former as *Dream of the Red Chamber* and to Wu's late Qing rewrite as *New Story*. Subsequent citations of *New Story* are given in in-text parentheses.
5 For the stone motif in the earlier *Water Margin* and *Journey to the West*, as well as their intertextual relations to *Dream of the Red Chamber*, see Wang Jing, *The Story of Stone*.
6 See also Huters, *Bringing the World Home*, 156. Wu Jianren was actively involved in the politics of his time. When the first installment of *New Story* appeared in the Shanghai *Nanfang bao* in 1905, Shanghai businesses and intellectuals were holding Chinese boycotts of American trade to protest the United States' Chinese exclusion laws. Wu resigned as editor at an

American-owned newspaper in Hankou to protest the US policy and organized public rallies in support of the boycott. The same year was also when an Asian power defeated a European one for the first time in the Russo-Japanese War, an event that proved that Japan's modernizing efforts, much more thorough as compared with those undertaken in China, had paid off.

7 *New Story* thus follows what Anthony C. Yu identifies in *Dream of the Red Chamber* as the "act of proleptic reading," where the stone's narrative exists as a "summarized, hence completed, process of reading and reception . . . and where no actual reader can antedate or supersede" the dramatized figure of Vanitas or Kongkong Daoren (*Rereading the Stone*, 118). I will discuss Old Youth, this figure of the first reader (and copy editor and translator) in *New Story* toward the end of this chapter.

8 Tsien, *Written on Bamboo and Silk*, 69.

9 Tsien, *Written on Bamboo and Silk*, 69.

10 Wang Jing, *The Story of Stone*, 69.

11 Wang Jing, *The Story of Stone*, 51.

12 Wang Jing, *The Story of Stone*, 74. *New Story* does not dwell on the role of the jade in Baoyu's psyche, hence my sole focus on the stone motif. For a discussion of the jade in *Dream of the Red Chamber* as a rarer and aestheticized variant of the stone symbolizing purity and chastity, and imbued with more normative moral values as the mortal token of Baoyu's time on Earth before his transformation back into Nüwa's mythical stone, see Wang Jing, *The Story of Stone*, 95–172.

13 Xu Yuanji, "Lun wan Qing tongxun," 154.

14 Xu Fei and Mao, "Liu Mei youtong," 98–101.

15 Judge, *Print and Politics*, 18; Yeh, "Creating the Urban Beauty."

16 See Judge, *Print and Politics*, 36; Vittinghoff, "Social Actors."

17 "Jiqi zaoren zhi qiyi."

18 Gan, "Jiqi ren (fu zhaopian)."

19 "Jiqi yuyan (lu *Guowen bao*)."

20 Delekesilei, "Jiqi jingshen lun," 12–13.

21 Reed, *Gutenberg in Shanghai*, 65.

22 Reed, *Gutenberg in Shanghai*, 53.

23 Wagner, *Joining the Global Public*, 108.

24 Quoted in Wagner, *Joining the Global Public*, 109.

25 Tsien, *Written on Bamboo and Silk*, 92.

26 Reed, *Gutenberg in Shanghai*, 68.

27 Reed, *Gutenberg in Shanghai*, 55.

28 Reed, *Gutenberg in Shanghai*, 71.

29 Quoted in Reed, *Gutenberg in Shanghai*, 60.

30 Manovich, *The Language of New Media*, 36.

31 Manovich, *The Language of New Media*, 36.

32 Manovich, *The Language of New Media*, 54.

33 Hung, "On Rubbings," 45, 51.

34 Quan, "Shiban hua jifa, 1," 60.

35 Quoted in Reed, *Gutenberg in Shanghai*, 85.

36 Reed, *Gutenberg in Shanghai*, 85.

37 Hu, "Wofo Shanren zuo pin kao lüe," 90.

38 Wang Jing, *The Story of Stone*, 3, 6.

39 For a discussion of the notion of intermediality and its relation to intertextuality and remediation, see Rajewsky, "Intermediality, Intertextuality, and Remediation."

40 Hanan, *Chinese Fiction*, 173.

41 A prime example of how print predominates the study of media is Des Forges's *Mediasphere Shanghai*. The book explicitly borrows Régis Debray's notion of mediasphere to show that cultural production in late nineteenth- and early twentieth-century Shanghai consisted of overlaps between "textual and visual fields" in which "fiction and nonfiction books, newspapers, magazines, illustrated collections, and eventually, recorded performances, film, and radio" cross-referenced each other "across boundaries between different texts, genres, and media" (*Mediasphere Shanghai*, 1–2). Despite such attention to material media and mediation as a position between two opposing sides, Des Forges focuses exclusively on installment fiction—its convincing argument for the significance of genre fiction for understanding Shanghai modernity notwithstanding—while only occasionally referencing entertainment news media and the pictorial press. For a similar critique, see Mittler's review of Des Forges's book, "Mediasphere Shanghai."

42 Huters, *Bringing the World Home*, 159–60.

43 Gitelman, *Paper Knowledge*, 8. Michael Warner cautions against the teleology of print only to conflate it with the rise of the bourgeois public sphere. For the ritual burning of scrap paper with writing on it, see Des Forges, "Burning with Reverence."

44 Gitelman, *Paper Knowledge*, 3, 6, 8.

45 Gitelman, *Paper Knowledge*, 3.

46 Gitelman, *Paper Knowledge*, 5–6. Gitelman adopts this "deflationary" view of documents from Bruno Latour.

47 In Ma, "Stone, Jade, Medium," I examine how *New Story* and its inherited narrative structure anticipate the problem of reflexivity that preoccupied second-wave cybernetics and systems theory. The problem of Baoyu's transformation from a third-person center of consciousness into stone form raises the theoretical question of the distinction between a self-observing system and a primitive mode of recording medium. *New Story*'s metafictionality, or what I have refined as the novel's meta-mediatic quality, set against the backdrop of mechanical reproductions helps to pin down in narrative terms what can be overtly abstract and disciplinarily outfield terms used in cybernetics and systems theory such as autopoiesis, first introduced in the field of biology by Humberto Maturana and Francisco Varela to explain the self-organization of living systems. See also Clarke, *Neocybernetics and Narrative*.

48 On biographical writings and Chinese historiography, see Durrant, *The Cloudy Mirror*; Hardy, *Worlds of Bronze and Bamboo*; Mann, "Scene-Setting."

49 Quoted in Wagner, "Joining the Global Imaginaire," 109.

50 Reed, *Gutenberg in Shanghai*, 18–21. In another of his novels, *Ershi nian mu-duzhi guai xianzhuang (Strange Phenomena Observed during the Last Twenty Years)*, Wu Jianren reproves the commercial booksellers of his day.

51 Huters, *Bringing the World Home*, 96. Zhou's dictum was enthusiastically adopted by Zhu Xi (1130–1200) and became vital for prose composition in the Ming and Qing dynasties.

52 Yu Weidong, Xu, and Zhang, "Morality and Nature," 363. According to the authors, *dao* corresponds to the category of being in Western metaphysics.

53 Huters, *Bringing the World Home*, 24.

54 Schmitt, "Tidal Conrad," 15.

55 Schmitt, "Tidal Conrad," 15.

56 Felski, *The Limits of Critique*, 84.

57 Huters, *Bringing the World Home*, 33.

58 On the history of the Xiechang Matchstick Company, see Zhu, *Kepa de Shanghai ren*.

59 Huters, *Bringing the World Home*, 60.

60 To apply the logic of Niklas Luhmann's systems theory, the stone-jade inscription does not by itself qualify as a system—that is, it does not produce meaning on its own. Instead, it constitutes the environment from which other systems—consciousness, society, and other interactions in the narrative—emerge. "Every change in a system is a change in the environment of other systems; every increase in complexity in one place increases the complexity of the environment for all other systems" (Luhmann, *Social Systems*, 177).

61 Clarke, *Neocybernetics and Narrative*, 10–12. In his work integrating Luhmann's social systems theory with media and narrative theory, Clarke cautions against the cultural and theoretical tendency on the part of thinkers such as Kittler to "off-load the duties of cognitive systems onto informatics structures," and reads such an off-loading as signifying "an allegory of desire" (*Neocybernetics and Narrative*, 20).

62 Pan, "Qingren de Mingpian," 65. To the best of my knowledge, the Chinese history of trading cards, name cards, and visiting cards has not been studied in English-language scholarship. For a study of the American context, see Jay, *The Trade Card in Nineteenth-Century America*.

63 Des Forges, "Burning with Reverence," 139, 145.

64 Des Forges, "Burning with Reverence," 141.

65 Des Forges, "Burning with Reverence," 139.

66 Ji Zhaojin, *A History of Modern Shanghai Banking*, 48.

67 Wu Yunxian, "Lüe Lun Huifeng yinhang," 64.

68 Ji Zhaojin, *A History of Modern Shanghai Banking*, 49–50.

69 Ji Zhaojin, *A History of Modern Shanghai Banking*, 48–49.

70 The Eight-Nation Alliance set up in 1900 consisted of troops from Germany, Japan, Russia, Britain, France, the United States, Italy, and Austria-Hungary. Military forces from these nations occupied China for more than a year after the signing of the Boxer Protocol in 1901.

71 Aiken and Lu, "The Evolution of Bookkeeping in China"; Chen, "The Rise and Fall of Debit-Credit Bookkeeping in China"; Gardella, "Commercial Bookkeeping in Ch'ing China and the West"; Ji Xu-dong and Wei, "The Evolution of Bookkeeping Methods in China"; Lin, "Chinese Double-Entry Bookkeeping before the Nineteenth Century."

72 Américi, "Preparing the People for Capitalism," 12–14, 17.

73 Américi, "Preparing the People," 17.

74 Germain, *Dollars through the Doors*, 36, 110.

75 Cheng Linsun, *Banking in Modern China*, 147–48.

76 Isaacson, *Celestial Empire*, 78–80.

77 Luo Xiaojing, "Lixiang guomin," 175.

78 Huters, *Bringing the World Home*, 107.

79 Wang, *Fin-de-Siècle Splendor*, 304.

80 Liu, *The Freudian Robot*, 18.

81 Kittler, *Gramophone, Film, Typewriter*, 16.

82 Hayles, *How We Became Posthuman*. In information theoretical terms, there are no messages prior to its "encoding" in a signal transmitted through a medium, as when ink is pressed on paper or electrical pulses run through telegraph wires (*How We Became Posthuman*, 18). Our often cavalier use of the word *information* takes the signal for the medium, whereas in Claude E. Shannon's mathematical theory of information, the latter as message only exists in material bodies.

83 Paulson, *The Noise of Culture*, ix, 160.

84 Paulson, *The Noise of Culture*, ix.

85 Clarke, "Information," 163–64.

86 Hayles, *How We Became Posthuman*, 25.

87 Hayles, *How We Became Posthuman*, 25.

88 Hayles, *How We Became Posthuman*, 18.

89 Chen Yimin, "Mingpian gujin tan," 95.

90 Pan, "Qingren de mingpian," 66.

91 Quoted in Huang, "Centralized Minimalism," 22–23.

92 Quoted in Huang, "Centralized Minimalism," 23.

93 Earlier in the Barbaric Realm, Baoyu disputes with a speaker at a public forum who proposes that China must not reform because the very word for reform (*weixin*) is absent in Chinese. Since the classics evoke words such as *weixin*, Baoyu argues that it would be ridiculous to insist on the foreign origins of political reforms—another instance of a measured patriotism noticeably absent when he enters the Civilized Realm. This episode, together with the political climate of the time, suggests that it is unexpected for Wu to idealize the Civilized Realm as an authoritarian regime, and that it is not an accident that Baoyu's dream proposes the political alternative. Even though Liang Qichao extols the notion of an "enlightened authoritarianism," he counts constitutional reform as its essential component. For a lengthier discussion on these intellectual ideas, see Wang Guowei, "Lun Wu Jianren."

NOTES TO CHAPTER TWO

94 Zinda, "Propagating New 'Virtues.'" A primary school textbook *Elementary Ethics* (published in 1906 by the Commercial Press in Shanghai) established the primacy of a moral education (*deyu*), with instruction in patriotism to be the root of all studies. Yan Fu, in an article published in the same year, similarly stresses the importance of moral education since the metaphysical basis of *Dao* is more fundamental than knowledge of physical matters (*qi*) ("Propagating New 'Virtues,'" 696).

95 Huang, "Centralized Minimalism," 23–25.

96 Huang, "Centralized Minimalism," 25.

97 For an erudite study of the unpredictability of paperwork both real and imagined, see Kafka, *The Demon of Writing*. I include *New Story* in this section of the book on records (*ji*) precisely because the novel's construction of the ideal bureaucratic machine and its paperwork has not been studied. For a novel that more explicitly thematizes this topic, see Li Baojia, *Officialdom Unmasked*.

98 Reed, *Talons and Teeth*, 9.

99 Reed, *Talons and Teeth*, 11.

100 Reed, *Talons and Teeth*, 1–2, 12, 31–32.

101 Reed, *Talons and Teeth*, 1.

102 Reed, *Talons and Teeth*, 32.

103 Reed, *Talons and Teeth*, 31–32, emphasis added.

104 See Creel, "The Beginnings of Bureaucracy in China"; Kaske, "Metropolitan Clerks"; Lau and Lee, "Bureaucratic Corruption"; Mann, *Local Merchants and the Chinese Bureaucracy*; Michael, *The Origin of Manchu Rule in China*.

105 Kafka, *The Demon of Writing*, 341.

106 Yu, *Rereading the Stone*, 118.

107 Quoted in Mann, "Scene-Setting," 633.

108 Yu, *Rereading the Stone*, 166–68.

109 Yan Se, "Real Wages," 42.

110 Quoted in Wagner, *Joining the Global Public*, 109.

111 Wagner, "Joining the Global Imaginaire," 109.

112 Wang, *Fin-de-Siècle Splendor*, 283.

113 Huters, *Bringing the World Home*, 170.

114 Huters, *Bringing the World Home*, 279–80.

115 Huters, *Bringing the World Home*, 155, 211. Earlier, in the Jiangnan Arsenal, Baoyu sees workers emerging from the factories covered in soot and is reminded of this earlier scene with Beiming in the temple.

116 Haitian du xiaozi, "Nüwa shi," 448–50.

117 Haitian du xiaozi, "Nüwa shi," 476–82.

118 Dooling, *Women's Literary Feminism*, 20.

119 Tsu, "Female Assassins." Women writers, on the other hand, were more interested in science for its "serious intellectual content," leaving men to write about female assassins as a more "novel and possibly more lucrative endeavour" (177–78).

120 Tsu, "Female Assassins," 174–76.

121 Tsu, "Female Assassins," 174.

Chapter Three. Lyrical Media

1 Liang, *Liang Qichao quanji*, 1:219.

2 Liang, *Liang Qichao quanji*, 1:217.

3 Lőrincz, "Instrumentality and Referentiality."

4 Lőrincz, "Instrumentality and Referentiality," 327, 331. Lőrincz's exploration of the relation between "instrumental technicity and textual dynamics" in Thomas Kling's poetry (327), or what he calls the "technicity inherent in any poiesis" (331) is illuminating in this regard.

5 Liang, *Liang Qichao quanji*, 1:217. For a useful overview of poetic materiality in English literary criticism, see Ford, "Poetry's Media." Ford argues that the inherent relationality in the medium concept means that critics such as Derek Attridge, Gerald Bruns, and Daniel Tiffany variously sought the medium of poetry "downwards" or "regressively" to some layer of physicality beneath language (449–50), when the embeddedness of physicality within language can foreground mediality itself.

6 Foundational works debating the literal and the figurative in Chinese and Western comparative poetics include Yu, *The Reading of Imagery in the Chinese Poetic Tradition*; Yeh, "Metaphor and Bi"; Owen, *Readings in Chinese Literary Thought*; Owen, *Traditional Chinese Poetry and Poetics*; Saussy, *The Problem of a Chinese Aesthetic*. I will return to comment on Yu's and Yeh's positions on the incompatibility between Western and Chinese imageries, as well as Saussy's deconstructive reading, later in this chapter.

7 Tang Xiangbing, "'Poetic Revolution,'" 248. For a study of how poetic forms envision the formation of the Japanese nation, see Tuck, *Idly Scribbling Rhymers*.

8 Later in this chapter, I will briefly discuss a representative work on female mediumship and media technologies in nineteenth- and early twentieth-century Great Britain and the United States. There exists, to the best of my knowledge, no substantive study of the same intersecting phenomenon in China of the same period.

9 Liang, *Liang Qichao quanji*, 1:219.

10 Schmidt, *Within the Human Realm*, 48.

11 Schmidt, *Within the Human Realm*, 9.

12 Schmidt, *Within the Human Realm*, 14.

13 Huang Zunxian, "Jin bieli." When necessary, I refer to J. D. Schmidt's translations in *Within the Human Realm*, 269–72. Whereas Schmidt's translation of "Jin bieli" as "Modern Parting" retains the temporal significance given in the Chinese original, an alternative translation of the poems as "Parting with My Beloved" omits the meaning of the contemporary and the now. See Chang and Owen, *The Cambridge History of Chinese Literature*, 421. Curiously, Chang and Owen also claim that Huang wrote this set of poems to his wife from overseas, while the masculine pronoun *jun* used by the female speaker contradicts any autobiographical link. I agree more with Schmidt that the poems' "lack of any demonstrable connection with Huang's personal experi-

ences suggests he conceived them as experiments in using modern technology to revivify a genre of [parting] poetry that had reached a dead end long before his time" (*Within the Human Realm*, 186–87).

14 Liang, *Liang Qichao quanji*, 1:219. The other poem of Huang's that Liang singles out is "Wu tai furen shou shi" ("A Birthday Poem for Madame Wu").

15 Schmidt, *Within the Human Realm*, 187–88. For another study of the themes of separation in Chinese poetry, see Lavrač, "On Parting, Separation and Longing."

16 Schmidt, *Within the Human Realm*, 182.

17 Huang Zunxian, "Renjing lu shi cao xu," 68–69.

18 Schmidt, *Within the Human Realm*, 51–52.

19 Huang Zunxian, "Jin bieli," 121.

20 Huang Zunxian, "Jin bieli," 121; Schmidt, *Within the Human Realm*, 189.

21 Gang Hou, "Wan jiezhang Wang jun binpu."

22 Xu Zili, "Dianhua."

23 Jian Hao, "Liusheng qiji" and "Dianhua," 108–9.

24 Liang, *Liang Qichao quanji*, 1:219.

25 Robertson, "Voicing the Feminine," 69.

26 Robertson, "Voicing the Feminine," 69.

27 Schmidt, *Within the Human Realm*, 188.

28 Wang, *The Lyrical in Epic Time*, 1.

29 Wang, *The Lyrical in Epic Time*, 3.

30 Saussy, "Outside the Parenthesis," 854.

31 Huang Zunxian, "Jin bieli," 121.

32 Yeh, "Metaphor and Bi," 246, 252.

33 Huang Zunxian, "Renjing lu shi cao xu," 68.

34 Yu, *The Reading of Imagery*, 57.

35 Yu, *The Reading of Imagery*, 59.

36 Yu, *The Reading of Imagery*, 59.

37 Yu, *The Reading of Imagery*, 60–61.

38 Yu, *The Reading of Imagery*, 63.

39 Yu, *The Reading of Imagery*, 63.

40 Huang Zunxian, "Jin bieli," 121.

41 Schivelbusch, *The Railway Journey*.

42 Huang Zunxian, "Jin bieli," 121.

43 Mullaney, *The Chinese Typewriter*, 110–12. Infrequently used characters were left to the discretion of individual operators, who could designate them a position in the approximately 3,000 blank spaces reserved for such purposes.

44 Mullaney, *The Chinese Typewriter*, 110–12.

45 Huang Zunxian, "Jin bieli," 121. I prefer a literal translation of shu as "trees" to make a point of the riddle's play between physical infrastructure and nature. Schmidt's translation, on the other hand, reads: "In front of my gate two rows of straight poles, / March in perfect order to a place over the horizon" (Schmidt, *Within the Human Realm*, 270).

46 Schmidt, *Within the Human Realm*, 188–89.

241

47 Yu, *The Reading of Imagery*, 76, original emphasis.
48 Chapter 5 studies the representation of infrastructural form.
49 Yu, *The Reading of Imagery*, 76.
50 Yu, *The Reading of Imagery*, 76.
51 Huang Zunxian, "Renjing lu shi cao xu," 68.
52 Yu, *The Reading of Imagery*, 76.
53 Owen, *Traditional Chinese Poetry and Poetics*; Yeh, "Metaphor and Bi."
54 Saussy, *The Problem of a Chinese Aesthetic*, 29–30.
55 Liang, *Liang Qichao quanji*, 1:219.
56 Lőrincz, "Instrumentality and Referentiality," 328.
57 See Yu, *Rereading the Stone*, esp. 137–50, for a discussion of the mirror motif.
58 Huang Zunxian, "Jin bieli," 122.
59 For studies of the links between visuality and life-writing, see Rugg, *Picturing Ourselves*; Derrida, *The Ear of the Other*.
60 Schmidt, *Within the Human Realm*, 271.
61 Doane, "Indexicality"; Doane, "The Indexical and the Concept of Medium Specificity."
62 Doane, "The Indexical and the Concept of Medium Specificity," 136.
63 Doane, "Indexicality," 2.
64 Doane, "The Indexical and the Concept of Medium Specificity," 135–36.
65 Doane, "The Indexical and the Concept of Medium Specificity," 136.
66 Huang Zunxian, "Jin Bieli," 122.
67 "Words of light" refers of course to William Henry Fox Talbot's name for the medium of photography. For a classic work explicating citation, history, and photography in Walter Benjamin, see Cadava, *Words of Light*.
68 Cadava, *Words of Light*, xxvi.
69 Huang Zunxian, "Jin bieli," 122.
70 Blom, "The Autobiography of Video," 281.
71 Huang Zunxian, "Jin bieli," 121–22.
72 Gitelman, *Always Already New*, 5.
73 Huang's poetry evokes Walter Benjamin's well-known definition of history as the "seizing hold of a memory" in "Theses on the Philosophy of History."
74 Blom, "The Autobiography of Video," 282–83.
75 Simondon, *On the Mode of Existence*, 26, 58.
76 Massumi et al., "'Technical Mentality' Revisited," 30.
77 Simondon, *On the Mode of Existence*, 57–58. Simondon's example of the invention of the Guimbal turbine illustrates what he means by technical mentality. In this mechanism, the water-powered turbine is connected to a generator inside a crankcase of pressurized oil. The oil that both lubricates the generator and transfers heat to it meets the water activating the turbine, which also cools the heat. The multiple functions of both water and oil create a differential—the pressure of the oil exceeding that of the water surrounding it—and it is this differential that allows for the insertion of the generator into the penstock containing the turbine, which in turn allows the water to cool the heat in the oil. The invention of the turbine presupposes that the

interactions of the oil and water would work; yet this solution can only be "virtual" since the problem of an overheated generator does not exist prior to the insertion of the generator into the conduit. In other words, invention comes about "because there is a leap that takes place and is justified by means of the relation that it brings about within the milieu that it creates." The "condition of possibility," that is, the technical context or what Simondon calls "milieu" realizes "this turbo-generator couple." Massumi stresses the importance of circular causality in Simondon's thinking of concretization: "before the oil and the water entered into relation, the respective multifunctionalities were not in effect" since they could only come "from the future" ("'Technical Mentality' Revisited," 25). The inventor's thoughts thus do not originate an invention in the traditional sense by following a steady path from model to materialization. Instead, invention demands a thinking of self-conditioning emergence, the "autonomous taking-effect of a futurity" (26).

78 Massumi, "'Technical Mentality' Revisited." Both the "cognitive schema in thought" and the "schema of concretization in turbine-technicity . . . 'resemble' each other in the sense that they exemplify the same ontogenetic process." Simondon calls this the process of "individuation" (34).

79 Simondon, *On the Mode of Existence*, 60.

80 Wu Shengqing, *Modern Archaics*. Wu broadly defines the "ornamental lyricism" of comparison (*bi*) and affective imagery (*xing*), beyond its formal aesthetics, as a "social practice, an elegant lifestyle, and a concomitant cultural and intellectual ideal" (2).

81 This is where I depart from Blom's anti-anthropomorphic position in "The Autobiography of Video."

82 Schmidt, *Within the Human Realm*, 188.

83 Galvan, *The Sympathetic Medium*, 12–13.

84 Galvan, *The Sympathetic Medium*, 12.

85 Galvan, *The Sympathetic Medium*, 12.

86 Galvan, *The Sympathetic Medium*, 13.

87 Robertson, "Voicing the Feminine," 71.

88 Liu E, *Lao Can you ji*.

89 See Wang, *Fin-de-Siècle Splendor*, 37.

90 Chow, *Woman and Chinese Modernity*, 127.

91 Chow, *Woman and Chinese Modernity*, 127.

92 Chow, *Woman and Chinese Modernity*, 127.

93 Wang, *Fin-de-Siècle Splendor*, 37, 39.

94 Liang Qichao, "On the Relationship." For a lengthier engagement with this foundational text, see this book's introduction.

95 Wang, *Fin-de-Siècle Splendor*, 39. See also Cai, "The Rethinking of Emotion," for a discussion of emotions in Gong Zizhen.

96 Wang, *Fin-de-Siècle Splendor*, 41.

97 Wang, *Fin-de-Siècle Splendor*, 41.

98 Tani Barlow explores the construction of womanhood in Chinese feminism with what she calls the "catachresis" or concept-metaphor of women in

modern Chinese intellectual history in *The Question of Women in Chinese Feminism.*

99 Judge, "Talent, Virtue, and the Nation," 796, 800–802.

100 Judge, "Talent, Virtue, and the Nation," 800.

101 Judge, "Talent, Virtue, and the Nation," 800.

102 Judge, "Talent, Virtue, and the Nation," 801–2.

103 For translations of and essays on He-Yin's works, see Liu, Karl, and Ko, *The Birth of Chinese Feminism.*

104 Judge, "Talent, Virtue, and the Nation," 801. For an analysis of women's lyric writing of the early twentieth century, in particular the works of Lü Bicheng (1883–1943), see Wu Shengqing, *Modern Archaics.* Nanxiu Qian's recent monograph, *Politics, Poetics, and Gender in Late Qing China,* reassesses late Qing poetry from an explicitly gendered perspective, focusing on the poet-reformer Xue Shaohui and her colleagues. Qian, however, assesses Xue's literary aesthetics in terms of her reformist politics, and limits feminist subjectivity to its role in nurturing the family and the state (19–20).

105 Hu, *Tales of Translation,* 4.

106 Dooling, *Women's Literary Feminism,* 12.

107 De Lauretis, *Technologies of Gender,* 2–3.

108 De Lauretis, *Technologies of Gender,* 2.

109 De Lauretis, *Technologies of Gender,* 2.

110 For a critical analysis of Lu Xun's account, see Cheng, "Gendered Spectacles."

111 Hu, "Qiu Jin's Nine Burials," 140. The open-ended referent of the name Qiu Jin as a constructed entity diverges increasingly "from the historical personage bearing the same name" as others enshrine monuments in commemoration of her martyrdom. In *The Question of Women,* Barlow corroborates this view by conceptualizing women as a historical catachresis that gathers the ubiquity and ambiguity of a proper noun into "highly ideated elements of lived experience" (2).

112 Judge, "Talent, Virtue, and the Nation," 801.

113 Hu, *Burying Autumn,* 99, fig. 3.01.

114 Hu, *Burying Autumn,* 121, fig. 3.03.

115 Hu, *Burying Autumn,* 137, fig. 3.05.

116 Huang Hua, "Shi xin yingxiong yi you ci," 75. Qiu Jin's stay in Japan ended on a tragic note when one of her classmates, Chen Tianhua, committed suicide in protest of the local government's legislative restrictions on overseas Chinese students' activities.

117 Qiu Jin, "Ziti xiaozhao." I rely on Hu Ying's translation in *Burying Autumn,* "Self-Inscription on a Photograph, Dressed as a Man" (153).

118 Hu, *Burying Autumn,* 154. Hu, on the other hand, argues that the speaker immediately posits the inauthenticity of both female and male bodies in its first two lines, a view that does not take into account the role played by the photographic image.

244

119 Hu Ying's translation manifests the "you," which is absent in the original Chinese, while Li-Li Chen's translation renders the line in passive voice such that emphasis is put on what the old friends are told rather than on the person telling them. Chen's translation of the last two lines reads: "At future meetings with old friends, / They'll be told— / I've swept away all that's trivial, / all that's just / surface dust." See Qiu Jin, "Inscribed on a Photograph of Myself Dressed as a Man," 656–58.

120 Mann's *Precious Records* examines the importance of Buddhism for "the community life and domestic regime of every mid-Qing householder" (190–91). For a discussion of Wu Zhiying's continuing of this female devotional practice in the late Qing context, see Hu, "Qiu Jin's Nine Burials," 154.

121 Doane, "Indexicality," 2.

122 Doane, "Indexicality," 2.

123 Wu Shengqing, "A Paper Mirror," 323.

124 Doane, "The Indexical and the Concept of Medium Specificity," 131.

125 Hu, *Burying Autumn*, 151.

126 Doane, "The Indexical and the Concept of Medium Specificity," 140.

127 Doane, "The Indexical and the Concept of Medium Specificity," 136.

128 Ngai, *Ugly Feelings*, 159. Ngai makes a similar argument in her analysis of Hedy's mimetic behavior in the 1992 American film *Single White Female* as the "undoing of identification" based on "the other's transformation after the fashion of what the self is not."

129 Hu, *Tales of Translation*, 110–11.

130 Mann, quoted in Hu Ying, *Tales of Translation*, 110.

131 Mann, quoted in Hu Ying, *Tales of Translation*, 110. Examples of the genre abound in this period: Sophia Perovskaia and Madame Roland, among many others, appeared in Qiu Jin's publication.

132 Xia, *Wan Qing nüxing*, 121–29.

133 Ngai, *Ugly Feelings*, 149–51.

134 Hu, "Gender and Modern Martyrology," 124.

135 Hu, "Gender and Modern Martyrology," 125–27.

136 Quoted in Hu, "Gender and Modern Martyrology," 126.

137 Hu, "Gender and Modern Martyrology," 127–28.

138 Hu, "Gender and Modern Martyrology," 130.

139 Hu, "Gender and Modern Martyrology," 125, 128.

140 Hu, *Tales of Translation*, 107; Judge and Hu, "Introduction," 2. In addition to her call for Chinese women to follow the likes of "Madame Roland, Mary Lyon, Sophia [Perovskaia], [Harriet] Beecher [Stowe] and Joan [of Arc]," Qiu Jin also compared her own patriotism to an account of a woman of Qishi by Liu Xiang (77–6 BCE) in his *Lienü zhuan* (*Biographies of Exemplary Women*, ca. 34 BCE), the "urtext of the Chinese women's biographical tradition" (Hu, *Tales of Translation*, 107). Suffice it to say that the lines of exemplary women became entangled with those of translated tales of foreign women around the turn of the twentieth century and are therefore discontinuous and messy.

141 Hu, *Burying Autumn*, 196–97.

142 Hu, *Burying Autumn*, 197.

143 Hu, *Burying Autumn*, 117.

144 Hu, *Burying Autumn*, 198.

145 Hu, *Burying Autumn*, 131.

146 Hu, *Burying Autumn*, 118.

147 Hu, *Burying Autumn*, 131.

148 Hu, Burying Autumn, 129.

149 Hu, *Burying Autumn*, 12–13. Hu notes the prevalence of this trope between Qiu Jin, Wu Zhiying, and Xu Zihua. It might be interesting to compare this rhetoric of friendship predicated on the friend's absence with Jacques Derrida's examination of this trope in *Politics of Friendship*.

150 Hu, *Burying Autumn*, 198.

151 Judge, "Talent, Virtue, and the Nation," 801.

152 Quoted in Hu, *Burying Autumn*, 206.

153 Quoted in Hu, *Burying Autumn*, 206.

154 On a classical work on photography's relations to death, see Barthes, *Camera Lucida*.

155 Wang, *The Lyrical in Epic Time*, 42.

156 Massumi, *Parables for the Virtual*, 28.

157 Chow, *Women and Chinese Modernity*, 18–23. While Chow studies the sentimental in the specific medium of film, her attention to the envelopment of the sentimental within its communicative medium helps highlight different valences of visibility in earlier forms such as photography and print.

158 According to Anna Gibbs, "media and bodies appear as vectors, and affect itself as the primary communicational medium for the circulation of ideas, attitudes and prescriptions for action among them" (quoted in Rentschler, "Affect," 12).

Chapter Four. 1900

The first epigraph, excerpted from a longer Boxer verse, is cited in Lu Yunting, *Yihe tuan de shehui biaoyan*, 150. The complete telegram sent by Sheng can be found in Guo Jiwu, "Dongnan hubao," 38.

1 Marvin observes how electricity introduced new words, often haphazardly so, into nineteenth-century English. See *When Old Technologies Were New*, esp. 3–8.

2 Guo Jiwu, "Dongnan hubao," 38.

3 Zhou, *Historicizing Online Politics*, 19–38.

4 Zhou, *Historicizing Online Politics*, 28–29. Roger R. Thompson attributes the increase in telegraph lines' destruction to the military budget. The budget crisis ensuing from the indemnity for the Sino-Japanese War of 1894–95 meant that fewer soldiers were available for line security in north China (Thompson, "The Wire," 401).

5 Parks and Starosielski, "Introduction." For other representative studies on infrastructure, see Star, "The Ethnography of Infrastructure"; Larkin, "The Politics and Poetics of Infrastructure"; Rankin, "Infrastructure and the International Governance of Economic Development"; Aouragh and Chakravartty, "Infrastructures of Empire."

6 See Baark, *Lightning Wires*; Shi, *Dianbao tongxin*; Sun, *Wan Qing dianbao*; Thompson, "The Wire"; Wook, "Dashed Expectations"; Zhou, *Historicizing Online Politics*.

7 Parks and Starosielski, "Introduction," 5.

8 Parks and Starosielski, "Introduction," 5.

9 Wenzlhuemer, "The Telegraph and the Control of Material Movements," 628.

10 Wenzlhuemer, "The Telegraph and the Control of Material Movements," 628.

11 Wenzlhuemer, "The Telegraph and the Control of Material Movements," 644.

12 Pfeiffer, "The Materiality of Communication," 12.

13 Pfeiffer, "The Materiality of Communication," 12.

14 Pfeiffer, "The Materiality of Communication," 12.

15 Hayles, *How We Think*, 125–26.

16 Sun, *Wan Qing dianbao*, 11. For further examples of these neologisms, see Liu, *Translingual Practice*, 351.

17 Baark, *Lightning Wires*, 71.

18 Quoted in Lei, "Wan Qing dianbao he tielu," 71.

19 Zhou, *Historicizing Online Politics*, 28–29.

20 Hayles, *How We Think*, 124.

21 Quoted in Lei, "Wan Qing dianbao he tielu," 71.

22 Baark, *Lightning Wires*, 75.

23 For more on such organic metaphors, see Peters, "Technology and Ideology."

24 Sun, *Wan Qing dianbao*, 33.

25 Hayles, *My Mother Was a Computer*, 3.

26 Carey, "Technology and Ideology"; Hayles, *How We Think*, 126.

27 Zhou, *Historicizing Online Politics*, 41. For instance, newspapers publishing international news conveyed by telegraph often had to go through overland couriers and steamers. Zhou documents how the first news conveyed by telegraph that was printed in *Shanghai xinbao* in 1869 took twenty-two days from its dispatch from London via a Russian telegraph station bordering Manchuria, overland by courier to Tianjin, before the news reached Shanghai by steamer.

28 Zhou, *Historicizing Online Politics*, 43–44. Before the advent of telegraphy, *Jingbao* (*Report from the Capital* or *Peking Gazette*) was the main print publication compiling edicts, announcements, and memorials in Beijing, which were then excerpted and sold to various newspapers such as *Shanghai xinbao* and *Shenbao*. After the opening of the Tianjin-Shanghai line in 1881, official telegrams classified according to degrees of urgency and priority made "official communication between the court, local officials, and overseas diplomats" much faster and more efficient. Newspapers could, for example,

publish an official edict (*diandu* or *dianzou*) telegraphed from Beijing in a matter of a day or two.

29 Zhou, *Historicizing Online Politics*, 55.

30 See Peters, "Radio."

31 Carey, "Technology and Ideology," 319.

32 Zhou, *Historicizing Online Politics*, 55–56.

33 Zhou, *Historicizing Online Politics*, 57.

34 Zhou, *Historicizing Online Politics*, 57.

35 Zhou, *Historicizing Online Politics*, 55, 59–60.

36 Quoted in Sun, "Zaizao 'zhongxin,'" 47.

37 "Beijing bianluan zhuandian huideng."

38 Zhou, *Historicizing Online Politics*, 65–66.

39 "Benguan xinwen."

40 "Tongsheng zhongfeng."

41 Sun, "Zaizao 'zhongxin,'" 48.

42 "Beijing bianlun zhuandian huideng."

43 Shih, "Against Diaspora," 30.

44 Zhou, *Historicizing Online Politics*, 248n3.

45 Quoted in Hevia, *English Lessons*, 282.

46 Wang-Fan, *Yihe tuan zhanzheng*, 19–22.

47 For a discussion of the significance of German toys marketed during the Boxer Rebellion, see Bowersox, *Raising Germans*, 18–53.

48 See Hevia, *English Lessons*, 195–240. The Allied forces refer to the Eight-Nation Alliance made up of Germany, Japan, Russia, Britain, France, the United States, Italy, and Austria-Hungary.

49 Hevia, "The Photography Complex."

50 Leyda, *Dianying*. These films include *Beheading a Chinese Boxer* and *Boxer Attack on a Missionary Outpost*, as well as Scottish film pioneer James Williamson's 1900 newsreel *Attack on a Chinese Mission*, which featured the chasing technique in montage sequences. See also Haddad, "The Wild West Turns East." In the same year, the American studio Lubin Company, also purporting to have shot in China, filmed *Chinese Massacring the Christians* using American Indian stereotypes to portray the Boxers attacking a missionary home similar to Western plots of Indians invading a pioneer cabin (Haddad, "The Wild West Turns East," 24–25). American Mutoscope and Biograph produced *Tortured by Boxers* (1900) as well as *Rescue of a White Girl from the Boxers* (1900), both employing standard themes of civilization and savagery found in narratives of Anglo-Indian conflict with close to no knowledge of the actual events in China (26). The American Vitagraph Company imitated Georges Méliès's *La Chine contre les Allies* (1900) in *The Congress of Nations* (1900), satirizing the foreign legations' noble attempt to rescue China from its own savages in Méliès's original (5–6). For how the Japanese Yoshizawa Company produced "reportage" films popularly shown in Japanese movie houses converted from live theater venues, see Desser, "Japan."

51 Hevia, "The Photography Complex," 80–81.

248

52 Hevia, "The Photography Complex," 80–81.

53 Ricalton, *James Ricalton's Photographs*, 159.

54 Ricalton, *James Ricalton's Photographs*, 159.

55 Ricalton, *James Ricalton's Photographs*, 159.

56 Ricalton, *James Ricalton's Photographs*, 161.

57 Hevia, "The Photography Complex," 100.

58 Hevia, "The Photography Complex," 100.

59 Hayles, *Writing Machines*, 22. Another anecdote of Ricalton's role in this growing media network is his showing of a program of Thomas Edison's films in China, which inspired the earliest Chinese film journalism, "Guanmeiguo yingxi ji" ("Viewing American Films"), published in *Youxi bao* (Games Magazine), September 5, 1897. See Leyda, *Dianying*, 2–3.

60 Ricalton and Lucas, "Introduction," 30–32.

61 Krauss, "Photography's Discursive Spaces."

62 Ricalton, *James Ricalton's Photographs*, 166.

63 Ricalton, *James Ricalton's Photographs*, 166.

64 Elliott, "American Photographs."

65 Elliott, "American Photographs," 167. Elliott rejects the explanation that the intrepid traveler was unwilling to mute the atrocities committed by the Allied soldiers, or that the traveler was constrained by market factors such as editorial and public preferences for less gruesome photographic images of war (165).

66 Quoted in Elliott, "American Photographs," 167.

67 Ricalton, *James Ricalton's Photographs*, 166.

68 Hevia, "The Photography Complex," 80–81.

69 "Racialized specimen" is discussed in Jones, "Portable Monuments." The "yellow poor" can be found in Fraser, "The Face of China."

70 Ricalton, *James Ricalton's Photographs*, 176.

71 Ricalton, *James Ricalton's Photographs*, 159.

72 Ricalton, *James Ricalton's Photographs*, 202.

73 Jones, "Portable Monuments," 617.

74 Ricalton, *James Ricalton's Photographs*, 202.

75 Bolter and Grusin, *Remediation*.

76 For a discussion of the relation between early photography and telegraphy, see Batchen, "Electricity Made Visible."

77 Cohen, *China Unbound*, 100.

78 Cohen, *China Unbound*, 101.

79 Carey, "Technology and Ideology," 305.

80 Star, "The Ethnography of Infrastructure."

81 Parks and Starosielski, *Signal Traffic*, 7.

82 "Beijing bianluan wenti."

83 Ricalton, *James Ricalton's Photographs*, 159.

84 Cohen, *History in Three Keys*, 84–86; Shi, *Dianbao tongxin*, 106.

85 Cohen, *History in Three Keys*, 84. Young, unemployed male peasants became attracted to the group's promise of food and invulnerability (34). Areas not as

seriously impacted by natural disasters such as Zhili province, "in many ways the most logical site for the center of an antiforeign and anti-Christian explosion," experienced job losses in the transport sector (36).

86 Quoted in Cohen, *History in Three Keys*, 86.

87 Cohen, *History in Three Keys*, 10.

88 Cohen, *History in Three Keys*, 10.

89 Cohen, *History in Three Keys*, 34.

90 Geoghegan, "Mind the Gap," 901.

91 Geoghegan, "Mind the Gap," 900–902. These techniques include "codes, electrics, song and dance, political address, scientific experimentation, parlor games, group meditation, [and] experimental photography."

92 Geoghegan, "Mind the Gap," 900.

93 As Cohen observes, Chinese historians have rarely studied the Boxers alongside similar phenomena in other societies (Cohen, *China Unbound*, 86).

94 For a reconsideration of the Boxers' religious and magical practices as strategies offering protection and emotional security, see Cohen, *History in Three Keys*, 119–45.

95 Cohen, *History in Three Keys*, 123–27; *Gengzi jishi*.

96 Cohen, *History in Three Keys*, 127.

97 Cohen, *History in Three Keys*, 127, 334n35.

98 Geoghegan, "Mind the Gap," 300n3.

99 Smith, *China in Convulsion*, vol. 1.

100 Cohen, *History in Three Keys*, 33.

101 Thompson, "The Wire," 410–11.

102 Quoted in Guo Jiwu, "Dongnan hubao," 38. The urgency of Sheng's message is captured in the second epigraph to this chapter (see unnumbered note, above).

103 Thompson, "The Wire," 405–6; Mullaney, *The Chinese Typewriter*. Upon receiving a telegram through this telegraph-courier relay, the recipient then had to convert the four-digit numbers back into Chinese characters. A telegraph operator equated each Chinese character to its unique four-digit number according to the 1871 code developed by Septime Auguste Viguier. The 1871 code adds another layer of mediation: "the first mediating between Chinese characters and Arabic numerals, the second mediating between Arabic numerals and the long and short pulses of telegraphic transmission" (Mullaney, *The Chinese Typewriter*, 101–2). As a result, Chinese script was, in Mullaney's words, "doubly governed" compared with its English, French, German, and Russian counterparts.

104 Thompson, "The Wire," 414.

105 Zhou, *Historicizing Online Politics*, 75–77.

106 Thompson, "The Wire," 411–14, 418.

107 Star, "The Ethnography of Infrastructure," quoted in Thompson, "The Wire," 416.

108 Marvin, *When Old Technologies Were New*, 4–5.

109 Marvin, *When Old Technologies Were New*, 5.

110 Marvin, *When Old Technologies Were New*, 4.

111 Sheng, *Yihe tuan yundong*.

112 Sheng, *Yihe tuan yundong*, 38:81.

113 Sheng, *Yihe tuan yundong*, 43:98.

114 Sheng, *Yihe tuan yundong*, 46:109.

115 Sheng, *Yihe tuan yundong*, 50:21.

116 Sheng, *Yihe tuan yundong*, 55:138.

117 Sheng, *Yihe tuan yundong*, 58:152.

118 Sheng, *Yihe tuan yundong*, 73:192, 73:194.

119 For Sheng's reprimand, see Sheng, *Yihe tuan yundong*, 77:209.

120 Sheng, *Yihe tuan yundong*, 95:261.

121 Sheng, *Yihe tuan yundong*, 97:269.

122 Sheng, *Yihe tuan yundong*, 97:269.

123 Sheng, *Yihe tuan yundong*, 92:258.

124 Sheng, *Yihe tuan yundong*, 106:299.

125 Sheng, *Yihe tuan yundong*, 117:336.

126 Thompson, "The Wire," 412. In her memoir, Mary Hooker also noted the British minister Sir Robert Hart's bitter objection to sending uncoded telegrams (Hooker, *Behind the Scenes in Peking*, 145).

127 Sheng, *Yihe tuan Yundong*, 174:513, 17:515.

128 Sheng, *Yihe tuan Yundong*, 179:525. See also 170:499.

129 Sheng, *Yihe tuan Yundong*, 194:578, 201:603.

130 Sheng, *Yihe tuan Yundong*, 201:603.

131 Sheng, *Yihe tuan Yundong*, 235:695.

132 Shi, *Dianbao tongxin*, 126–29.

133 Thompson, "The Wire," 422.

134 Shi, *Dianbao tongxin*, 135.

135 Pfeiffer, "The Materiality of Communication," 3.

136 Smith, *China in Convulsion*, vol. 2. According to Jones, this image, like most of those in Smith's two-volume account, was probably reprinted from a contemporary stereograph ("Portable Monuments," 614).

137 Hevia, "The Photography Complex," 86.

138 Hevia, "The Photography Complex," 86.

139 Jones, "Portable Monuments," 614.

140 Smith, *China in Convulsion*, 2:629–30n32, emphasis added.

Chapter Five. A Medium to End All Media

A version of part of this rewritten chapter appeared in *Science Fiction Studies* 40, no. 1 (March 2013): 55–72. as "'A Tale of New Mr. Braggadocio': Narrative Subjectivity and Brain Electricity in Late Qing Science Fiction."

1 Quoted in Zhang Zhongmin, "Bunao de zhengzhi xue," 147.

2 Quoted in Zhang Zhongmin, "Bunao de zhengzhi xue," 147.

3 Quoted in Zhang Zhongmin, "Bunao de zhengzhi xue," 147.

4   Wu Yixiong, "Wan Qing shi qi xifang renti shengli zhishi," 79–80. Early
    translations of the telegraph emphasizing the "wire" (*xian*) resonate with the
    period's fascination with the wire- or thread-like features of nerves.

5   Quoted in Li Suyun, "Xifang shenjing de yiru," 132.

6   See Yan Jianfu, *Cong "shenti" dao "shijie,"* 210n5.

7   Tan, *Renxue*, 60.

8   Thacker, *Biomedia*, 6.

9   Cochran, *Chinese Medicine Men*, 40.

10 Zhang Zhongmin, "Bunao de zhengzhi xue," 147; Zhang Zhongmin, "Jindai
    Shanghai de mingren yiyao guanggao," 156. The pharmaceutical entrepreneur
    was searching for an English-sounding, sophisticated derivative of the literal
    translation of his family name, Huang, as "Yellow" when he came up with the
    character of Dr. Yale. Huang also gave Dr. Yale the initials T. C., romanized
    versions of his own initials in dialect pronunciation. As for the origin of the
    drug, Huang had bought the formula from a Chinese pharmacist, who had
    intended it to be used as a sedative (Cochran, *Chinese Medicine Men*, 40).
    Huang's collaboration with famous Shanghai literati such as Sun Yusheng
    (1864–1940) and Wu Jianren, author of *New Story of the Stone*, deserves
    separate study. An advertisement in June 1910 published Wu's praise for the
    drug "Huanwo linghun ji" (The Recovery of My Soul) along with a photo of
    the writer, who received three hundred dollars for the endorsement. See also
    Cochran, *Chinese Medicine Men*, 40–42.

11 Xu Nianci, "New Tales of Mr. Braggadocio." I rely on Isaacson's excellent En-
    glish translation, and reference the original Chinese text when necessary.

12 Xu Nianci, "New Tales," 15.

13 Xu Nianci, "New Tales," 16.

14 Xu Nianci, "New Tales," 28.

15 Xu Nianci, "New Tales," 28.

16 On Xu Nianci's satire, see Zhang Zhongmin, "Bunao de zhengzhi xue," 151.
    Other stories commissioned by Huang Chujiu include the travel narrative
    "Kong qiqiu" ("Hot-Air Balloon"), set in England and featuring the World's
    Fair and new technologies, and fiction with more traditional plots such as
    the detective story "Santou an" ("The Case with the Three Heads"), both
    published in 1905. For an analysis of how Chinese capitalism grew with
    trade rather than industrialization, see Huang Yiping, *Jindai zhongguo jingji
    bianqian*.

17 Xu Nianci, "New Tales," 38.

18 Xu Nianci, "New Tales," 38.

19 See A Ying, *Wan Qing xiaoshuo shi*; Yang Guomin, *Wan Qing xiaoshuo*; Lai,
    Qing mo xiaoshuo.

20 Isaacson, *Celestial Empire*, 109.

21 Isaacson, *Celestial Empire*, 109.

22 Quoted in Ren, "Wan Qing kehuan xiaoshuo," 101. Xu published these
    thoughts in a 1907 article in *Xiao shuolin*.

23 For Wang Tao's (1828–1897) update of literary (*wenyan*) stories, see Lu Hsiao-peng, "Waking to Modernity."

24 Chu, *Do Metaphors Dream of Literal Sleep?*, 5.

25 Chu, *Do Metaphors Dream of Literal Sleep?*, 1–4.

26 For a classic analysis of the relationship between the social and the political in Western philosophy, see Arendt, *The Human Condition*; see also Pitkin, *The Attack of the Blob*. For a more nuanced treatment that takes into consideration the rise of mass media, see Baudrillard, *In the Shadow of the Silent Majorities*.

27 Chu, *Do Metaphors Dream of Literal Sleep?*, 7.

28 Hayles, *My Mother Was a Computer*, 18.

29 Hayles, *My Mother Was a Computer*, 18.

30 Frederic Jameson's description of capital as a "totalizing or systemic concept" that "no one has ever met or seen" applies here to the social with equal aplomb ("Cognitive Mapping," 354.) Elsewhere, I have discussed the problem of comparison in literary studies vis-à-vis this issue of totality. See Ma, "To Compare Otherwise."

31 Xu Nianci, "New Tales," 19–20.

32 Xu Nianci, "New Tales," 20.

33 Xu Nianci, "New Tales," 22.

34 Xu Nianci, "New Tales," 36.

35 Xu Nianci, "New Tales," 36.

36 Xu Nianci, "New Tales," 36. Readers of Chinese literature will undoubtedly detect traces of Lu Xun's social criticism here. For a study of Lu Xun's early interests in biology and science fiction, see Liu, "Life as Form."

37 Choy, *Discourses of Disease*, 6.

38 Choy, *Discourses of Disease*, 6. Both *New Story of the Stone* and *Stone of the Goddess Nüwa*, which I discuss in chapter 2, prioritize diagnosis and cure through the then-fantastical technologies and medical procedures such as proto-X-ray devices and painless dissections.

39 Liang, "On the Relationship," 74.

40 Liang, "On the Relationship," 77–79.

41 Xu Nianci, "Yu zhi xiaoshuo guan." On how later Qing literary journals like *Xiaoshuo lin* and *Yueyue xiaoshuo* (*Monthly Fiction*) moved away from the earlier period's singular focus on politics toward a more aesthetic approach, see Du, "Bu zhi shi zhengzhi."

42 Woloch, *The One vs. the Many*, 12.

43 Woloch, *The One vs. the Many*, 25.

44 Xu Nianci, "New Tales," 39.

45 Xu Nianci, "New Tales," 38.

46 Woloch, *The One vs. the Many*, 116–19. According to Woloch, the Bennet sisters aggregate to form a "minor minor character."

47 Xu Nianci, "Xin faluoxiansheng tan," 20. The character *qun* heightens the sense of the collective that I am examining.

48 Xu Nianci, "New Tales," 38.

49 Woloch, *The One vs. the Many*, 30.

50 Woloch, *The One vs. the Many*, 27.

51 Lu Hsiao-peng, "Waking to Modernity," 746–47.

52 Woloch, *The One vs. the Many,* 19. The nineteenth-century European novel is particularly poised to address the question of the one versus the many given its contradictory contributions to "depth psychology" on the one hand and "social expansiveness" on the other. Xu's claim that Chinese fiction is more realistic than Western fiction in its portrayal of multiple characters of course oversimplifies matters ("Xiaoshuo lin yuanqi"). On an alternative interpretation of characterization in the Chinese narrative tradition that emphasizes singular characters, see Plaks, "Towards a Critical Theory."

53 Woloch, *The One vs. the Many*, 38.

54 Woloch, *The One vs. the Many*, 38.

55 Woloch, *The One vs. the Many*, 38.

56 Woloch, *The One vs. the Many*, 38.

57 Isaacson, *Celestial Empire*, 114. Xu's use of the term *linghun* to refer to soul evokes the *hun-po* theory of the soul, though there is a lack of a systematic explanation for the number of *hun* and *po* souls one has, their relationship to the corporeal body, and their existence after death. The distinction between "soul" (*linghun*) and "physical body" (*quke*) does ascribe to the *Book of Rites'* associations of "the *hun* with vital energy and ascent to heaven and the *po* with the physical body and a descent into earth" (Brashier, quoted in Isaacson, *Celestial Empire*, 114). On the other hand, Xu could have been influenced by Christian theological discussions of body-soul dualism published in missionary publications. In any case, neither a purely folkloric nor Christian theology can fully explain Mr. Braggadocio's transformation. Later in this chapter, I show that the intellectual lineage of his soul- and bodily-selves is less important than the communicative roles that they play—both separately and together—in the narrative.

58 Xu Nianci, "New Tales," 36.

59 Xu Nianci, "New Tales," 16–17.

60 Xu Nianci, "New Tales," 17.

61 Xu Nianci, "New Tales," 17. I supplement Isaacson's translation with the Chinese original in Xu Nianci, "Xin Faluoxiansheng tan," 2.

62 Xu Nianci, "New Tales," 17.

63 Jiang, "From the Technique," 141. Whereas Dorothy Ko has inscribed modern Chinese national consciousness as an outside gaze, "a point of view that lies outside the boundaries of the national body" ("From the Technique," 141), Jiang adds that Mr. Braggadocio's extraterrestrial adventures engage simultaneously in "two opposite processes: that of distancing, of viewing China from the outside in, and of centralizing," focusing on China's internal problems and power struggles ("From the Technique," 141).

64 Doleželová-Velingerová, "Narrative Modes," 56.

65 Doleželová-Velingerová, "Narrative Modes," 56. See also Hanan, *Chinese Fiction*, 165; Zhao, *The Uneasy Narrator*, 66.

66 Doleželová-Velingerová, "Narrative Modes," 66.

67 Doleželová-Velingerová, "Narrative Modes," 72.

68 See Woloch, *The One vs. the Many*.

69 Thacker, *Biomedia*, 6.

70 Thacker, *Biomedia*, 6.

71 Xu Nianci, "New Tales," 17.

72 Thacker, *Biomedia*, 6.

73 Xu Nianci, "New Tales," 18.

74 Xu Nianci, "New Tales," 18.

75 Xu Nianci, "New Tales," 19.

76 Xu Nianci, "New Tales," 19.

77 Xu Nianci, "New Tales," 19.

78 Thacker, *Biomedia*, 6.

79 Thacker, *Biomedia*, 6.

80 Thacker, *Biomedia*, 9–10.

81 Thacker, *Biomedia*, 10.

82 Xu Nianci, "New Tales," 20.

83 Xu Nianci, "New Tales," 26.

84 Xu Nianci, "New Tales," 30.

85 Jiang, "From the Technique," 134.

86 Xu Nianci, "New Tales," 19.

87 Xu Nianci, "New Tales," 27.

88 Xu Nianci, "New Tales," 31. See Isaacson, *Celestial Empire*, 119, for an analysis of Mr. Braggadocio's atypical observations on evolutionary biology.

89 Xu Nianci, "New Tales," 32.

90 Xu Nianci, "Xin faluoxiansheng tan," 15.

91 Xu Nianci, "New Tales," 31.

92 I take the term "*arche*-fossil" from Meillassoux, *After Finitude*. Meillassoux raises the question of the *arche*-fossil, and the ancestrality of reality anterior to human life-forms, for the philosophy of speculative realism, arguing that only the latter enables us to grasp the "in-itself" by getting out of transcendentalism and the centrality of the subject (4). This argument, however, would have to contend with the problem of literary narration. The mysterious reappearance of Mr. Braggadocio's old diary must be seen in light of the larger problem of the story's first-person narration of disparate selves, adding a past subjectivity into an already multiplied perspective. Who or what begins the narration that we are presently following? Does the found diary amplify the human-centric view, which means that one can make sense of the beginning of life only in the presence of a living observer and human records? Is it at all possible to think the existence of prehistoric life before human consciousness?

93 Xu Nianci, "New Tales," 32; Xu Nianci, "Xin Faluoxiansheng tan," 16.

94 Xu Nianci, "New Tales," 35.

95 Luan, "Jindai kexue xiaoshuo yu linghun," 49.

96 Liu, "Force of Psyche," 248–49.

97 Liu, "Force of Psyche," 249–50.
98 Geoghegan, "Mind the Gap," 901–2.
99 Wood, *Ideal Suggestion*, 34.
100 Wood, *Ideal Suggestion*, 99.
101 Wood, *Ideal Suggestion*, 108–10.
102 Wright, "Tan Sitong and the Ether Reconsidered," 569.
103 Tan, *Renxue*, 47. See also Wright, "Tan Sitong and the Ether Reconsidered," 556.
104 Tan, *Renxue*, 60.
105 Tan, *Renxue*, 60. As electricity, ether even mediates emptiness itself.
106 Quoted in Wright, "Tan Sitong and the Ether Reconsidered," 557.
107 Xu Nianci, "New Tales," 36.
108 Xu Nianci, "Xin Faluoxiansheng tan," 18.
109 Xu Nianci, "New Tales," 36–37.
110 Xu Nianci, "New Tales," 37.
111 Xu Nianci, "New Tales," 37.
112 Xu Nianci, "New Tales," 37.
113 Woloch, *The One vs. the Many*, 116–19.
114 Xu Nianci, "New Tales," 38.
115 Liu, "Force of Psyche." William James linked the New Thought movement to social evolutionism and religious mysticism. Wood's particular version of mind therapy or mind cure evidenced the popularity of self-education as a tool for social individuation. Fryer began his translation after China's defeat in the First Sino-Japanese War in 1895 and showed his awareness of the political and social climate of the period by inserting into Wood's preface his personal comments on "opium houses, crimes, wars, disasters and famine" to emphasize, as Liu puts it, "the importance of the education of the mind and heart of man" (249, 253).
116 Xu Nianci, "New Tales," 38; Yang Guomin, *Wan Qing xiaoshuo*, 19. Mr. Braggadocio's selfish concern with individual profit over national progress conforms to Yang's observation that intellectuals of the period shifted from a focus on ethics to "wealth and strength" (*fuqiang*).
117 Wu Hongcheng and Zhao, "Wan Qing shiye jiaoyu."
118 Wu Hongcheng and Zhao, "Wan Qing shiye jiaoyu," 31.
119 Li Fu-ying, "Wan Qing 'wushi' 'zhiyong' de jiaoyu guanli sichao yu sheye jiaoyu," 69.
120 Quoted in Wu Hongcheng and Zhao, "Wanqing shiye," 34.
121 Yang Guomin, *Wan Qing xiaoshuo*, 23.
122 Xu Nianci, "New Tales," 38.
123 Harvey, *The New Imperialism*, 141.
124 Tsu, *Failure, Nationalism, and Literature*.
125 For the reception and association of Marx's "Fragment on Machines" with post-Fordism and the Italian Marxist tradition of Operaismo, see Pasquinelli, "Italian Operaismo and the Information Machine"; Trott, "The 'Fragment on Machines.'"

126 Marx, *Grundrisse*, 676–78.

127 Marx, *Grundrisse*, 681, 685. Hence while *matières instrumentales* (French in the original) such as coal, wood, grease, and oil have use values for the production process, the same materials also have use values outside production and can be consumed noncommercially (680).

128 Marx, *Grundrisse*, 692.

129 Marx, *Grundrisse*, 693.

130 Marx, *Grundrisse*, 694.

131 Marx, *Grundrisse*, 694, emphasis added.

132 Harvey, *The New Imperialism*, 149.

133 Marx, *Grundrisse*, 706.

134 Virno, "General Intellect," 4.

135 On "general social labor" in capital, see Marx, *Grundrisse*, 694.

136 Virno and Hardt, *Radical Thought in Italy*. For critics of immaterial labor (variously referred to as cognitive labor) who oppose the concept's downplaying of the continuing exploitation of physical and material work by Third World workers and women of color, see Camfield, "The Multitude and the Kangaroo"; Weeks, "Life within and against Work," 17.

137 Lazzarato, "Immaterial Labor," 133.

138 Lazzarato, "Immaterial Labor," 135–36.

139 Lazzarato, "Immaterial Labor," 140.

140 Lazzarato, "Immaterial Labor," 137.

141 Marx, *Grundrisse*, 694.

142 Lazzarato, "Immaterial Labor," 137

143 Lazzarato, "Immaterial Labor," 142.

144 Lazzarato, "Immaterial Labor," 142.

145 Liang, "Lun shengli fenli," 76. Liang's use of *xinli*, which I translate as mental labor, must be differentiated from Henry Wood's and Tan Sitong's interest in mental powers or the power of thought (*xinli*).

146 Liang, "Lun shengli fenli," 81–82.

147 Liang, "Lun shengli fenli," 84.

148 Liang, "Lun shengli fenli," 88.

149 Lazzarato, "Immaterial Labor," 133.

150 Williams, *Marxism and Literature*, 159–62.

151 Williams, *Marxism and Literature*, 159.

152 Williams, *Marxism and Literature*, 162.

153 Williams, *Marxism and Literature*, 162.

154 Williams, *Marxism and Literature*. New technologies in printing and publishing that shape the field of writing and literature, for instance, depend on new working relationships between artists. Whereas the seventeenth-century author was a "solitary handworker, alone with his 'medium,' he had in earlier periods worked closely with dramatists, and later phases of development, with other media industries such as cinema and television" (162–63).

155 Marx, *Grundrisse*, 694.

Conclusion: Stone, Woman, Wireless

1 For scholarship on media archaeology, see Ernst, "Media Archaeography"; Huhtamo and Parikka, *Media Archaeology*; Parikka, *What Is Media Archaeology?*

2 Mitchell and Hansen, "Introduction," xxii.

3 Galloway, Thacker, and Wark, *Excommunication*, 7–9.

4 Karl, *The Magic of Concepts*, 13.

5 Karl, *The Magic of Concepts*, 13.

6 Galloway, "What Is New Media?"

7 Jameson's multivolume series on the "poetics of social forms" include *Postmodernism*, *Archaeologies of the Future*, and *A Singular Modernity*. For an interview with Jameson on his ongoing project, see Cevasco, "Imagining a Space That Is Outside." In *Fiery Cinema*, Bao focuses "the politics of media" on the "production of mass affect," refining the former term from post-1968 film scholarship interested in political modernism (21, 24–25). Liu traces the rise of digital media in post-Mao 1980s China (*Information Fantasies*, 22–23).

8 Williams, *Television*, 127.

9 Galloway, Thacker, and Wark, *Excommunication*, 7.

10 Chen Wen-lian, "Wan Qing funü jiefang."

11 See Caffentzis, "A Critique of Cognitive Capitalism"; Federici, "On Affective Labor"; Fuchs, "Cognitive Capitalism or Informational Capitalism?" For critiques of Michael Hardt and Antonio Negri's *Empire*, and the authors' responses, see Lazzarato, "Immaterial Labor"; Hardt et al., "The Global Coliseum."

12 Hao, *Folding Beijing*; Ren and Xu, "Interpreting Folding Beijing."

13 Chen Qiufan, *Huang chao*. Hereafter, I cite page numbers of the Chinese original in parenthesis in the main text to distinguish it from the English translation (*Waste Tide*), which will only be referenced in the notes.

14 For the novel's indebtedness to cyberpunk, see Wang Shuoqiang, "Huang chao yu Chen Qiufan de chonggou shijie."

15 Chen Qiufan, email message to author, July 18, 2019. I am incredibly grateful to Chen for permitting me to cite our personal email exchanges here.

16 For an important discussion of new media and embodiment, see Hansen, *New Philosophy for New Media*.

17 Chen Qiufan, *Waste Tide*, 133–34.

18 Chen Qiufan, email message to author, July 18, 2019.

19 Liptak, "One of China's Best Sci-Fi Authors"; Liptak, "An Animated Adaptation of Chinese Sci-Fi Novel"; Cheung, "New Golden Age for Science Fiction."

20 Chen Qiufan, *Waste Tide*, 134.

21 Hayles, *My Mother Was a Computer*, 17–18.

22 I thank Shawn Ho Yong Chuan, my former student at Yale–NUS College, for this insightful observation.

23 Woloch, *The One vs. the Many*, 25.

24 Woloch, *The One vs. the Many*, 12.

25 Thacker, *Biomedia*, 6.

26 For a recent polemic on information control's challenge to the validity of capitalism as an analytical category, see Wark, *Capital Is Dead*.

27 One of this book's claims is that the dialectics between the technological-material and the theoretical-ethical cannot be summed up by neat equations, and therefore remains an essential task for the cultural humanities. That is to say, while I acknowledge the authority of the sciences and more quantitative disciplines in the field of technological innovations, my definition of mediation throughout this book wrests the study of the *relations* between technology and culture back *to* and *for* the humanities. This is my modest contribution to what Christopher Newfield urges as an "epistemic parity" between numerical culture and the study of literatures, languages, and culture. See Newfield, "The Trouble with Numerical Culture." For a classic exposition of the "old-fashioned [Marxist] question" of the relation between global cultural systems and the economic order, see Arjun Appadurai, "Disjuncture and Difference in the Global Cultural Economy."

BIBLIOGRAPHY

A Ying. *Wan Qing xiaoshuo shi* [A history of late Qing fiction]. Beijing: Dongfang chubanshe, 1996.

Acland, Charles R. *Residual Media*. Minneapolis: University of Minnesota Press, 2007.

"Aidisen xin chuang jisheng jixing qi shuo" [On Edison's invention of the phonograph]. *Gezhi huibian* 6 (1891): 46.

Aiken, Maxwell, and Wei Lu. "The Evolution of Bookkeeping in China: Integrating Historical Trends with Western Influences." *Abacus* 34, no. 1 (2002): 140–62.

Allen-Robertson, James. "The Materiality of Digital Media: The Hard Disk Drive, Phonograph, Magnetic Tape and Optical Media in Technical Close-Up." *New Media and Society* 19, no. 3 (2017): 455–70.

Altman, Rick. *Silent Film Sound*. New York: Columbia University Press, 2007.

Américi, Laurence. "Preparing the People for Capitalism: Relations with Depositors in a French Savings Bank during the 1820s." *Financial History Review* 9, no. 1 (2002): 5–19.

An Haibo. "Wan Qing de 'guang yu chengxiang': Lingnan Zou Boqi de sheying lilun yu shijian" [Light and imaging in the late Qing dynasty: The photographic theory and practice of Zou Boqi]. *Zhuangshi* 286, no. 2 (2017): 142–43.

Anker, Elizabeth S., and Rita Felski. *Critique and Postcritique*. Durham, NC: Duke University Press, 2017.

Aouragh, Miriyam, and Paula Chakravartty. "Infrastructures of Empire: Towards a Critical Geopolitics of Media and Information Studies." *Media, Culture and Society* 38, no. 4 (2016): 559–75.

Appadurai, Arjun. "Disjuncture and Difference in the Global Cultural Economy." In *Modernity at Large: Cultural Dimensions of Globalization*, 27–47. Minneapolis: University of Minnesota Press, 1996.

Apter, Emily. *Against World Literature: On the Politics of Untranslatability*. New York: Verso Books, 2014.

Arendt, Hannah. *The Human Condition*, 2nd ed. Chicago: University of Chicago Press, 2013.

Baark, Erik. *Lightning Wires: The Telegraph and China's Technological Moderniza-tion, 1860–1890*. Westport, CT: Greenwood Press, 1997.

Bachner, Andrea. *Beyond Sinology: Chinese Writing and the Scripts of Culture*. New York: Columbia University Press, 2014.

Bao Weihong. *Fiery Cinema: The Emergence of an Affective Medium in China, 1915–1945*. Minneapolis: University of Minnesota Press, 2015.

Barlow, Tani. *The Question of Women in Chinese Feminism*. Durham, NC: Duke University Press, 2004.

Barthes, Roland. *Camera Lucida: Reflections on Photography*. Translated by Richard Howard. New York: Farrar, Straus and Giroux, 1981.

Batchen, Geoffrey. "Electricity Made Visible." In *New Media, Old Media: A History and Theory Reader*, edited by Wendy Hui Kyong Chun and Thomas Keenan, 27–44. New York: Routledge, 2006.

Baudrillard, Jean. *In the Shadow of the Silent Majorities*. Translated by Paul Foss. Los Angeles: Semiotext(e), 2007.

Bazin, André. *What Is Cinema?* Translated by Timothy Barnard. Montreal: Caboose, 2009.

"Beijing bianluan wenti" [Question of the crisis in Beijing]. *Thien Nan Shin Pao*, June 15, 1900. Accessed December 23, 2017. NUS Libraries Database.

"Beijing bianluan zhuandian huideng" [Summary of telegrams on the Beijing crisis]. *Thien Nan Shin Pao*, February 9, 1900. Accessed December 23, 2017. NUS Libraries Database.

"Benguan xinwen" [Editorial news]. *Thien Nan Shin Pao*, April 23, 1900. Accessed December 23, 2017. NUS Libraries Database.

Benjamin, Walter. "Theses on the Philosophy of History." In *Illuminations: Essays and Reflections*, translated by Harry Zohn, 253–64. New York: Schocken Books, 2011.

Best, Stephen, and Sharon Marcus. "Surface Reading: An Introduction." *Representations* 108, no. 1 (2009): 1–21.

Blom, Ina. "The Autobiography of Video: Outline for a Revisionist Account of Early Video Art." *Critical Inquiry* 39, no. 2 (2013): 276–95.

Bolter, J. David, and Richard A. Grusin. *Remediation: Understanding New Media*. Cambridge, MA: MIT Press, 2000.

Bowersox, Jeff. *Raising Germans in the Age of Empire: Youth and Colonial Culture, 1871–1914*. Oxford: Oxford University Press, 2013.

Brinkema, Eugenie. *The Forms of the Affects*. Durham, NC: Duke University Press, 2014.

Bush, Christopher. *Ideographic Modernism: China, Writing, Media*. Oxford: Oxford University Press, 2012.

Cadava, Eduardo. *Words of Light: Theses on the Photography of History*. Princeton, NJ: Princeton University Press, 1997.

Caffentzis, George. "A Critique of Cognitive Capitalism." In *Cognitive Capitalism, Education and Digital Labor*, edited by Michael Peters and Ergin Bulut, 23–57. New York: Peter Lang, 2011.

Cai Zong-qi. "The Rethinking of Emotion: The Transformation of Traditional Literary Criticism in the Late Qing Era." *Monumenta Serica* 45 (1997): 63–100.

Cai Zong-qi. "*Wen* and the Construction of a Critical System in 'Wenxin Diaolong.'" *Chinese Literature: Essays, Articles, Reviews* 22 (2000): 1–29.

Caldwell, Bruce J. "Praxeology and Its Critics: An Appraisal." *History of Political Economy* 16, no. 3 (1984): 363–79.

Camfield, David. "The Multitude and the Kangaroo: A Critique of Hardt and Negri's Theory of Immaterial Labour." *Historical Materialism* 15, no. 2 (2007): 21–52.

Carey, James W. "Technology and Ideology: The Case of the Telegraph." *Prospects* 8 (1983): 303–25.

Cevasco, Maria Elisa. "Imagining a Space That Is Outside: An Interview with Fredric Jameson." *Minnesota Review*, no. 78 (2012): 83–94.

Chang Kang-i Sun and Stephen Owen, eds. *The Cambridge History of Chinese Literature*, vol. 2: *From 1375*. Cambridge: Cambridge University Press, 2010.

Chen Depeng. "Wenhua jiegou yu 'zhongti xiyong' wenhua guan de dansheng ji qi yingxiang" [Cultural structure and the birth and influence of the cultural concept of 'Chinese essence and Western means']. *Pingdingshan xueyuan xuebao* 22, no. 4 (2007): 34–41.

Chen Qiufan. *Huang chao* [The waste tide]. Shanghai: Shanghai ZUI, 2013.

Chen Qiufan. *Waste Tide*. Translated by Ken Liu. New York: Tom Doherty Associates, 2019.

Chen Shimin. "The Rise and Fall of Debit-Credit Bookkeeping in China: History and Analysis." *The Accounting Historians Journal* 25, no. 1 (1998): 73–92.

Chen Wen-lian. "Wan Qing funü jie fang si chao xin qi de yuanying ji te dian" [The rise of women's liberation thought in the late Qing]. *Journal of Heng Yang Teachers' College* 1, no. 24 (2002): 93–98.

Chen Yimin. "Mingpian gujin tan" [Namecards past and present]. *Xungen*, no. 6 (2014): 94–98.

Chen Zhanbiao. "1878 nian Guo Songtao de shibo youli" [Ambassador Guo Songtao at Expo 1878]. *Dang'an chunqiu* 6 (2010): 16–18.

Cheng, Eileen J. "Gendered Spectacles: Lu Xun on Gazing at Women and Other Pleasures." *Modern Chinese Literature and Culture* 16, no. 1 (2004): 1–36.

Cheng Linsun. *Banking in Modern China: Entrepreneurs, Professional Managers, and the Development of Chinese Banks, 1897–1937*. Cambridge: Cambridge University Press, 2003.

Cheng Xiuhua, ed. *Zhongguo dianying fa zhan shi* [A history of Chinese cinema]. Beijing: Zhongguo dianying chuban she, 1998.

Cheung, Rachel. "New Golden Age for Science Fiction in China, and What It Has to Offer." *South China Morning Post*, May 14, 2017.

Chow, Rey. *Woman and Chinese Modernity: The Politics of Reading between West and East*. Minneapolis: University of Minnesota Press, 1991.

Choy, Howard Y. F. *Discourses of Disease: Writing Illness, the Mind and the Body in Modern China*. Leiden: Brill, 2016.

263

Chu, Seo-Young. *Do Metaphors Dream of Literal Sleep? A Science-Fictional Theory of Representation*. Cambridge, MA: Harvard University Press, 2010.

Chun, Wendy Hui Kyong, and Thomas Keenan, eds. *New Media, Old Media: A History and Theory Reader*. London: Psychology Press, 2006.

Clark, Justin T. *City of Second Sight: Nineteenth-Century Boston and the Making of American Visual Culture*. Chapel Hill: University of North Carolina Press, 2018.

Clarke, Bruce. "Information." In *Critical Terms for Media Studies*, edited by W. J. T. Mitchell and Mark B. N. Hansen, 157–71. Chicago: University of Chicago Press, 2010.

Clarke, Bruce. *Neocybernetics and Narrative*. Minneapolis: University of Minnesota Press, 2014.

Cochran, Sherman. *Chinese Medicine Men: Consumer Culture in China and Southeast Asia*. Cambridge, MA: Harvard University Press, 2006.

Cohen, Paul A. *China Unbound: Evolving Perspectives on the Chinese Past*. London: Routledge, 2003.

Cohen, Paul A. *History in Three Keys: The Boxers as Event, Experience, and Myth*. New York: Columbia University Press, 1997.

Crary, Jonathan. *Techniques of the Observer: On Vision and Modernity in the Nineteenth Century*. Cambridge, MA: MIT Press, 2012.

Creel, H. G. "The Beginnings of Bureaucracy in China: The Origin of the Hsien." *Journal of Asian Studies* 23, no. 2 (1964): 155–84.

De Lauretis, Teresa. *Technologies of Gender: Essays on Theory, Film, and Fiction*. Bloomington: Indiana University Press, 1987.

Delekesilei, "Jiqi jingshen lun" [On the spirit of the machine]. *Xiehe bao*, April 16, 1914, 12–13.

Derrida, Jacques. *The Ear of the Other: Otobiography, Transference, Translation— Texts and Discussions with Jacques Derrida*. Translated by Christie McDonald. New York: Schocken Books, 1985.

Derrida, Jacques. *Politics of Friendship*. Translated by George Collins. London: Verso, 2005.

Des Forges, Alexander Townsend. "Burning with Reverence: The Economics and Aesthetics of Words in Qing (1644–1911) China." *PMLA* 121, no. 1 (2006): 139–55.

Des Forges, Alexander Townsend. *Mediasphere Shanghai: The Aesthetics of Cultural Production*. Honolulu: University of Hawai'i Press, 2007.

Desnoyers, Charles A. "Introduction." In *A Journey to the East: Li Gui's A New Account of a Trip around the Globe*. Translated by Charles A. Desnoyers, 1–74. Ann Arbor: University of Michigan Press, 2004.

Desnoyers, Charles A. "Translator's Preface." In *A Journey to the East: Li Gui's A New Account of a Trip around the Globe*. Translated by Charles A. Desnoyers, v–ix. Ann Arbor: University of Michigan Press, 2004.

Desser, David. "Japan." In *The International Movie Industry*, edited by Gorham Anders Kindem, 7–21. Carbondale: Southern Illinois University Press, 2000.

Doane, Mary Ann. "The Indexical and the Concept of Medium Specificity." *differences: A Journal of Feminist Cultural Studies* 18, no. 1 (2007): 128–52.

Doane, Mary Ann. "Indexicality: Trace and Sign: Introduction." *differences: A Journal of Feminist Cultural Studies* 18, no. 1 (2007): 1–6.

Doleželová-Velingerová, Milena. "Literary Historiography in Early Twentieth-Century China (1904–1928): Constructions of Cultural Memory." In *The Appropriation of Cultural Capital: China's May Fourth Project*, edited by Milena Doleželová-Velingerová and Oldrich Král, 123–66. Cambridge, MA: Harvard University Asia Center, 2001.

Doleželová-Velingerová, Milena. "Narrative Modes in Late Qing Novels." In *The Chinese Novel at the Turn of the Century*, edited by Milena Doleželová-Velingerová, 55–86. Toronto: University of Toronto Press, 1980.

Dong Huining. "'Feiying ge huabao' yanjiu" [Study on 'Feiyingge Illustrated']. *Nanjing yishu xueyuan xuebao: meishu yu sheji ban* 1 (2011): 104–11.

Dooling, Amy D. *Women's Literary Feminism in Twentieth-Century China*. New York: Palgrave Macmillan, 2005.

Du Huimin. "Bu zhi shi zhengzhi—tan wan Qing houqi xiaoshuo qikan yijie guannian de duoyang xin shanbian" [Not only politics—on the multifaceted changes of later Qing fiction journals]. *Xiandai yuwen* 6 (2009): 53–56.

Durrant, Stephen W. *The Cloudy Mirror: Tension and Conflict in the Writings of Sima Qian*. Albany: State University of New York Press, 1995.

Durrant, Stephen, Wai-yee Li, and David Schaberg. *Zuo Tradition / Zuozhuan: Commentary on the "Spring and Autumn Annals."* Seattle: University of Washington Press, 2016.

Edison, Thomas A. "The Latest Offerings of Science." *Daily Graphic*, June 8, 1878, 662–63.

Edison, Thomas A. "The Phonograph and Its Future." *North American Review* 126, no. 262 (1878): 527–36.

Elliott, Jane. "American Photographs of the Boxer Rising." *History of Photography* 21, no. 2 (1997): 162–69.

Elliott, Jane. *Some Did It for Civilisation, Some Did It for Their Country: A Revised View of the Boxer War*. Hong Kong: Chinese University Press, 2002.

Elman, Benjamin A. "Naval Warfare and the Refraction of China's Self-Strengthening Reforms into Scientific and Technological Failure, 1865–1895." *Modern Asian Studies* 38, no. 2 (2004): 283–326.

Elman, Benjamin A. *On Their Own Terms: Science in China, 1550–1900*. Cambridge, MA: Harvard University Press, 2005.

Elsaesser, Thomas, and Malte Hagener. *Film Theory: An Introduction through the Senses*. London: Routledge, 2015.

Ernst, Wolfgang. "'Media Archaeography: Method and Machine versus History and Narrative of Media.'" In *Media Archaeology: Approaches, Applications, and Implications*, edited by Jussi Parikka and Erkki Huhtamo, 239–55. Berkeley: University of California Press, 2011.

Ernst, Wolfgang. *Sonic Time Machines: Explicit Sound, Sirenic Voices, and Implicit Sonicity*. Amsterdam: Amsterdam University Press, 2016.

Everett, Jeffery. "Organizational Research and the Praxeology of Pierre Bourdieu." *Organizational Research Methods* 5, no. 1 (2002): 56–80.

265

Fang Ming, Dong Zenqiang, and Chen Jiantang. *Zhongguo jindai minzhu sixiang shi, 1840–1949* [A history of contemporary Chinese nationalism, 1840–1949]. Beijing: Renmin chubanshe, 2014.

Federici, Sylvia. "On Affective Labor." In *Cognitive Capitalism, Education and Digital Labor*, edited by Michael Peters and Ergin Bulut, 57–73. New York: Peter Lang, 2011.

Felski, Rita. "Context Stinks!" *New Literary History* 42, no. 4 (2011): 573–91.

Felski, Rita. *The Limits of Critique*. Chicago: University of Chicago Press, 2015.

Ford, Thomas H. "Poetry's Media." *New Literary History* 44, no. 3 (2013): 449–69.

Fraser, Nancy. "Heterosexism, Misrecognition, and Capitalism: A Response to Judith Butler." *Social Text* 52–53 (1997): 279–89.

Fraser, Sarah E. "The Face of China: Photography's Role in Shaping Image, 1860–1920." *Getty Research Journal*, no. 2 (2010): 39–52.

Fryer, John. "Chinese Education—Past, Present, and Future, Pt. 1." *Chinese Recorder*, July 1897, 329–35.

Fuchs, Christian. "Cognitive Capitalism or Informational Capitalism? The Role of Class in the Information Economy." In *Cognitive Capitalism, Education, and Digital Labor*, edited by Michael Peters and Ergin Bulut, 75–119. New York: Peter Lang, 2011.

Fuller, Matthew. *Media Ecologies: Materialist Energies in Art and Technoculture*. Cambridge, MA: MIT Press, 2005.

Furth, Charlotte. *The Limits of Change: Essays on Conservative Alternatives in Republican China*. Cambridge, MA: Harvard University Press, 1976.

Galloway, Alexander R. *The Interface Effect*. Cambridge: Polity Press, 2013.

Galloway, Alexander R. *Protocol: How Control Exists after Decentralization*. Cambridge, MA: MIT Press, 2004.

Galloway, Alexander R. "What Is New Media?: Ten Years after the Language of New Media." *Criticism* 53, no. 3 (2011): 377–84.

Galloway, Alexander R., Eugene Thacker, and McKenzie Wark. *Excommunication: Three Inquiries in Media and Mediation*. Chicago: University of Chicago Press, 2014.

Galvan, Jill Nicole. *The Sympathetic Medium: Feminine Channeling, the Occult, and Communication Technologies, 1859–1919*. Ithaca, NY: Cornell University Press, 2010.

Gan Yonglong. "Jiqi ren (fu zhaopian)" [Robot (with photo)]. *Dongfang zazhi* 8, no. 8 (1911): 22.

Gang Hou. "Wan jiezhang Wang jun Binpu" [Mourning my sister's husband Wang Binpu]. *Xinshe caokan* 7 (1889): 4.

Gardella, Robert P. "Commercial Bookkeeping in Ch'ing China and the West: A Preliminary Assessment." *Ch'ing-Shih Wen-t'i* 4, no. 7 (1982): 56–72.

Gengzi jishi [Record of the Boxer Rebellion]. Beijing: Kexue chuban she, 1959.

Geoghegan, Bernard Dionysius. "After Kittler: On the Cultural Techniques of Recent German Media Theory." *Theory, Culture and Society* 30, no. 6 (2013): 66–82.

Geoghegan, Bernard Dionysius. "Mind the Gap: Spiritualism and the Infrastructural Uncanny." *Critical Inquiry* 42, no. 4 (2016): 899–922.

Germain, Richard. *Dollars through the Doors: A Pre-1930 History of Bank Marketing in America*. Westport, CT: Greenwood Publishing, 1996.

Gitelman, Lisa. *Always Already New: Media, History, and the Data of Culture*. Cambridge, MA: MIT Press, 2008.

Gitelman, Lisa. *Paper Knowledge: Toward a Media History of Documents*. Durham, NC: Duke University Press, 2014.

Gitelman, Lisa. *Scripts, Grooves, and Writing Machines: Representing Technology in the Edison Era*. Stanford, CA: Stanford University Press, 1999.

Gitelman, Lisa, and Geoffrey B. Pingree. *New Media, 1740–1915*. Cambridge, MA: MIT Press, 2003.

Gu Yi. "What's in a Name? Photography and the Reinvention of Visual Truth in China, 1840–1911." *Art Bulletin* 95, no. 1 (2013): 120–38.

Guillory, John. "Genesis of the Media Concept." *Critical Inquiry* 36, no. 2 (2010): 321–62.

Guo Changhai and Qiu Jingwu, eds. *Qiu Jin yanjiu ziliao: wenxian ji* [Research material on Qiu Jin, 2 vols.]. Ningxia: Ningxia renmin chubanshe, 2007.

Guo Jiwu. "Dongnan hubao yu wan Qing zhengju" [The mutual defense pact of the Southeastern provinces and late Qing politics]. PhD diss., Minzu University of China, 2010.

Guo Songtao. *Lundun yu Bali riji*. Changsha: Yuelu shushe, 1984.

Haddad, John R. "The Wild West Turns East: Audience, Ritual, and Regeneration in Buffalo Bill's Boxer Uprising." *American Studies* 49, nos. 3–4 (2008): 5–38.

Haitian du xiaozi [Lone Howler]. "Nüwa Shi" [Stone of the goddess Nüwa]. In *Zhongguo jindai xiaoshuo zaxi* 20, 439–536. Nanchang: Baihua zhou wenyi chuban she, 1991.

Hanan, Patrick. *Chinese Fiction of the Nineteenth and Early Twentieth Centuries: Essays by Patrick Hanan*. New York: Columbia University Press, 2004.

Hansen, Mark Boris Nicola. *New Philosophy for New Media*. Cambridge, MA: MIT Press, 2004.

Hao Chang. *Chinese Intellectuals in Crisis: Search for Order and Meaning 1890–1911*. Berkeley: University of California Press, 1987.

Hao Jingfang. *Folding Beijing*. Translated by Ken Liu. *Uncanny: A Magazine of Science Fiction and Fantasy*, 2016.

Hardt, Michael, et al. "The Global Coliseum: On Empire." *Cultural Studies* 16, no. 2 (2002): 177–92.

Hardy, Grant. *Worlds of Bronze and Bamboo: Sima Qian's Conquest of History*. New York: Columbia University Press, 1999.

Hartley, John. *Communication, Cultural and Media Studies: The Key Concepts*. London: Routledge, 2012.

Harvey, David. *The New Imperialism*. Oxford: Oxford University Press, 2003.

Hayles, Katherine. *How We Became Posthuman: Virtual Bodies in Cybernetics, Literature, and Informatics*. Chicago: University of Chicago Press, 1999.

Hayles, Katherine. *How We Think: Digital Media and Contemporary Technogenesis*. Chicago: University of Chicago Press, 2012.

267

Hayles, Katherine. *My Mother Was a Computer: Digital Subjects and Literary Texts*. Chicago: University of Chicago Press, 2010.

Hayles, Katherine. *Writing Machines*. Cambridge, MA: MIT Press, 2016.

Hayot, Eric. *Chinese Dreams: Pound, Brecht, Tel Quel*. Ann Arbor: University of Michigan Press, 2012.

Hayot, Eric, Haun Saussy, and Steven G. Yao, eds. *Sinographies: Writing China*. Minneapolis: University of Minnesota Press, 2007.

Hevia, James L. *English Lessons: The Pedagogy of Imperialism in Nineteenth-Century China*. Durham, NC: Duke University Press, 2003.

Hevia, James L. "The Photography Complex: Exposing Boxer-Era China (1900–1901), Making Civilization." In *Photographies East: The Camera and Its Histories in East and Southeast Asia*, edited by Rosalind C. Morris, 79–120. Durham, NC: Duke University Press, 2009.

Hill, Michael Gibbs. *Lin Shu, Inc.: Translation and the Making of Modern Chinese Culture*. Oxford: Oxford University Press, 2012.

Hon Tze-ki. "Zhang Zhidong's Proposal for Reform: A New Reading of the *Quanxue Pian*." In *Rethinking the 1898 Reform Period: Political and Cultural Change in Late Qing China*, edited by Rebecca E. Karl and Peter Gue Zarrow, 77–98. Cambridge, MA: Harvard University Asia Center, 2002.

Hooker, Mary. *Behind the Scenes in Peking*. London: John Murray, 1911.

Hu Shudu. "Wofo Shanren zuopin kaolüe—changpian xiaoshuo bufen" [A survey of the works of Wofo shanren—section on long novels]. *Zhongshan daxue xuebao* 3 (1980): 86–102.

Hu Ying. *Burying Autumn: Poetry, Friendship, and Loss*. Cambridge, MA: Harvard University Asia Center, 2016.

Hu Ying. "Gender and Modern Martyrology: Qiu Jin as Lienü, Lieshi, or Nülieshi." In *Beyond Exemplar Tales: Women's Biography in Chinese History*, edited by Joan Judge and Ying Hu, 121–37. Berkeley: University of California Press, 2011.

Hu Ying. "Qiu Jin's Nine Burials: The Making of Historical Monuments and Public Memory." *Modern Chinese Literature and Culture* 19, no. 1 (2007): 138–91.

Hu Ying. *Tales of Translation: Composing the New Woman in China, 1898–1918*. Stanford, CA: Stanford University Press, 2000.

Huang Hua. "Shi xin yingxiong yi you ci—Zhongri xuezhe bixiao de Qiu Jin zhuangsu" [The beginning knowledge of the female hero: The different outfits of Qiu Jin under the records of Chinese and Japanese writers]. *Fünu yanjiu luncong* 128, no. 2 (2015): 73–80.

Huang, Philip C. C. "Centralized Minimalism: Semiformal Governance by Quasi Officials and Dispute Resolution in China." *Modern China* 34, no. 1 (2008): 9–35.

Huang Yiping. *Jindai zhongguo jingji bianqian* [Economic changes in contemporary China]. Shanghai: Shanghai renmin chubanshe, 1992.

Huang Zunxian. "Jin bieli, si shou" [Modern parting: Four poems]. In *Huang Zunxian quanji*, edited by Chen Zhen, vol. 1, 121–22. Beijing: Zhonghua shuju, 2005.

Huang Zunxian. "Renjing lu shi cao xu" [Preface to "Poetry from the Hut within the Human Realm"]. In *Huang Zunxian quanji*, edited by Chen Zhen, vol. 1, 68–69. Beijing: Zhonghua shuju, 2005.

Huhtamo, Erkki, and Jussi Parikka, eds. *Media Archaeology: Approaches, Applications, and Implications*. Berkeley: University of California Press, 2011.

Hui Yuk. *The Question Concerning Technology in China: An Essay in Cosmotechnics*. Falmouth, UK: Urbanoic Media, 2016.

Hung Wu. "Inventing a 'Chinese' Portrait Style in Early Photography." In *Brush and Shutter: Early Photography in China*, edited by Frances Terpak and Jeffery W Cody, 69–90. Los Angeles: Getty Research Institute, 2011.

Hung Wu. "On Rubbings: Their Materiality and Historicity." *Writing and Materiality in China: Essays in Honor of Patrick Hanan*, edited by Judith T. Zeitlin and Lydia H. Liu, 29–72. Cambridge, MA: Harvard University Asia Center, 2003.

Huters, Theodore. *Bringing the World Home: Appropriating the West in Late Qing and Early Republican China*. Honolulu: University of Hawai'i Press, 2005.

Iovene, Paola. *Tales of Futures Past: Anticipation and the Ends of Literature in Contemporary China*. Stanford, CA: Stanford University Press, 2014.

Isaacson, Nathaniel. *Celestial Empire: The Emergence of Chinese Science Fiction*. Middletown, CT: Wesleyan University Press, 2017.

Jameson, Fredric. *Archaeologies of the Future: The Desire Called Utopia and Other Science Fictions*. London: Verso, 2005.

Jameson, Fredric. "Cognitive Mapping." In *Marxism and the Interpretation of Culture*, edited by Cary Nelson and Lawrence Grossberg, 347–57. Urbana: University of Illinois Press, 1988.

Jameson, Fredric. *Postmodernism, or, The Cultural Logic of Late Capitalism*. Durham, NC: Duke University Press, 1991.

Jameson, Fredric. *A Singular Modernity*. London: Verso Books, 2013.

Jay, Robert. *The Trade Card in Nineteenth-Century America*. Columbia: University of Missouri Press, 1987.

Ji Xu-dong and Wei Lu. "The Evolution of Bookkeeping Methods in China: A Darwinist Analysis of Developments during the Twentieth-Century." *Accounting History* 18, no. 3 (2013): 317–41.

Ji Zhaojin. *A History of Modern Shanghai Banking: The Rise and Decline of China's Financial Capitalism*. London: Routledge, 2016.

Jian Hao [Hero of the Sword]. "Liusheng jiqi" [The phonograph] and "Dianhua" [The telephone]. *Guoming ribao huibian* 4 (1904): 108–9.

Jiang Jing. "From the Technique for Creating Humans to the Art of Reprogramming Hearts: Scientists, Writers, and the Genesis of China's Modern Literary Vision." *Cultural Critique* 80 (2012): 131–50.

"Jiqi yuyan (lu Guowen bao)" [A machine fable (from Guowen bao)]. *Zhixin bao*, no. 94 (1899).

"Jiqi zaoren zhi qiyi" [A strange tale of the human-creating machine]. *Huanqiu Zhongguo xuesheng bao* 1, no. 2 (1906).

Jones, Andrew F. "Portable Monuments: Architectural Photography and the 'Forms' of Empire in Modern China." *positions: asia critique* 18, no. 3 (2010): 599–631.

269

Jones, Andrew F. *Yellow Music: Media Culture and Colonial Modernity in the Chinese Jazz Age.* Durham, NC: Duke University Press, 2001.

Jones, Paul. "The Technology Is Not the Cultural Form? Raymond Williams's Sociological Critique of Marshall McLuhan." *Canadian Journal of Communication* 23, no. 4 (1998): 423–54.

Judge, Joan. *Print and Politics: "Shibao" and the Culture of Reform in Late Qing China.* Stanford, CA: Stanford University Press, 1996.

Judge, Joan. "Talent, Virtue, and the Nation: Chinese Nationalisms and Female Subjectivities in the Early Twentieth Century." *American Historical Review* 106, no. 3 (2001): 765–803.

Judge, Joan, and Ying Hu. "Introduction." In *Beyond Exemplar Tales: Women's Biography in Chinese History*, edited by Joan Judge and Ying Hu, 1–16. Berkeley: University of California Press, 2011.

Kafka, Ben. *The Demon of Writing: Powers and Failures of Paperwork.* New York: Zone Books, 2012.

Kafka, Ben. "Media/Medium (of Communication)." In *Dictionary of Untranslatables: A Philosophical Lexicon*, edited by Barbara Cassin, 626–29. Princeton, NJ: Princeton University Press, 2014.

Karl, Rebecca E. *The Magic of Concepts: History and the Economic in Twentieth-Century China.* Durham, NC: Duke University Press, 2017.

Kaske, Elisabeth. "Metropolitan Clerks and Venality in Qing China: The Great 1830 Forgery Case." *T'oung Pao* 98, nos. 1–3 (2012): 217–69.

Keulemans, Paize. *Sound Rising from the Paper: Nineteenth-Century Martial Arts Fiction and the Chinese Acoustic Imagination.* Cambridge, MA: Harvard University Asia Center, 2014.

Kittler, Friedrich A. *Discourse Networks 1800/1900.* Translated by Michael Metteer and Chris Cullens. Stanford, CA: Stanford University Press, 1992.

Kittler, Friedrich A. *Gramophone, Film, Typewriter.* Translated by Geoffrey Winthrop-Young and Michael Wutz. Stanford, CA: Stanford University Press, 1999.

Klein, Lucas. *The Organization of Distance: Poetry, Translation, Chineseness.* Leiden: Brill, 2018.

Kluitenberg, Eric. "Introduction." In *Book of Imaginary Media: Excavating the Dream of the Ultimate Communication Medium*, 7–26. Rotterdam: NAi Publishing, 2006.

Krauss, Rosalind. "Photography's Discursive Spaces: Landscape/View." *Art Journal* 42, no. 4 (1982): 311–19.

Lacey, Nick. *Image and Representation: Key Concepts in Media Studies.* London: Palgrave Macmillan, 1998.

Lacey, Nick. *Narrative and Genre: Key Concepts in Media Studies.* London: Macmillan, 2000.

Lai Fangling. *Qing mo xiaoshuo yu shehui zhengzhi bianqian* [Late Qing fiction and societal, political change]. Taipei: Daan chubanshe, 1994.

Larkin, Brian. "The Politics and Poetics of Infrastructure." *Annual Review of Anthropology* 42, no. 1 (2013): 327–43.

Larsen, Neil. "Literature, Immanent Critique, and the Problem of Standpoint." *Mediations* 24, no. 2 (2009): 48–65.

Latour, Bruno. *We Have Never Been Modern*. Translated by Catherine Porter. Cambridge, MA: Harvard University Press, 2012.

Latour, Bruno. "Why Has Critique Run Out of Steam? From Matters of Fact to Matters of Concern." *Critical Inquiry* 30, no. 2 (2004): 225–48.

Latour, Bruno, and Steve Woolgar. *Laboratory Life: The Construction of Scientific Facts*. Princeton, NJ: Princeton University Press, 1979.

Lau Chong-chor and Rance P. L. Lee. "Bureaucratic Corruption in Nineteenth-Century China: Its Causes, Control, and Impact." *Southeast Asian Journal of Social Science* 7, nos. 1–2 (1979): 114–35.

Lavrač, Maja. "On Parting, Separation and Longing in the Chinese Poetic Tradition." *Interlitteraria* 20, no. 2 (2015): 105–22.

Lazzarato, Maurizio. "Immaterial Labor." In *Radical Thought in Italy: A Potential Politics*, edited by Paolo Virno and Michael Hardt, 132–47. Minneapolis: University of Minnesota Press, 1996.

Lei Yi. "Wan Qing dianbao he tielu de xingzhi zhi zheng" [Conflicts between the telegraph and the railway in the late Qing]. *Yanhuang chunqiu* 10 (2007): 70–73.

Levine, Caroline. *Forms: Whole, Rhythm, Hierarchy, Network*. Princeton, NJ: Princeton University Press, 2015.

Levine, Caroline. "Strategic Formalism: Toward a New Method in Cultural Studies." *Victorian Studies* 48, no. 4 (2006): 625–57.

Lewis, Mark Edward. *Writing and Authority in Early China*. Albany: State University of New York Press, 1999.

Leyda, Jay. *Dianying: An Account of Films and the Film Audience in China*. Cambridge, MA: MIT Press, 1972.

Li Baojia, *Officialdom Unmasked*. Translated and abridged by T. L. Yang. Hong Kong: Hong Kong University Press, 2001.

Li Fu-ying. "Wan Qing 'wushi' 'zhiyong' de jiaoyu guanli sichao yu sheye jiaoyu [Being pragmatic and being usable: The ideological trend of education management and the education about industry and commerce during the late Qing dynasty]." *Journal of Educational Science of Hunan Normal University* 5, no. 3 (2006): 67–70.

Li Gui. *A Journey to the East: Li Gui's A New Account of a Trip around the Globe*. Translated by Charles A. Desnoyers. Ann Arbor: University of Michigan Press, 2004.

Li Suyun. "Xifang shenjing de yiru ji qi du jingluo yanjiu de yingxiang tanyuan" [Translation of Western nerves terminology and its impact on neurological research]. In *Conference Proceedings of the Zhongguo zhongyi kexue yuan zhengjiu yanjiu shuo*, October 1, 2010, 131–35.

Liang Qichao. *Liang Qichao quanji* [Collected works of Liang Qichao], edited by Shen Peng, 10 vols. Beijing: Beijing chuban she, 1999.

Liang Qichao. "Lun shengli fenli" [On wealth production and wealth consumption]. In *Yinbing shi quanji* [Collected works from Yinbing Studio]. Tainan: Dafu shuju, 1999.

Liang Qichao. "On the Relationship between Fiction and the Government of the People." In *Modern Chinese Literary Thought: Writings on Literature, 1893–1945*, edited by Kirk A. Denton, translated by Nai Cheng Gek, 74–81. Stanford, CA: Stanford University Press, 1996.

Liang Qichao. "Yin bingshi ziyou shu" [Freedom book from Yinbing Studio]. In *Ershi shiji Zhongguo xiaoshuo lilun ziliao* [Collected works of twentieth-century Chinese literary theory], edited by Xia Xiaohong and Chen Pingyuan, vol. 1, 23. Beijing: Beijing daxue chubanshe, 1989.

Lin Z. Jun. "Chinese Double-Entry Bookkeeping before the Nineteenth Century." *The Accounting Historians Journal* 19, no. 2 (1992): 103–22.

Liptak, Andrew. "An Animated Adaptation of Chinese Sci-Fi Novel The Three-Body Problem Is in Development." *The Verge*, June 21, 2019.

Liptak, Andrew. "One of China's Best Sci-Fi Authors Is Getting an English-Language Collection." *The Verge*, February 9, 2019.

Liu E. *Lao Can you ji* [Travels of Lao Can]. Beijing: Renmin wenxue chubanshe, 1957.

Liu Guanglei. "Wan Qing chuanbo guannian de yanbian yu baihua baokan de yingxiang" [On the development of the concept of communication in late Qing dynasty and its influence on vernacular newspapers]. *Guangdong jishu shifan xueyuan xuebao* 11 (2013): 14–21.

Liu, Joyce. "Force of Psyche: Electricity or Void? Reexamination of the Hermeneutics of the Force of Psyche in Late Qing China." *Concentric: Literary and Cultural Studies* 35, no. 2 (2009): 245–76.

Liu, Lydia He. "Life as Form: How Biomimesis Encountered Buddhism in Lu Xun." *The Journal of Asian Studies*, 68, no. 1 (February 2009): 21–54.

Liu, Lydia He. *The Clash of Empires: The Invention of China in Modern World Making*. Cambridge, MA: Harvard University Press, 2006.

Liu, Lydia He. *The Freudian Robot: Digital Media and the Future of the Unconscious*. Chicago: University of Chicago Press, 2010.

Liu, Lydia He. *Translingual Practice: Literature, National Culture, and Translated Modernity—China, 1900–1937*. Stanford, CA: Stanford University Press, 1995.

Liu, Lydia He, Rebecca E. Karl, and Dorothy Ko, eds. *The Birth of Chinese Feminism: Essential Texts in Transnational Theory*. New York: Columbia University Press, 2013.

Liu Xiao. *Information Fantasies: Precarious Mediation in Postsocialist China*. Minneapolis: University of Minnesota Press, 2019.

Liu Xihong. *Yingyao siji* [Private diary in an English carriage]. In *Yingyao siji and Suishi Ying E ji*, edited by Zhu Chun, Yang Jian, and Zhong Shuhe, 39–227. Changsha: Yuelu shu she, 1985.

Liu Zhimin and Li Jingting. "Lun Nüwa de chuangxin gongde—zaoren, butian" [On Nüwa's virtues of creation—making humans, mending heaven]. *Shehui kexue luntan* 9, no. 2 (2008): 193–95.

"Liusheng xinji" [A new sound recording machine]. *Zhixin Bao* 54 (1898): 25–27. Accessed July 16, 2015. CNBKSY.

Lörincz, Csongor. "Instrumentality and Referentiality in Poetry (Thomas Kling)." *Configurations* 18, no. 3 (2010): 327–44.

Lovink, Geert. *My First Recession*. Rotterdam: V2 Publishing, 2003.

Lu Hsiao-peng. "Waking to Modernity: The Classical Tale in Late-Qing China." *New Literary History* 34, no. 4 (2003): 745–60.

Lu Xun. "Wenhua pian zhi lun" [Aberrations in cultural development]. In *Lu Xun quan ji* [Collected works of Lu Xun], vol. 1, 44–62. Xianggang: Wenhua yanjiu she, 1973.

Lu Yunting. *Yihe tuan de shehui biaoyan: 1887–1902 nian jian Huabei diqu de xiwu huodong* [The Boxers' social performance: Huabei region's occult activities, 1887–1902]. Shanghai: Shanghai guji chubanshe, 2014.

Luan Weiping. "Jindai kexue xiaoshuo yu linghun: you 'Xin faluo xiansheng tan' shuo kai qu" [Recent science fiction and the soul: Beginning with "Xin faluoxiansheng tan."] *Zhongguo xiandai wenxue yanjiu chongkan* 3 (2006): 46–68. Accessed January 7, 2015. doi:10.16287/j.cnki.cn11-2589/i.2006.03.003.

Luhmann, Niklas. *Social Systems*. Stanford, CA: Stanford University Press, 1995.

Luo Dajing. *Helin yulu* [The glittering dew drops of Helin], 16 vols. Beijing: Zhonghua shuju, 1983.

Luo Xiaojing. "Lixiang guomin de xiandai wutuobang" [The ideal "citizen"'s "modern utopia"—a new critique of late Qing utopian fiction]. *Jiangsu shehui kexue* 1 (2011): 175–81. Accessed December 10, 2011. doi:10.13858/j.cnki .cn32-1312/c.2011.01.015.

Ma Shaoling. "Stone, Jade, Medium: A Neocybernetic New Story of the Stone (1905–1906)." *Configurations* 26, no. 1 (2018): 1–26.

Ma Shaoling. "To Compare Otherwise: Dialectics and the Work of Comparison in Structural Totality." *Mediations* 31, no. 1 (2017): 27–46.

Mann, Susan. *Local Merchants and the Chinese Bureaucracy, 1750–1950*. Stanford, CA: Stanford University Press, 1987.

Mann, Susan. *Precious Records: Women in China's Long Eighteenth Century*. Stanford, CA: Stanford University Press, 1997.

Mann, Susan. "Scene-Setting: Writing Biography in Chinese History." *American Historical Review* 114, no. 3 (2009): 631–39.

Mannoni, Laurent. *The Great Art of Light and Shadow: Archaeology of the Cinema*. Translated by Richard Crangle. Exeter, UK: University of Exeter Press, 2015.

Manovich, Lev. *The Language of New Media*. Cambridge, MA: MIT Press, 2002.

Mao Zedong. *Mao Zedong on Dialectical Materialism: Writings on Philosophy, 1937*. New York: M. E. Sharpe, 1990.

Marvin, Carolyn. *When Old Technologies Were New: Thinking about Electric Communication in the Late Nineteenth Century*. Oxford: Oxford University Press, 1990.

Marx, Karl. *Grundrisse: Foundations of the Critique of Political Economy*. Translated by Martin Nicolaus. London: Penguin, 2005.

Massumi, Brian. *Parables for the Virtual*. Durham, NC: Duke University Press, 2002.

Massumi, Brian, et al. "'Technical Mentality' Revisited: Brian Massumi on Gilbert Simondon." In *Gilbert Simondon: Being and Technology*, edited by Arne De Boever, Alex Murray, Jon Roffe, and Ashley Woodward, 19–36. Edinburgh: Edinburgh University Press, 2012.

McDermott, Joseph P. "The Ascendance of the Imprint in China." In *Printing and Book Culture in Late Imperial China*, edited by Cynthia J. Brokaw and Kai-Wing Chow, 55–106. Berkeley: University of California Press, 2005.

McLuhan, Marshall. *Understanding Media: The Extensions of Man*. Corte Madera, CA: Gingko Press, 2003.

Meillassoux, Quentin. *After Finitude: An Essay on the Necessity of Contingency*. London: Bloomsbury Publishing, 2009.

Menke, Richard. "The Medium Is the Media: Fictions of the Telephone in the 1890s." *Victorian Studies* 55, no. 2 (2013): 212–21.

Michael, Franz H. *The Origin of Manchu Rule in China: Frontier and Bureaucracy as Interacting Forces in the Chinese Empire*. Hemel Hempstead, UK: Octagon Books, 1965.

Mitchell, W. J. T., and Mark B. N. Hansen, eds. *Critical Terms for Media Studies*. Chicago: University of Chicago Press, 2010.

Mitchell, W. J. T., and Mark B. N. Hansen. "Introduction." In *Critical Terms for Media Studies*, edited by W. J. T. Mitchell and Mark B. N. Hansen, vii–xxii. Chicago: University of Chicago Press, 2010.

Mitchell, W. J. T., and Mark B. N. Hansen. "Time and Space." In *Critical Terms for Media Studies*, edited by W. J. T. Mitchell and Mark B. N. Hansen, 101–13. Chicago: University of Chicago Press, 2010.

Mittler, Barbara. "Mediasphere Shanghai: The Aesthetics of Cultural Production (Review)." *Harvard Journal of Asiatic Studies* 69, no. 2 (2009): 478–87.

Morton, David. *Sound Recording: The Life Story of a Technology*. Baltimore: Johns Hopkins University Press, 2006.

Mullaney, Thomas S. *The Chinese Typewriter: A History*. Cambridge, MA: MIT Press, 2017.

Newfield, Christopher. "The Trouble with Numerical Culture—Profession." *MLA Profession, Humanities RX*.

Ngai, Sianne. *Ugly Feelings*. Cambridge, MA: Harvard University Press, 2009.

Ouellette, Laurie, and Jonathan Gray, eds. *Keywords for Media Studies*. New York: New York University Press, 2017.

Owen, Stephen. *Readings in Chinese Literary Thought*. Cambridge, MA: Harvard University Asia Center, 1996.

Owen, Stephen. *Traditional Chinese Poetry and Poetics: Omen of the World*. Madison: University of Wisconsin Press, 1985.

Pan Honggang. "Qingren de Mingpian" [Qing peoples' name cards]. *Dushu Wenzhai* 7 (2009): 65–68.

Pang Laikwan. *The Distorting Mirror: Visual Modernity in China*. Honolulu: University of Hawai'i Press, 2007.

Parikka, Jussi. "New Materialism as Media Theory: Medianatures and Dirty Matter." *Communication and Critical/Cultural Studies* 9, no. 1 (2012): 95–100.

Parikka, Jussi. *What Is Media Archaeology?* Hoboken, NJ: Wiley, 2013.

Parks, Lisa, and Nicole Starosielski. "Introduction." In *Signal Traffic: Critical Studies of Media Infrastructures*, edited by Lisa Parks and Nicole Starosielski, 1–30. Urbana: University of Illinois Press, 2015.

274

Parks, Lisa, and Nicole Starosielski, eds. *Signal Traffic: Critical Studies of Media Infrastructures*. Urbana: University of Illinois Press, 2015.

Pasquinelli, Matteo. "Italian Operaismo and the Information Machine." *Theory, Culture and Society* 32, no. 3 (2015): 49–68.

Paulson, William R. *The Noise of Culture: Literary Texts in a World of Information*. Ithaca, NY: Cornell University Press, 1988.

Peng Ying-cheng. "Lingering between Tradition and Innovation: Photographic Portraits of Empress Dowager Cixi." *Ars Orientalis* 43 (2013): 157–74.

Peters, John Durham. *The Marvelous Clouds: Toward a Philosophy of Elemental Media*. Chicago: University of Chicago Press, 2015.

Peters, John Durham. "Radio: Broadcasting as Dissemination (and Dialogue)." In *Speaking into the Air: A History of the Idea of Communication*, 206–26. Chicago: University of Chicago Press, 1999.

Peters, John Durham. "Technology and Ideology: The Case of the Telegraph Revisited." In *Thinking with James Carey: Essays on Communications, Transportation, History*, edited by Jeremy Packer and Craig Robertson, 137–56. New York: Peter Lang, 2006.

Pfeiffer, Karl Ludwig. "The Materiality of Communication." In *Materialities of Communication*, edited by Hans Ulrich Gumbrecht and Karl Ludwig Pfeiffer, 45–69. Stanford, CA: Stanford University Press, 1988.

Pitkin, Hanna Fenichel. *The Attack of the Blob: Hannah Arendt's Concept of the Social*. Chicago: University of Chicago Press, 1998.

Plaks, Andrew. *Archetype and Allegory in the Dream of the Red Chamber*. Princeton, NJ: Princeton University Press, 2015.

Plaks, Andrew. "Towards a Critical Theory of Chinese Narrative." In *Chinese Narrative: Critical and Theoretical Essays*, edited by Andrew Plaks, 309–52. Princeton, NJ: Princeton University Press, 2016.

Preece, W. H. "The Phonograph." *Journal of the Society of Arts* 26, no. 1329 (1878): 534–37.

"The Principles of the Telephone Applied to the Phonograph." *Scientific Monthly* 21, no. 6 (1925): 666–68. doi:10.2307/7737.

Qian Jiang. "Translation and the Development of Science Fiction in Twentieth-Century China." *Science Fiction Studies* 40, no. 1 (2013): 116–32.

Qian Nanxiu. *Politics, Poetics, and Gender in Late Qing China: Xue Shaohui and the Era of Reform*. Stanford, CA: Stanford University Press, 2015.

Qiu Jin. "Inscribed on a Photograph of Myself Dressed as a Man." In *Women Writers of Traditional China: An Anthology of Poetry and Criticism*, edited by Kang-i Sun Chang, Haun Saussy, and Charles Yim-tze Kwong, translated by Li-li Chen, 656–58. Stanford, CA: Stanford University Press, 1999.

Qiu Jin. "Ziti xiaozhao" [Self-inscription on a photograph]. In *Qiu Jin yanjiu ziliao* [Research material on Qiu Jin], edited by Guo Changhai and Qiu Jingwu, 94. Ningxia: Ningxia renmin chubanshe, 2007.

Quan Xianguang. "Shiban hua jifa, 1" [Techniques of lithography, 1]. *Meiyuan* 2 (1994): 60.

275

Rajagopal, Arvind. "Communicationism: Cold War Humanism." *Critical Inquiry* 46, no. 2 (2020): 353–80.

Rajewsky, Irina. "Intermediality, Intertextuality, and Remediation: A Literary Perspective on Intermediality." *Intermédialités/Intermediality* 6 (2005): 43–64.

Rankin, William J. "Infrastructure and the International Governance of Economic Development, 1950–1965." In *Internationalization of Infrastructures: Proceedings of the 12th Annual International Conference on the Economics of Infrastructures*, edited by Jean-Francois Auger, Jan Jaap Bouma, and Rolf Künneke, 61–75. Delft: Delft University of Technology, 2009.

Rawski, Evelyn S. "Reenvisioning the Qing: The Significance of the Qing Period in Chinese History." *Journal of Asian Studies* 55, no. 4 (1996): 829–50.

Reed, Bradly. *Talons and Teeth: County Clerks and Runners in the Qing Dynasty.* Stanford, CA: Stanford University Press, 2000.

Reed, Christopher A. *Gutenberg in Shanghai: Chinese Print Capitalism, 1876–1937.* Honolulu: University of Hawai'i Press, 2004.

Ren Dongmei. "Wan Qing kehuan xiaoshuo zhong de 'kexue'—yi 'Xin faluo xiansheng tan' weili" [The early transmission of the term *science* as seen from the spread of scientific novels in the late Qing dynasty—the case of "Xin faluo xiansheng tan"]. *Shandong wenxue* 9 (2016): 100–102.

Ren Dongmei and Chenmei Xu. "Interpreting Folding Beijing through the Prism of Science Fiction Realism." *Chinese Literature Today* 7, no. 1 (2018): 54–57.

Rentschler, Carrie A. "Affect." In *Keywords for Media Studies*, edited by Laurie Ouellette and Jonathan Gray, 12. New York: New York University Press, 2017.

Ricalton, James. *James Ricalton's Photographs of China during the Boxer Rebellion: His Illustrated Travelogue of 1900*, edited by Christopher J. Lucas. Lewiston, NY: Edwin Mellen Press, 1990.

Ricalton, James, and Christopher J. Lucas. "Introduction: The Life and Career of James Ricalton." In *James Ricalton's Photographs of China during the Boxer Rebellion: His Illustrated Travelogue of 1900*, edited by Christopher J. Lucas, 1–60. Lewiston, NY: Edwin Mellen Press, 1990.

Robertson, Maureen. "Voicing the Feminine: Constructions of the Gendered Subject in Lyric Poetry by Women of Medieval and Late Imperial China." *Late Imperial China* 13, no. 1 (1992): 63–110.

Rooney, Ellen. "Form and Contentment." *MLQ: Modern Language Quarterly* 61, no. 1 (2000): 17–40.

Rooney, Ellen. "Symptomatic Reading Is a Problem of Form." In *Critique and Postcritique*, edited by Elizabeth S. Anker and Rita Felski, 127–52. Durham, NC: Duke University Press, 2017.

Rudolph, Jennifer M. *Negotiated Power in Late Imperial China: The Zongli Yamen and the Politics of Reform.* Ithaca, NY: East Asia Program, Cornell University, 2008.

Rugg, Linda Haverty. *Picturing Ourselves: Photography and Autobiography.* Chicago: University of Chicago Press, 2007.

Ryan, Marie-Laure. *Narrative across Media: The Languages of Storytelling.* Lincoln: University of Nebraska Press, 2004.

Said, Edward W. *Culture and Imperialism*. New York: Doubleday, 2012.

Saussy, Haun. *Great Walls of Discourse and Other Adventures in Cultural China*. Cambridge, MA: Harvard University Asia Center, 2001.

Saussy, Haun. "No Time Like the Present: The Category of Contemporaneity in Chinese Studies." In *Great Walls of Discourse and Other Adventures in Cultural China*, 91–117. Cambridge, MA: Harvard University Asia Center, 2001.

Saussy, Haun. "Outside the Parenthesis (Those People Were a Kind of Solution)." *Modern Language Notes* 115, no. 5 (2000): 849–91.

Saussy, Haun. *The Problem of a Chinese Aesthetics*. Stanford, CA: Stanford University Press, 1993.

Sayers, Jentry. "An Archaeology of Edison's Metal Box." *Victorian Review* 38, no. 2 (2012): 39–41.

Schivelbusch, Wolfgang. *The Railway Journey: The Industrialization and Perception of Time and Space*. Berkeley: University of California Press, 1986.

Schmidt, J. D. *Within the Human Realm: The Poetry of Huang Zunxian, 1848–1905*. Cambridge: Cambridge University Press, 2007.

Schmitt, Cannon. "Tidal Conrad (Literally)." *Victorian Studies* 55, no. 1 (2012): 7–29.

Schwartz, Benjamin Isadore. *In Search of Wealth and Power*. Cambridge, MA: Harvard University Press, 1964.

Schwartz, Benjamin Isadore. "The Limits of 'Tradition versus Modernity': The Case of the Chinese Intellectuals." In *China and Other Matters*, 45–64. Cambridge, MA: Harvard University Press, 1996.

Sebastian, Thomas, and Judith Geerke. "Technology Romanticized: Friedrich Kittler's *Discourse Networks 1800/1900*." *Modern Language Notes* 105, no. 3 (1990): 583–95.

Serres, Michel. *The Parasite*. Translated by Lawrence R. Schehr. Minneapolis: University of Minnesota Press, 2007.

Sheng Xuanhuai. *Yihe tuan yundong—Sheng Xuanhuai dang'an ziliao xuanji zhi qi* [The Boxer movement—selected works from Sheng Xuanhuai's files]. Edited by Tinglong Gu and Xu Lu Chen, vol. 7. Shanghai: Shanghai renming chuban ju, 2001.

Shi Bing. *Dianbao tongxin yu Qingmo Minchu de zhengzhi bianju* [Telegraph communications and political change in late Qing and early Republican China]. Beijing: Zhongguo shehui kexue chuban she, 2012.

Shih Shu-Mei. "Against Diaspora: The Sinophone as Places of Cultural Production." In *Global Chinese Literature*, edited by Jing Tsu and David Der-Wei Wang, 29–48. Leiden: Brill, 2010.

Si Chunling. "Wan Qing Huifeng Yinhang Yanjiu (1865–1894)" [A study of the Hong Kong and Shanghai Banking Corporation in the late Qing dynasty (1865–1894)]. MA diss., Hebei Normal University, 2009.

Siegert, Bernhard. "Cacography or Communication? Cultural Techniques in German Media Studies." *Grey Room* 29 (2008): 26–47.

Simondon, Gilbert. *On the Mode of Existence of Technical Objects*. Translated by Cecile Malaspina and John Rogove. Minneapolis: University of Minnesota Press, 2017.

277

Smith, Arthur Henderson. *China in Convulsion*, 2 vols. New York: F. H. Revell, 1901.

Snow, C. P. *The Two Cultures*. Cambridge: Cambridge University Press, 1993.

Stalling, Jonathan. *Poetics of Emptiness: Transformations of Asian Thought in American Poetry*. New York: Fordham University Press, 2010.

Star, Susan Leigh. "The Ethnography of Infrastructure." *American Behavioral Scientist* 43, no. 3 (1999): 377–91.

Starr, Chloe F. *Red-Light Novels of the Late Qing*. Leiden: Brill, 2007.

Steen, Andreas. *Zai yule yu geming zhi jian: liusheng ji, changpian, he Shanghai de yinyue gongye de chuqi, 1878–1937* [Between entertainment and revolution: Phonograph, records, and the origins of Shanghai's music industry]. Translated by Lü Shu and Wang Weijiang. Shanghai: Shanghai ci shu chubanshe, 2015.

Stiegler, Bernard. "Derrida and Technology: Fidelity at the Limits of Deconstruction and the Prosthesis of Faith." In *Jacques Derrida and the Humanities: A Critical Reader*, edited by Tom Cohen, 238–70. Albany: State University of New York Press, 2002.

Stiegler, Bernard. *Technics and Time, 1: The Fault of Epimetheus*. Stanford, CA: Stanford University Press, 1998.

Sun Li. *Wan Qing dianbao ji qi chuanbo guannian 1860–1911* [Late Qing telegraphy and its communicative perspectives]. Shanghai: Shanghai shuju, 2007.

Sun Li. "Zaizao 'zhongxin': dianbao wangluo yu wan Qing zhengzhi de kongjian chonggou" [The rise of the telegraph network and the reconstruction of policy space in the late Qing dynasty]. *Xinwen yu chuanbo yanjiu* 12 (2015): 37–61.

Suvin, Darko. *Positions and Presuppositions of Science Fiction*. London: Palgrave Macmillan, 1988.

Tan Sitong. *Renxue* [A study of benevolence]. Beijing: Gaodeng jiaoyu chuban she, 2010.

Tang Hongfeng. "Huandeng yu dianying de bianzheng—yi zhong dianying kaogu xue de yanjiu" [The dialectics between the magic lantern and cinema: A media archaeology of Chinese cinema]. *Shanghai daxue xuebao (shehui kexue ban)* 33, no. 2 (2016): 40–60. doi:10.3969 /j.issn1007-6522.2016.02.004.

Tang Xiaobing. "'Poetic Revolution,' Colonization, and Form at the Beginning of Modern Chinese Literature." In *Rethinking the 1898 Reform Period: Political and Cultural Change in Late Qing China*, edited by Rebecca E. Karl and Peter Gue Zarrow, 245–68. Cambridge, MA: Harvard University Asia Center, 2002.

Taussig, M. T. *Mimesis and Alterity: A Particular History of the Senses*. London: Routledge, 1993.

Thacker, Eugene. *Biomedia*. Minneapolis: University of Minnesota Press, 2004.

Thompson, Roger R. "The Wire: Progress, Paradox, and Disaster in the Strategic Networking of China, 1881–1901." *Frontiers of History in China* 10, no. 3 (2015): 395–427.

Tian, Chenshan. *Chinese Dialectics: From Yijing to Marxism*. Lanham, MD: Lexington Books, 2005.

Tong, Qingsheng. "Guo Songtao in London: An Unaccomplished Mission of Discovery." In *China Abroad*, edited by Elaine Yee Lin Ho and Julia Kuehn, 1–16. Hong Kong: Hong Kong University Press, 2009.

"Tongsheng zhongfeng" [To feel together in loyal anguish]. *Thien Nan Shin Pao*, March 5, 1900.

Trott, Ben. "The 'Fragment on Machines' as Science Fiction; or, Reading the Grundrisse Politically." *Cambridge Journal of Economics*, 42, no. 4 (2018): 1107–22.

Tsien Tsuen-hsuin. *Written on Bamboo and Silk: The Beginnings of Chinese Books and Inscriptions*. Chicago: University of Chicago Press, 2004.

Tsu Jing. *Failure, Nationalism, and Literature: The Making of Modern Chinese Identity, 1895–1937*. Stanford, CA: Stanford University Press, 2005.

Tsu Jing. "Female Assassins, Civilization, and Technology in Late Qing Literature and Culture." In *Different Worlds of Discourse*, edited by Nanxiu Qian, Grace Fong, and Richard Smith, 167–96. Leiden: Brill, 2008.

Tsu Jing and Benjamin A. Elman. "Introduction." In *Science and Technology in Modern China, 1880s–1940s*, edited by Tsu Jing and Benjamin A. Elman, 1–14. Leiden: Brill, 2014.

Tsu Jing and Benjamin A. Elman, eds. *Science and Technology in Modern China, 1880s–1940s*. Leiden: Brill, 2014.

Tuck, Robert. *Idly Scribbling Rhymers: Poetry, Print, and Community in Nineteenth-Century Japan*. New York: Columbia University Press, 2018.

Tucker, Herbert F. "Tactical Formalism: A Response to Caroline Levine." *Victorian Studies* 49, no. 1 (2006): 85–93.

Virno, Paolo. "General Intellect." *Historical Materialism* 15, no. 3 (2007): 3–8.

Virno, Paolo, and Michael Hardt, eds. *Radical Thought in Italy: A Potential Politics*. Minneapolis: University of Minnesota Press, 1996.

Vismann, Cornelia. "Cultural Techniques and Sovereignty." *Theory, Culture and Society* 30, no. 6 (2013): 83–93.

Vittinghoff, Natascha. "Social Actors in the Field of New Learning." In *Mapping Meanings: The Field of New Learning in Late Qing China*, edited by Michael Lackner and Natascha Vittinghoff, 75–119. Leiden: Brill, 2004.

Wagner, Rudolf G., "Joining the Global Imaginaire: The Shanghai Illustrated Journal Dianshizhai huabao." In *Joining the Global Public: Word, Image, and City in Early Chinese Newspapers, 1870–1910*, edited by Rudolf G. Wagner, 105–74. Albany: State University of New York Press, 2012.

Wagner, Rudolf G., ed. *Joining the Global Public: Word, Image, and City in Early Chinese Newspapers, 1870–1910*. Albany: State University of New York Press, 2012.

Waley-Cohen, Joanna. "The New Qing History." *Radical History Review* 88 (2004): 193–206.

Wang, David Der-wei. *Fin-de-Siècle Splendor: Repressed Modernities of Late Qing Fiction, 1849–1911*. Stanford, CA: Stanford University Press, 1997.

Wang, David Der-wei. *The Lyrical in Epic Time: Modern Chinese Intellectuals and Artists through the 1949 Crisis*. New York: Columbia University Press, 2015.

Wang Guowei. "Lun Wu Jianren pingpan xianshi biaoda lixiang de jiezuo 'Xin Shitouji'" [On Wu Jianren's critique of reality and his idealist masterpiece "New Story of the Stone"—also on Wu's idea of "civilized despotism."] *Daizong xuekan: Taian jiaoyu xueyuan xuebao* 1 (2001): 42–46.

Wang Hui. "The Fate of 'Mr. Science' in China: The Concept of Science and Its Application in Modern Chinese Thought." *positions: asia critique* 3, no. 1 (1995): 1–68.

Wang Jing. *The Story of Stone: Intertextuality, Ancient Chinese Stone Lore, and the Stone Symbolism in Dream of the Red Chamber, Water Margin, and The Journey to the West*. Durham, NC: Duke University Press, 1992.

Wang Qian. *"Dao" "ji" zhi jian: Zhongguo wenhua beijing de jishu shexue* [Between 'dao' and 'ji': The cultural background to Chinese philosophy of technology]. Beijing: Renmin chuban she, 2009.

Wang Shuoqiang. "Huang chao yu Chen Qiufan de chonggou shijie" [*Waste Tide* and Chen Qiufan's multiple worlds]. *Kepu chuangzuo*, no. 2 (2017): 42–44.

Wang-Fan Yiqian. *Yihe tuan zhanzheng de guoji yulun yan jiu: 1900–1901* [Boxer rebellion and international coverage, 1900–1901]. Shanghai: Fudan University Press, 2015.

Wardrip-Fruin, Noah, and Nick Montfort. *The New Media Reader*. Cambridge, MA: MIT Press, 2003.

Wark, McKenzie. *Capital Is Dead*. London: Verso Books, 2019.

Weeks, Kathi. "Life within and against Work: Affective Labor, Feminist Critique, and Post-Fordist Politics." *Ephemera* 7, no. 1 (2007).

Wellbery, David, and Friedrich A Kittler. "Foreword." In Friedrich A. Kittler, *Discourse Networks 1800/1900*, vii–xxxiii. Stanford, CA: Stanford University Press, 1992.

Wenzlhuemer, Roland. "The Telegraph and the Control of Material Movements: A Micro-Study about the Detachment of Communication from Transport." *Technology and Culture* 58, no. 3 (2017): 625–49.

Williams, Raymond. *Marxism and Literature*. Oxford: Oxford University Press, 1977.

Williams, Raymond. *Television: Technology and Cultural Form*. London: Psychology Press, 2003.

Wilson, George M. "Edward Said on Contrapuntal Reading." *Philosophy and Literature* 18, no. 2 (1994): 265–73.

Winthrop-Young, Geoffrey. "Cultural Techniques: Preliminary Remarks." *Theory, Culture and Society* 30, no. 6 (2013): 3–19.

Winthrop-Young, Geoffrey, and Michael Wutz. "Translator's Introduction." In Friedrich A. Kittler, *Gramophone, Film, Typewriter*, xi–xxxviii. Stanford, CA: Stanford University Press, 1999.

Wolfson, Susan J. "Reading for Form." *MLQ: Modern Language Quarterly* 61, no. 1 (2000): 1–16.

Wolfson, Susan J., and Marshall Brown, eds. *Reading for Form*. Seattle: University of Washington Press, 2016.

Woloch, Alex. *The One vs. the Many: Minor Characters and the Space of the Protagonist in the Novel*. Princeton, NJ: Princeton University Press, 2009.

Wood, Henry. *Ideal Suggestion through Mental Photography; a Restorative System for Home and Private Use, Preceded by a Study of the Laws of Mental Healing*. Boston: Lee and Shepard, 1893.

Wook, Yoon. "Dashed Expectations: Limitations of the Telegraphic Service in the Late Qing." *Modern Asian Studies* 39, no. 3 (2013): 832–57.

Wright, David. "John Fryer and the Shanghai Polytechnic: Making Space for Science in Nineteenth-Century China." *British Journal for the History of Science* 29, no. 1 (1996): 1–16.

Wright, David. "Tan Sitong and the Ether Reconsidered." *Bulletin of the School of Oriental and African Studies* 57, no. 3 (1994): 551–75.

Wright, Mary Clabaugh. *The Last Stand of Chinese Conservatism: The T'ung-Chih Restoration, 1862–1874*. Stanford, CA: Stanford University Press, 1962.

Wu, Guo. "Gailiang de di xian—'tiyong,' 'daoqi' yu Zheng Guanying sixiang" [The bottom line for reform: The thought of Zheng Guanying and the doctrine of Chinese learning as essence, Western learning as utilities, the dichotomy between *dao* and *qi*]. *Guizhou shifan daxue xuebao (shehui kexue ban)* 131, no. 6 (2004): 60–63. doi:10.16614/j.cnki.issn1001-733x.2004.06.013.

Wu Hongcheng and Zhao Yingxia. "Wan Qing shiye jiaoyu sichao shulun" [Intellectual trends of practical education during the late Qing]. *Hebei daxue xuekan (zhexue shehui kexue ban)* 41, no. 3 (2016): 30–31.

Wu, Jianren. *Ershi nian muduzhi guai xianzhuang* [Bizarre happenings witnessed over two decades]. Shenyang: Chun feng wen yi, 1994.

Wu Jianren. *Xin shitouji* [New Story of the Stone]. In *Zhongguo jingdai xiaoshuo daxi*, vol. 7, 151–402. Nanchang: Jiangxi renmin chubanshe, 1988.

Wu Shengqing. *Modern Archaics: Continuity and Innovation in the Chinese Lyric Tradition, 1900–1937*. Cambridge, MA: Harvard University Asia Center, 2013.

Wu Shengqing. "A Paper Mirror: Autobiographical Moments in Modern Chinese Poetry." *Journal of Chinese Literature and Culture* 3, no. 2 (2016): 312–34.

Wu Yixiong. "Wan Qing shiqi xifang renti shengli zhishi zai huao chuanbo yu bentu hua" [The spread of Western knowledge of human physiology during the late Qing]. *Zhongshan daxue xuebao (shehui kexue ban)* 49, no. 3 (2009): 78–94.

Wu Yunxian. "Lüe lun Huifeng yinhang zai jindai Zhongguo de jige fazhan jieduan ji qi qishi" [A brief discussion of HSBC bank's recent development in China]. *Beijing lianhe daxue xuebao (renwen shehui kexue ban)* 2, no. 4 (2004): 63–68. doi:10.16255/j.cnki .11-5117c.2004.04.012

Xia Xiaohong. *Wan Qing nüxing yu jindai Zhongguo* [Late Qing women and contemporary China]. Beijing: Beijing University Press, 2004.

Xiao Guomin. "'Xiyang zazhi' de bianzhuan xue: wan Qing shi dafu shouci zouxiang xiyang de jiti shuxu" [Study of the editorial process of "Western magazine": A collective narration of late Qing intellectuals' first turn toward the West]. In *Bijiao wenxue yu shijie wenxue zhuankan* 1 (2014): 240–76.

"Xin chuang ji sheng qi tu shuo" [An illustrated text on the new phonograph]. *Gezhi huibian* 5 (1890): 47–50.

Xu Chenchao. "Wan Qing shi qi guoren yu liu sheng ji de jiechu yi ji liu sheng ji zai Zhongguo de chuanbo he yingxiang" [Late Qing receptions of the phonograph and its popularization and influence]. *Journal of Kaifeng Institute of Education* 36, no. 3 (2016): 14–15.

Xu Fei and Mao Shizhen. "Liuemi youtong yu Zhongguo dianxin de zaoqi fazhan" [American-educated youths and their roles in the early development of the telegraph in China]. *Zhongguo ke ji lun tan* 2 (2005): 98–101. doi:10.13580/j.cnki.fstc.2005.03.023.

Xu Nianci. "New Tales of Mr. Braggadocio." Translated by Nathaniel Isaacson. *Renditions* 77–78 (2012): 15–38.

Xu Nianci [Donghai juewo]. "Xiaoshuo lin yuanqi" [The origins of Forest of Fiction]. *Xiaoshuo lin* 1 (1907): 1–2.

Xu Nianci. "Xin faluoxiansheng tan" [New tales of Mr. Braggadocio]. In *Qingmo-Minchu xiaoshuo shuxi kexue ban*, edited by Yu Runqi, 1–20. Beijing: Zhongguo wenlian chuban she, 1997.

Xu Nianci. "Yu zhi xiaoshuo guan" [My views on fiction]. *Xiaoshuo lin* 1, no. 1 (1908): 1–8.

Xu Yuanji. "Lun wan Qing tongxun ye de jindai hua" [Modernization of late Qing telecommunications]. *Shanghai shehui kexueyuan xueshu jikan* 4, no. 19 (1987): 151–59.

Xu Zili. "Dianhua" [Telephone]. *Lujiang Bao* 76 (1904): 19.

Yan Fu. "Lun shi bian zhi ji" [On the speed of world change]. In *Jing xuan Yan Fu*, edited by Lang Liu, 247–51. Xiamen: Lujiang chuban she, 2007.

Yan Jianfu. *Cong "shenti" dao "shijie": wan Qing xiaoshuo yu xin gainian ditu* [From the "body" to the "world": Late Qing fiction and a new conceptual cartography]. Taipei: Guoli Taiwan daxue chuban zhongxin, 2014.

Yan Se. "Real Wages and Skill Premia in China, 1858–1936." Social Science Research Network Scholarly Paper, 2011. https://papers.ssrn.com/abstract=1785230.

Yang Guomin. *Wan Qing xiaoshuo yu shehui jingji zhuanxin* [Late Qing fiction and socioeconomic transformations]. Shanghai: Dongfang chuban gongsi, 2005.

Yang Xiaoming and Zheng Yaofei. "Guo Songtao keji guan chu tan" [Preliminary discussion on Guo Songtao's views on technology]. *Kexue Jishu Yu Bianzheng Fa* 26, no. 2 (2009): 75–79.

Yao, Steven G. *Foreign Accents: Chinese American Verse from Exclusion to Postethnicity*. New York: Oxford University Press, 2010.

Yeh, Catherine Vance. "Creating the Urban Beauty: The Shanghai Courtesan in Late Qing Illustrations." In *Writing and Materiality in China: Essays in Honor of Patrick Hanan*, edited by Judith T. Zeitlin and Lydia H. Liu, 397–447. Cambridge, MA: Harvard University Asia Center, 2003.

Yeh, Catherine Vance. *Shanghai Love: Courtesans, Intellectuals, and Entertainment Culture, 1850–1910*. Seattle: University of Washington Press, 2006.

Yeh, Michelle. "Metaphor and Bi: Western and Chinese Poetics." *Comparative Literature* 39, no. 3 (1987): 237–54.

Yi Dexiang. *Donghai xihai zhi jian—wan Qing shixi riji zhong de wenhua guanzha, renzheng yu xuanze* [Between the eastern and western seas: Cultural observation, recognition, and selection in late Qing diplomatic diaries]. Beijing: Beijing University Press, 2009.

Young, Robert. *Colonial Desire: Hybridity in Theory, Culture and Race*. London: Routledge, 2010.

Yu, Anthony C. *Rereading the Stone: Desire and the Making of Fiction in Dream of the Red Chamber*. Princeton, NJ: Princeton University Press, 2001.

Yu Cuiling. "Riji fengbo yu Shenbao jiufen: Guo Songtao huiyu de xifang meijie yinsu lunxi" [The diary controversy and the conflict in Shenbao: The role of Western media in Guo Songtao's defamation]. In *Beijing shifan daxue xuebao* 194, no. 2 (2006): 76–81.

Yu, Pauline. *The Reading of Imagery in the Chinese Poetic Tradition*. Princeton, NJ: Princeton University Press, 2000.

Yu Weidong, Xu Jin, and Zhang Lin. "Morality and Nature: The Essential Difference between the Dao of Chinese Philosophy and Metaphysics in Western Philosophy." *Frontiers of Philosophy in China* 4, no.3 (2009): 360–69.

Yue Meng. "Hybrid Science versus Modernity: The Practice of the Jiangnan Arsenal, 1864–1897." *East Asian Science, Technology, and Medicine* 16 (1999): 13–52.

Zhang Deyi. *Suishi Ying-E ji* [An account of my journey with the British and Russian emissary]. In *Yingyao siji, Suishi Ying-E ji*, edited by Zhu Chun, Yang Jian, and Zhong Shuhe, 267–847. Changsha: Yuelu shu she, 1985.

Zhang Longxi. "Western Theory and Chinese Reality." *Critical Inquiry* 19, no. 1 (1992): 105–30.

Zhang Longxi. "What Is Wen and Why Is It Made so Terribly Strange?" *College Literature* 23, no. 1 (1996): 15–35.

Zhang Xiantao. *The Origins of the Modern Chinese Press: The Influence of the Protestant Missionary Press in Late Qing China*. New York: Routledge, 2007.

Zhang Zhi. "Wan Qing kexue xiaoshuo chuyi: dui wenxue zuopin ji qi sixiang beijing yu zhishi shiye de kaocha" [On late Qing science fiction: A survey of literary works, their ideological backgrounds, and knowledge horizons]. *Kexue wenhua pinglun* 6, no. 5 (2009): 69–96.

Zhang Zhongmin. "Bunao de zhengzhi xue: 'Ailuo Bunao zhi' yu wan Qing xiaofei wenhua de jiangou" [The politics of brain health: Ailuo Brain Tonic and the construction of consumer culture in the late Qing]. *Xueshu yuekan* 43, no. 9 (2011): 145–54.

Zhang Zhongmin. "Jindai Shanghai de mingren yiyao guanggao—yi wenren yu yao wei zhong xin" [Celebrity medical advertising in modern Shanghai: Focusing on the literati's promotion of medicine]. *Xueshu yuekan* 47, no. 7 (2015): 153–62.

Zhao I-heng. *The Uneasy Narrator: Chinese Fiction from the Traditional to the Modern*. Oxford: Oxford University Press, 1995.

Zhong Shuhe. "Lun Guo Songtao" [On Guo Songtao]. In *Lundun Yu Bali Riji*, 1–49. Changsha: Yuelu shu she, 1984.

Zhong Shuhe. "'Yong xia bian yi' de yi ci shibai" [A failed case in the program of "sinicizing the barbarians"]. In *Yingyao siji*, 1–34. Changsha Shi: Yuelu shu she, 1985.

Zhou Yongming. *Historicizing Online Politics: Telegraphy, the Internet, and Political Participation in China.* Stanford, CA: Stanford University Press, 2006.

Zhu Yan. *Kepa de Shanghai ren: xiaoxiao gangkou* [The frightening Shanghainese: A small harbor]. Chengdu: Shihui wenhua chuanbo gongsi, 2011.

Zinda, Yvonne Schulz. "Propagating New 'Virtues.'" In *Mapping Meanings: The Field of New Learning in Late Qing China*, edited by Michael Lackner and Natascha Vittinghoff, 687–710. Leiden: Brill, 2005.

INDEX

Pages numbers followed by f indicate figures.

Boxer Rebellion media coverage and representation: *China through the Stereoscope*, 160–65, 166f, 169; infrastructural damage, 165–67, 168f; infrastructure failures, 178; international, 158–59, 166–67; James Ricalton, 158–64

Boxers, 149, 170–73, 249n85

the brain: interconnectivity, 202; interest in, 181–82, 198; mental powers, 197–98; social, 202–3. *See also* "New Tales of Mr. Braggadocio"

breakdowns, 180

Brinkema, Eugenie, 24, 223n67

Cao Xueqin. *See Dream of the Red Chamber*

Carey, James, 154–55, 169

characterization, 187–88

Chen Depeng, 7

Cheng Linsun, 92

Chen Qiufan, 210. *See also Waste Tide*

Chen Yi, 153–54

China through the Stereoscope, 160–65, 166f, 169

Chineseness, 157

Chinese novels (*xiaoshuo*), 27–29

Chinese writing, 53–54, 75–76

Chow, Rey, 129, 144, 246n157

Choy, Howard Y. F., 186

chuan. See transmission

cinema, 65–67

civilization terms (*wenming*), 95

Cixi, Empress Dowager, 156–58, 174

Clarke, Bruce, 237n61

clerks and runners, 83, 97–101

Cohen, Paul A., 171, 249n85, 250n93

communication's religious significance, 171–72

communication theory, 11, 96

comparative philosophical studies, 221n49

comparison, 119–23, 126

connectivity. *See* interconnectivity (*tong*)

contrapunctal reading, 67–68

Crary, Jonathan, 65

creation narratives, 74–75, 195

Cui Guofu, 115–16

cult of feelings, 141

cultural contact, 42

cultural materialism, 10, 14–15, 22, 26

dao. See the Way

deixis, 31, 124, 133, 136–37, 142

Deleuze, Gilles, 42

democratic thought, 233n151

denotative, 87

denotative reading, 87

Derrida, Jacques, 23, 25–26

Des Forges, Alexander Townsend, 90, 236n41

dethronement crisis (*Jihai jianchu*), 156–58, 169–70

diplomatic reports on the West (*shixi ji*): overview, 40; *An Account of My Embassy to the West*, 45, 227n12; guidelines for writing, 41–42; imaginary media, 44–45; Latourian modernity, 73–74; Ministry of Foreign Affairs, 41–42, 73; temporal factors, 57; truth, 43–44; Western dismissals of, 40–41. See also *An Account of My Journey with the British and Russian Emissary*; *London and Paris Diaries*; *Private Diary in an English Carriage*

disease discourses, 186–87

Doane, Mary Ann, 124, 136–37

Doleželová-Velingerová, Milena, 191

Dooling, Amy D., 107, 131–32

Dream of the Red Chamber, 75, 82, 101–3. See also *New Story of the Stone*

Dr. Yale's Brain Tonic, 181, 183, 206, 251n10

Duara, Prasenjit, 60

Dunstheimer, G. G. H., 171

Edison, Thomas: in Guo Songtao's diary, 56–57; and James Ricalton, 161; kinetoscope, 66–67, 73; phonograph idea, 58, 231n102; phonograph marketing, 54–55; phonograph-telephone

288

289

media archaeology, 207–8

media forms *versus* forms of media, 3

media infrastructural studies, 150–51

media studies: Marshall McLuhan, 14–15, 208–9, 228n30; mediation in, 10, 221n38; new, 14–15, 80, 208; Qing China, 1, 13, 17. *See also* Williams, Raymond

mediation: overview, 2–3, 8, 259n27; absent devices, 66; as active process, 122; arsenals, 38–39; definition, 19; diary example, 2–3; figurative uses, 22; formalist theory, 15–16; gender, 114; history, 5–6; *versus* homology, 15; linguistic, 12–13; meaning-making, 67; media devices, 2; in media studies, 10, 221n38; in media theory, 207–8; metamediality, 82; *New Story of the Stone*, 82–83, 102, 207; "New Tales of Mr. Braggadocio," 197, 207; precarious, 208–9; in Qing *fin de siècle* studies, 12–13; relationship to media, 22; role in media, 10–12, 19; technical, 150; telegraph codes, 120–21; unworkable interfaces, 43; as worlding process, 5

mei character, 76

Meillassoux, Quentin, 255n92

meiti term, 1

Menke, Richard, 48

mental powers, 197–98, 200, 257n145. See also *Ideal Suggestion through Mental Photography*

metafiction, 82, 104

metamediality, 82–83

metaphors: *versus* allegory, 121–22; materiality, 37, 112; "Modern Parting," 119; nationalism discourses, 181–82; steamships, 112; technologies as, 123; telegraphy, 152, 154

mimetic technologies, 38

Ministry of Foreign Affairs, 41–42, 73

mirror images, 93–94, 105, 123–25

Mitchell, W. J. T., 232n134

"Modern Parting": overview, 115–16; autobiographical reflexivity, 126; biographical aspects, 240n13; dream

meetings, 116, 125–26; female speaker, 117–18, 120–21, 128; feminine sentimentality, 31–32, 117; influences, 115–16; Liang Qichao on, 113, 145; mechanisms of feeling, 119–27, 144; metaphor, 119; mirror images, 123–25; photography, 116, 123–27; poetics, 118–20, 123, 126; riddles, 120–21, 124; stimulation, 119; technological change, 126–27, 144; telegraphy, 116–17, 120–23, 126–27, 241n45; title, 115–16, 240n13; vehicles, 116–17, 119–20, 125

moral education, 98–99, 200, 239n94

More, Thomas, 94

Mullaney, Thomas S., 120–21, 223n71, 250n103

name cards. *See* visiting cards

nationalist discourses: anatomy metaphors, 181–82; of creation, 195; creation myths, 195; feminine exemplarity, 138–39, 142–43, 145, 197, 217; femininity, 130–32; gender, 138–39

Naxiu Qian, 244n104

Needham paradigm, 10

neuroanatomy. *See* the brain

Newfield, Christopher, 259n27

new media studies, 14–15, 80, 208. *See also* remediation

New Qing History, 5

newspapers, 154–157, 247n28

New Story of the Stone: overview, 74–75, 207; book cart episode, 86–87, 93, 111, 145, 163; Boxer Rebellion, 91; bureaucracy, 84, 98–100, 239n97; character-testing mirror, 93–94, 105; character transformations, 102, 104–6; Chinese inventions, 94–95; Chinese learning, 93; clerks and runners, 83, 97–98, 100–101; communications and messages, 97–101; as diary, 93; *versus Dream of the Red Chamber*, 103; genre inconsistencies, 30; governmental forms, 98–99; historical contexts, 76–77, 83–84, 87; identity, 31, 89, 94; individual-institution relations,

292

Ricalton, James: Boxer Rebellion reporting, 159–65, 166f, 169; and Edison, 161, 249n59; photography *versus* writing, 162–63
Richard, Timothy, 40
Robertson, Maureen, 117–18, 129
Rooney, Ellen, 18

Said, Edward, 67–68
Saussy, Haun, 6, 13, 118, 122
Sayers, Jentery, 60–61
Schjellerup, H. C. F. C., 120
Schmidt, J. D., 114–15, 117, 124, 241n45
Schmitt, Cannon, 18, 87
School for the Diffusion of Languages, 38–39
science fiction: definition, 225n142; first Chinese, 225n140; minor characters, 189; political contexts, 30; representation theory, 185; sexual politics, 212; translations into Chinese, 225n140. See also *New Story of the Stone*; "New Tales of Mr. Braggadocio"; *Waste Tide*
"Self-Inscription on a Photograph": overview, 25, 133; bodies, 135, 138, 244n118; feminine sentimentality, 32, 113; historical contexts, 138; modeling, 143; photograph, 133, 134f, 137–39; semiotics of, 135–37; text, 134–36, 245n119
Self-Strengthening Movement: arsenal manufacturing, 38, 227n8; education, 200; essence (*ti*) *versus* applicability (*yong*), 8; failure of, 8; imitation of Western techniques and crafts, 45–46; technological ideologies, 7, 38; Western learning responses, 7
self-writings. See biography
Seo-Young Chu, 185
Serres, Michel, 219n5
Se Yan, 103
Shanghai, 76–77, 80, 83, 236n41
Shannon, Claude, 96, 219n5, 238n82
Shen Fu, 191

Sheng Xuanhuai, 149, 173–78
Shui-mei Shih, 157
Simondon, Gilbert, 126–27, 242n77, 243n78
Sino-Japanese War, 5, 8, 91, 184, 200–201, 246n4, 256n115
Six Chapters of a Floating Life, 191
Smith, Arthur H., 173, 179–80
Snow, C. P., 9, 221n32
social units, 185–86
sonic time, 59
Spiritualism, North American, 172
Star, Susan, 169
steamships, 111–12, 116–17, 119–20, 125
stereography, 160–62, 165. See also *China through the Stereoscope*
Stiegler, Bernard, 25, 74
stimulation, 119–23, 126
stone inscriptions: *Dream of the Red Chamber*, 75, 82, 101–3; and lithography, 81, 88; *New Story of the Stone*, 76–78, 85, 88, 102, 104–6, 237n60; significance of, 75–76
The Stone of the Goddess Nüwa (*Nüwa Shi*), 106–8, 253n38
stone rubbings, 81
The Story of the Stone. See *Dream of the Red Chamber*
surface *versus* symptomatic reading, 18
Sutherland, Thomas, 91
Suvin, Darko, 225n142
Su Zhe, 115

Taiwanese independence, 155–56
Tang Caicheng, 32
Tang Hongfeng, 66
Tan Sitong, 182, 198–99, 202, 257n145
Tao Qian, 94
Taussig, Michael, 38
technesis, 22–23
technical education, 200–201
technical mediation, 150
technical mentality, 242n77
technical objects, 126–127, 243n78
techno-ethnocentrism, 11–12
the technological real, 22–24

293

technology: figurations of, 145; functionalist models, 22–23; machines, 24–25, 77, 202; mimetic, 38; nationalist femininity, 131–32; print-nonprint integration, 48–49; themes of, 123; vocabulary for, 149. *See also* Western technology adoption

technotexts, 25–26

telegrams: "Modern Parting," 116–17, 120–23, 126–27, 241n45; newspapers printing, 154–57; scholarship on, 151; Taiwanese independence, 155–56; as technotexts, 25

telegraphy: Boxer attacks on, 159–60, 165–67, 173–76, 178; Boxer Rebellion uses, 173–77; Chinese codes, 120–21, 241n43, 250n103; Chinese Telegraphy Bureau, 4; communication-transportation separation, 169; courier network, 174–75; debates over, 149–50; dethronement crisis, 156–58, 170; expansion, 76, 149–50; imaginaries, 32; Imperial Telegraph Administration, 149–50, 174–75, 177–78; infrastructure destruction (peacetime), 150, 246n4; Janus metaphor, 152, 154; representations of, 151; resistance to, 150, 153–54; sovereignty, 177–78; spatial distortion, 154; structural perspectives, 151; Taiwanese independence, 155–56; temporal distortion, 154; terms for, 86, 153

telephones: Guo Songtao's account, 47–49, 53, 231n104; phonograph combinations, 60–61; *versus* phonographs, 57–58

telescribes, 60–61

television, 14–15

temporality: diplomatic reports, 57; industrialized, 120; linear, 60; media, 59–60, 232n134; sonic, 59; telegraphy, 154; Western ordering of, 65

textuality, 54–55, 61–62

Thacker, Eugene, 70, 182, 192–94, 206

theory *versus* reality, 6–8

Thompson, John, 64–65, 232n131

Thompson, Roger R., 246n4

tong. See interconnectivity

translation: at Jiangnan Arsenal, 38–39; Michael Gibbs Hill on, 13, 222n54; "Modern Parting," 117, 124, 241n45; "Self-Inscription on a Photograph," 245n119

transmission (*chuan*): overview, 113; approach to, 207–9; character for, 113, 126; emotional, 140; externalization of emotions, 144; Guo Songtao's use of, 56–58; portraiture, 64; science fiction, 217; telegraphy, 86; and *zhuan*, 113, 126, 144

travel journals (*youji*), 40

travel narratives, 46–47

typewriters, 38, 226n5

unworkable interfaces, 43, 72–73, 228n31

use value, 202, 257n127

utopian fiction, 94

Viguier, Septime Auguste, 120

Virno, Paolo, 203

visiting cards, 89–90, 97, 237n62

visuality, 61–62, 231n124

Wade, Thomas Francis, 227n24

walls, 180

Wang, David, 118, 129–30, 143, 222n51

Wang, David Der-wei, 233n168

Wang Guowei, 130

Wang Hui, 51

Wang Jing, 82

Wang Tao, 32

Wang Ziren, 129

Wark, MacKenzie, 70

Warner, Michael, 236n43

Waste Tide: overview, 33, 210–11; female medium, 214; feminine instrumentality, 215–16; minor characters, 215; *versus* "New Tales of Mr. Braggadocio," 211–12, 214–17; sexual politics, 211–12, 214, 217; split consciousness,

294

INDEX